DAVID H. BREEN is a member of the Department of History at the University of British Columbia.

The ranching frontier in Canada has been regarded traditionally as simply a northward extension of the American cattle kingdom, a picturesque but only marginally important precursor to general agrarian settlement. In this book Professor Breen maintains that the role of the Canadian cattlemen cannot be dismissed so lightly.

Breen shows that between 1874 and 1924 the Canadian cattlemen formed a powerful political and economic force which was often directly opposed and actively hostile to the more numerous farm population. He also demonstrates that the Canadian ranch community existed as a social entity distinct from the surrounding agricultural population as well as from its American counterpart. His assessment centres on two main themes: the evolution of dominion land and settlement policy, and the economic and political contest between cattlemen and grain farmers for territorial control.

Breen focuses initially on the era of the open range (1874–96), then discusses the period of government-sponsored mass settlement (1896–1911), and concludes with an evaluation of the cattlemen's effectiveness as a political pressure group after prolonged drought drove the farmers from the region (1911–24).

DAVID H. BREEN

The Canadian Prairie West and the Ranching Frontier 1874–1924

UNIVERSITY OF TORONTO PRESS
Toronto Buffalo London

©University of Toronto Press 1983
Toronto Buffalo London
Printed in Canada

ISBN 0-8020-5548-6

Canadian Cataloguing in Publication Data

Breen, David H.
  The Canadian Prairie West and the ranching frontier

  Bibliography: p.
  Includes index.
  ISBN 0-8020-5548-6

  1. Cattle trade – Prairie Provinces – History.
  2. Land use, Rural – Prairie Provinces – History.
  3. Ranchers – Prairie Provinces – Political activity.
  I. Title.

  HD 9433.C33P72   338.1′762′009712   C82-094615-X

All photos in this book have been reproduced courtesy of the Glenbow Archives,
Calgary, Alberta, with the exception of the federal government poster warning against
squatting, which is reproduced courtesy of the Public Archives of Canada.

Cover: Bow River Horse Ranch near Cochrane 1900

For Patricia

Contents

Tables

Maps

Preface

The ranching frontier in the Canadian west, unlike its American counterpart, has not been accorded the honour of a separate niche in the nation's historiography. The colonization of the Canadian prairie has traditionally been described almost entirely in terms of cereal agriculture. What passing reference is directed to this phase of western development invariably draws attention to the picturesque 'American' character of the ranching frontier in Canada.[1] Also common is the idea that the cattle industry was hardly established before it was displaced by the onrush of prairie settlement. The inference is that the ranching period is of limited and short-lived consequence in western history and, if we are to understand western development or discover a western ethos, we must quickly turn to look at the prairie homesteader. While this emphasis may not be unreasonable given the farmers' overwhelming numbers and geographic predominance, a closer look at these long-held assumptions about the ranching frontier is long overdue. The conventions that the cattlemen's frontier in Canada was simply a short-lived social and cultural adjunct of the American cattle kingdom, that the ranching minority and the farm majority were cut from essentially the same social fabric, and that Canadian cattlemen, despite a vested economic interest against open settlement, simply succumbed to greater numbers and were easily integrated into the mainstream to contribute to a common agrarian heritage are open to question.

In the endeavour to examine the broad sweep of prairie settlement, the rancher has been too quickly dismissed as the 'picturesque' representative of a momentary interlude before the arrival of the homesteader and 'progressive' development. Such cursory attention has failed to give due recognition to the peculiar nature of settlement in a large portion of the Canadian prairie and consequently our knowledge of the ranchers' place in western and national history has remained misguided and superficial.

The central purpose of this book is to show that there is what might be legitimately described as a ranching frontier in the Canadian historical experience and that before 1900 the prospect of beef production, as much as of prairie grain, underlay the Canadian government's thoughts about western development; that Canadian cattlemen existed as a powerful political and economic force which, for the better part of four decades, was often directly opposed to and often actively hostile towards the larger farm population; and that the Canadian ranch community existed as a social entity in many ways distinct from the surrounding agricultural population as well as from its American counterpart. To develop these ideas, focus is placed on two main themes: the evolution of dominion land and settlement policy in the semi-arid region and the economic and political contest between cattlemen and grain farmers for territorial control.

The book is divided chronologically into three periods beginning with the era of the open range, 1874–96. Attention initially is upon the small cattlemen who proved the suitability of the south-western Canadian prairie for stock-raising, and then upon the large cattle companies whose presence made the region part of Montreal's economic hinterland. Particular notice is paid also to the social-cultural composition of the nascent ranching community that coloured the already developing economic contest between rancher and farmer.

During the second period, 1896–1911, cattlemen were confronted by a government program of mass settlement that seriously threatened their industry's economic viability and at the same time intensified the social tension peculiar to this part of the Canadian west.

In the concluding period, 1911–22, the agrarian advance was turned by the ranchers' improved political and economic fortunes as well as by a prolonged drought that drove farmers from the region. In the light of this development, federal land policy in the dry region is evaluated and the cattlemen's continued effectiveness as a political pressure group is measured through their carefully orchestrated campaign to ensure retention of their large leaseholds, their strenuous efforts to retain access to the Chicago market in face of the protection-minded American Congress, and their part in a movement that eventually forced the British government to abandon its long-standing embargo on the importation of live cattle.

Whatever merit this book possesses owes much to the insights, assistance, and continuous encouragement of others. Without my wife Patricia's good humour and unfailing support throughout years of research and writing, this endeavour would not have been possible. I shall always be indebted to Lewis G. Thomas, who supervised the PHD dissertation from which the book emerged. His knowledge of, and feeling for this subject, like that of retired Chief Archivist of the Glenbow-Alberta Institute, Sheilagh Jameson, the other person whose assistance was crucial and to whom I am especially grateful, came from a ranch country heritage and had a dimension that went beyond mere documents and books. Professors Lewis H. Thomas and Roderick C. Macleod at the University of Alberta contributed patient and helpful advice. Dr Patrick Dunae helped me refine my thoughts about the character and contribution of English gentlemen ranchers, Dr Max Foran was always available to discuss Calgary's complex relationship with the ranching fraternity, and Professor Simon Evans has graciously allowed me to reproduce some of the maps that he prepared for his dissertation on the ranching frontier. The professional staff at the Public Archives of Canada and especially at the Glenbow-Alberta Institute in Calgary were always helpful, and I extend my appreciation to them. My research has been supported by funds from the Canada Council, the J.S. Ewart Foundation at the University of Manitoba, and the University of British Columbia.

This book has been published with the help of a grant from the Social Science Federation of Canada, using funds provided by the Social Sciences and Humanities Research Council of Canada, and a grant from the Publications Fund of the University of Toronto Press.

Ft Macleod 1882

Cowhands, 1880s, Stuart Ranch near Calgary

Senator Matthew H. Cochrane 1823–1903

William Pearce 1848–1930

Public Notice!

Whereas, it is stated that squatting to some extent is being done on the lands under lease to the

British American Ranch Company,

Situate on both sides of the Bow River, west of Calgary, the public are hereby notified that the

Government Will in no Way recognize such Squatting,

The COMPANY having lately relinquished Townships 24 in Ranges 2 and 3 West of the 5th Principal Meridian, on the understanding that its rights to the remainder of such lease would be fully protected

A M BURGESS,

Deputy of the Minister of the Interior.

Ottawa, August 20th, 1887

'No squatting' poster

PART I

THE FORMATIVE PERIOD: CATTLE COMPANIES AND THE
OPEN RANGE 1874-96

1

The ranching frontier in Canada 1874–82: the 'free grass' years

After the American Civil War, the cattle kingdom expanded north and east from south-western Texas into what was then popularly known as the Great American Desert. By 1876–8 it had spread over the entire Great Plains area of the United States. The cattle-raising techniques employed by the northward-moving Texans were of Mexican origin and had been acquired and perfected during the preceding three decades. This form of stock-raising was distinguished from eastern stock-farming by the use of the horse and by the necessity of immense unfenced acreages where cattle could graze freely on natural vegetation. While these early cattlemen had developed a system of stock-rearing perfectly adapted to their physical environment, the possibility of expanding herds beyond the size required to meet the limited needs of military posts and mining towns and thus utilizing fully the enormous pastoral resources available depended upon a connection with the eastern urban market. As one prominent historian of the American west has cogently explained, the western railroad was the one essential upon which the whole future of this new frontier rested, and 'the passing of the first stock train bound for the Chicago market meant that [the] utilization of the northern ranges had begun in earnest.'[1] The tremendous incentive to move western range cattle east was the product of market conditions. A steer worth under ten dollars in Texas could be sold to eastern buyers for thirty to forty dollars.

The first substantial movement of Texas cattle northward came in 1866. This drive, into the feeding areas of Kansas and Missouri rather than to a shipping point was not entirely successful, and it was not until the following year when the Kansas Pacific Railway reached a point some 200 miles west of Kansas City at Abilene that direct shipment to the lucrative eastern market became possible. The 1867 cattle drive established what became the most famous of all cattle trails, the Chisholm Trail, along which larger Texas herds made their way northward each subsequent year. Though increasing dramatically in volume through the late sixties and early seventies, the business was still haphazard. Of the estimated 630,000 head of cattle that crossed the Red River boundary of northern Texas in 1871, most were shipped directly to eastern markets, only about 100,000 head being used to stock the ranges of southern Wyoming and western Nebraska. As soon as the cattlemen crossed the Red River they were in Indian territory and until the final disposition of the plains Indian was accomplished in the late seventies, permanent location in eastern Montana and northern Wyoming was a precarious proposition at best. With the invasion of Indian country by miners and ranchers, hostilities became frequent, but it was not until after the defeat of General George A. Custer on the Little Big Horn River in eastern Montana Territory in June 1876 that a determined federal effort was made to break the power of the northern tribes. As hostilities ended in 1878, stockmen began to move into the Powder River and Big Horn country of northern Wyoming and from the sheltered valleys of western Montana on to the eastern plains.

At the same time would-be ranchers began to move small herds into the foothills of the south-western North-west Territories in Canada. Contrary to the usual interpretation, the ranching frontier as it moved into Canadian territory was not a gradual movement northward after the ranges to the south filled up. Rather, development of the cattle industry in the Canadian south-west was coincident with that of the north-western American plains. Though the cattle kingdom did not develop as rapidly or as extensively in Canada as it did south of the border, it was none the less an integral part of the startling continental expansion which began in 1875 and within three years saw cattle grazing as far north as the Bow River Valley, some 200 miles beyond the international boundary. The domain of the nascent Canadian cattle kingdom ran southward from Calgary along the foothills of the Rocky Mountains to the American boundary.

The movement of cattle into the Canadian foothills country at this time is hardly surprising. In terms of climate and topography the region was very similar to western Montana. A unique climatic feature, the 'chinook,' brought warm, dry winter winds which regularly melted the snow and exposed grass for winter pasture. This desiccating wind also brought cattlemen an indirect advantage. Excessive summer evaporation of surface moisture rendered much of the region semi-arid, and hence less favourable for agriculture than regions further north. Consequently, the number of settlers with whom the ranchers later had to contend was limited until after the turn of the century, when dry-land farming techniques were better understood. The south-west's stock-raising possibilities were further enhanced by the highly nutritious short grass vegetation, by the numerous coulees which furnished natural shelter, and by the large number of

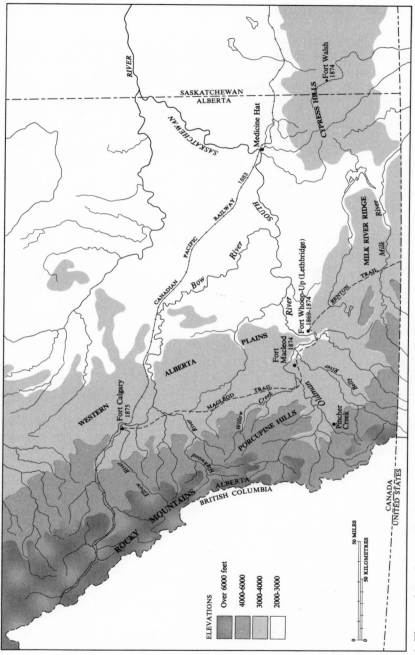

1 The ranching frontier in Canada. Reprinted from *The Prairie West to 1905*, general editor, Lewis G. Thomas, map by Geoffrey Matthews, ©Oxford University Press

streams available for stock-watering. This tremendous natural potential was well known to the former fur and whiskey traders from Ft Benton, Montana, who were among the first to take advantage of this new opportunity.

No white men were more familiar with the high border country than the Ft Benton traders. Arriving first with the American Fur Company, they were part of the commercial frontier that began moving north and west up the Missouri River in the 1830s. Company traders bartered with Indians at posts along the Missouri and Marias rivers on the southern flank of Blackfoot territory. The Hudson's Bay Company also shunned the lands of the hostile Blackfoot Confederacy. After several tentative southward incursions beginning in 1822–3, they retreated to more familiar and hospitable territory and endeavoured to capture what they could of the Blackfoot trade from Rocky Mountain House and Ft Edmonton. It was gold fever in the late 1850s and 1860s that ultimately drew white adventurers to linger in the region while they explored streams and rivers. Though the gold-seekers soon departed for more promising areas, they helped prepare the way for southern traders. Organized trade moved across the border into the heart of Blackfoot country in 1869 and the success of this first venture brought scores of others.[2] The American frontier crossed the boundary with the Yankee traders. Given the name 'Whoop-up Country,' the area was made part of Ft Benton's economic hinterland. Financed mainly by Ft Benton merchants I.G. Baker and T.C. Power and liberally supplied with trade whiskey, the traders debauched, bullied, and fought with the Indians and each other. The Blood, Blackfoot, and Piegan, equipped with new rapid-firing rifles and in competition with white and métis hunters, fell upon the last great buffalo herds in their quest for the hides that the traders prized.

If the land of the Blackfoot was known to frontiersmen as hostile territory, to educated opinion outside it was considered a barren northward extension of the Great American Desert. This view was the legacy of the Hind and Palliser expeditions which traversed the western interior in the late 1850s. In 1858, as the transfer of Hudson's Bay Company lands to Canada was being discussed, Professor Henry Youle Hind of the University of Toronto was sent west by the Canadian government to report on a possible transportation route and upon the region's general prospects. Hind's assessment of the southern plains was scarcely encouraging. He dismissed the entire region south of the South Saskatchewan as a 'treeless plain, with a light and sometimes drifting soil, occasionally blown up into dunes, and not, in its present condition, fitted for the permanent habitation of civilized man.'[3]

The Hind expedition overlapped a more extensive survey of the plains portion of the Hudson's Bay Company territory commissioned by the imperial government. Led by Captain John Palliser, the British expedition thoroughly assessed the region drained by the North and South Saskatchewan rivers and came to an equally negative conclusion about the settlement potential of the short grass prairie.

The general barrenness and absense of valuable timber along this whole region of country has been the cause of great disappointment to us, as all the previous accounts we had heard of the south branch of the Saskatchewan or Bow River, had led us to believe, that it would have been a most desirable place for settlers, but having now examined all that river, we find the whole region ... by no means a desirable district for settlement.[4]

These reports, particularly the latter, apparently precluded successful farming on the southern plains and eventually became weapons in the ranchers' arsenal during their protracted and often bitter struggle to discourage agricultural settlement.

Palliser's prognosis as it related to the entire region was not as bleak as Hind's, for the dry area, subsequently known as Palliser's Triangle, was held to be bordered by a fertile belt attractive for settlement. While these fertile lands to the north and east spanned a broad area, the more promising territory at the western edge of the dry country was but a narrow strip. Pressed by the mountains on one side and an arid waste on the other, and thus confined to the foothills country that paralleled the Rocky Mountains from the international boundary to the Bow River valley, was a ribbon-like oasis that merited special attention. Palliser, like many cattlemen who came to the area a generation later, was drawn to the region's singular beauty. He likened the foothills country to similar lands in Switzerland and the Tyrol, noted the wooded, well-watered character of the landscape as well as the nutritious grasses, and alleged that the climate was 'far preferable to that of either Sweden or Norway.'[5] Palliser's thoughts foreshadowed the preference of later observers to ascribe to the region a unique and attractive character.

After the expeditions of Palliser and Hind, discussions concerning the territory's future continued intermittently. When confederation of the British North American colonies in 1867 finally demonstrated the feasibility of Canadian administration, the British Colonial Office used its persuasive influence to speed the transfer of title. Negotiations were finally concluded in 1869 and the Hudson's Bay Company relinquished its sovereignty to the imperial government, which in turn passed the territory to the new dominion a year later.

In 1870, however, it still appeared that the south-western portion of this new acquisition would continue to be ignored, at least as an area of potential settlement. Captain W.F. Butler, sent by the Canadian government in 1870 to comment on the state of affairs in the interior west of Red River, reiterated the contentions of Hind and Palliser: 'the great plains lying between the Red Deer River and the Missouri [constitute] a vast tract of country which, with few exceptions, is arid, treeless, and sandy – a portion of the true American desert ...'[6] What drew Ottawa's attention to this part of the territory was Butler's account of Indian warfare, the rapidly disappearing buffalo, and the debauching of the native tribes by the numerous American whiskey traders. While the government pondered the question of how best to establish law and order in the region without imposing too heavy a burden on the treasury, the situation continued to deteriorate. Ultimately the massacre in June 1873 of about thirty Assiniboine Indians in the Cypress Hills by a party of white wolf hunters and whiskey traders from Ft Benton prompted a decision.[7] With some fear that the entire region might be engulfed by the Indian wars then raging in the American west, and to bolster Canadian sovereignty in the North-west Territories, the federal government dispatched a small force of soldier-policemen under Captain G.A. French in 1874.

The coming of the North-West Mounted Police was of central importance to western development in general and to the stock-raising industry in particular. Their arrival coincided with the beginning of the rapid expansion of the cattle industry in the American west, and their presence meant that the cattlemen's empire could be established simultaneously in Canadian territory. That presence soon assured the two prerequisites for the development of a stock-raising industry – a market and security. Certain American and former Hudson's Bay Company traders in the vicinity who had long recognized the territory's ranching potential quickly took advantage of the new situation. The pattern here parallels the origin of the stockmen's enterprise in the United States. The first stockmen in the Canadian west were local residents who responded to the presence of small immediate markets, created in the first instance by the police, and a short time later by the purchases of the Department of the Interior for Indian needs. As the western cattleman preferred to let his cattle graze largely unattended on the range, the basis of his livelihood was vulnerable and he was always concerned about the safety of his herd. In quickly suppressing the whiskey trade and in establishing a friendly rapport with the Indian population, the police also provided a measure of protection essential to the cattle industry's development.

The presence of the police at this juncture is significant in another respect. Members of the force witnessed the arrival of the first small herds in the south-west between 1874 and 1876. Thus by 1877 there were a number of men whose terms of enlistment were due to expire who were well aware of the growth and success of the ranching industry in the United States and of the unequalled opportunities close at hand. These former policemen were the core about which the Canadian ranching industry later developed and were in large measure responsible for drawing the attention of other easterners to the region's ranching potential.

During the summer of 1875, the police at Ft Macleod were joined by Joseph MacFarland, an Irishman with long experience in the American west who settled and kept a small herd in the vicinity of the new fort.[8] Others were quick to follow MacFarland's lead, among them George Emerson, a former Hudson's Bay man who had frequented the area since the mid-sixties and who also brought in a small herd from Montana. Their presence is confirmed in the 1876 report of the police Comptroller, Frederick White, who in addition to announcing his pleasure that the liquor traffic was now suppressed, observed that 'a number of Americans have crossed the border and engaged in stock raising and other pursuits' and that a small village had sprung up around the fort.[9]

These settlers were soon joined by a few of the thirty-nine policemen whose terms of engagement had expired during the year.[10] In 1877 more enlistment contracts terminated and additional officers and men became cattlemen. Inspector W.F. Shurtliff and Superintendent W. Winder sought the best of both worlds and made a joint purchase of stock which they left in the keeping of others while they continued in the force.[11] This practice was common enough to draw public criticism and on one occasion compelled Prime Minister Macdonald to address the charge of police impropriety. The flow of former policemen into the nascent cattle industry was such that by 1880, before the arrival of the big cattle companies, they made up the dominant element within the ranch community.[13] Their presence, of course, had an important impact on the region's evolving social milieu. Their attitude to law and order, for example, contrasted with that of ranchers south of the boundary and assured that vigilante justice would rarely be a part of the Canadian cattlemen's modus operandi.

The settlement of ranchers near Ft Macleod between 1875 and 1877 was paralleled to a lesser extent in the Bow River valley some 150 miles farther north. Though Ft Macleod for the first decade was the recognized capital of the Canadian cattle kingdom, Ft Calgary soon was a rival claimant. The arrival of cattle in this region actually predated that of southern herds by two years. The first cattle in the Canadian south-west were those brought in in 1873 from Ft Garry by the Methodist missionary John McDougall to his father's new mission at Morleyville on the Bow River. A second herd was brought to the mission the following year from Montana by Kenneth McKenzie.[14] The first large herd, some 450 head, was driven into the valley across the Rockies from the Columbia Lake district in August 1875 by John Shaw.[15]

This incredible cattle drive years before the rest of the country was even aware that a functional pass through the southern Rockies existed was a product of the British Columbia cattle industry's desperate search for new markets as gold-mining communities began to decline in the late 1860s. By 1874 interior cattlemen had identified seven possible trails to their most promising external market, the towns on the south-western coast. Cattle from the Kamloops area were common arrivals in New Westminster from the mid-1870s.[16] The willingness of British Columbia ranchers to accept the challenge of terrain and distance in their search for markets is clearly underlined in the great cattle drive undertaken by Thaddeus Harper in 1876–7. With nine hired cowhands Harper drove nearly 2000 head of British Columbia cattle to San Francisco.[17] Hard-pressed British Columbia cattlemen, like their counterparts in Washington and Oregon, also looked for potential markets east of the Rockies. In the United States the movement of cattle from west to east was much more massive. Large herds from the Pacific northwest were driven through the mountains into Montana to join with Texas cattle in stocking the plains. This meant that the early herds established in northern Montana and the Canadian south-west were built as much from western as from Texas stock. The famous Cochrane herd of about 6000 head which was later driven into the Bow River valley from Montana had this bi-regional origin.

A clear signal that cattle-raising in the south-west could begin in earnest came in 1877 with the signing of Indian Treaty Number 7. At Blackfoot Crossing the assembled south-west tribes, in return for promises and assurances of support if and when hard times should come, agreed to 'cede, release, surrender, and yield up to the Government of Canada for Her Majesty the Queen and her successors forever, all their rights, and privileges whatsoever to the lands …'[18] The Indians' renunciation of their title to the land and the government's promise to supply them with cattle[19] provided a strong stimulus to the incipient industry. The treaty also meant implicitly that the 'free grass' era in Canadian ranching history would be short-lived, for now that the lands were available and the industry proven, eastern official and business interests began to think in terms of large-scale stock-raising.

Gradual expansion of the industry continued with the promise of an expanding market. Within a year of the treaty's signing it was apparent that the Blackfeet were in difficulty. Police Commissioner James Macleod warned Ottawa that settling the Indians down to pastoral pursuits would be slower than anticipated, that the buffalo were rapidly disappearing and would not last more than three years, and that soon starving Indians could pose a serious threat.[20] Beef rations would have to be supplied and the Commissioner recommended that the government prepare for this situation by going into the cattle business.

He suggested that a large herd could be established in the Bow River country, where pasturage was abundant and cattle could graze outdoors all winter. 'There is no question in my mind as to the investment,' Macleod said enthusiastically. 'Many men in Montana have made fortunes in this business; why should not the Government utilize the magnificent domain lying idle in the West ...' This unqualified assurance was supported by a report of the mildest winter since the arrival of the force, a winter alleged to have brought little or no snow and to have been interrupted only by an 'occasional cold day.'

Such local optimism was directly reflected in the industry's continuing growth as the number of former policemen and others joining the ranchers' ranks began to increase at a faster rate. By 1878 it was necessary for the Territorial Council to pass the first ordinance respecting marketing of stock.[21] There is no evidence for the tradition that the disillusioned ranchers deserted the territory in 1879 in face of the depredations of starving Indians.[22] In truth, that year followed the pattern set by the previous four and was marked by the arrival of many would-be ranchers, including the usual number of discharged police, certain eastern Canadians, and the first well-to-do Britons.[23] Also in 1879 the government decided to act upon Macleod's 1878 advice and reduce expenses by establishing a ranching enterprise of its own. One thousand head of breeding cattle were brought from Montana to be used as foundation stock to increase local meat supplies for the Indians. The decision was timely; during the winter of 1880 daily rations were provided at Ft Macleod for 200-300 starving Indians.[24] This action seems to have lessened the problem of Indian cattle-killing that had begun to increase through 1878.

By 1880 the cattle-grazing industry was firmly established in the Canadian south-west. At Ft Macleod and Pincher Creek, thirty miles west, the nuclei of definite communities had been established.[25] In all there were about 200 individuals scattered between the American boundary and the Bow River valley who had begun small-scale ranching ventures. Already the community had developed distinctive social characteristics. In addition to the former policemen, who tended to reflect the values of their middle class Ontario background,[26] and the Canadian and American traders already mentioned, there was another group of Canadians. They were mainly from the Eastern Townships and, it would appear, from Compton County in particular. One of the first police officers to leave the force in order to pursue a ranching career was Captain William Winder of Lennoxville, Quebec. While on leave in 1879, Winder apparently discussed the possibility of forming a large cattle company with a number of well-to-do farmers and merchants and in so doing was at least indirectly responsible for arousing the interest of the most successful stock breeder in the Townships, Senator Matthew H. Cochrane. Though large investors began to investigate the region's potential, they were not prepared at this stage to commit capital until the government's intentions regarding the proposed transcontinental railway were clearly understood. This concern about railways and access to large urban markets, however, was not such an immediate concern to those who thought in more humble terms and who began to leave the Townships in growing numbers to start ranching in the west on a smaller scale.[27]

Several factors probably account for the interest evident in the Townships. The region's connection with and interest in the west dated from fur-trade days. For example, George Emerson, a former Hudson's Bay trader and one of the earliest ranchers in the region, was from this part of Quebec. More important perhaps was the attention the south-west gained in the press through the exploits of the newly created federal police force. Such general interest gained particular strength in the Townships for two reasons. The increasing French-Canadian immigration into the region was accompanied by a growing social pressure which encouraged many of the English-speaking population to contemplate the possibilities of new lands in the west. This was particularly true of younger sons whose future in the Townships seemed limited by the competition for land.[28] At the same time the particular attraction of the grazing lands of the south-west over other western regions was related to the presence of a long-established stock-raising industry in the Townships, particularly in prosperous Compton County, where cattle-raising was the single most important industry.[29] As a result there were many farmers and merchants in the region acquainted with the cattle business who could evaluate the stock-raising potential of the prairie south-west with a practised eye and special interest.

The embryonic ranching community, predominantly of eastern Canadian origin but including a minority of American and Canadian frontiersmen, was joined between 1879 and 1881 by another group that contributed to the Canadian cattle kingdom's distinctive social milieu. From 1879 there began to arrive a number of Englishmen who typically wrote 'gentleman' under the heading 'previous occupation' on their homestead applications. Unlike Louis Garnet, one of the first to arrive in 1879, most did not insist on appearing for dinner in evening dress in order to 'keep from reverting to savagery,'[30] or go to the expense of having a piano delivered to the ranch while the railway was still several hundred miles distant, but Garnet's eccentricities are indicative of the social order which was to evolve. These prospective ranchers invariably had sufficient capital to establish their own ranches, and they were generally members of the middle and upper strata of British society. Most arrived with the moral and financial backing of influential friends at home and in Canada. Charles Inderwick and F.W. Godsal, for example, came west with considerable funds and the personal recommendations of the Marquis of Lorne. Others had close relations in the upper echelons of British parliamentary and military circles.[31]

Probably most numerous among Britons were those drawn from the lesser landed gentry, who either sold or left small properties, expecting to regain their economic status in the Canadian west at a time when British agriculture was particularly hard-pressed to meet the competition of agricultural imports.[32] Hartford and Sampson, the Oxford-trained proprietors of the Bar XY, were typical of many well-educated second sons who could not be supported by the family estate at home. It was customary for the family in Britain to support these individuals with an annual remittance until they could become comfortably established in their new occupation. Associated with this group were many Anglo-Irish who left threatened estates in southern Ireland. Other families of the English establishment were represented in the Canadian west by sons whose military pensions and gratuities provided sufficient capital to allow them to become ranchers. The country abounded with ranchers whose former military rank remained a common prefix to their surnames.[33]

The country was so filled with expatriate Britons, according to the Canadian wife of one rancher, that social discourse was hopelessly confined to 'their childhood – the opera – military tournaments – Henley ...'[34] She was also critical of what she deemed to be the rather condescending attitude of many of her neighbours towards Canadians. 'There are so many Englishmen here,' she wrote to a friend in the spring of 1884; 'they nearly all have no tact in the way they speak of Canadians and Canada, and the last straw to me is the way in which they say "but we do not look on you as a Canadian!" They mistake this for a compliment. It makes my Canadian blood boil.' At the same time her own insistence that the cowboys on her ranch appear properly attired with collar and tie for dinner suggests that despite her complaints she probably fitted without too much difficulty into the evolving social mould, as did many of her Canadian compatriots.

The English character and the presence of so many Englishmen 'of good family' were consistently reported by visitors and residents of the region before the turn of the century. British journalists travelling with the Marquis of Lorne on his western tour in 1881 were much impressed with the foothills country around Ft Macleod and Pincher Creek. The representative of the *Edinburgh Courant* observed that 'quite a little colony had been attracted by the beauty and fertility of the country, and among them men of high English Family ...'[35] Five years later in the opening address to the Territorial Council, Lieutenant Governor Edgar Dewdney commented that the Provisional District of Alberta had over the past number of years 'received a very important addition to its population, consisting principally of wealthy families' chiefly engaged in stock-raising.[36] Writing in *Blackwood's Edinburgh Magazine* of Canadian ranch life in the late 1890s, Moira O'Neill observed that the country 'abounded' with Englishmen and that the region was 'emphatically a land of the Younger Son.'

Herself chatelaine of a ranch near High River, O'Neill emphasized that life for an 'English lady' on a ranch was not that of a household drudge; though homes were not as refined as in Britain, no walls could compare with her cedar-panelled ones as the 'ideal background for water colours, china, and books.' Above all she stressed the beauty of the countryside, where one could 'find great refreshment in the shady side of a big haystack, and Bacon's "History of the Reign of Henry VII".'[37] The life-style of some wealthier ranchers at the turn of the century was accurately presented in Canada's first encyclopaedia, wherein many cattlemen were noted as having 'established themselves in charming homesteads, surrounded by the same kind of comfort and refinement which Englishmen associate with the life of an English country house.' By way of qualification the author did remind his readers that there were many stages of development from the small lumber shack 'to the stone house spreading its red roofed verandahs in the midst of well-kept lawns and flower gardens ...'[38]

Though the squirearchy or 'race of "ranch patriarchs",' which Professor W. Brown of the Agricultural College at Guelph felt should be established in the pastoral regions of the south-west,[39] did not quite develop, a distinctive society peculiar to the Canadian cattle kingdom did evolve. At the apex of the region's social pyramid was a wealthy and politically powerful élite composed principally of Britons and eastern Canadians. The outward manifestations of this early ranching society included among other things the fox hunt, in which the lowly coyote was the unhappy substitute for the fox, a polo league of international calibre, Chinese cooks, governesses, tutors and schools in the 'Old Country' and eastern Canada, and winters in Calgary, Victoria, or Great Britain, depending on financial status. This group was definitely a minority, but they were none the less the arbiters of a social standard, artificial though it may have been.

As indicated, the foundations of this society had been established as early as 1881, before the era of the cattle companies began. Up to this time the Canadian cattle kingdom had been the preserve of the small rancher. The first hint that this phase, the era of free grass, was about to end came when the Department of the Interior reported in 1879 that certain individuals already were successfully engaged in the stock-raising industry in the foothill region, and then pointedly predicted that there was 'every possibility of the further development by gentlemen of experience in stock-farming, and possessed of large capital both from Great Britain and the older Provinces.'[40] The report might be recognized as the government's declaration of intent to promote the interest of cattle companies and large stockmen.

Officials in Ottawa were eager to see the establishment of a large stock-raising industry in a region hitherto considered to be practically a desert. Because it brought investment and limited settlement to a region considered too dry for cereal agriculture, ranching seemed to fit perfectly into the general framework of western development. In addition there was the immediate and pressing problem of meeting Indian beef requirements as the last buffalo herds disappeared from the northern plains. Dr Duncan McEachran, Chief Veterinary Inspector and a prominent early ranch manager and owner, cynically summarized government policy towards the Indians at the time as operating on the premise that it was 'cheaper to feed [Indians] than to fight them.'[41] The expense was none the less significant. For Ft Benton's I.G. Baker Company alone, Canadian government beef contracts were worth more than $500,000 a year in the late 1870s. This major and growing expense, coupled with the limited success of the government-sponsored ranching enterprise intitiated in 1879, was another factor that prompted the interest of Macdonald's Department of the Interior officials in establishment of a large-scale cattle industry in the western foothills.

There were at the same time many eastern capitalists, particularly in Montreal, who were increasingly interested in the possibilities of western stock-raising. But real development was precluded until several outstanding concerns could be resolved. Larger investors had been reluctant to establish themselves in a region where land tenure, as it was known in the east, had yet to be defined, where land use or 'range right' was determined only by a vague mutual understanding between parties, rather than by legal contract, and where it seemed cattle were simply turned loose on the prairie. More important, the Liberal government of Alexander Mackenzie, faced with a severe depression, showed little enthusiasm for construction of the transcontinental railway which was the prerequisite for establishment of cattle export markets.

The situation altered dramatically in 1878 when Sir John A. Macdonald and his Conservative party were returned to power and gave first priority to completion of a railway to British Columbia. The prospect of railway construction crews at work across the west promised a substantial increase in the immediate local market. This, with the fortuitous coincidence of the British government's decision in 1879 to impose an embargo on live cattle imports from the United States, which promised to give Canadian cattle a privileged position in the British market, presented the possibility of huge export sales and engendered much enthusiasm. Hereafter potential stock-raisers and land speculators took a lively interest in the grazing lands of the Canadian south-west.

Given the government's desire to see rapid expansion of the ranching frontier in Canada as well as the definite interest of certain eastern capitalists, it remained for the two sides to come to some mutually agreeable arrangement by which expansion could occur. Of first concern was the matter and manner of land tenure. This question was eventually resolved after much negotiation between the Canadian Prime Minister and Senator Matthew H. Cochrane. As possibly the most prominent stock-breeder in Canada and as one engaged in the stock business most of his life, Cochrane was naturally interested in the possibilities of western stock-raising.

He was born in 1824 on a farm in Compton County, Quebec, and resided there except for twenty-three years in Boston, where he eventually prospered in the manufacture of shoes and leather goods. He returned to Canada in 1864 and continued his business in Montreal. By the mid-eighties, in partnership with Charles Cassils, his firm employed some 300 people and had a yearly business volume of about $500,000. This business success, which assisted his appointment to the Senate, provided the initial resources to support his main preoccupation, animal husbandry. Cochrane was determined to make his way to the forefront of British and American cattle-breeding circles. With astute judgment and liberal expenditure he achieved quick and remarkable success. In 1868, for example, he purchased the cow 'Duchess 97th,' paying 1000 guineas, until then the highest price ever paid for a shorthorn cow in Great Britain. The British shorthorn was a favoured breed in the latter half of the nineteenth century and Cochrane's pedigreed herd was soon internationally acclaimed. By the late 1870s he was exporting breeding stock to Great Britain and the United States. At a British auction in 1877 his 'Fifth Duchess of Hillhurst' sold for a record 4300 guineas. The handsome financial success of his prize-winning shorthorn exports led Cochrane to expand operations at his now-famous Hillhurst farm in Compton County to include purebred Hereford and Aberdeen Angus herds.[42]

Cochrane's intimate acquaintance with the British and United States pedigreed cattle markets meant that he was also conscious of the dramatic growth through the late 1870s of North American live cattle exports to the British consumer market (see Table 1). While growth of the British market led to a tremendous increase in beef production in Quebec's Eastern Townships and in the farming areas of Ontario, Cochrane sensed that the greatest profit potential lay in the mass production of quality beef. The key to this vision was access to grazing lands on the far western frontier.

Cochrane's first official request for grazing lands along the Bow River west of Calgary came on 26 November 1880.[43] Shortly thereafter he sent to the government tentative plans for his proposed ranching scheme, along with a request for certain considerations not specifically covered by provisions in the Dominion

Lands Act. Before 1881, grazing regulations were ill defined. The first Dominion Lands Act in 1872 anticipated that stock-raising in the west would follow the traditional eastern pattern, that it would be primarily a small-scale activity conducted to supplement farmers' other agricultural endeavours. Consequently, unoccupied pasture could be leased only to bona fide homesteaders.[44] A grazing lease could be cancelled on six months' notice and the land made available for homesteading or other purposes. When the suitability of certain parts of the western territory for stock-raising became apparent by 1876 the act was amended to permit leasing of grazing land to non-residents, individuals, or companies. Cancellation notice was extended to two years and the lessee's commitment to agricultural settlement was no longer required.[45] In the grazing country, however, none of the early ranchers bothered with such a formality. In this regard Canadian practice followed the American pattern, where it was mutually understood by the small local stockmen that 'range rights,' or the use of a particular area, was acquired by the first cattleman to bring his herd into the valley of a stream or river.

Cochrane prefaced his proposal to Prime Minister Macdonald with what he considered to be the advantages that would accrue to the government and the nation were a viable ranching industry established. He stressed that the government would no longer be obliged to purchase beef supplies for the police and Indians from foreigners and would at the same time be favouring growth of industry on its own side of the border. In addition to tying his own interests to Macdonald's National Policy, he emphasized the benefits of such an enterprise to future immigrants to the Territories. They would have the opportunity to stock their farms with improved breeds of cattle and horses rather than with inferior animals from the United States and without having to face the excessive cost of transportation from Ontario. Cochrane also expressed the belief that a large cattle export trade could be developed. He estimated that the cost of establishing in the west a herd of 2000-3000 animals including about seventy-five purebred bulls would be about $125,000. To warrant this large outlay he asked to lease an area sufficient to expand the herd to 10,000 and the right to purchase an acreage within the leased tract sufficient for ranch buildings and for a certain amount of winter protection and forage.[46]

Last of all, Cochrane assured Macdonald that the lands he desired along the Bow River were to be the best of his knowledge unoccupied and offered no special attraction to farm settlers. This general outline was followed about two months later with a more specific and somewhat expanded proposal. In return for a larger commitment, which Cochrane estimated would represent an investment of about $500,000 within two years, he requested the right eventually to purchase 10,000 acres of his choice within the bounds of the lease. He asked in addition that he be allowed to purchase outright all lands along the lease's outer boundary. He argued that such government co-operation was necessary if the government wished to ensure successful inauguration of improved stock-breeding on an extensive scale in the North-West Territories.[47]

Macdonald and his cabinet met intermittently throughout the spring of 1881 to consider Cochrane's propositions. The cabinet's general attitude towards the scheme was favourable, perhaps because Cochrane's case was so ably supported by his good friend, Compton neighbour and Minister of Agriculture, John H. Pope. The only issue that appears to have generated any substantial debate was how much land within the leasehold a lessee should be permitted to purchase outright, as well as the price to be charged for these acres. Macdonald was prepared to concede that Cochrane's request for a base of freehold land from which to operate his ranch could be considered a legitimate security, but he judged the request for 10,000 acres excessive and he was not prepared to allow purchase of land along lease boundaries. The government's response to Cochrane's proposal therefore was that the senator be allowed to purchase, at $2.00 an acre, 5000 acres selected from within a leased tract of 100,000 acres, also to be selected by Cochrane. An annual rental of ten dollars per 1000 acres and a provision for return of the lease to the Crown on two years' notice was also suggested.[48]

Before final approval in cabinet, the government's draft terms were submitted for Cochrane's consideration. In subsequent discussions the senator persuaded the government to reduce the price to be charged the lessee for homestead land within the leasehold from $2.00 to $1.25 per acre, although he was unable to get a firm commitment as to the amount of land that could be purchased at this price.[49] It was further agreed that Cochrane would have the first choice of grazing lands in the west and that during 1881 and 1882 lease-holders would be permitted to stock their leases with duty-free American cattle.[50] On the basis of this understanding Cochrane completed organization of his ranch company and arranged for purchase of cattle in Montana.

It was not until a half year later, in December 1881, a month after the first Cochrane herd had reached the Bow River valley, that an order-in-council finally introduced the government's new grazing lease policy to the Canadian public. Leases of up to 100,000 acres were to be granted for a period not exceeding twenty-one years. The rental was set at one cent per acre per year, or $10.00 for every 1000 acres. In order to deter speculators and ensure a means of cancellation, the lessee was obliged to place on the tract one head of cattle for every ten acres embraced by the lease within three years of the assignment.[51] This provision was also intended to set the maximum number of cattle that could be put on a lease and thus prevent over-stocking. The government reserved as well the right to terminate the contract for any reason on two years' notice.[52] To Cochrane's chagrin, the lessee's right of purchase was left somewhat vague, permitting the option of purchase within the leasehold 'for a home farm and corral,' without specifying the amount of land that could be bought. Beyond this the senator was surprised to learn that under the newly announced policy the per acre cost of such lands had been restored to the original $2.00.

Ottawa's less generous attitude perhaps is explained by the fact that as negotiations had proceeded through 1881 the government became aware that interest in western stock-raising had greatly increased and that there was a vigorous demand for leases. 'Ranching fever,' as the press came to describe this interest, promised to make it less difficult to attract risk capital to the west and the government consequently reverted to a somewhat stronger position than it had taken in the discussions with Cochrane in the spring. Moreover, Senator Cochrane had already made his commitment and his presence in the west ensured that others would follow. Cochrane felt betrayed. He insisted that he had been promised the right to five per cent of the land leased at $1.25 per acre and had his solicitor press the claim, using as evidence a note to this effect from Macdonald to J.H. Pope on 12 May 1881.[53] He continued to advance his demand for the next two years, for instance, lamenting in June 1883 that winter losses had cost the company over $100,000, and that he would not have invested a dollar in the enterprise had it not been for the promise.[54] His efforts were to no avail and the issue dragged on for a full decade before it was finally settled at a conclave of ranchers and government officials in 1892. Cochrane's plea was probably thwarted by the commanding position his company had already assumed despite the alleged handicap of which he complained. Cochrane and his associates controlled and had excluded all others from a fifty-mile stretch of the river valley from Calgary to the mountains in the west.

Implementation of the new lease system marked the close of the first developmental phase of the Canadian ranching frontier. With the lease structure came the era of the large cattle companies and rapid expansion of the western stock-raising industry. The usual romanticism and traditional focus of attention on this second period of development, a period that some have labelled the cattle kingdom's 'golden age,' should not obscure the fact that it was the small stockmen between 1875 and 1880 who proved the region's potential and laid the necessary foundation for the company era. Important as the Cochrane Ranch was, the history of stock-raising in the Canadian west does not begin with it. There were already thousands of cattle grazing on the range when the company men arrived. In the ten months immediately preceding arrival of the first company herd (the 6634 Cochrane cattle) in September 1881, seventeen independent local stockmen in the Ft Macleod region, for example, had brought in at least 5000 head.[55] Cattle had grazed in the Bow River valley for almost a decade before Cochrane's celebrated herd was driven into the valley.

The new system greatly changed the position of the independent stockmen and to this extent fundamentally altered the pattern of development that had evolved in the ranch country before 1881. Ottawa's grazing lease policy not only heralded the arrival of the cattle companies, it made it much more difficult for additional small stock-raisers to get started. First there was the problem of obtaining a lease. This was absolutely essential if a would-be rancher was to have sufficient grazing land to accommodate a herd of cattle and if he was to obtain his cattle at the most advantageous price. Only leaseholders were accorded the right to import their foundation stock from the United States duty free. Settlers and small stockmen who were non-leaseholders were required to pay the regular twenty per cent customs levy. Moreover, leases were assigned from the distant federal capital and individuals applying from the west often found that the desired range had been given to someone in the east who had important friends in Parliament. Within a few years most of the preferred grazing land in the Rocky Mountain foothills had been leased to eastern-based cattle companies.

The alternative for the small rancher without capital was to apply for a 160-acre homestead and take his chances ranging a few head of cattle on the surrounding countryside. But this choice had limitations as well; if the land desired was under lease, homestead entry was not permitted. In effect the lease regulations contained a 'no-settlement' clause. The fact that the lease could be cancelled on two years' notice offered little hope for an intending homesteader. In practice it meant that a prospective homesteader, even if he could convince the government that certain lands should be withdrawn from the lease, would be compelled to wait for two years after the notice of cancellation had been sent to the lessee. Many prospective settlers as it turned out were not prepared to wait two, three, or four years and consequently moved to lands further north. This provision thus had a profound effect on the early history of the region. It set in motion a conflict between the large stockmen and companies on one side and many small stock-raisers and would-be farmers on the other. It was a conflict that was to last, with varying degrees of bitterness, until World War I. The new lease system in effect gave control of the region to the big operators.

The establishment of the lease system with which this period ends is significant in another context. Borrowed from the Australian experience, the idea of leasing grazing land rather than allowing it to be used as public pasture is another reflection of the different tradition north of the 49th parallel. Acceptance of the established imperial principle that leasehold tenure for pastoral purposes was a logical intermediate condition before a territory was opened up to general farm settlement had an important effect.[56] It ensured that the Canadian range would develop in a manner significantly different from the American pattern. Indeed, the promotion and administrative role of the federal government in the range cattle industry distinguishes the Canadian from the American experience.

'Free grass' was the motive force behind the vast expansion of the American cattle industry in the 1870s. Theoretically the range was free to all. In practice, the traditional phenomenon of the American frontier, squatter sovereignty, determined what land could be used by whom. Such sovereignty was based upon the custom of priority; when a cattleman drove his herd into some promising valley and found cattle already present he went elsewhere. Early legislation in the cattle country provided punishment for those who drove stock from their 'accustomed range.' Though directed against cattle rustling, such laws indirectly recognized the fact that by grazing in a certain area the stock-owner gained a prescriptive right to the range over one who might come later. Such a system worked well in the American west as long as there were new valleys into which the industry could expand, but as the range became more crowded such ill-defined range rights proved difficult to defend by legal means. In contrast, in the Canadian west, through leasing the public domain the government maintained a much more direct control of land use and, perhaps as much by accident as by design, largely prevented the ruinous overstocking that afflicted much of the American ranch country by the mid-1880s. At the same time, by establishing a clear basis of legal ownership, leases helped prevent the range wars that occasionally developed south of the border among ranchers disputing one another's rights to a particular range.

While introduction of the lease system clearly brought about a sharp change in the operational structure of the western cattle industry and thus ended the first phase of development on the Canadian ranching frontier, the new policy also promoted continuity in the region's evolving social pattern. The lease policy tended to reinforce those already observable social characteristics that perhaps were the most important legacy of the free grass period. Now that it was necessary to have a grazing lease, those best served were applicants with the most influence in the east and particularly, as will be shown, those with the best-placed friends in the Conservative party. The new policy therefore measurably strengthened the region's Canadian orientation. With this political preference went an accompanying class bias. It required more capital to start a ranch than it did to farm; consequently ranching tended to attract people with greater resources. Therefore, by making it even more difficult for small stock-raisers to get started, the new lease policy served further to define the class base from which the ranch population would be drawn.

The people attracted to the ranch country during the founding period thus stand in sharp contrast to those described in the traditional literature. In a social demographic context the Canadian cattle kingdom was not simply a northward extension of the American ranching frontier. A majority of those who came to the southwest corner of the Canadian prairie were people who were collectively very different from the American ranch community and, it must be stressed, distinct from the larger western farm population with whom they are usually included. This social difference, in fact, compounded the economic and political differences which divided the farm and ranch communities. The vast majority of the newcomers to the western foothills were not frontiersmen or those whose families had moved progressively westward for several generations as the frontier advanced, as was more characteristic in the United States. Contrary to the traditional interpretation, the Canadian cattlemen of the period were representatives of the metropolitan culture of the east and of the stratified society of rural Britain. The social orientation was eastward rather than southward. Though in essence the economic character of the ranching enterprise and the stock-raising techniques were largely the same on both sides of the border, this must not be allowed to obscure the fact that the social structure which evolved north of the boundary during this period was uniquely Canadian.

2

The cattle companies and the 'beef bonanza' 1882–91

The ranching industry should not be considered simply as an arid land adaptation. The advantage of ranching compared to alternative patterns of land use within the same region is determined in the long run by return on investment. Ranching is not a subsistence occupation. If grain-growing, for example, offers a greater return, then the ranching industry predictably contracts. Cattle ranching as it developed in North America in the early 1880s was strictly a business operation and in this sense is a product of the Industrial Revolution. The industry depends on large urban markets as well as a massive processing and transportation infrastructure to link producer and consumer. The required technology came with the westward advance of the railway after the American Civil War and the subsequent development of the refrigerator ship in 1879,[1] which meant that cheaply grown western beef gained access to the high-priced markets of the eastern United States and Europe. The situation presented intense speculative appeal, as the rapid organization of numerous heavily capitalized cattle companies attests. In the broadest sense the phenomenal expansion of the ranching frontier in the late 1870s and early 1880s is as much an expansion into the working class areas of London, Manchester, and cities of the American seaboard as into the grasslands of the north-western plains.

The vast expansion of the North American stock-raising industry during the late 1870s was greatly stimulated by the dramatic increase in beef exports to Great Britain. Beef shipments to Britain from the United States, which began in 1874, amounted in 1876 to only a few hundred head, and then suddenly climbed to approximately 75,000 head in 1879.[2] British annual imports of fresh beef increased from 1732 tons in 1876 to an average of 30,000 tons between 1878 and 1880, of which eighty to ninety per cent came from the United States.[3] The increasing demand for beef in Great Britain coincided with a decline in her own production. Persistent outbreaks of cattle plague, foot and mouth disease,

TABLE 1

Exports of live cattle from North America to
Great Britain 1874-84

Year	Canadian live cattle	American live cattle	
		I	II
1874	63	–	123
1875	455	299	110
1876	638	392	224
1877	4,007	11,538	5,091
1878	7,433	68,540	24,982
1879	20,587	74,117	71,794
1880	32,680	154,814	125,742
1881	49,409	103,693	134,361
1882	41,519	47,686	68,008
1883	37,894	154,631	76,091
1884	53,962	138,661	169,257

SOURCE: data for Canadian exports from *Statistical Year
Book of Canada for 1900* (Ottawa: Government Printing
Bureau 1901) 99. Data for American exports from W.D.
Zimmerman, 'Live Cattle Export Trade between United
States and Great Britain, 1868–1885,' *Agricultural History*
XXXVI (January 1962) 50. Column I is derived from British
sources, column II from US sources.

and pleuropneumonia compelled destruction of several million head of British
cattle during the 1860s and 1870s.[4] In a situation where British demand was
increasing as herds were being depleted and where the price of beef had
accordingly risen, a highly profitable market for North American cattle thus
emerged almost immediately.

Both the Canadian government and cattle producers were alert to the potential of this market. Government officials, conscious of Great Britain's growing
predominance as an importer of Canadian agricultural produce, paid special
heed to developments in this sector. Under the guidance of Dr Duncan McEachran, Chief Veterinary Inspector, shipping facilities at embarkation ports were
improved and regulated. Farmers in Ontario and Quebec quickly responded to
improving beef prices with enormous production increases.[5] As live cattle
became a major shipping commodity, other commercial interests, particularly
the Montreal-based Allan and Dominion Steamship lines, also developed interest in the north Atlantic cattle trade.

The magnitude of cattle imports was such that by 1878 there was growing
concern among British farmers over the competition of cheaper imported
American beef. At the same time financial circles, particularly in Edinburgh,

became excited about the investment potential of American cattle ranching. Popular journals were soon filled with the reports of enthusiastic visitors and investment agents who described the tremendous potential profits. In 1879 such optimistic assessments were officially confirmed in a British Royal Commission on Agriculture established to assess the competitive threat. Two of the assistant commissioners sent to America to investigate explained that the key to the western stockman's success was free public land. After the purchase of a herd and a minimal amount of river or steam frontage for watering, the cattleman faced no operational expenses save that of herding his cattle. They reported that it was 'generally acknowledged that the average profit of the stock-grower has been for years fully 33 per cent.' With the singular advantage of 'land for nothing, and an abundance of it,' ranching was described as clearly the most profitable branch of American farming.[6] Such was the tenor of numerous books, articles, and pamphlets that continued to appear until the crisis of 1886. Books such as General James S. Brisbin's *Beef Bonanza or How to Get Rich on the Plains* discussed cheap land and fabulous profits and gained wide attention.[7] British newspapers carried quotations from American sources which claimed profits averaging 100 per cent for each of the five years between 1877 and 1882.[8] Even more conservative estimates of profits ranging from 33½ to 66½ per cent by writers such as the Scot, J.S. Tait, in a small brochure entitled 'The Cattle-fields of the Far West,'[9] were sufficient to create an investment craze.

The arithmetic of profit was blatantly straightforward; a good calf worth five dollars at birth could be fed on almost free grass and would bring forty-five to sixty dollars when ready for market three or four years later. By 1879 the great 'cattle boom' was underway and by 1883 a host of British financiers and titled investors had established heavily capitalized individual and company enterprises. The foreign-controlled giants of the industry, the Prairie Cattle Company, Ltd, the Texas Land and Cattle Company, Ltd, the Matador Land and Cattle Company, Ltd, the Hansford Land and Cattle Company, Ltd, the Western American Cattle Company, Ltd, and the Swan Land and Cattle Company, Ltd, some of whom later extended their operations into Canada, were all formed in this period. In 1882, for example, ten major British-American cattle companies were incorporated, the smallest, the Western Land and Cattle Company, capitalized at $575,000 and the largest, the Matador Land and Cattle Company, at $2,000,000.[10]

Ranching fever developed simultaneously in Canada as Canadian capitalists, particularly those already involved in the new eastern-based cattle export trade, discovered that a comparable grazing area, already proven by small stockmen, existed in their own west. Enthusiasm grew following the 1879 British embargo on American live cattle imports. This disease control measure, which compelled the slaughter of American cattle on arrival in port, promised to leave the feeder market open to Canadian producers. It was here that the western steer had the greatest price advantage, an advantage the Canadian Minister of Agriculture estimated to be worth about twenty dollars a head over comparable US animals.[11]

The possibilities appeared highly attractive and the Canadian press joined those of the United States and Great Britain in proclaiming this new Eldorado. The Winnipeg *Times*, for example, asserted: 'Our North-West Territories afford choice locations where the veriest novice could embark in the raising of horses or cattle, almost without limit, and with a sure promise of great reward.'[12] The credibility and reach of such optimistic local appraisals were given a great boost through the wide coverage that attended the Marquis of Lorne's western tour in the summer of 1881. Correspondents from the *Edinburgh Courant*, *Edinburgh Scotsman*, *London Graphic*, *London Times*, and the *London Telegraph* who accompanied the Governor General's party commented upon the rich soil of Manitoba and Saskatchewan, but it was the foothills ranch country with its magnificent moutain backdrop which really caught their imagination. Lorne and his friends spoke of the beauty of the region, the well-watered and wooded nature of the terrain, and the obvious ranching possibilities attested to by the ranchers already established in the area.[13] Opinions from the popular press were supported as well by the most reputable professionals. John Macoun, the respected and nationally known Dominion Field Naturalist and Botanist, in his controversial but widely read book *Manitoba and the Great North-West*, predicted a glowing future for the ranching industry in the Canadian west, saying that the region must become 'the chief stock-raising country in America.'[14] Such glowing reports from visitors to the cattle country persisted to the turn of the century.[15] Contrary views received practically no publicity.[16] Given such optimistic assessments, Canadian and some British investors sought locations in the foothills of the Canadian Rockies. Capitalists saw in this region the opportunity for rapid and immense gain, an almost intoxicating prospect in a period which, in Canada at least, was one of severe recession.

The stock-raising techniques which promised such substantial rewards required considerable capital and thereby excluded most of those outside the financial circles of eastern metropolitan centres. The first group of capitalists that gathered about Senator Cochrane is typical of those attracted and warrants detailed attention.

Shareholders in the Cochrane Ranche Company, Ltd, incorporated 5 May 1881 and capitalized at $500,000, included Senator M.H. Cochrane, his son

James, Dr Duncan McEachran, James Walker, and J.M. Browning. Other shareholders by 1885 were L.H. Massue, George A. Drummond, James Gibb, and
E.T. Brooks.[17] The Scottish-born McEachran was the leading Canadian veterinary surgeon of his day and founder of the Montreal School of Comparative and
Veterinary Medicine. His concern over the danger of importing diseased animals was instrumental in establishment of quarantine stations in 1876 at all
principal ports of entry and later in the creation of the Health of Animals Bureau
in Ottawa. From 1884 until 1902 McEachran served as Chief Veterinary
Inspector of Canada and in this position was always a powerful ally of the large
stock-raisers. His own stock-raising interests included a farm at Ormstown in
the Eastern Townships and a directorship in the Cochrane Ranche Company as
well as the managership and vice-presidency of t..e English-owned Walrond
Ranche Company. Colonel James Walker, former Superintendent of the North-
West Mounted Police and first resident manager of the ranch, terminated his
investment in the company when he resigned his managership after two years of
disastrous stock losses. The company's business manager, John Milne Browning
of Longueuil, was one of Quebec's leading estate agents. He had managed the
extensive holdings of the Right Honourable Edward Ellice, which included the
seigneury of Beauharnois. Browning also possessed extensive agricultural holdings of his own and served for some years as President of the Quebec Council of
Agriculture. The Seigneur of Trinité and St Michel, Louis Huet Massue, was an
extensive farmer and stock-raiser and was, from 1878 to 1887, Conservative MP
for Richelieu. Scottish-born George A. Drummond was one of the most prominent members of the Montreal financial community. He was the major owner of
the Canada Sugar Refining Company and was successively director, vice-
president, and president of the Bank of Montreal. In 1888 he was called as a
Conservative to the Senate and in 1904 received a knighthood. Edward T.
Brooks was also a well-known Conservative politician. From 1872 to 1882,
when he was appointed a judge of the Superior Court, he had represented the
constituency of Sherbrooke. Brooks's other business interests are indicated by
his presence on the boards of directors of several Eastern Townships railway
ventures. The remaining shareholder, James Gibb, cannot be definitely
identified.

The wealth and political power represented on the shareholder list of this one
ranching company bears witness to the kind of support that cattlemen could
command when necessary. When to these names are added those directors of
other ranching companies the list reads like a 'who's who' of the Canadian
parliamentary and financial worlds. Another patriarch of the Canadian cattle
kingdom, the North-West Cattle Company, was mainly owned by the Allan

family. The majority interest of these powerful owners of the Montreal-based Allan Steamship Lines was augmented by that of Charles and Frederick Stimson. Their presence typically joined Montreal capital with practical stock-raising experience from the Eastern Townships.[18] Charles was a well-to-do Montreal leather goods merchant and Frederick, who was sent to manage the ranch, was a farmer and stock-raiser from Compton.

The Compton-Montreal connection is also illustrated within the organization of the Winder Ranche Company. It was formed in May 1880 when Winder, formerly of Compton County, Quebec, was on leave from the NWMP at Ft Macleod. Shareholders included Winder, Charles Stimson, Winder's brother-in-law and also a shareholder in the Allan ranching venture, George Barry, a Montreal merchant, W.M. Ramsay, a well-known Montreal financier, J.M. Lemoine, a Compton stock-raiser, and John L. Gibb and Charles Sharples, both Quebec City businessmen.[19] Although the shareholders of this smaller company could not command the same influence within the power structure as Cochrane or the Allans, they were all part of a closely knit cattle company fraternity that tied together all levels of the Quebec business community and made Montreal the financial capital of the nascent Canadian cattle kingdom.

The formation of these companies was in fact part of a frantic rush on the part of Canadian businessmen between 1881 and 1883 to use what influence they could to obtain western leases lest they be left out of what business opinion of the day judged to be a 'sure thing.' In applying for the Winder lease, Charles Stimson urged the Deputy Minister of the Interior to act quickly on their behalf, as a Halifax group with the support of the Honourable Charles Tupper was after the same range.[20] Though B.W. Chipman and his Halifax partners did not obtain the lands of their first choice they were, through Tupper's influence, able to obtain a lease elsewhere.[21] Influential conservative businessmen and barristers from Ottawa formed the Stewart Ranch Company.[22] In Toronto a group associated with the brother of the federal Minister of Justice, C.J. Campbell, acquired a 100,000-acre lease.[23] In Winnipeg a powerful group of contractors gathered about the railroader, Donald D. Mann, to found the Glengarry Ranche Company.[24] The activities of similar groups of business and professional men, supported by the local Conservative MP or senator, in St John, Windsor, Oshawa, Niagara, Hamilton, Collingwood, Barrie, and Port Hope, all seeking leases for proposed ranching enterprises,[25] testify to the extent of the ranching craze in Canada.

As a group, investors in the various ranching ventures, speculative or otherwise, carried great political and economic weight. Some, such as A.W. Ogilvie, the Montreal milling magnate, T.N. Gibbs of Oshawa, and J. Boyd of St John, in addition to being important businessmen had, like Cochrane, the advantage of being Conservative members of the Senate. Conservative members of the House of Commons were even more numerous in their involvement with various ranching enterprises.[26] The award of the big grazing leases by order-in-council to so many friends of the government during April 1882, just two months before the 1882 election, was perhaps more than coincidence. With their influential eastern directors and head offices in Montreal or Ottawa, cattlemen enjoyed the advantage of close contact with the seats of political and financial power. Though decisions made thousands of miles from the base of operations often resulted in inefficient ranch management, an eastern headquarters nevertheless enabled leaders of the ranch community to operate more effectively as a political pressure group.

Aggressive interest in the grazing lands of western Canada emanated also from Great Britain. While the British capital invested in the Canadian cattle industry was small compared to its vast inflow into the American west during these years, British interests were included among the larger ranching enterprises. Of the four great patriarchs of the Canadian range, the Cochrane Ranche Company, Ltd, the North-West Cattle Company, Ltd, the Oxley Ranche Company, Ltd, and the Walrond Ranche Company, Ltd, the latter two were British-owned. The Oxley Ranche Company was established in 1882 under the guidance of Alexander Staveley Hill, a British Conservative MP and a personal friend of John A. Macdonald. The other major shareholder was the Earl of Lathom, who at the time was Lord Chamberlain.[27] Lathom, a well-known Hereford breeder, had become interested in the Canadian west in 1881, when Senator Cochrane's son visited his farms to purchase Hereford bulls to be sent to the new ranch on the Bow River.[28]

In 1883 British interests led by Sir John Walrond-Walrond founded the Walrond Ranche Company. Like many of his fellow investors, Sir John was also a former Conservative parliamentarian. Lord Clinton and Dr Duncan McEachran were the other major shareholders.[29] McEachran also acted as General Manager. In addition to the two major British companies, a number of smaller ones were established. The Alberta Ranche Company, owned by Sir Francis de Winton, the Marquis of Lorne, Canada's Governor General, and Sir F.F. Mackenzie, added Britain's bluest blood and much social prestige to the ranch fraternity.[30] Viscount Boyle, Lord Castleton, Rear Admiral Thomas Cochrane, and certain other titled Britons took properties of their own to join numerous others of the lesser gentry who had already begun ranching, and in general strengthened the British social milieu characteristic of the Canadian ranching community.

The eastern Canadian and British orientation of the ranching community was greatly strengthened with the arrival of the cattle companies. As a result, the influence of Ft Benton rapidly declined. The eastern and metropolitan influence wielded by company directors was also enhanced by the men sent west to manage affairs. Examination of the management of the most important ranch companies from 1881 to 1892 reveals that, with few exceptions, resident managing directors were Canadian or British. Members of the managerial ranks, if they were not part owners or personal friends of principal shareholders, were recruited from eastern business circles. The manager of the very successful Allan enterprise, Fred Stimson, had been a successful merchant and farmer in the Eastern Townships before coming west to superintend the North-West Cattle Company. Though most of these individuals could not claim an Oxford training, like Arthur Springett, the son-in-law of Alexander Galt and manager of the Oxley Ranche, the majority were well educated. Men and officers of the NWMP often came from a similar background, and in the early years were sometimes favoured as ranch managers because of their knowledge of the country. The Marquis of Lorne sent a former member of his household staff to manage the Alberta Ranche, while Dr McEachran chose to retain close personal direction of the Walrond Ranche Company.[31]

The men sent west to manage the ranches during the company era contributed in an important way to the peculiar nature of the ranching frontier in Canada. By virtue of their cultural and educational backgrounds, the managerial staff of western ranch companies was simply a transplanted part of the eastern managerial class. The Canadian range was never in the hands of 'wild and woolly' westerners,[32] either American or Canadian. The ranch country was instead under the supervision of middle and upper middle class easterners, who were often educated and professional men. Power in the Canadian west was exercised not by men carrying six-shooters and wearing chaps but rather by men in well-tailored waistcoats who often knew the comfortable chairs in the St James and Rideau clubs. Unlike in the American west, early management did not arise from the indigenous frontier population.[33]

The homogeneity of the Canadian and British managerial class suggests that American influence, contrary to popular belief, was restricted to the few American foremen and cowboys whose duties were confined mainly to the physical management of cattle.[34] Moreover, after 1885 the number of Americans constantly diminished and by 1890 even most cowboys were Canadian or British. American company influence was essentially restricted to one large company, the Circle Ranche, owned by the Conrad brothers and I.G. Baker of Ft Benton, Montana. Its manager, Howell Harris, a reformed American whiskey trader, presented a respected voice of experience in early ranch councils, but neither his influence nor that of several other American foremen such as George Lane of the Bar U or J. Lamar of the Walrond predominated during the early period.

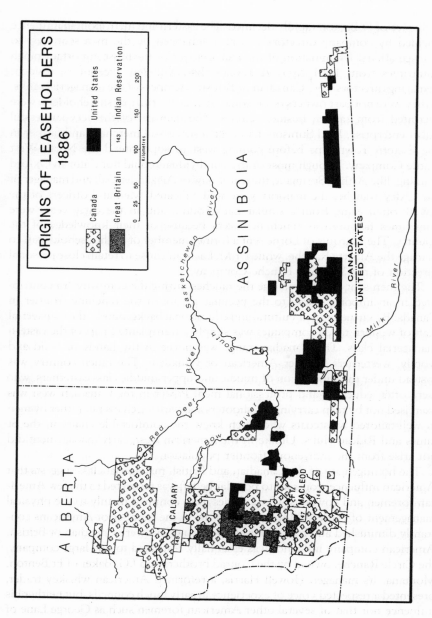

ORIGINS OF LEASEHOLDERS
1886

Canada

Great Britain

United States

Indian Reservation

143

0 25 50 100 150 200
Kilometres

ALBERTA

ASSINIBOIA

CALGARY

FT. MACLEOD

Red Deer River

Bow River

South Saskatchewan River

Milk River

CANADA
UNITED STATES

145

142

146

147

148

2 Origins of leaseholders 1886. Courtesy S.M. Evans, 'The Passing of a Frontier: Ranching in the Canadian West 1882–1912,' PHD thesis, University of Calgary 1976

Though these few undeniably contributed to the economic foundation of the Canadian cattle industry, especially as the large cattle companies were being established, their presence seems to have had little effect upon the ranch community's social or political development before World War I.

The arrival of the company men brought to a close the first stage in development of the ranching frontier in the Canadian west. They were the representatives of metropolitan commerce and with them came a new system of land tenure that took control from the small 'free grass' stockmen of the initial period and gave it to the large operators. From the early eighties the cattle business ceased to be a frontier industry. Although the small stockman did not disappear, his influence in the cattle community became less compared with that exercised by the owners and managers of the larger companies. As well, he was forced to alter drastically the manner in which he conducted his business. Often he found that the land on which he had ranged his cattle was now part of another's lease, and in applying for a lease of his own, which many refused to do, his remoteness put him at a distinct disadvantage in dealing with Ottawa.

On the practical side the small rancher was confronted with other serious problems. His own small herd was manageable; many of his animals were raised on the range close to his homestead and were inclined to remain in the area. When the companies arrived with vast herds purchased hundreds of miles to the south, the small owner lost control of his cattle. As the big companies did not fence their leases, their cattle wandered over tremendous areas, mixing with the stock owned by the smaller ranchers and taking these animals with them as they drifted. It became of little use to provide winter feed as the cattle were mixed and scattered. If he remained in business the small stock-raiser was forced to adopt, at considerable disadvantage to himself, the manner of operation of the large outfits. This tended to reduce his calf crop as he could no longer effectively supervise his herd during the calving season, and at the same time increased his expenses as he now had to attend the one- to two-month-long spring round-up. Faced with these new conditions, some smaller cattlemen sold their cattle; others, refusing to be driven out, continued their operations in the hope of eventually gaining the advantage of size. Their growing differences with the big concerns are clearly evident within the early stock-growers' organizations.

Cattlemen's protective associations are a feature characteristic of the range cattle industry from its earliest days and offer a particularly useful window through which to examine the ranchers and their enterprise at any given time. Where the cattle of various owners were simply turned loose on the plains to feed and multiply, to be gathered only in the spring to establish ownership of the new calf crop and again in the late summer or early fall to select animals for market, a large measure of co-operative endeavour was essential. Agreement had to be reached on marks and brands that denoted ownership and there was always the volatile question of unbranded cattle whose ownership was uncertain – 'mavericks' as they were known to cattlemen. Contesting claims had to be adjudicated. Consent had to be reached on round-up times and on the means of controlling range bulls. The informal gatherings of local ranchers that dealt with these issues in the earliest period developed into more sophisticated bodies as the cattle industry expanded and matured. The function of cattlemen's associations grew easily from simply monitoring day-to-day operations of the stock industry in a particular locality to addressing problems relating to ranchers' extraregional concerns: markets, transportation, and government land policy.

As the product of a production technique peculiar to a particular economy, the ranchers' associations differed greatly from organizations typically established by farmers. The range cattlemen, despite their vaunted independence, demanded a degree of community protection that farmers and other western settlers never required, as attested by the number of police posts and special summer stations in the ranching country during the early period. The ranch community always reacted vigorously to any suggestions that the NWMP be eliminated or reduced in number. Another fundamental difference between stockmen and their farming neighbours is reflected in the basic nature of their respective organizations. Unlike the western farmer, the stockgrower did not seek co-operative effort to remedy the wants growing out of isolation such as roads, schools, social amenities, and increased land values. His motivation towards organization came not because of isolation, but because that isolation was threatened. In this sense his organization is unique in the western experience. His problems tended to increase as the number of ranchers and later of farmers increased. Settlement was a potential threat to his range and his rewards were potentially greatest when his isolation was most complete.

Ranchers' organizations as they evolved in Canada during the early eighties were patterned on the stock-growers' associations in Wyoming, which had evolved by 1879 into the powerful Wyoming Stock-Growers' Association. The Montana Stock-Growers' Association was also formed in 1879 but did not become a permanent body with regular meetings until the summer of 1884. The Canadian cattlemen's organizations also date from this period, from the arrival of the large cattle companies. Company directors had their eye on the British market. They had begun therefore to import quality breeding stock and purebred bulls from eastern Canada and Great Britain in order to upgrade the range herds purchased in the United States. This valuable stock, often left unattended on the range, prompted their concern about cattle theft and the control of inferior range bulls that might compromise efforts to improve herds. An effective ranchers' association was seen therefore as an important step towards achieving a desired code of range practice.

The first stock association on the Canadian range was formed in 1882 in the Pincher Creek region, the first area to have any concentration of ranch population. The Pincher Creek Stock Association, with Jim Christie as president, was the successor of more informal groups that had organized the general round-ups over the previous three seasons. It was soon apparent that the structure of this first organization was unworkable. Communications were too primitive to enable a single association at Pincher Creek to effectively meet the needs of the entire ranch country. Motivation to organize a stronger, more appropriate alliance came mostly from the larger ranchers who, at this point, were mainly new to the region and as yet remained a background force. Another group that had a strong interest in promoting a viable regional cattlemen's association and who had the authority and prestige to press openly for action to achieve this, was the NWMP. Late in 1882, former Commissioner James Macleod, aware that attending to ranchers' problems was beginning to demand an inordinate amount of police time, called upon ranchers to form an association.[35]

Heeding Macleod's advice, cattlemen assembled in the spring of 1883. The pro tem chairman, John Herron of the Stewart Ranch, declared that the purpose of the meeting was to unite all stockmen in order to protect their interests. Cattlemen were informed that if they wanted the government to make stock laws for them they must propose them.[36] Joseph McFarland, the first rancher in the country, was accorded the honour of being the first president, while Matthew Dunn and Frederick S. Stimson were selected as vice-presidents. Following the election of officers and discussion of general business, the meeting concluded by establishing a reward of $100 for information leading to the conviction of any person charged with any of the three most serious ranch crimes: cattle-killing, horse-thieving, and fire-setting. The new organization, the South-Western Stock Association, was structured as a general or regional association on the American model. With representation from local stock associations to be established in each main ranching districts – Pincher Creek, Kootenai, Kipp, Willow Creek, and High River – it was anticipated that the Association would efficiently serve the interests of all cattlemen.

While small stockmen were the prominent group in the first association and initially well represented in the second, between 1883 and 1885 the company men emerged as the controlling force. Nearly all those present at the third annual meeting of the Association were representatives of companies or large individual holdings. The list of elected officers in 1885 is revealing: John R. Craig (Oxley Ranche), president; Frederick S. Stimson (North West Cattle

Company), first vice-president; William Winder (Winder Ranch Company), second vice-president; and W. Black, secretary-treasurer. C.C. McCaul was named solicitor and the management committee consisted of Donald W. Davis (former whiskey trader and later MP); F.W. Godsal; G. Levigne (Mount Head Ranche Company); J. Garnett, O.S. Main, William F. Cochrane (Cochrane Ranche Company); and J. Dunlap (Cochrane Ranche Company).[37] The top three executive positions were thus controlled by the large companies and the committee of management was entirely composed of company men or large leaseholders. In short, corporate leaders of the ranch community had taken over at the expense of smaller operators. They included the most powerful members of the community and were capable of exerting much local and extraterritorial pressure, but they could not yet legitimately claim to represent the collective voice of the ranch community.

The division between large and small rancher was compounded later in 1885 by a geographic division which further split the group. Northern ranchers decided that a group headquartered in Ft Macleod was too removed to look after their interests properly, and hence formed the North-West Stock Association.[38] Thus divided, the industry was more vulnerable to increasing outside pressure for open settlement, but it was not until the government announced a proposed change in the lease structure in 1886 that ranchers were reminded of their common interests. New government interest in settlement following the North-West Rebellion prompted a special meeting of the South-Western Stock Association to draft a petition to the Minister of the Interior, in which he was reminded that the south-west was not agricultural land and was essentially stock country. The company spokesman argued that they had been induced by the government to invest large sums of money in the western stock business and that in consequence 'the Government [was] bound to afford such protection by such legislation as may be necessary to the safe and profitable carrying on of the industry induced.'[39] The stock industry's concern regarding growing agitation for open settlement and abolition of the lease system as well as growing uncertainty regarding government policy is reflected in their request that the government set up a commission to meet with the stockmen to discuss the general question of leases and settlement.

With this added incentive to reunite as an economic and political unit, a large group of ranchers assembled in Ft Macleod on 4 March 1886. It was generally acknowledged that the old association was the subject of widespread discontent, and that it was not representative. The secretary of the South-Western Stock Association thus summed up the requirements of a new general stock association: the new association must in its membership offer clear advantages to all; each district should conduct its own local round-up; each district should send delegates to general association meetings; the question of mavericks must be settled; incorporation was necessary to achieve legal status; international relations should be established with the association in Montana; and the new organization should employ stock detectives to guard the Association's interests.[40]

But even before the cattlemen could address the main issue of reorganization they divided on the question of mavericks, always one of the most delicate problems in ranch country. It was well understood that after a day's branding at the general round-up there would be a number of calves whose mothers, and hence ownership, could not be determined. Range custom solved the dilemma by dictating that such cattle be sold by the association to finance its operations and thereby benefit all stockmen equally. Many small ranchers, especially those not belonging to the association, resented the Association's claim and were much more concerned about losing a few calves than were the owners of large herds. One individual at the meeting attempted to argue that mavericks legally belonged to the Crown. Doc Frields, a Texan from the Walrond Ranche, was quite disturbed by this logic and insisted that 'the Queen has got no cattle in this country, and she is a Jo Dandy if she gets ere a maverick from the W.R.' In the end, regardless of dissatisfaction expressed, no one could present a better solution. Tensions surrounding this issue remained throughout the period of the range cattle industry.

The discussion of mavericks out of the way, the ranchers worked to formulate the basis for a new and representative organization. Consequently a committee consisting of S. Pinhorne, W.F. Cochrane, W. Bell, F.W. Godsal, and J.J. Barter was appointed to draw up and distribute a constitution and by-laws before the next meeting. Though a very deliberate and ostensibly sincere attempt was being made to make this association a lasting one, membership of the appointed committee had a rather ominous appearance to some smaller ranchers. It was composed entirely of large ranchers, which suggests that this group felt the most urgent need for a strong association. The *Macleod Gazette*, aware of complaints, reminded its readers that this committee was only to draft by-laws, that it had no power, and that the larger ranchers were not trying to gain advantage. 'Let the small men come to the meeting,' the editor counselled, 'and give free expression to their views.'[41]

A large gathering assembled on 13 April 1886 in Ft Macleod to discuss the constitution of the proposed association. The minutes record a protracted and somewhat bitter debate between large and small owners. John R. Craig, President of the old association, after much debate succeeded in taking the floor to explain that he saw no reason why confidence should have been lost in his association. The men of the old association, he maintained, were men of experience in the country who knew people in the east and in England with whom ranchmen had to deal. They would not 'be taught by men who came here with very crude notions of what they wanted ...'[42] Northern ranchers stalked out of the meeting and all semblance of order disintegrated. Finally, the meeting adjourned for a second attempt in the evening.

The evening's discussion resulted in the founding of a new association, the Canadian North-west Territories Stock Association. Most discussion centred about the proposed constitution and reveals much about the composition and attitudes of the ranch community at this time. One rancher present noted that most settlers had a few cattle and that some clear distinction had to be made between settlers and dealers in livestock. The last people ranchers wanted in their new organization were 'sod-busters.' The point of greatest contention concerned the individual rancher's voting strength or, in other words, who was going to control the new association. The manager of the Oxley Ranche, speaking for the large ranchers, proposed that 'the districts vote on delegates according to the number of cattle owned.' A number of cattlemen immediately objected, claiming that 'this was the very thing that split up the old Association.' Smaller ranchers expressed their fear that 'big companies would be able to elect their own men as delegates' on this basis. One rancher warned that he 'could not see the use of the small men joining' if the motion were adopted. The large ranchers countered by reminding the gathering that, if members paid dues to the association in proportion to the number of cattle owned, they should exercise proportionate voting rights. The large ranchers' solicitor emphatically stated that 'it was absurd to propose that the men with 5,000 cattle could be outvoted by the man with 100 head.' Chaos ensued when one dissenter, after appropriately affirming that 'he was a Conservative to the backbone,' rebelled against the idea of 'two or three getting together and thinking that they were going to run the world.' When the chairman was able to bring order out of the profanity that followed, the question was put and the motion was carried by a considerable majority. As a result, voters at district meetings were entitled to vote in proportion to the number of cattle owned. The scale was as follows: one vote for 500 head and under; two votes for 500 to 1000 head; three votes for 1000 to 2000 head; four votes for 3000 to 4000 head; five votes for 5000 to 8000 head; six votes for 8000 to 12,000 head; seven votes for 12,000 to 17,000 head.[43] Thus the struggle for power within the ranch organization was temporarily resolved in favour of the large ranchers, but it is important to note, as the vote indicated, that only a small minority of ranchers opposed domination by the larger operators. Most smaller cattle owners realized that they had essentially the same economic goals and that unity was essential if stock-owners were to withstand the threat of general settlement. In addition, there seems to have existed within the ranch community a degree of social contiguity that bound many cattlemen together regardless of the number of head of cattle owned.

The assembled ranchers were also compelled to return to the contentious issue of mavericks that they had begun to discuss the month previous. It was decided after considerable discussion that stray calves should be advertised in four successive issues of the Ft Macleod and Calgary newspapers and then, if not claimed to satisfaction, they should be sold and the receipts turned over to the district association. While this pacified some cattlemen, the issue remained a major source of controversy between large and small stockmen for the next two decades. Many small stockmen could not afford to attend the various general round-ups and repeatedly charged the association with arbitrary action.

The first meeting of the Canadian North-west Territories Stock Association was held in Ft Macleod on 11 May 1886. Regional delegates elected John Herron as President and John J. Barter and J. Dunlap as Vice-Presidents. Charles E.D. Wood, editor of the *Macleod Gazette*, was appointed Secretary-Treasurer.[44] This new assembly was much more representative of the ranch community and struck a much better balance geographically and economically than had the older associations. Within two weeks Wood could claim that 'almost every stockman in the Pincher Creek, Willow Creek and High River districts belongs to the new association.'[45] Its success was further exemplified later in the month when it disposed of collected mavericks with no complaints tendered.[46]

The Association was the first formed by the ranchmen that could claim to speak for almost the whole community. Its formal constitution gave it considerable control over the conduct of ranching and ranchers. The avowed purpose of the organizers was 'the advancement and protection of the interests of stockmen' by moulding the cattlemen into a carefully controlled and closely knit group.[47] Membership was occupationally restricted; a system of fines and penalties was authorized to be exacted for infraction of by-laws, such as failure to help a neighbour fight a prairie fire, failure to notify the association before undertaking a cattle drive, or branding between round-ups. Refusal to abide by the regulations or to pay assessments and fines resulted in expulsion from an association that offered its members many obvious benefits, not least of which was a united front against the most feared threat to the cattleman's ascendancy – massive agrarian settlement.

The collective support of the ranch community for the leadership exercised by the large cattle ranchers through their control of the association was generally forthcoming and if there were differences they were usually of degree rather than principle. Besides, whatever differences existed within the community could be ignored by large stockmen. Their control of the range and of the stock associations allowed them to dictate how the industry would be conducted locally. Control of the general association also provided a platform from which large stock-growers could claim to speak as the legitimate and official spokesmen of the cattle industry to the world outside. By virtue of their local political and economic control, coupled with their intimate metropolitan connections, the cattlemen by 1886 had assumed the status of a regional élite. In addition, a homogeneous social background was bolstered by common vocational interests; all of which led to the development of a closely knit community of interest set apart from other western groups. It was an aggressive and self-sustaining society. Given their remarkable position, the western ranch community might be legitimately described as a 'cattle compact.'

The encompassing strength of this compact was manifest in many ways. The question of duty and quarantine on American cattle might be taken as a case in point. When Senator Cochrane negotiated the terms of the government's proposed lease structure with Prime Minister Macdonald he secured the leaseholders' right to bring cattle from the United States duty-free between 1881 and 1883. The cattle companies had this deadline extended three times, eventually to 31 August 1886, while they stocked their leases.[48] During this time settlers protested bitterly that they were being denied the same advantage and forced to pay the twenty per cent levy.[49] The law provided for the entrance of cattle 'solely for ranching purposes' and the farmer, or even the intending stockman without a lease, was not allowed by the customs department to include his cattle in this provision.

Once the companies had stocked their leases they became ardent protectionists.[50] What the big ranchers feared was that the few seeking entry to the Canadian range from the south might be the vanguard of a general invasion. It was apparent by the early 1880s to many, both in Canada and the United States, that the American range was vastly overstocked and Canadian cattlemen, along with high officials within the Department of the Interior, feared an impending flood of American cattlemen and their herds.[51] Stockmen in the Canadian foothills had been greatly alarmed by the arrival in August 1886 of a herd of 8000 cattle belonging to the influential Powder River Cattle Company of Cheyenne, Wyoming. It seems in fact that the final six-month extension of the duty-free provision had been gained through the engaging connivance and well-placed London contacts of the company's British manager and part owner, Moreton Frewen.[52] Canadian stockmen protested that the Americans had ruined their range and now wanted to crowd into Canada, where they would eventually bring about the same unfortunate overgrazing. For this reason the big leaseholders after 1886 began to argue in favour of the customs levy and in addition proposed that a rigorous veterinary inspection be added.[53] When it was rumoured after the disastrous winter of 1886–7 that the agents of American cattle companies were in Ottawa seeking leases, vigorous protests against the Americans were renewed.[54] In response the government imposed a stiff quarantine, impounding Canada-bound cattle at the border for ninety days. This measure almost completely ended importation of American range cattle and at the same time stalled the northward diffusion of American ranchers onto the open plains immediately north of the Montana boundary.

It was not long before small stockmen and settlers began to charge that companies were merely protecting their own high profits, as much of the range was still unstocked. Critics noted also that the government's adviser in quarantine matters, Dr McEachran, had a vested interest in the restriction of American imports.[55] The cattle companies were none the less determined at this juncture to protect their British market, and to calm British fears that diseased American cattle could reach their ports by way of Canada had the quarantine regulations tightened even further so as to apply also to the cattle in possession of settlers seeking entry into Canada.[56] An attempt by a senior government official to intercede with the Deputy Minister on behalf of the settlers was turned down with the caution 'we have the whole influence of the cattlemen in the Calgary District against us in this matter.'[57] The quarantine on all American cattle remained for some years until the large stock-growers eventually petitioned the government for removal in the hope that the Americans might reciprocate by allowing them to export to the Chicago market.[58]

In addition to exercising such strong influence on the government in its tariff policy towards the cattle industry, the cattle compact also exercised its persuasiveness to advantage in the crucial matter of land regulations. Above all other issues in the range country stood the matter of ownership and control of land, especially lands adjoining streams and rivers. The same kind of influence used to obtain leases in the first instance was also used to obtain title to choice land along streams and rivers. In recognition of the value of such properties to stock-raisers, the government in 1886 began to set aside for public use at strategic locations areas known as stock-watering reserves, in order to prevent a few individuals or companies from monopolizing vast territories. This was done at the ranchers' request and squatters or would-be settlers were kept off, by force if necessary. Yet it seems that certain well-placed cattlemen on occasion had such reservations cancelled and then purchased to become part of their own deeded holdings, despite the strong objections of smaller stockmen and Department of the Interior officials. In one such case involving a water reserve on Pincher Creek, the recommendation of William Pearce, the department official with final authority on such matters, that a rancher's request to purchase the reserve be denied, was countermanded by the Deputy Minister after a visit was made in support of the request by the rancher's MP, D.W. Davis.[59] Pearce resisted to the end, insisting that such reserves were necessary if harmony was to prevail and small stockmen were to be protected, especially where water was scarce, as he claimed it was in this instance. Pearce was no doubt pleased to forward to his superior the letters of protest once the notice of sale became public.[60]

Water reserves in the area were completely eliminated several years later when the government allowed another purchase, again despite Pearce's persistent opposition. In this instance, Davis, who, in addition to his parliamentary position also happened to be a rancher, again interceded on behalf of an applicant. In the end Pearce was informed confidentially by the Minister's Secretary that it was 'very desirable, for reasons which will be so obvious to you that I need not enlarge upon them, to meet [the applicant's] wishes, and I have now to ask.you whether or not, on a review of all the circumstances, you could withdraw your opposition to the granting of [the] application.'[61] In this manner a lengthy section of Pincher Creek fell under the control of two individuals.

While the cattlemen were often in vigorous competition among themselves for certain lands, there was another competitor for use of the rangelands whom they unanimously sought to exclude. The sheepman made his presence felt shortly after the arrival of the cattle companies and against this 'odious' individual cattlemen quickly closed ranks in order to drive him from the region or at least restrict his area of operation. Sheep cropped the grass more closely than did cattle and when in competition for the same range successfully drove the cattle before them. With the knowledge that on any fully or overstocked range sheep and sheepman could stay longest, stockmen adopted a posture of unstinting hostility from the moment of their earliest arrival. The Department of the Interior was reminded of the vicious feuds between sheepmen and cattlemen in the American west and in 1882 an order-in-council was passed at the cattlemen's request that sheep-grazing be prohibited without special ministerial permit.[62]

With one important exception the stockmen were able to maintain a united front to contain the sheep rancher. This exception, which first opened the door to limited sheep-grazing in the south-west, was the work of Senator Cochrane and illustrates the great influence exercised by individuals within the ranch community, in this case even against the wishes of the community itself. After suffering extensive stock losses during the winter of 1882-3 Cochrane was convinced that the Bow River valley was situated too far north and took a second lease far to the south near the American boundary. Cochrane proposed to move his cattle to this southern range and put sheep on his northern holdings. To achieve this, he reversed his stand of the year before, and through one of the company's shareholders advised the Minister of the Interior that there was room for both cattle and sheep in the territory and that in fact the high and colder Bow River country was better suited for sheep.[63] The Minister acceded to the request and gave special approval. Stockmen in the south-west were greatly alarmed and pressed the government to set a boundary which would confine sheep-grazing to the north. The boundary suggested by the South-Western Stock Association was Sheep Creek, about thirty miles south of Calgary.[64]

The great antipathy between cattleman and sheepman was never understood in the east. The *Winnipeg Times*, for example, charged that 'the cattlemen of the west cannot be accused of modesty. They want the whole country to themselves; sheep are not to be permitted to come between the wind and their nobilities.'[65] Despite appearances, it was not a 'dog-in-the-manger' attitude. The two forms of ranching could not co-exist on the same open range and this was fully understood by government officials in the west. The stock association's boundary request was fully supported by William Pearce, who lectured his superiors in Ottawa that 'from what [he] had seen in Colorado, New Mexico, and California, [he was] satisfied that sheep will in a very few years ruin the best cattle range.'[66] The government granted the boundary request and later, after a petition from stock-raisers in the Bow River valley, and after Cochrane had abandoned his sheep-raising enterprise, the sheepmen were further restricted.[67] Eventually, they were pushed from the foothills country altogether and on to the plains of south-eastern Alberta and south-western Assiniboia, where separate sheep-grazing reservations were established in 1890 and 1892. Here they remained largely unchallenged until the turn of the century, when they were again faced with their old adversary, the cattleman, who had retreated in turn onto the plain in face of the farmer's advance. The conflict was renewed and sheepman were confronted with further restrictions.[68]

Their competition for the western range was easily controlled by the solidly entrenched cattlemen. The real struggle was with the other major competitor for the stockman's domain, the farmer. The granger, or 'sod-buster' as he was more uncharitably known in cattle country, posed a serious threat almost from the beginning and taxed the full resources of the ranch establishment in a struggle that lasted nearly three decades. In the foothills and on the south-west plains the settler had the tenuous position of an interloper. Here the prospective farmer ran the risk of forcible eviction. Relations were characteristically acrimonious and the smouldering threat of armed violence seemed ready on several occasions to erupt and destroy the heralded peace of the 'last best west.' While Canadian history does not record armed altercations such as those that on occasion broke out on the American range, the economically and politically powerful Canadian cattlemen were no less determined to protect their large and profitable holdings in face of general settlement. They were obviously not anxious to see the farmer's barbed-wire fences and plowed furrows encroach upon the great grazing leases.

The foundation upon which the Canadian ranching empire rested was the lease system and it was against this system the would-be settler directed his protests. By virtue of their early establishment and great size, about a dozen ranch companies rapidly achieved domination of the region, absorbing most of the purely speculative ventures. The Cochrane Ranche Company, for example, acquired the lands of the Rocky Mountain Cattle Company, the Anglo-Canadian Ranch Company, and the Eastern Townships Ranch Company, giving Senator Cochrane control of 334,500 acres.[69] By 1884, two-thirds of all stocked land in the south-west was controlled by ten companies. The extent of company control is underlined by the fact that the four venerable giants of the Canadian range, the Cochrane Ranche Company Ltd, the Walrond Ranche Company Ltd, the Oxley Ranche Company Ltd, and the North-West Cattle Company Ltd, held almost half of such lands. Settlers, who were arriving in increasing numbers by the mid-eighties, were thus confronted with a very sparsely settled countryside in which most suitable homestead land was not open for settlement. Most prospective settlers, when presented with this situation, continued to the better-watered lands north of Calgary. A minority, no doubt aware of the well-publicized financial success of ranching operations and probably with a mind to become small-scale stock-raisers themselves, squatted on the extensive leaseholds. The cattlemen realized that if even a few squatters were allowed on the big leases they would soon be joined by others, and consequently maintained a posture of open hostility.

The campaign for open settlement in the south-west actually began with the establishment of the first big ranches in 1882. In strongly worded editorials, the *Macleod Gazette* urged the government to allow homesteads to be taken on leased lands.[70] The *Gazette* charged that certain ranchers were acting 'mean and ugly' towards intending settlers and that because of the existing situation the Canadian west was being labelled by American immigration agents a territory where 'landlordism' prevailed.[71] The first public protest meeting followed shortly thereafter. This meeting, in October 1882, scarcely six months after the assignment of the great leases, was the precursor of nearly three decades of settlers' opposition to federal land policy in the south-west. The fifty-odd people assembled at Ellis's billiard hall in Calgary denounced the government's land reservations as 'manifestly unjust to the many settlers and pioneers who [had] come hither to make their homes,' and resolved, after lively debate, that it would be in the best interests of the North-West Territories if the great grazing leases were cancelled at once and the American grazing system adopted.[72] The

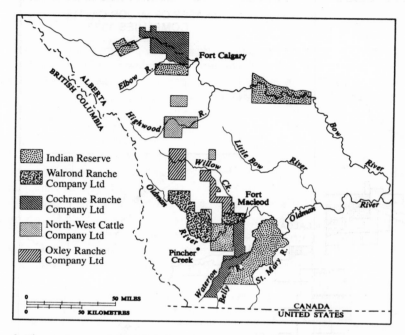

3 The cattle companies 1884. Reprinted from *The Prairie West to 1905*, general editor, Lewis G. Thomas, map by Geoffrey Matthews, ©Oxford University Press

consequent petition made little impression, other than causing a certain annoyance to A.M. Burgess, Deputy Minister of the Interior, who apparently took umbrage at the suggestion that certain government policies were retarding western settlement. He completly discounted the petitioners' complaint that nearly all agricultural land was taken up with grazing leases and government reserves as totally at variance with the facts. At this point the department had complete confidence in its lease policy and contemptuously dismissed the suggestion that the American grazing system be adopted, with the assurance that 'the Government had well considered the advantages and disadvantages of the ranging system of the United States, respecting which the Minister had information from much more reliable sources than evidently were accessible to those who passed this resolution ...'[73]

Despite Burgess's defence of the lease system, glaring abuses were evident. As the Toronto *Globe* explained in its report of the Calgary meeting, while a few operations such as the Cochrane Ranche were legitimate, many leases had been granted to people who had neither the ability nor the inclination to do anything

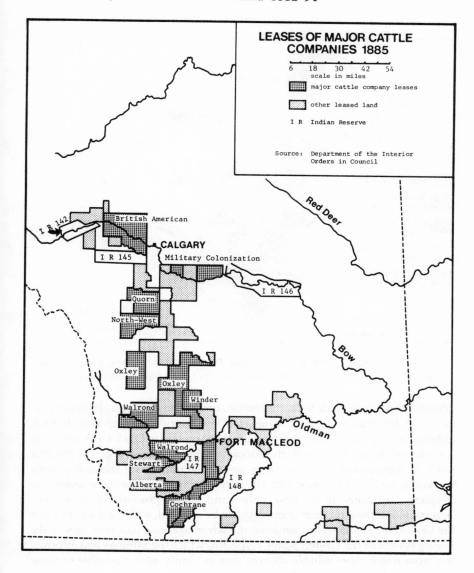

4 Leases of major cattle companies 1885. Courtesy S.M. Evans, 'The Passing of a Frontier: Ranching in the Canadian West 1882-1912,' PHD thesis, University of Calgary 1976

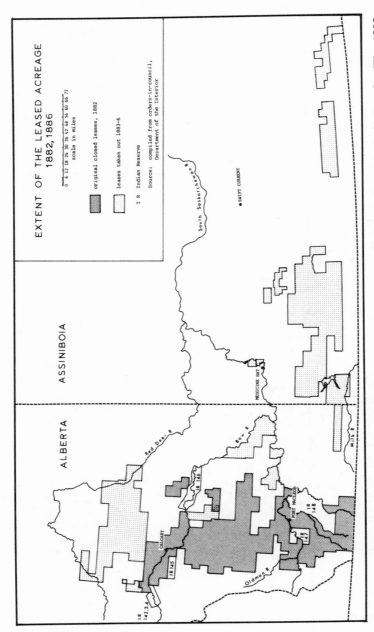

EXTENT OF THE LEASED ACREAGE
1882, 1886

0 6 12 18 24 30 36 42 48 54 60 66 72
scale in miles

▨ original closed leases, 1882

☐ leases taken out 1883–6

I R   Indian Reserve

Source: compiled from orders-in-council,
Department of the Interior

ALBERTA   ASSINIBOIA

South Saskatchewan R.

● SWIFT CURRENT

MEDICINE HAT

Red Deer R.

Bow R.

CALGARY

IR 146

IR 145

IR 142,3,4

Oldman R.

FORT MACLEOD

IR 148

IR 147

Milk R.

5 Extent of the leased acreage 1882, 1886. Courtesy S.M. Evans, 'The Passing of a Frontier: Ranching in the Canadian West 1882–1912,' PHD thesis, University of Calgary 1976

more than hold their property on speculation, hoping to be bought out by others honestly desiring to bring in and breed stock. In support of this contention the *Globe* listed numerous companies and individuals such as one Major Barnes (Baynes), a son-in-law of Senator Cochrane, who possessed two and one-half townships (57,600 acres) upon which, it was alleged, only half a dozen horses were kept.[74] Numerous companies having no stock whatsoever were identified as having leases of up to four townships. These great acreages seem to have consistently impressed the eastern press and public. Typical of such concern regarding what appeared to be the creation of great landed estates in the west was the subsequent dark warning of the Toronto *News* that a 'New Ireland' was in the making.[75]

Persistent allegations to this effect in the Ft Macleod paper were given broader coverage by the Toronto and Montreal press and eventually brought forth an official defence of government policy. Acting Minister of the Interior Sir David Macpherson explained to the Ft Macleod editor that the ranchers had 'gone in there with large capital and taken great risks,' and because they were paying rent for the land there consequently existed a contract between the cattlemen and the government which entitled the former to full federal protection. Ottawa was convinced that, given the almost unlimited availability of lands elsewhere, there was no need to tolerate squatting in the grazing region. Macpherson warned that 'no favour can be extended to the class of speculative squatters who are not agriculturalists, who have or who may be dotting themselves down on lands which are held under lease for grazing purposes, and upon other Dominion lands.'[76]

Macpherson's warning went unheeded and settlers continued to arrive throughout the spring and summer of 1883. In September a group of these settlers who had located in the Porcupine Hills, in the heart of the ranching country near Ft Macleod, forwarded a petition to the Department of the Interior. They complained that they had been encouraged to settle in the north-west by pamphlets published and distributed by the department, only to be informed after having erected houses and ploughed the land that the properties claimed were under prior lease.[77] The settlers requested that their lands be freed and that leaseholders be given a notice of cancellation in two years as provided within the terms of the lease. The Department of the Interior was unsympathetic and brusquely informed the petitioners that the lease had been in effect when they settled and that they were therefore in the hands of the lessee, who had power to evict trespassers.[78] The 'trespassers' were summarily forced off their claims. With the exception of one who persisted for sixteen years before finally gaining title to his initial homestead,[79] settlers moved north to more hospitable country.

Aware that their prosperity was directly related to extensive land holdings and an open, unfenced range, stockmen initiated a vigorous defence of their interests and as the pressure of settlement and the consequent number of evictions increased throughout the summer of 1884, the animosity between ranchers and prospective settlers grew in proportion. One contemporary observer reported that the entire foothill region from the American border to Calgary, 150 miles to the north, was divided into two hostile camps. Explaining that the struggle between the 'two clans' had recently assumed a serious turn, F. Girard, a doctor on the Blood Indian reserve, warned the government of impending violence. Taking the side of the farmers, Girard alleged:

Everywhere the will of the strongest is the law to which they [the farmers] have to submit. The Stock Raisers claim this right, though they have no title to it, and proclaim loudly and in every way: 'No farmers in this Country we have no need for them. The land is good but for pasture and nothing else; why, then, attempt, uselessly, to establish farms. Farmers coming here to establish themselves choose the lands on the rivers. It is a nuisance for us, because our cattle will soon be unable to reach water. Down with farming!'[80]

The essential difficulty, as Girard observed, was the 'monopoly exercised by lease-carriers.' Wherever farmers attempted to locate they were informed that the land was part of this or that lease. As there was no land office in Ft Macleod, an official check was difficult and costly. Consequently many settlers eventually squatted on whatever property suited them, only to be quickly faced with a legal suit which they could not hope to win. After the usual proceedings the would-be settler was condemned to pay costs and expelled. Girard predicted that such expulsions would continue in increasing numbers.

The readiness with which ranchers were inclined to use their legal advantage in 1884 precipitated a crisis in the following spring.[81] On Sunday, 5 April 1885, a large group of harried settlers responded to a word-of-mouth summons to meet at the farm of John Glenn on Fish Creek, several miles south of Calgary. It was plain to all assembled that this was the propitious moment for decisive action. Property rights had to be settled before spring seeding, only two months off. But most important was the ominous and weighty significance of the defeat of a NWMP and militia force at Duck Lake only ten days before. This defeat signalled the outbreak of the North-West Rebellion and it was clear to all those gathered for the meeting that Ottawa would be most sensitive to settlers' grievances at a time when the initiative lay with the rebels.

Sam Livingston, one of the first settlers in the region, was elected chairman, and in his opening remarks vividly summarized settlers' grievances. Livingston complained that though he had improved and cultivated his property near Calgary for nine years and had been entitled long ago to a patent for his lands, this had been denied. He observed that between 'government reserves, leases, school lands, and Hudson's Bay lands, a man was unable to find a spot to settle,' and that if he did settle he was certain 'to be chased by someone, either by the police, land agents, or government officials of some kind ...' Reflecting the mood of the gathering, he concluded that a settler was 'worse off than a wild animal, as a wild animal had a closed season in which he could not be hunted but a settler was chased at all seasons of the year.' In Livingston's view the current situation left no alternative but a resort to arms. Rather than be 'driven out' like some forty or fifty other settlers with whom he claimed personal acquaintance, he announced his determination to defend his claim with his Winchester.[82] Taking up this impassioned cry, John Glenn, host of the gathering, related that he too had been unsuccessful during the several years past in his attempt to obtain a land title – as indeed was the case with most of those present. Glenn declared that he also was prepared to defend his claim by force of arms should the authorities try to compel him to leave. If settlers were not immediately given their full rights Glenn announced that he would be compelled to burn his place and leave and, if this came to pass, he threatened to leave few ranchsteads standing behind him.

The ranch companies were the natural focus of the meeting's hostility. They held the lands that Livingston, Glenn, and their compatriots wanted. One of those assembled told of his eviction at the behest of the Bow River Ranche Company, while another protested his expulsion from the Cochrane lease. Several intending settlers claimed that they had sworn affidavits and had paid government agents to have titles drawn but had received no answer from the federal authorities. The testimonial of James Barwis underlined the sense of final resolve and desperation. He had been removed once from his chosen property, had since returned, and now declared: 'I hold it now and will defy all comers.'[83] Unable to obtain legal titles, subjected to continued harassment, and in despair at the thought of being kept on the run, many settlers thought armed resistance the only recourse unless the federal government could be persuaded to open the leases and grant them 'full and equal' rights. With this object in view the impatient crowd formed the Alberta Settlers' Rights Association as the official vehicle to forward to the Prime Minister their urgent request that all land suitable for agricultural purposes held under lease in southern Alberta be opened for settlement, and that all townships near Calgary be opened immediately for homestead entry.[84]

Anticipating that the farm population would soon comprise a majority, the petitioners insisted that it was absolutely necessary that the region be represented in parliament at Ottawa without delay. Federal representation was lauded as 'the only means of quieting the present discontent among the settlers in the Territories,' and the recent defeat in the dominion parliament of such a proposal by the Conservative government drew forth the dark and timely caution that immediate action was required 'to prevent a repetition of the trouble which now unhappily exists in these Territories.' To make it explicit to the Prime Minister where a refusal of their requests might lead and to indicate their possible allegiance during the coming struggle for the north-west, the petitioners concluded their telegram with a resolution that 'the halfbreeds in these Territories are entitled to and should receive the same privileges as regards lands as have already been conceded their brethren in Manitoba.'

Despite their reckless temper, it is doubtful that the small company gathered at John Glenn's farm would have joined the insurgents had their appeal gone unanswered. While the settlers were almost certainly prepared to fight for their homesteads, their bravado in announcing their right to rebel was simply to impress a government they knew to be in a corner. In this they were partially successful. Given the highly volatile situation in the west, the government was at first very much concerned. Federal authorities had been warned of the impending meeting at Glenn's farm and were decidedly apprehensive regarding the situation in and around Calgary.[85] On 10 April, Department of the Interior officials received 'quit the city notices' signed with the traditional 'triple 7' seal of American vigilance commitees.[86] The order to leave the city at once was not obeyed but nervous officials kept Ottawa informed of the activities of those individuals known to have attended the protest meeting. Official assessment of the gathering was that most of those present were not bona fide settlers but agitators from the town who, as one official remarked, were 'known and are watched.'[87] As rebel forces in the north were defeated, imminent pressure eased, but it was none the less clear that the demands of the several hundred new settlers around Calgary could no longer be ignored with political impunity. It was also clear that the real issue concerning the majority of new inhabitants was land tenure rather than representative institutions.

Responding directly to the petition, Prime Minister Sir John A. Macdonald instructed his Minister of the Interior, Sir David Macpherson, to have all ranches inspected and 'all leases cancelled without mercy where there has been a substantial breach of the conditions.'[88] Macdonald was quite aware of the speculation that had occurred and had from the beginning become increasingly disenchanted with his leaseholding friends. Writing in the summer of 1883 to the Honourable Alexander Campbell, his old law partner and fellow Privy Councillor, regarding the ranching scheme of Campbell's brother, Macdonald had protested:

Some 8 or 9 companies got Ranches on giving the assurance that they were both able and willing to stock them. It turns out that they all lied and merely got their leases for the purpose of selling them ... These speculators now club together to make one large company with a [range] the size of a province to speculate upon, and propose to hawk this around Europe.[89]

While cancellation of speculative leases eliminated some glaring abuses, the problem of opening lands in the immediate vicinity of Calgary remained. To this end two government reserve townships were opened. The most desirable lands in the area, however, and the region in which most squatting had occurred, were in the Bow River valley from the edge of the village of Calgary westward to the mountains. These lands were held by the most politically powerful of all the ranch groups, Senator Cochrane and his Montreal business associates. Moreover, his company was one of the few in the region that was meeting lease conditions.

It was to secure part of this river valley from Cochrane, to allay the ranchers' apprehension of federal abandonment, and to counter the growing clamour in the opposition press, that Deputy Minister of the Interior A.M. Burgess was sent to tour the region. In his subsequent report to Parliament he strongly defended government policy and asserted that there was no conflict of interest between rancher and settler, that the government was not withholding home-stead titles, and that agitation was the result of 'insinuations of ignorant and mischievous people, and the impression created by loose statements in the press.'[90] While it is notable that he did not mention discussion with farmers in the south-west, he did provide authority for his view with the assurance that he had 'discussed the subject with a large number of the range managers.' The government was trying to buy time to solve a difficult political dilemma. Publicly committed to a policy that gave settlement precedence over all other matters in the west, it was confronted by an exceedingly powerful minority interest within the Conservative party that wanted to discourage, if not prevent, settlement in a sizable part of the southwestern section of the North-West Territories.

Though cattlemen were ready to use all the resources at their disposal to restrict settlement, they were not entirely the villains they are generally made out to be. North American historigraphical bias has immortalized the sturdy westward-moving pioneer farmer as the emblem of democracy and progress and characterized cattlemen as autocratic and obstructionary. The true picture is hardly so black and white. Apart from the basic question of the region's suitability for agriculture, ranchers had a number of legitimate complaints.

Many so-called settlers were not really settlers at all, but rather small-time speculators who squatted on the choice part of a lease hoping to be bought off.

Settlers planning to make a permanent home usually chose locations on creek bottoms or near springs, and soon began to fence off ranchers' water supply. Others were not interested in farming but instead hoped to become cattlemen, despite limited or non-existent capital, by stealing the beginnings of a herd of their own from among the numerous strays from the great herds on the open range. This kind of cattle rustling was always a serious threat, especially to ranchers with large herds who found it nearly impossible to keep track of all their cattle. Many settlers found the temptation too great, as did the chairman of the founding meeting of the Alberta Settlers' Rights Association, Sam Livingston. Although he demanded recognition of settlers' rights, he had little regard for ranchers' property rights. About a month prior to the settlers' April meeting, W.F. Cochrane, writing to his father, reported the contents of a recently received letter from Livingston: 'He [Livingston] had heard where 7 or 8 of our cows were, and a Hereford bull and offered to turn over the cows on condition of receiving a bill of sale for the bull.'[91] Cochrane then wrote to the manager of company property near Calgary to make enquiries and to offer to pay to get the cattle back. 'We might as well buy the cows off him. If he wants to buy a Hereford bull we will sell him one.'[92] In spite of their great economic power the large ranchers were very vulnerable to the malice of those they offended. Regarding possible action against a known horse thief, Cochrane cautioned: 'he is a man that is not very safe to make an enemy of as he is just mean enough to burn the range off or do any mean trick out of revenge.'[93] The setting of prairie fires also offered another avenue of reprisal that could be accomplished without fear of apprehension and was potentially devastating to the rancher.

During 1885 and 1886 the cattlemen marshalled their local and national forces for the struggle that had begun to gain momentum. The electoral contest in the late summer of 1885 to determine the district's first representative in the Territorial Council at Regina clearly illustrates the attitude of the ranch community at this time. The candidate representing the more moderate element, Lord Boyle,[94] took the position that limited settlement was necessary and inevitable. At the same time he opposed the view of many smaller ranchers that speculative leases held by absentee owners should be cancelled. Boyle's group cautiously agreed to certain changes in the lease structure. G.C. Ives, the other candidate, represented the more extreme stand against any settlement, allegedly stating in his platform that 'the poor man ... has no business in this section of Alberta ... [especially the] agriculturalist, who is too poor to be able to purchase stock.'[95] Though the contest was bitter, and though, as the Macleod Gazette reported, 'worse than insults were hurled at Lord Boyle' at a public assembly in Pincher Creek, he emerged victorious.

With the election over, the government was anxious to alleviate the squatter problem in the south-west, which promised to become an increasing political liability. The problem faced by Ottawa was how to amend the lease system and at the same time not antagonize the powerful ranch lobby. A compromise that would permit limited settlement and still protect the interests of the established ranchers was the obvious solution. With this object in mind, the government became increasingly receptive to the idea of a water reserve system. From the cattlemen's point of view such a measure was definitely attractive. If the range could not be controlled through a closed-lease system, it was apparent that the same ends might be gained even more efficiently through control of the region's springs, streams, and river fronts. If a satisfactory system of stock water reserves could be established they were amenable to changes in the lease structure.

Certain members of the eastern ranch establishment had in fact approached the Minister of the Interior, Sir David Macpherson, the year before to request that certain reserves be set aside for stock-watering purposes. Macpherson in turn instructed the Department's senior official in the west, William Pearce, Superintendent of Mines, to confer with the stockmen on the matter.[96] Meanwhile the settlers' strong opposition to the federal lease policy, which had emerged before and during the North-West Rebellion, caused the new Minister of the Interior, Thomas Daly, as well as several senior officials within the department in Ottawa, to question the political expediency of the water reserve proposal. Pearce, however, argued convincingly for the policy. He drew attention to the fact that when squatters were permitted to take up bottom lands along the rivers they immediately fenced their properties, thus preventing stock from reaching water and shelter during winter storms. To illustrate the nature of the problem and the extent to which it had already developed, Pearce cited recent homesteading along the Belly River between Ft Kipp and Slide Out, where eighteen settlers had fenced and made inaccessible twenty-five continuous miles of river, thus rendering the surrounding 30,000 acres of good winter pasture valueless.[97] The Superintendent insisted that if the settlers' contention was correct – that only valley bottoms were suitable for growing vegetables or grain – it was unwise to attempt to settle the watercourses and render the remainder of the south-west useless. He maintained, moreover, that the bottom lands were predominantly characterized by a stone and gravel surface and that less than five per cent of them were arable.

Pearce's intent was to dispel the impression created by the eastern press that squatters in the south-west were intending farmers who were prevented from following their chosen vocation by a misguided federal land policy that favoured ranch interests. He consistently maintained throughout the entire territorial period that the region was best suited for grazing and that few squatters had any intention of putting the land to crop but rather intended to raise stock. Consequently legislation was required, not to assist and encourage a potential farming population, but rather to regulate and facilitate the ranching industry already in existence. The most immediate need in this regard, and one that would be to the advantage of large companies, as well as the small stock-raiser, was a system of water reserves.

Pearce saw the system of water reserves not as a means by which ranch companies could retain control of the region but rather as a device to ensure that the land would be used to its fullest potential and as a means of protecting the smaller stockman. Fully cognizant of the government's commitment to settlement and of the nature of the main opposition to a water reserve system, Pearce emphasized the important benefits that would accrue to the small stock-raiser. Citing the precedent set in the American free range country, he argued that experience had shown 'that the large capitalists invariably drive out the small ones' and that they accomplished this mainly by placing men on and pre-empting all the bottoms. By denying others access to water they gained free pasturage on the lands thus rendered useless to anyone else.[98] As a means of preventing the consequent 'lawlessness' which Pearce implied was typical of the United States and would surely follow in Canada, he recommended that the government make certain reservations for water and shelter that would guarantee access to all. For the sake of political expediency he suggested that it would be best if the initiative came from the stock associations and he expressed his confidence that the public would endorse such a policy.

In November 1885 Pearce accordingly sent an unofficial letter to the stock associations at Ft Macleod and High River urging that they make a formal request to the government that reserves be set aside for stock-watering and shelter.[99] The first response to Pearce's request came eventually from the northern ranchers in the North-West Stock Association. Taking Pearce's hint, the cattlemen requested that a committee be appointed by the government to confer with stockmen concerning the setting aside of water and shelter reserves, the reservation of hay bottoms, and the creation of cattle trails to marketing points.[100]

This connivance between the cattlemen and Pearce was viewed with some misgiving by Deputy Minister Burgess. Anxious to check the growing impression that the department was pro-ranch, Burgess warned the Minister that since reservations would exclude settlers from a considerable section of the North-West Territories, the Department should not base its decision solely on the basis of representations from an interested class.[101] Pearce, on the other hand, in his advice to the Minister, was untroubled by uncertainty as to the desirability of the ranchers' proposals. Throughout his long and important career in the west he was convinced that much of the south-west was unsuitable for farming unless irrigated.

While Minister of the Interior Thomas White was initially sceptical of the water reserve proposals earlier put forth by certain Montreal ranch company directors and supported by Pearce, he recognized the possibility of using the request for such reserves as the basis of compromise. It was imperative, however, that the government not have to face the accusation from small ranchers as well as the pro-settlement press that it was acting solely in the interests of the larger concerns. The water reserve proposal had to be assured of the cattlemen's collective support.[102] When it thus became apparent in the late spring of 1886 that the ranchers had resolved their internal differences through complete restructuring of the old stock association and that the newly organized political arm of the ranching community, the Canadian North-West Territories Stock Association, was definitely a representative body, the Minister made plans to journey to Ft Macleod to discuss personally the lease and water reserve issues with the cattlemen.

The fact that White was prepared to undertake this long and still arduous journey to a district not yet accessible by rail, in order to negotiate government policy, is testimony to the ranchers' political influence in government circles. At the consequent public meeting in Ft Macleod, White prefaced his remarks with the acknowledgment that the region was 'the best ranching country on the continent of America.'[103] He cautiously expressed his government's preference for a 'reasonable settlement,' and explained that all new leases would provide for homestead entry. White also expressed his hope that, while the previously granted twenty-one-year closed leases would be honoured, Senator Cochrane's recent promise to give up certain lands to which settlement seemed to be tending might be followed as an example. In return for the stockmen's co-operation White promised that a system of stock watering and shelter reservations would be established on rivers, creeks, and streams throughout the Territories and that farmers would not be allowed to fence cattle trails.[104]

On the basis of White's general assurances and promises of federal consideration, the ranchers forwarded memorials with specific proposals in order to press the government to take legislative action. The first memorial, from Senator Cochrane, Sir Hugh Allan, and other eastern presidents of the most important ranch companies, and the second, from the Canadian North-West Territories Stock Association, stressed ranchers' primary concern that access to and control of strategic watering places be assured.[105] But there was also a new demand in the petitions. Pointing to the seriously overcrowded American range, the petitioners asked that restrictions on the entry of American cattle be tightened further and that the lease-stocking requirements be reduced to one animal for every thirty acres leased from one animal for every ten. Hoping to impress upon the government the need for quick action with regard to their requests, the Association declared that the situation on the Canadian range was in danger of serious deterioration. Pointing to squatters and others who would enter their leases, the ranchers warned that: 'the efforts of individuals to resist these unfair encroachments upon their legal rights have produced elsewhere encounters and consequences most prejudicial to the well-being of the community, and in the long run with disastrous results to the industry itself.'

Deputy Minister Burgess found this allusion alarming. It lent weight to an earlier warning, in a confidential memorandum from Pearce, that the possibility of serious trouble between the leaseholders and homesteaders had to be seriously considered.[106] As noted above, Burgess lacked Pearce's conviction that the south-west was largely unsuited to agriculture and that since the squatters present in the region really intended to become stock-raisers rather than farmers, the whole problem could be resolved simply by setting aside water reserves which ensured equal access to this essential resource. Consequently, in his final recommendations on the matter to his superior Burgess prefaced his evaluation of the cattlemen's requests with the caution that certain forces were beyond the control of government:

there can be no doubt that when an actual settler desires the land for the purpose of making his home upon it, it would be impossible, even if it were expedient, to keep him out. It is not meant by this that one or two speculative settlers should be allowed to disturb a whole grazing ranche, but when the wave of settlement reaches the confines of the grazing country, if that country be found fit for the purposes of actual settlement, it will in my humble opinion be impossible to maintain it for purely grazing purposes.[107]

Beyond this, there were areas where Burgess felt government assistance to the ranching industry was feasible. He recommended acceptance of the cattlemen's plan to prevent overstocking, though he thought that twenty acres per animal rather than thirty would be sufficient. His position with regard to water reserves was similar. While agreeing that such reserves were necessary, he expressed his anxious but fruitless concern that there be a provision for cancellation upon a year's notice.[108]

Despite Burgess's hesitancy, the government, by order-in-council in December 1886, finally inaugurated the system of permanent water reservations that Pearce requested and withdrew from settlement or lease the first of a large number of such areas.[109] This initial list was expanded zealously under Pearce's guidance. In some parts of the south where settlement had not yet become a problem and where few requests for reserves were forthcoming, Pearce nudged the ranchers to action by reminding leaseholders that, while they had the right to evict squatters, the lease did contain the provision for cancellation on two years' notice, whereupon the entire lease area, including pasture and springs, would be open to settlement. On the other hand, if certain springs and creeks on the lease were set aside in the form of stock-watering reservations, Pearce argued that the public would understand that even if the lease were cancelled, settlement or fencing on certain lands would not be allowed. Such a step, Pearce explained, would 'prevent Ranchmen being harrassed [sic] by a very objectionable class of squatters whose aim is largely to levy black-mail, at least it is so asserted.'[110]

The petitioners' other request, reduction of lease-stocking requirements, did not receive federal approval until 19 March 1888. While it is debatable that this new provision was responsible for stemming the anticipated invasion of American cattle, it did have important consequences on the south-western range. By persuading the government to reduce these obligations by half, one animal for every twenty acres rather than one for every ten acres, the cattlemen made it much easier to retain their vast holdings. Heretofore the main lever used by the federal government to cancel leases had been the failure to meet lease-stocking requirements.

In all, the government response to the settlers' demands of 1885 was little more than a gesture designed to divert public clamour. The dismayed editor of the *Macleod Gazette* pointed out that the new regulations permitting homestead entry applied only to new leases. As most of the area was still covered by the old form of lease the situation regarding increased settlement remained largely unchanged.[111] In fact, the position of the cattlemen was greatly strengthened. With new water and shelter reserves on creeks, rivers, and springs throughout the ranching country, the ranchers gained a measure of indirect control outside the big leases that they had not had before.

The ranchers had every reason to be pleased with a government in which they were so intimately represented and their attachment is well illustrated by the returns of the first federal election in which they participated in 1887. The Liberal party, identified as the 'farmers'' party in the south-west, received only three of the 301 votes cast in the ranching communities of Ft Macleod and Pincher Creek.[112] Earlier, at a mass gathering held at Ft Macleod to discuss federal representation, ranchers had been particularly careful to disassociate themselves from certain farm groups elsewhere in the Territories who were also seeking a voice at the federal level. Those assembled were told: 'This meeting [is] no Farmers' Union. We [are] a different class of men, and propose to raise no Grit howl (hear, hear). Nor [do we] wish to harass the Government, [so] the resolution

[will] be respectfully submitted for consideration.'[113] The cattlemen's allegiance to the Conservative party was almost universal and it remained an enduring characteristic of the regional political structure until well after the turn of the century.

The government's new lease policy, cancellation of some speculative leases, and opening government reserve land near Calgary for homesteading brought only brief tranquillity to the Canadian range. The presence of the railway meant that settlement pressure was greatest near Calgary, especially along the Bow valley. The newly opened government reserve was quickly taken up, but the much-sought-after valley land that Senator Cochrane had promised to relinquish did not materialize for several years. Consequently the old struggle soon resumed and the Minister of the Interior was compelled to return to the west for the second consecutive summer to arbitrate between the contending groups. The *Calgary Herald* noted cynically that the settlers would be 'glad to see him, once more, and once more have the promise that those townships are to be withdrawn from the Cochrane lease.'[114] While Cochrane had agreed in principle to release two townships, he was not prepared to finalize the understanding without Ottawa's firm commitment to uphold the 'no-settlement' provision of the lease as it applied to the remaining six townships, as well as compensation in the form of additional lands to be added to his southern lease.

As Cochrane and the government negotiated, the situation grew continually worse and agreement was no sooner final than Cochrane was constrained to call upon Ottawa to honour its promise of unstinting support in keeping squatters off the remainder of the northern lease now held by Cochrane under the name of the British North American Ranch Company.[115] The appeal to Ottawa was bolstered with a threatening extract from a recent report of the ranch manager.

Morrison was out among some of the settlers the other day, pretending to be looking for land – asked one man if the B.A.R. Co. [British American Ranch Company] could not turn him off if he settled on their lease and the fellow's anser was 'Oh just show them a box of matches and they will leave you alone,' and then proceeded to tell how he was on one of the townships lately thrown open, but if he had not gotten his way before long he would have done some burning.[116]

The government, in keeping with the understanding, reassured the company of its full support.[117] Newspaper advertisements and handbills signed by the Deputy Minister were posted, specifically warning citizens to stay off leased lands along the Bow River belonging to the British North American Ranch Company, as the government would 'in no way recognize such squatting.'[118] The *Calgary Herald* in turn warned the federal government not to contemplate assisting the company to eject settlers as 'the squatters are not the kind of men to relinquish their rights merely because an arbitrary and unjust order has been issued against them.'[119]

For the next five years the Bow River valley remained in a state of constant turmoil and the Department of the Interior was the recipient of petitions, threats, and counter-threats from the contending parties.[120] The eventual decision of the Bow River Horse Ranche to bring matters before the courts pushed the Department of the Interior into a difficult corner. Given the lease provisions, the legal outcome was never in doubt and the department knew it would have to support an extremely unpopular decision. A local political friend of the new Minister of the Interior, Edgar Dewdney, warned of the possible consequences of the anticipated court decision. The friend explained that the settlers, knowing that their case had no chance in a court of law, had 'resolved to stand by each other and defend themselves with their wincheter [sic] rifles ... in case they are sherrifed [sic] off.'[121] The Deputy Minister was also fully cognizant of the awkward position in which the case had placed the department. He informed Dewdney that they would be forced to decide whether the ranchers should be sustained, or whether the department should give two years' notice of cancellation. Burgess recommended that the desirable solution would be a compromise wherein the company would give up the portion of the land lying nearest Calgary.[122] In the end, persistent efforts at compromise failed, and this, along with a crisis developing on the southern range, eventually forced the government to seek cancellation of all old closed leases.

In the south the editor of the *Macleod Gazette*, supported by the eastern press, renewed his campaign for open settlement. On this occasion the editor, C.E.D. Wood, was careful to confine his attack to the large ranch companies, hoping to take advantage of the differences between this group and smaller proprietors. Wood began his offensive in May 1888 with a strong editorial attack on the British-owned Oxley Ranche Company, charging that it had only half the cattle required to meet the lease-stocking requirements on its 287,000 acres and should therefore be compelled to give up excess acreage.[123] It was, however, upon the Walrond Ranche Company that the paper's main attention was focused over the next five years. Most large ranch companies policed their leaseholds with rigorous vigilance, but this British-owned company seems to have pursued a particularly aggressive policy towards would-be settlers. The stern evictions ordered by manager, Duncan McEachran, particularly enraged the *Gazette* editor. Wood's allegation that employees of the Walrond Ranche had 'run several good settlers out of the country' brought forth not a denial of such activities but McEachran's contemptuous response that he was sad to have aroused the wrath of Macleod's 'journalistic giant' and the warning that unless the *Gazette* altered its offensive policy he would start a new journal to be run in the interests of the stock industry.[124]

Wood was not to be easily dissuaded, for it was more than Ft Macleod's commercial development that motivated him. An earlier battle in court to protect his own claim to a small ranch against a leaseholder who had tried to evict him added a personal dimension to his cause.[125]

By winter the Walrond-settler feud had reached Parliament. The government was roundly condemned for not following its own publicly declared policy of open settlement. The Opposition charged that the cattlemen benefited from government policies developed mainly 'in the interest of the speculator and moneyed man, and uniformly against the interest of the settler and the poor man.' The Department of the Interior's defence of the stockmen's interests was similarly condemned and it was urged that this department be instructed to operate 'in a spirit favourable to the settlers.'[126]

Responding to press and parliamentary outcry, Dewdney cancelled some old leases whose holders had failed to comply with lease-stocking requirements. Though this was little more than a token gesture which did not interfere with any of the legitimate ranching operations, the dispute did make a significant impression upon the ranch community. During the initial stages of the controversy, cattlemen found themselves without a reliable way to conduct a public defence of their cause. They now sought to make good this deficiency through reorganization of the *Calgary Herald*. The *Alberta Livestock Journal* and the *Calgary Weekly Herald* were consolidated to form a new publication entitled the *Calgary Herald and Alberta Livestock Journal*. This new company was headed by the former rancher and new Conservative MP, D.W. Davis. His associates included Fred Stimson, manager of Sir Hugh Allan's North-West Cattle Company, and A.D. Braithwaite, local manager of the Bank of Montreal.[127] By so augmenting their metropolitan influence with the most influential newspaper in the south-west, cattlemen gained much wider public coverage of their counter-arguments to the persistent accusations of the pro-settlement press.

The new paper protested, for example, that the Bow River Horse Ranche had been unfairly criticized for evicting squatters from its lease. The eviction, according to the *Herald*, was clearly justified. 'If a farmer finds a person destroying his crops he summarily arrests him for trespass, and he has a perfect right to do so. Has not a rancher got an equal right to protect himself against trespass?'[128] It was argued that since it was the cattlemen who had opened up the country, 'common justice' demanded that their investment be protected. So much land was available elsewhere, the paper claimed, that 'no great hardship [was] sustained by an intending squatter in being summarily ordered off a lease when he first arrives.'

Further reorganization of the *Herald* the following year, which placed the paper's direction under Senator James Lougheed, Alexander Lucas,[129] and several other local Tories, tied the journal more directly to the Conservative party. Editorial policy towards the stockmen remained unchanged. The editor's affirmation that 'it is the policy of this journal to give special attention to the stock growers' interests' and the promise 'to put the policy in practice by all proper means and at every favourable opportunity ...'[130] was consistent with the conviction of many prominent Calgary businessmen that the future of the south-west, and more particularly of their city, was intimately bound to the prosperity of the cattle industry, in which many of them had invested.

Consolidation of ranch strength in Calgary was not unnoticed by the *Macleod Gazette*. The 'evil architect' of this manoeuvre in Wood's view was Dr McEachran, who the *Calgary Herald* now lauded as 'one of the ablest government officials we have.'[131] By this time the economic sanctions initiated by the cattlemen in retaliation against Wood's outspoken criticism had begun to take effect. The four largest ranch companies, the Oxley, Walrond, Cochrane, and North-West, had withdrawn their cattle and horse brand advertisements and twenty-four lesser companies and individuals followed suit. Many others allowed their paid-up advertisements to run until the next year's rental was due and then declined to renew their contracts. Diminished revenue forced the *Gazette* to begin its eighth year of publication reduced from eight to four pages, and caused the despondent editor to lament that the government had left 'the best country they have to the wolves and coyotes and the Walrond Ranche.'[132]

The unparalleled political influence and domination of the large stockmen during the decade 1881–91 was closely related to their initial economic success. The rapid corporate expansion into the grazing country was predicated upon the anticipation of substantial return on investment. The cattle companies were thus looked upon by their eastern owners as strictly business ventures. For this reason it was the yearly balance sheet as much as the pressure of settlement that would, in the final analysis, determine the longevity of the cattle kingdom as it existed in 1891.

The want of accurate statistics for the early period makes a detailed assessment of the cattle industry at this stage almost impossible, but none the less a general picture can be drawn. Prior to the company period, signalled by the arrival of the first big Cochrane herd (6634 head) in the spring of 1881, it can be estimated that about 15,000 head of cattle were grazing on the Canadian range.[133] By the autumn of 1884, three and a half years later, some 43,784 head had followed the Cochrane cattle north. This foundation stock brought from the United States, along with limited imports from eastern Canada and Great Britain, was increased to an estimated 110,516 head by the end of 1889.[134]

TABLE 2

Stock owned by non-leaseholders, January 1890

District	Name of stockholder (owning 400 head or more)	Cattle	Horses
Medicine Hat	German colony	500	25
	total stock owned by non-leaseholders with 400 head or more	500	25
	total stock owned by all non-leaseholders in Medicine Hat district	1,950	216
Ft Macleod	C.O. Card	700	10
	Joseph McFarland	600	10
	James Pierce	400	8
	Samuel Bird	400	8
	Shirley and Co., Oregon (cattle in quarantine)	1,200	10
	Cornish Cattle Co.	500 (+)	
	A.M. Morden	500	10
	Black Bros	400	10
	C. Smith	450	50
	total stock owned by non-leaseholders with 400 head or more	5,150	116
	total stock owned by all non-leaseholders in Ft Macleod district	6,765	1,425

These cattle were mainly owned by the large stockmen, as shown in Tables 2–4, which identify all stockholders with 400 or more head of cattle. The stock owned by settlers was excluded from this first enumeration by the Department of the Interior on the grounds that it was too insignificant.[135] Livestock production in the Canadian west was completely dominated by leaseholders, and this was true until well after the turn of the century.

The best means of determining economic distribution within the cattle community is through the number of cattle owned, on the same basis as cattlemen ranked one another. Lease size, which impressed contemporary eastern observers as well as subsequent historians, is much less significant. A lease has only potential value until it is stocked and it is the number of cattle rather than the size of the lease that determines the rancher's worth. Tables 2–4, listing all the large ranchers in the southwest, clearly indicates the distribution of economic power within the ranch establishment and the stock-raising industry. It is apparent that the region and the industry were dominated by relatively few individuals and companies with herds over 400 head, who were in turn superseded by a closely knit 'compact' of eighteen individuals and companies with

TABLE 2 continued

District	Name of stockholder (owning 400 head or more)	Cattle	Horses
Calgary	Sampson	700	6
	Ross and Podger	480	25
	George Emerson	700	10
	W.R. Hull and Bros	700	40
	total stock owned by non-leaseholders with 400 head or more	2,580	81
	total stock owned by all non-leaseholders in Calgary district	6,426	1,210
Maple Creek	Judd	500	
	Shurtliffe and Wood	450	40
	total stock owned by non-leaseholders with 400 head or more	950	40
	total stock owned by non-leaseholders in district	2,335	150
All districts	total stock owned by non-leaseholders with herds of 400 or more in all districts	9,180	262
	total stock owned by non-leaseholders in all districts	17,476	3,001

SOURCE: RG15, B2a, Vol. 23, 192192, 'Stock Returns' 15 January 1890. The big companies were inclined to exaggerate their stock returns in order to appear to meet lease-stocking requirements. The four large herds of over 10,000 head shown in Table 3 are probably in excess of the actual number by 1000 to 1500 head. Throughout the entire lease period the big leases were generally understocked.
(+) = estimated

herds over 1000. Of the estimated 109,298 head of cattle on the Canadian range in 1889, approximately 96,793 or eighty-nine per cent were owned by fifty-seven 'large' operators having 400 head or more. About sixty-nine per cent of the cattle were owned by ranchers with herds of 1000 or more. A herd of 400 cattle, the minimum herd size from which the 'large' stockmen have been arbitrarily ranked, represented a conservatively estimated investment of $10,000.[136] In the 1880s and 1890s this was no small amount, especially relative to the farmer or squatter, whose assets were usually valued in hundreds of dollars. Cattlemen, even at the lower end of the range hierarchy, enjoyed an economic status vastly superior to their few farm neighbours.

Though beef prices varied according to market factors, though many companies suffered the disadvantage of distant and sometimes inefficient management, and though there were substantial losses on some ranches during the

TABLE 3

Stock on leaseholds in the North-West Territories, January 1890

No. of ranch	Acres leased	Name of lessee (owning 400 head or more)	Cattle	Horses
1, 2, 35	157,960	North-West Cattle Company	10,410	832
22	23,000	Stewart Ranche Co.	2,149	330
25, 26, 34, 300	204,500	Cochrane Ranche Co.	10,433	81
28	100,000	A.B. Few	600 (†)	20
31	60,131	Military Colonization Co.	2,000	
35a	33,700	Moore and Martin		
36, 59a	85,336	C.W. Martin	5,000	1,250
38	10,000	Allfrey and Brooke	750 (†)	
42	34,788	Bow River Horse Ranche Co.	3	1,037
45	12,000	Wells and Brown	540	12
48	253,934	New Oxley (Canada) Ranche Co.	6,500	150
55	50,000	Winder Ranche Co.	1,800 (†)	500
65	6,000	Bell and Patterson	600 (†)	150
74, 82, 154	216,640	Walrond Ranche Co.	13,000	300
92	100,000	A.G. Conrad	6,000	100
94	20,000	F.W. Godsal	668	235
101	27,750	Alberta Ranche Co.	1,200	25
104	5,280	W. Bell-Irving	596	124
107	51,000	Thos. B.H. Cochrane, RN	800	40
108	6,000	D. McDougall	440	320
111	1,920	I. Walter Ings	600	50
122, 247, 264	45,282	George Alexander	1,680	86
123, 197	15,807	Walter C. Skrine	600	10
137	33,500	Brown Ranche Co.	1,000	70
146	80,000	Canadian Agricultural Coal and Colonization Co.	6,500	790
167	52,320	Glengarry Ranche Co.	1,262	13

unusually severe winter of 1886–7, operations throughout the period were generally profitable. The losses sustained by the Walrond Ranche Company during that winter, for example, were no doubt eased in the minds of the company's shareholders by the dividend of thirty five per cent paid the year before.[137] In 1886, when the paid-up shares of the North-West Cattle Company equalled $162,000, it reported a clear profit of $133,204.25.[138] Dividends of at least twenty per cent were not uncommon on other well-managed ranches.[139] In contrast to the dismal market faced by American stockmen, the Canadian market returned to a buoyant state in 1888. In that year the Calgary district alone marketed an estimated 5000 head of cattle, and, in spite of prices of fifty dollars per head and up for three-year-olds, it was impossible to meet eastern

TABLE 3 continued

No. of ranch	Acres leased	Name of lessee (owning 400 head or more)	Cattle	Horses
176	36,588	McDermid and Ross	1,200	70
185	40,000	H. Samson	1,400	30
189	8,960	Greeley and Marsh	750	12
193	38,750	Cypress Cattle Co.	1,172	135
217	5,120	W. Carter	550	10
225	17,000	Medicine Hat Ranche Co.	450	50
240	32,580	W.I. Conrad	2,500	180
248	11,000	A.E. Cross	500	150
263 I	–	H.W. Savony and others	900	150
268	7,040	F.W. and I.W. Ings	650	20
307	11,000	John Quirk	500	8
289, 309	55,000	Canadian Pacific Colonization Corp.	453	92
311	6,400	Boright and Parsons	400	10
313	4,640	E. Maunsell	560	25
323	2,560	R.G. Robinson	500	400
		total stock owned by leaseholders with 400 head or more	87,613	7,917
		total stock owned by all leaseholders	91,822	11,471

SOURCE: RG15, B2a, Vol. 23, 192192, 'Stock Returns' 15 January 1890. Reacting to persistent complaints from larger leaseholders that many small stockmen did not burden themselves with a lease, the Department in 1890 warned that such grazing would henceforth render the herd liable to seizure. It is evident that the size of some smaller leases above does not correspond to the relatively large herd size, and that such leases, apart from securing certain choice watering places, were meant simply as a token gesture.
(†×) = estimated
I = lease no. 263 not yet approved by order-in-council

demand.[140] By 1890, cattle companies had achieved their major goal; they had firmly established themselves in the lucrative British market, and the livestock industry was described as flourishing.[141] It was the attraction of this particular market that had been the driving force behind the Canadian cattle boom and finally, a decade after their establishment in the west, some larger Canadian ranchers were sending shipments in excess of 1000 head a year to the 'Old Country.'[142] (See Table 5).

The importance of the trans-Atlantic live cattle trade is another feature which distinguishes the Canadian range cattle industry from its American counterpart. For the American cattleman there was always a vast home market. Canadian producers were much more dependent on the more tenuous but also more lucrative British market.

TABLE 4

Ownership and distribution of cattle on the Canadian range 1889

Total cattle owned by	non-leaseholders	17,476
	leaseholders	91,822
	all stockmen	109,298
Total cattle in herds 400 or greater owned by	non-leaseholders	9,180
	leaseholders	87,613
	all stockmen	96,793
Total cattle in herds 1000 or greater owned by	non-leaseholders	nil
	leaseholders	75,206

SOURCE: RG 15, B2a, Vol. 23, 192192, 'Stock Returns,' 15 January 1890. Dept of the Interior, 15 January 1890. Although the size of a few herds had to be estimated, Pearce assured the Secretary that the aggregate was correct.

TABLE 5

Exports of live cattle 1881–1900*

Year ended 30 June	Cattle exported to					
	Great Britain		United States		All countries	
	Number	Value	Number	Value	Number	Value
1881	49,409	$3,157,009	7,323	$ 154,851	62,277	$3,464,871
1882	41,519	2,706,051	15,914	423,807	62,106	3,256,330
1883	37,894	3,209,176	23,280	516,585	66,396	3,898,028
1884	53,962	4,631,767	30,593	893,759	89,263	5,681,082
1885	69,446	5,752,248	67,758	1,411,642	143,003	7,377,777
1886	60,549	4,998,327	25,338	633,094	91,866	5,825,188
1887	63,662	5,344,375	45,765	887,756	116,274	6,486,718
1888	54,248	4,123,873	40,047	648,178	100,747	5,012,713
1889	60,000	4,992,161	37,360	488,266	102,919	5,708,126
1890	66,965	6,565,315	7,840	104,623	81,454	6,949,417
1891	107,689	8,425,396	2,763	26,975	117,761	8,772,499
1892	101,426	7,481,613	551	21,327	107,179	7,748,949
1893	99,904	7,402,208	402	11,032	107,224	7,745,083
1894	80,531	6,316,373	256	3,771	86,057	6,499,597
1895	85,863	6,797,615	882	19,216	93,802	7,120,823
1896	97,042	6,816,361	1,646	8,870	104,451	7,082,542
1897	120,063	6,454,313	35,998	509,138	161,345	7,159,388
1898	122,106	7,403,990	87,905	1,239,448	213,010	8,723,292
1899	115,476	7,129,430	92,834	1,298,170	211,847	8,522,835
1900	115,056	7,579,080	86,989	1,401,137	205,524	9,080,776

SOURCE: *Statistical Year Book of Canada for 1900* (Ottawa: Government Printing Bureau 1901) 98–9

* Does not include American cattle exported through Canadian ports

TABLE 6

Exports of wheat and wheat flour 1881-1900*

Year ended 30 June	Bushels	Value
1881	4,232,449	$ 4,766,928
1882	5,958,860	7,929,323
1883	8,068,165	8,397,443
1884	1,633,776	1,108,918
1885	2,897,952	2,522,817
1886	5,156,613	4,770,833
1887	7,972,684	7,067,282
1888	3,739,271	3,466,489
1889	1,081,219	1,117,189
1890	940,219	910,244
1891	3,443,744	2,971,662
1892	10,428,636	8,732,264
1893	11,117,717	8,801,061
1894	11,200,953	7,832,919
1895	9,829,076	6,198,221
1896	10,759,764	6,489,954
1897	9,753,185	7,085,048
1898	24,689,698	22,739,676
1899	13,907,927	10,890,275
1900	20,365,393	14,787,373

SOURCE: *Statistical Year Book of Canada for 1900*
(Ottawa: Government Printing Bureau 1901) 84, 86

* Does not include American wheat and wheat flour exported through Canadian ports

The growing significance of cattle exports to the Canadian economy was not lost upon the government. While wheat, wheat flour, and the other components of the agricultural products sector were barely holding their own, animal and dairy products exports were buoyant. (See Table 6.) This trade sector stood apart as a bright spot in an otherwise static list of export commodities during this decade.[143] The optimism with which the Canadian government looked to the development of the cattle trade is apparent in the Minister of Agriculture's 1883 *Report.*

The cattle trade of Canada has now ceased to be an experiment. It has grown to be one of the greatest lines of trade of the country ... It is an established fact too that Canada is destined to become one of the most important cattle raising countries in the world, possessing as it does, every facility for the conduct of an enormous trade ... Cattle raising here is now capable of unlimited extension, and is yet to be one of our most important export trades.[144]

The evidence suggests that Ottawa's first interest in the western plains was not cereal agriculture but stock-raising. This led the government to play a direct role in promotion and development of the Canadian cattle industry in a way that was foreign to the American experience and helped to define the distinctive character of the ranching frontier in Canada. Federal support for the interests of western ranchers therefore can be seen to reflect not only this group's remarkable political and business connections, but also the place of live cattle exports in the Canadian economy.

The economic condition of the industry in the early nineties was, of course, vital to its continued existence. As long as the profits to be realized were greater from grazing than from farming, the threat of an intruding farm population would be peripheral. The general subsistence level of agriculture as it was to be found in the west during the eighties and nineties was not a competitive factor; the full challenge of commercial agriculture would not be faced for another decade. For this reason the conflict within the cattle country before 1892 was mainly between the established rancher and newcomers of limited means who planned to claim a 160-acre homestead and expand their assets, often at their larger neighbour's expense, from one cow to a herd, and so become full-fledged stock-raisers themselves. The owner of a small but growing herd was looked upon with suspicion and feared lest his example be incentive to countless others. This antagonism between large and small stockmen, as indicated earlier, is reflected in the persistent internal strife within stockmen's associations.

The contest between larger cattlemen and their various competitors who sought entry into the south-west – sheepmen, farmers, and intending stock-raisers – was unequal. The economic and political power of the established cattlemen at this point was greater than any other single force in the North-West Territories except for the railway. Moreover, their position as a regional élite was immeasurably strengthened by the fact that they were fully integrated into a larger and more powerful national élite. Given the remarkable position of the cattlemen in the Canadian west during this period, the often-used regional description 'cattle kingdom' seems particularly accurate.

The years of the big ranchers' hegemony represents a distinct stage in the development and settlement of the Canadian west, and in this regard the occupation of the Canadian semi-arid region seems to follow the patterns manifest in the western United States, Argentina, Australia, and South Africa. In each region, before general farm settlement occurred, there was an interval that Australian historians have called 'the Pastoral Ascendancy.' On the Canadian plains frontier, the character of this pastoral ascendancy was distinguished by two features: the degree of the central government's administrative control and the nature of the incoming population. Apart from the police, the first mark of the federal presence in the ranch country was the lease system. It underlines a presence, on the frontier generally and in the cattle industry specifically, that was not part of the American tradition. The national government, as agent of the St Lawrence financial community, played a direct role in promotion of the cattle industry in the Canadian west and the land policy that emerged to guide development was the product of a particular British-Canadian mentality.

3

Grazing leases to stock-watering reserves: the cattle kingdom 1892–6

Squatters trying to occupy land within the great leaseholds were a persistent annoyance to cattlemen in the early 1890s. In the ensuing contest, power, privilege, and capital had to give way before the deep-rooted North American tradition of farmers' access to unsettled lands. The cattlemen and the government in which they were so well represented were compelled to abandon closed-lease tenure in favour of more subtle means of control.

The tension which threatened to erupt into an open range war during the summer of 1891 climaxed a decade of intermittent opposition to the large cattlemen's hegemony in the southwest. The crisis followed a year of deceptive calm that in part was the result of a temporary change in the editorial policy of the *Macleod Gazette*. Forced to recognize his financial vulnerability in face of the economic sanctions imposed by the ranch community, Wood abandoned his championship of the settlement cause and after the winter of 1889, avoided the lease or settlement question in his editorials. Wood's conciliatory overtures throughout 1890 did not, however, bring a return of the ranch community's subscriptions and the paper continued to languish as the number of ranch advertisements kept decreasing. In the end, the ranchers' intransigence pushed the *Gazette* to renew its challenge. If he was not to be forgiven by the local community for his past indiscretion, Wood's had now to express his belief in an increased farm population in order to ensure the paper's economic survival. Recognizing this, he gradually shifted his attention to the proposed construction of the Calgary and Edmonton Railway, which was to run from the American boundary to Edmonton. It seemed that this undertaking would bring the settlement that the region had hitherto failed to attract.

It was the particularly aggressive removal of squatters by the British-owned Walrond Ranche that brought Wood once more into direct confrontation with the ranchers. Reporting that an incendiary had put the torch to 300 tons of hay at the ranch, Wood insisted that the incident had to be considered as one of the

evil consequences of their manager's suicidal persecution of settlers. If settlers' houses are pulled down about their ears ... if, after making valuable improvements, settlers are turned out of house and home, and if, through some extraordinary influence with the government, the said manager [McEachran] can secure the cancellation of homestead entries, and secure government alliance in his war upon Canadian citizens, then retaliation is the only thing that the company can expect.[1]

This strong statement condoning violence, by a former policeman, illustrates the depth of frustration and despair felt by the ranchers' opponents. There was no way to meet the ranchers on equal terms and government contact or sympathy seemed almost non-existent.

The incident which had caused the incendiary attack and which set the *Gazette* and the ranch companies on a collision course seems to have originated in the eviction of several squatters from their homes in mid-winter.[2] Immediately following the fire, McEachran wrote to the Comptroller of the North-West Mounted Police implicating several families which had recently been evicted from the Walrond lease. McEachran described the incident as 'the inauguration of a reign of terrorism and lawlessness which if not checked at the commencement will doubtless extend, and there is no saying what complications will arise.'[3] McEachran asked that police detectives be employed in the area and that the Crown join with him in offering a $250 reward for the conviction of the party or parties responsible. Despite the recommendation of Joseph Royal, Lieutenant Governor of the Territories, that it would not be politically advisable for the Crown to be involved, McEachran was able, with the threat of a general range war, to prevail personally upon the Deputy Minister of Justice to instruct the Lieutenant Governor to offer this reward.[4]

Wood began his second attack on the cattlemen almost alone. To his chagrin the citizens and businessmen of the town refused open support of his cause.[5] They had suffered indirectly as a result of the *Gazette*'s previous contest with McEachran, and chose to remain discreet by-standers while the most serious feud to develop on the Canadian range unfolded. Public attention was again drawn to the actions of the Walrond Ranche Company several months later by an editorial in the *Gazette* charging that company cowhands had demolished the buildings of bona fide settlers on the Walrond lease.[6] The charge related to the eviction of the Dunbar family, who claimed to have settled on the property before the 1883 survey. After Dunbar squatted, the land was granted under the old non-settlement regulations to a prospective rancher. Though he had the right to evict squatters, the new proprietor had allowed Dunbar to remain. In 1887 this original lease was cancelled and in the following year the area was granted to the Walrond Ranche under the new form of lease permitting settlement. At this point Dunbar successfully applied for a homestead entry. Later, after improving his holding, Dunbar was informed that his entry had been cancelled by the Department of the Interior. The explanation given was that the land agent at Lethbridge had made a mistake in granting it.[7]

Cattlemen reacted to the mounting criticism of the press during the spring and summer of 1891 by policing their leases all the more vigorously; this in turn intensified the already inflamed relations between settler and rancher. The terse report from McEachran's ranch foreman about the eviction of one of Dunbar's neighbours illustrates the ranchers' determination, in face of the reluctance of the federal authorities, to enforce the 'no settlement' clause in the lease themselves.

two of the boys and myself went over to pull the house down and we met Dave [Cochrane] on our way over we told him what we was going to do he forbid us doing it but we went ahead and pulled it down just the same the whole tribe of them are boiling over with wrath, I hear Dunbars are saying that they are 6 or 8 of them are going to get together and put up a house some night and have Sam in it next morning I think this is only to make us uneasy at any rate we will only try to watch them the closer.[8]

Most ominous was the report's clear implication that without outside intervention, a vicious range feud or even an armed outbreak in the southwest was a distinct possibility. This was clear to McEachran, who immediately forwarded his foreman's letter to the Minister of the Interior and asked for police protection from 'the spirit of lawlessness which we have to contend with on [sic] the Dunbar family.' He reminded the Minister that the land was unsuited for agriculture, that the 'pauperism' of the Dunbars showed that farming could not succeed. McEachran couched his appeal for government support with the warning that his men would prevent trespass and that a collision with the squatters was likely.

The warning was not merely for dramatic effect. McEachran was genuinely alarmed by the deteriorating state of relations, as was the police superintendent S.B. Steele in the Ft Macleod district. On the basis of a report from a police scout sent to observe the situation in the Porcupine Hills, B. Steele informed the police commissioner of the 'very irritated feeling existing on all sides' and predicted that 'any more evictions would be followed by reprisals.'[9]

Eventually the storm reached the 1891 autumn session of Parliament. The Department of the Interior attempted to defend the position of the Walrond Ranche by explaining that the old lease regulations still applied to this new land grant because it had been given in exchange for a tract of land near Ft Macleod which that company had held under the old form. Hence McEachran had the legal right to evict squatters.[10] But the Opposition would not be assuaged by such legal niceties. After recounting the names of numerous settlers who had been evicted, J. McMullen, Liberal MP for North Wellington, proclaimed: 'in all the hardships that I have ever read of, and the ejectments that have taken place in unfortunate Ireland ... I have read of no case of hardship that exceeds the one I have now presented to the House ...'[11] Supporting a petition from twenty-five settlers in the Porcupine Hills, the Liberals demanded that the Walrond lease be cancelled and that all old leases be altered to allow homesteading.

Finally, Minister of the Interior Edgar Dewdney enunciated government policy on the matter. Using the arguments of the cattle compact, he cautioned that the large amount of capital invested in the ranching industry must be protected. He informed the House that there was good land available for settlement elsewhere. Dewdney argued that certain squatters made a business of settling on leased land, usually squatting on springs with the object of being bought out, and listed a number of examples to support his case. Developing the theme that ranchers were often victimized by squatters who settled and fenced stock-watering areas, he concluded: 'I think it speaks well for the ranchers and for everyone concerned that we have not had more difficulties.'[12]

Despite Dewdney's strong verbal defence in the House of the leaseholders, the ranchers remained uneasy about the government's future intentions, for Dewdney had remarked, under the pressure of Opposition charges, that some changes in the lease system might be considered if the expected land rush materialized following completion of the southern extension of the Edmonton and Calgary Railway.[13] As the confrontation continued into the spring of 1892, McEachran insisted upon a firm commitment from the government regarding leased properties and threatened to advise the directors of his company to withdraw completely from western operations unless the government guaranteed 'permanent possession of the land or undisturbed possession till the end of the present lease.'[14] The government for its part was certainly aware that the great weight of public opinion was with the squatters and was therefore reluctant to see the federal authority compelled to act as agent for the cattlemen, as would be the case if McEachran's demands were met.

The ranchers were, however, determined to leave no avenue of influence untried in their effort to hold federal support. From their point of view the

Dunbar dispute had become a vital test case. They realized that if settlers in the region once gained federal backing their cause was lost, and each squatter thus far established would bring numerous friends. This suspicion was certainly substantiated by Dunbar's testimonial to the *Macleod Gazette* that 'were it not for the present state of affairs in regard to settlement, he could induce forty good settlers from the neighbourhood of his old home to come here and locate.'[15] Senator Lougheed was quickly recruited to call upon Deputy Minister of the Interior A.M. Burgess to emphasize the cattle industry's concern and support McEachran's claim that every attempt had been made to treat the Dunbars justly. Burgess in turn promptly interceded with the Minister to suggest that if the facts were as McEachran stated, blame could hardly be accorded to the Walrond Ranche for the continued unfortunate state of affairs.[16]

The Dunbar case was finally concluded when the Department of the Interior, under attack from Wilfrid Laurier, leader of the Opposition, offered to give the Dunbars credit for improvements when they applied for a new location.[17] Significantly, settlement of the dispute involved compensation paid by the government, not by the Walrond Ranche. Ottawa not only supported the existing lease structure, but in this case paid the cost of settling the family elsewhere. The government had had the opportunity to call McEachran's bluff of withdrawal if it truly desired to open up the region. But as in the 1889 settlement imbroglio, the Conservative party had little desire to antagonize a group so intimately represented within its own membership. Bound to its powerful capitalist supporters in the east, the government was compelled to help maintain their outpost in the west.

In the final analysis the ranchers' victory none the less proved transitory, and in a sense 1891 might be seen as a turning point in the lease and settlement question in the southwest. The cattlemen had compelled the government to stand by them, honour the terms of the no-settlement lease, and see the squatters evicted. But their unyielding stand had also served to focus public attention. Never before had the government had to face such concerted opposition to its support of the cattle companies. Popular opinion outside the region clearly sided with the squatters and Ottawa was repeatedly called to account for the apparent disregard of the government's own longstanding commitment to western settlement. While the cattle interests were too powerful to ignore, the tide of criticism that advanced with the dispute in 1891 made it politically expedient to persuade the ranchers to compromise.

The excuse for effecting such a compromise was ultimately provided through the government's railway policy. In order to fulfil its land grant obligations to the Calgary and Edmonton Railway, then under construction south of Calgary, the government had to reach an understanding with the holders of the great leased tracts in the south-west. The need for railway land thus provided a lever that could be used to force ranchers to accept a negotiated change in the lease structure without leaving the government vulnerable to the accusation that it was abandoning its friends in favour of squatters and their Liberal supporters. On 21 December 1891, after a year of continuous feuding throughout the southwest, Dewdney invited representatives of the cattle interests to meet privately with him to discuss the land tenure issue. Included in the invitation for the ranchers' consideration was the proposal that leaseholders be allowed to purchase one-tenth of their leases at two dollars per acre and that the remainder be released under a new formula permitting settlement.

The ranchers hastened to respond to Dewdney's circular. Certain members of the corporate ranch establishment met in Montreal to decide on the course of action to be followed.[18] Those gathered in the financial centre of the Canadian cattle kingdom agreed that all leaseholders should be invited to be present at, or to send a representative to, a subsequent meeting to decide what sort of collective action should be taken and to arrange for a deputation to meet with the government. The leaseholders' appointees who eventually met with the Minister on 29 February 1892 included Senator Cochrane, Dr McEachran, and D.W. Davis, MP; three of Montreal's influential Conservative businessmen – Sir Hugh Allan, P.S. Ross, and W.M. Ramsay; three prominent ranch managers from the west – C. Stimson, C. Kerry, and D.H. McPherson; as well as the Ottawa attorney, J.A. Gemmill, who had long acted as a parliamentary lobbyist and legal adviser to various Alberta ranches.

Dewdney's broad, conciliatory assurance to the delegation that 'nothing would be done to disturb so large an industry,'[19] was tempered by the declaration that some leased areas would have to be given over to enable the government to meet its obligation to the Calgary and Edmonton Railway, and that a certain degree of settlement must eventually occur along the new line. On this occasion the cattlemen found the government adamant. It was apparent to Ottawa that there could never be order and stability in the southwest until the 'no-settlement' leases were cancelled. The Dunbar episode, for example, had hardly been concluded after extended negotiation and national outcry when McEachran's cowhands resumed the pulling down of settlers' houses.[20] The squatters for their part made it known that they were restraining their actions against the leaseholders, 'pending the decision of the Department of the Interior on this subject.'[21] Meanwhile the police kept the region under anxious surveillance for fear some incident might spark an open conflict. Aware that the government's decision was also eagerly awaited by important groups outside the south-west and aware, too, of the direction of popular feeling, the department was insistent that the 'no-settlement' leases be cancelled. Finding that the government's determination to alter its grazing lease policy could not be resisted, the cattlemen naturally bargained for the most favourable terms possible. Provisions of the compromise, if indeed any were firmly established, were not revealed to the public in the official communiqué, which announced only that a lengthy discussion had been held.

The *Macleod Gazette*'s reaction to the communiqué was one of immediate apprehension. Noting that only the ranch interest was being consulted in what appeared to be a secret conclave, the paper protested that Ottawa was following its customary policy of yielding to the ranchers' 'slightest demand.'[22] Even the prospect of permanently alienating one-tenth of the great leases seemed excessive to Wood, who demanded that the settlers be heard. The cattlemen's journal, the *Calgary Herald*, like the *Gazette*, assumed that a deal had been made. It was the two-dollar per acre levy, however, rather than the one-tenth reservation, which this paper deemed excessive.[23]

Finally, on 12 October 1892, an order-in-council gave notice that all leases which did not provide for the withdrawal of lands for homestead or railway purposes would be terminated in four years, on 31 December 1896. Ranchers were given the option of purchasing one-tenth of their leases at two dollars per acre, a price which the ranch lobby was later able to reduce to a dollar twenty-five per acre, or half the amount charged to homesteaders for pre-empted acres in the Ft Macleod region.[24] Despite the speculation of both the *Calgary Herald* and the *Gazette* that a 'deal' had been made, it was several years before the key to the agreement became generally known. As it turned out, the substance of the accord was the government's unwritten promise of a gradual but vast extension of the region's stock-watering reserves.

This change of government policy has been interpreted as the climax of a gradual desertion of the ranchers by the federal government in face of the increasing pressure of settlement.[25] The decline of the great ranches has been inferred from the subsequent decrease in the total lease acreage and the increase in the number of lessees as shown in Table 7. Noting this phenomenon, John Blue, for example, has concluded that by 1888 the day of the great rancher with his 100,000-acre ranch had ended.[26]

While it is true that the declining total acreage of leased land suggests greater government concern for settlement, it cannot be concluded that the government had abandoned the ranchers from the date the leased acreage begins to decline, or that the large ranches were destroyed. The great decline in the leased acreage before 1895 is largely accounted for by the cancellation of speculative holdings whose owners had little or no intention of ranching. Changes in government regulations were not intended to, nor did they, have any serious effect on the cattle compact, whose holdings remained relatively constant until 1895. What

TABLE 7

Grazing leases 1884–96

Year	Acres	Number of leases in force
1884	1,785,690.00	47
1888	3,252,378.00	111
1890	2,288,347.00	126
1892	1,801,209.11	142
1894	1,298,871.51	156
1895	904,186.73	185
1896	257,983.39	136

SOURCE: Canada, Department of the Interior,
Annual Reports (1884–96)

is significant is not that the total leased acreage was reduced, but who held the remaining acreage, and in what quantity. In this regard it is clear that reductions impinged slightly on the holdings of companies or individual members of the ranch establishment. The 163,868 leased acres of the Cochrane Ranch in 1894 represent only a modest decline from the 189,000 acres held in 1884. The Oxley and Walrond ranch holdings declined to 149,934 and 120,238 acres respectively from the 180,000 acres that each held in 1884. The leasehold of the North-West Cattle Company, on the other hand, increased from 59,000 to 157,925 acres during this decade.[27] It should be noted, moreover, that it is of questionable validity in the first place to speak of the decline of the cattle industry from a list of lease figures without a corresponding measurement of herd sizes. The rancher's circumstances are revealed more by herd size than by the expanse of a lease.

As a group, cattlemen retained their dominant position in the southwestern countryside after 1896 simply by transferring their operations to the largest deeded holdings in the North-West Territories through purchase of great blocks of their former leases from the new Calgary and Edmonton Railway at a dollar fifty per acre.[28] When the Cochrane Ranche Company decided to liquidate its assets in 1905 it had to dispose of 63,000 acres of deeded land.[29] The survival of this patriarch of the cattle kingdom in the Canadian south-west is typical. Both the North-West Cattle Company and the Walrond Ranche Company, for example, retained holdings in excess of 50,000 acres until the mid-twentieth century.[30] Though ownership of these old ranches altered, their continued existence along with newer grants such as the Medicine Hat Ranch, for example, which operated 270,000 acres in 1956, suggests that the large ranch has been an enduring feature in the Canadian south-west.[31]

Cattlemen, with the aid of their efficient metropolitan political and financial connections, remained undisputed masters of the rangelands in 1896 despite alterations in federal lease laws. The paramount factor in the continuation of such control was the stock-watering reserve system begun by William Pearce in 1886 and vastly expanded between 1892 and 1896 before the old no-settlement leases were opened. As in 1886, when the federal government negotiated lease changes with the cattlemen it was in fact this unwritten understanding that brought leaseholders to accept the principle of cancellation in 1892. The key individual then was the Department of the Interior's Superintendent of Mines, William Pearce. Persistent reminders from him that the Department had the obligation of a longstanding promise made in 1891 to the cattlemen at Ft Macleod to protect their interest through reservation of suitable stock-watering places finally induced Ottawa to proceed.[32] In October 1893 Pearce forwarded a long list of properties to be set aside, with the footnote that the list would be added to as additional leaseholds were wound up.

Cattlemen divided themselves into regional committees to draw up lists of reservations desired in their respective localities.[33] The lists were then sent to Pearce, who inspected the properties and then forwarded his recommendations to the Department in Ottawa. These selections were supplemented by the requests of individual ranchers and companies, and, in cases where ranchers failed to take the initiative, by Pearce himself.[34] By and large the selections made by the stockmen were approved, so that by 1894 springs, creeks, and river bottoms were well protected throughout the south-west and especially in the foothills region.

Once the reserves were established the Department, through Pearce's initiative and the ranchers' vigilance, vigorously prevented settlement on or even near them. Consequently the next rash of squatter evictions were from the water and shelter reservations rather than from the closed leases, as in the past. In the squatter's eyes, however, it mattered little whether the eviction was from a lease or a water reserve; it was an eviction from a chosen location none the less, and the bitterness of the previous decade was perpetuated. The shot fired at Dr McEachran through the window of his house on the Walrond Ranche in the summer of 1893 was symptomatic of this longstanding hostility and a reminder that the danger of the feud taking a violent turn was always a real possibility.[35]

In the spring of 1894 the Department prepared a form letter to warn squatters that certain lands were reserved.[36] In June those who had failed to take heed were notified to desist making improvements on lands which they had been told to vacate. Squatters were warned that they would 'be forcibly removed and if at any time thereafter any attempt be made to renew said improvements they [would] not only be forcibly removed but such further steps taken as [would] prevent if possible a repetition of the trespass.'[37] Pearce's zealous and unsympathetic attitude in these matters is well illustrated in his report of a visit to a homesteader who had claimed an adjacent, but unfortunately reserved, quarter section. 'I pointed out to her, that had it not been for the action of the government, this quarter section would long since have been acquired by parties who were here before they came to the country and that consequently she and her husband had no grievance whatever.'[38] Faced with the plea that they needed water for the house, Pearce conceded that a half-inch pipe might be used to bring the water, but warned the couple not to make any improvements as they would not get the land.

When by the summer of 1894 it became evident that written warnings were going unheeded, Pearce initiated formal eviction proceedings. He recommended that police in these cases simply follow the old method of removing squatters within leaseholds, except henceforth the directive would be sent to the police by the Department rather than by the leaseholder as in the past.[39] The past, and apparently continued modus operandi, consisted of giving the squatter notice that on a certain day steps would be taken to eject him forcibly if he had not vacated before then. The police officer in command of the nearest district was notified of the warning, and on the day indicated sent a detachment to the place in question to see that the peace was not disturbed as the buildings were pulled down. Such a procedure was, for example, outlined to the manager of the Marquis of Lorne's Alberta Ranche, with accompanying instructions that the offending parties squatting on water reserves within that lease be given three weeks' notice. Pearce then outlined his actions to the Deputy Minister along with the admonition that it would be unwise to countermand the instructions he had given.

I only desire to repeat, that weakening on the part of the Department at this juncture would be fatal to the welfare of the stock interest which are of paramount importance in the District south of Calgary. The squatters on the Alberta Ranche Company's lease state that in their opinion the letters sent them with reference to their vacating their present claims are merely 'bluff' on the part of the leaseholder and Government and the sooner their minds are disabused of this erroneous impression, the better for all parties concerned.[40]

Pearce was convinced that a determined stand had to be made, that if such squatters were not 'summarily ejected' within a year there would not be a valuable spring left and the district would be ruined as a stock-raising area.[41] The Department concurred.

Given this presumption, Pearce pursued squatters mercilessly. For the next two years he co-ordinated the efforts of cattlemen and police in the eviction proceedings. Notices of those who persisted in squatting were forwarded to the NWMP Comptroller to instruct his force to take possession of this or that property 'on behalf of Her Majesty.'[42] Though the Department also had an alternative to this method of eviction, namely legal proceedings, it was invariably decided to procure eviction of squatters by using the police to resume possession on behalf of the Crown and remove improvements belonging to such violators.[43] Legal proceedings in court had on occasion been tried, but this method took much too long to conclude and resulted in undue publicity.

The campaign against squatters came to a temporary halt in May 1896. In a private letter to Major S.B. Steele, NWMP Superintendent at Ft Macleod, Pearce suggested that it might be advisable that no further steps be taken against settlers on stock-watering reserves until after the federal election on 23 June. As the Superintendent explained: 'A crop of things spring up which, were it not that a general election is on, would never be resurrected.'[44] Pearce's decision to seek a month's moratorium is hardly surprising, for his actions in the south-west had aroused much opposition. With many leases still closed, and the increasing reservation of spring, creek, and river bottoms, the intending settler found homestead selection increasingly difficult. There was, moreover, the longstanding and widespread feeling that the Department of the Interior was under the thumb of those sympathetic to the cattle interests. To the farmer it seemed that cattlemen were being allowed to select all the best lands before the agriculturalist was allowed entry, in a deliberate act to squeeze them out. As one settler complained to the Department: 'The big stockmen claim most every section has been alloted [sic] and as they are the only ones that seems to know anything about it would you be kind enough to enlighten us a little about the matter?'[45] This query was followed with a petition from the few settlers in the region charging that the whole matter of water reserves was arranged by two or three stockmen whose intent was to reserve the range for stock-grazing purposes. The petitioners requested that the matter of water reserves in the locality be decided by the majority of residents at a public meeting.[46]

The settlers received little sympathy. D.W. Davis, resident in the region since whiskey trade days and Conservative MP for the District of Alberta, to whom the petitioners entrusted delivery of their memorial, advised the Minister against any changes in the system.[47] Pearce's response was more directly hostile. He repeated his longstanding argument that the object of making such reservations, including the one on which the petitioners had built their meeting hall, was for the benefit of all and the government had no intention of altering its course. Pearce had little faith in the notion that a public meeting might best decide on what reserves were necessary for their locality and dismissed the plea for a democratic resolution of the problem with the rejoinder:

Can you point out to me, if your request is granted, what ground we can bring forth in refusing any other applicants the right to squat on these reservations providing they go to the trouble of having a petition circulated as forwarded? The experience with petitions has, if I am not mistaken, been, that no great attention can be made to such documents. If those who are beneficially affected by squatting on these reservations are to constitute themselves as judges of the expediency or otherwise of granting such applications; then, good-bye to all ideas of reservations![48]

He was convinced that there could not be too many reservations in a district where the stock interest was paramount. Of the 115,000 acres under lease to the Quorn Ranch Company, for example, Pearce proposed to set aside some 9800 acres.[49] The fact that this acreage was concentrated about the water courses within the lease made settlement almost as difficult as if the old no-settlement lease had been retained. Pearce methodically set aside such lands along the foothills from Calgary to the American border and finally out on the southern plains in the vicinity of Medicine Hat and Maple Creek. Settlement was just beginning in the latter region in the mid-nineties and it was not until the spring of 1896 that ranchers in this region forwarded to Pearce the locations of desired reservation.[50] But by the summer an extensive system of water reservations had been established throughout the southwest.

Pearce's reserves were in large part responsible for the survival of the cattlemen's empire throughout a decade and a half of Liberal rule after 1896.[51] As one prominent stockman later remarked, this protection had 'practically excluded settlement' in his district.[52] The cattlemen were entirely cognizant of Pearce's contribution to their well-being over the years and in 1899 members of the ranch establishment gathered at the St James Club in Montreal to proffer a gift to him, in recognition of services rendered 'in the interests of the cattlemen.'[53] In 1911 when the Conservatives returned to power the vestiges of Pearce's reserve system remained.

The water reserve legislation, like the lease system before it, was an attempt on the part of the federal government to treat the south-west as a region distinct from the rest of the prairies. It stood in recognition of what the Department of the Interior deemed to be the country's peculiar physiographic qualities, and was designed to protect and encourage stock-raising interests. Such legislation presupposed a high degree of supervision, which in turn meant that the federal police were burdened with a set of responsibilities unique to this part of the North-West Territories. Such responsibilities were often onerous and sometimes unpleasant, as the lease and water reserve evictions bear witness, and in the eyes of the small minority opposed to such legislation the police tended to be identified as the agents of the region's vested interest.[54]

The NWMP's activity in the ranch-settler conflict reveals another facet of the cattlemen-police relationship and in light of its far-reaching character, a closer assessment is warranted. As noted earlier the nature of the cattlemen's occupation was such as to require protection on a day-to-day basis greater than that needed by any other economic group in the prairie west. The rancher's cattle, representing almost his entire capital investment, wandered freely over a vast expanse with only limited supervision. In the Canadian west the NWMP, in addition to the normal functions of a police force, were therefore called upon to protect ranchers' herds through a network of posts and regular patrols traversing the range country.

Cattlemen had come to rely upon the police since their arrival and with the coming of the big cattle companies became even more demanding, particularly in their requests for protection against the Indians. W.F. Cochrane in a letter to his father reported that the NWMP had been tardy in their promise to post men at Stand-Off to guard against Indians killing Cochrane cattle. If action was not soon forthcoming, Cochrane suggested, 'we'll tell him that if he does not do it we will write to headquarters about it.'[55] Captain Cotton quickly sent the required men, and subsequently swore before a gathering of the South-Western Stock Association that 'he had never forgotten their interests and never would.'[56] The cattlemen never considered security so complete or automatically forthcoming as to be taken for granted, and where police effort seemed lacking they were prepared to use whatever influence was required for improvement.

Police posts and patrols therefore were constantly increased to keep pace with expansion of the cattlemen's empire. By 1889 a vast surveillance network thoroughly covered the south-west. The cattlemen were served by five divisions, D and H headquartered at Macleod, K at Lethbridge, A at Maple Creek, and E at Calgary. Stationed within each division's territory were numerous detachments from which regular and 'flying patrols' operated in all directions. A Division supplied small detachments to Swift Current, Saskatchewan Landing, Dunmore, Bull's Head, Josephburg, Willow Creek, Graburn, Battle Creek, East End, and Medicine Hat, where one officer, four non-commissioned officers, and sixteen constables were stationed. From the outpost at Willow Creek patrols connected with those from K Division. Posts at Kennedy's Crossing far to the east near the international boundary, Pendant d'Oreille, Writing-on-Stone, and Milk River, as well as Fifteen-Mile Butte and Nine-Mile Butte on the old Ft Benton trail between Lethbridge and Milk River Ridge were maintained by K Division. Flying patrols from St Mary's River, about twenty miles south of Lethbridge, and the junction of the Little Bow and Belly rivers discouraged rustling in outlying regions. Daily patrols kept careful watch, the coming and going of strangers was closely checked, and ranchers and settlers were visited regularly.

Posts and patrols of the two divisions at Ft Macleod connected in the south with the Lethbridge Division and in the north with the Calgary Division at High River. Detachments from the Ft Macleod divisions of special concern to southern cattlemen included St Mary's, about twenty-five miles west of the Milk River Ridge detachment and about eight miles north of the international boundary; Lee's Creek; Milk River near the American border; Big Bend near the Cochrane Ranch at the south-west corner of the Blood Reserve; Kootenai Fork twelve miles north of Big Bend; Stand-Off on the Belly River near the junction of the Kootenai River (Waterton); and Kipp, on the Old Man River between Ft Macleod and Lethbridge. Detachments in the cattle country north of Ft Macleod were stationed at Leavings, about thirty miles north-west of Ft Macleod, and at Mosquito Creek, approximately twenty miles further north among some of the largest ranches. Police were also stationed at Porcupine Hills on Beaver Creek close to the Walrond Ranche, while a substantial detachment was maintained in the cattle town of Pincher Creek some miles up the Old Man River from Ft Macleod. D Division also operated a flying patrol south of Stand-Off to discourage cattle-killing by the Blood Indians. The northern ranching country was supervised by E Division. A detachment from it at Gleichen watched over the Blackfoot Reserve and the eastern and southern plains. The police at Morley patrolled the Stoney Reserve and the foothills country along the Bow River. The post at Sheep Creek looked after the region immediately south of Calgary, while the detachment at Pekisko further south, near the home ranch of the North-West Cattle Company, patrolled the foothills cattle country as far south as was necessary to intersect with the patrols of the Mosquito Creek unit of the Ft Macleod Division. The High River post watched over the Calgary–Ft Macleod Trail and patrolled the country to the east.[57] This remarkable surveillance of the ranch country was complemented by special summer patrols along the Montana boundary.

While the numerous detachments scattered throughout the cattle country were not intended to be simply guardians of the ranchers' interests and spent much of their time on routine police duties, their single most important function after the maintenance of peace and order was to prevent the killing and stealing of livestock. The thoroughness of their activity in this regard is suggested by the numerous reports in police files, some of which run to hundreds of pages, on cases which involved only a few head of livestock. Even more important than the thoroughness of their investigations was the preventive effect of their formidable network of posts and patrols, which kept cattle-stealing to a minimum before 1896. Each of the four largest ranches had a police detachment stationed within a few miles of its home ranch. The extent to which the Canadian range was patrolled is suggested by the more than 2000 mounted patrols performed by the Calgary Division alone during 1889. On no other

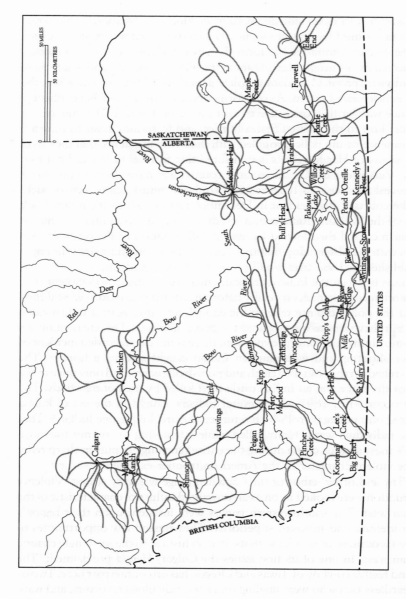

6 NWMP patrols and posts in ranch country 1888. Courtesy Special Collections, University of British Columbia Library, from Canada, Department of the Interior, 'Map Shewing Police Stations and Patrols throughout the North-West Territories, during the Year 1888'

frontier was the cattleman afforded such protection as he established his herds. The vigilante committee was consequently practically unknown on the Canadian range. Such a committee was formed on rare occasions when an individual was suspected by his neighbours of tampering with their herds, and where there was insufficient proof to initiate a police action, but in no instance was the ultimate penalty ever exacted. As one former policeman and rancher explained, the practice was for the committee to visit the suspect at night, get him out of bed, escort him to the United States border, and warn him never to return.[58]

The presence of the police, coupled with their firm insistence that they were the sole agents of Her Majesty's law, ensured that frontier justice did not gain currency. Violence in the Canadian cattle country was most uncommon. Police reports reveal that between 1878 and 1883 only five murder cases were brought before the courts.[59] An incident in December 1895 in which the tough Texas foreman of the Walrond Ranche beat an adversary to the draw and shot him in the stomach caused the Macleod Gazette to call attention to the rarity of such incidents with the observation that this was only the second time since the paper was established in 1882 that it had cause to report a gunfight.[60]

Relations between the Indians and cattlemen were equally non-violent. The ranchers often complained, especially before and during the North-West Rebellion, that the police did not take strong enough measures against Indian cattle thieves, but they were never prepared to act on their own. Despite continuous bitter complaining and some provocation, there is but one recorded incident of a rancher shooting and wounding an Indian caught stealing a horse.[61] The ranchers relied on the NWMP to catch and punish offenders, and only once in the history of the force was an Indian cattle thief killed by men of that body. The incident occurred in 1891 when several Indians, caught in the act of killing cattle, fired on a police patrol which returned the fire, killing one Indian.[62] That only one individual was actually killed while attempting to commit the range country's most serious crime during the entire ranching era puts in sharp relief the more violent character of the American frontier experience.

The 'law and order' ethos of the Canadian range was very strong. Violence and disruption were looked upon as an unwanted influence characteristic of the American west. The south-western papers were insistent upon their region's separate identity and inherent superiority. They missed few opportunities to compare favourably their west with its 'British justice' to the seemingly chaotic American west. In one of its first issues the Calgary Herald proclaimed: 'The rough and festive cowboy of Texas and Oregon has no counterpart here. Two or three beardless lads who wear jingling spurs and ridiculous revolvers, and walk with a slouch ... [but] the genuine Alberta cowboy is a gentleman ...'[63] The frequent reports of lynchings of cattle and horse thieves in Montana and

Wyoming were usually accompanied with a lecture on the deplorable absence of law on the American frontier.[64] Individuals who argued for or patterned their actions on the American model earned the enmity of all. Wood of the *Macleod Gazette*, for example, whose championship of the settlers' cause was longstanding and whose personal antipathy to the Walrond Ranche manager, Duncan McEachran, was expressed frequently in the *Gazette*, was not deterred from warning the squatter who shot at McEachran that 'the people of the Canadian North-West will object most decidedly to any attempt at a repetition of American western lawlessness.'[65] Wood's warning significantly implied not only that the guilty party was American, but also that the act itself was characteristically American. Such rowdyism as did from time to time occur was typically ascribed in its lighter form to the English remittance man and in its more serious form to expatriates from south of the border.[66] Given this feeling, the American cattleman or cowboy who moved north often found himself suspect and considered by his neighbours and the police as a potential threat to their 'orderly' society.

This anti-American bias reflected a fundamental difference in attitude to law and order in the cattle country on the two sides of the border. Citizens in the Canadian range country by and large accepted the premise that the law should be formulated and imposed from above. This point of view was almost directly opposite to that characteristic of the American frontier, where the cherished ideal was that such matters should be a local responsibility and hence be responsible to and directed by the citizenry below. With regard to law and order, the police, the ranch establishment, and the majority of south-western settlers were of common mind. They had, as the press repeatedly assured them, 'British law' and 'British justice' and with a conviction bordering on the conceit so characteristic of the late Victorian élite they looked frequently to the American cattle kingdom to be further assured of the superiority of their system. Even the few who dissented were more inclined to object to specific laws, or what they deemed to be the undue influence of certain groups, than to the nature of the governmental or judicial system. Given the cultural and social composition of the population on the Canadian range, the predominance of such ideas is not surprising. Cultural tradition, along with the commanding presence and efficiency of the NWMP, assured that the Canadian ranching frontier was essentially non-violent despite the universal tension that pitted cattleman against Indian, sheepman, and settler.

Conformity of attitude in the cattle country during the early period brought a degree of stability uncharacteristic of most frontier societies. This had much to do with the social bonds that, before 1896, drew the majority of ranchers and policemen so closely together. Both groups were cut from essentially the same social fabric, so that the social and cultural milieu of the larger ranch community was reproduced in miniature within the police force. About a fifth of the officers in the period after 1885 were from the British Isles and Canadian officers were recruited almost entirely from upper class families in Ontario, Quebec, and the Atlantic provinces.[67] They came from the same families that dominated the professions, the church, the military, the government, and the civil service, as well as the nation's business community. They came, in short, from the same group that comprised the ranch establishment and many moved easily from the life of police officer to ranch-owner. Like many big leaseholders who had gained their lands through political connections, the officer class was recruited with careful attention to the dictates of party patronage, which meant that both groups had a vested interest in the well-being of the Conservative party. The constables of the force fitted a similar mould. They were not the social rejects that comprised the ranks of most nineteenth-century frontier military garrisons. They came in almost equal balance from the farms and the clerical and skilled trades of the east, and as such represented that part of the population that was most upwardly mobile in the late nineteenth century.[68] The composition of the force tended, moreover, to remain static in a social sense as there was generally a waiting list for enlistment which allowed the force to be selective in its recruitment. The process of selection was also continued after enlistment through the high rate of desertion. Those who rejected the standards and demands of police work soon departed with the covert blessing of the force, leaving a body relatively homogeneous in attitude and background.

At the community level, members of the force, particularly officers, identified with and were readily accepted by leading local citizens. Cattlemen for their part were careful to establish and maintain close relations with the force. The commanding officer of E Division at Calgary was always granted honorary membership in the Ranchmen's Club, Calgary's oldest and most select fraternity. The close relationship which developed with the NWMP was also advanced for reasons which went beyond the utilitarian motives both parties recognized. The police and the ranchers had arrived on the grasslands at about the same time and a close affinity had developed quite naturally. The bonds of friendship were strengthened by the fact that so many ranchers were originally members of the force. As already noted, the class background of the police and the larger stockmen was remarkably similar and they tended to see the world from the same perspective. For these reasons it was usually much easier for the police to identify with the cattle kingdom, with its strong British overtones and equestrian tradition, than with the few frontier squatters and the American dry-land farmers who later moved into the southern region. The police officers and important ranch families understood that they were of the same social station and there was consequently much social interchange between the two groups.

NWMP officers and their wives were frequent guests at ranch homes and social gatherings sponsored by the ranch community.[69] This social congeniality lent a special character to the Canadian cattle kingdom that lasted until World War I.

Despite their close social contacts with the NWMP, cattlemen did not take the support of the police for granted nor did they presume to seek assistance beyond the letter of the law. Procuring police support to help persuade Ottawa to change unfavourable legislation was another matter, and in this regard the stockmen were not reticent.[70] They saw the police as vital to protection of their economic interests and traditionally ended their association meetings, which the police frequently attended, with a vote of thanks and a request for continued support.[71] Such practice was really a matter of good manners between men who understood each other and their respective needs very well. What the cattlemen feared most were the recurring proposals for reductions in the force. These they were always quick to protest, and always they were ready to defend the force's reputation.

The cattlemen's mastery of the range until the turn of the century is attributable not only to the powerful institutional support upon which they could call, such as the police at the local level or supporters within the Conservative party at the national level, but also to the internal consolidation of the ranch community which took place in the mid-nineties. Growing uncertainty about federal support after the Dunbar case and increased external pressure motivated cattlemen to resolve their differences during the four-year period of grace before the old leases were abolished. This sense of urgency was compounded with the defeat of the Conservative government in the summer of 1896. In addition to seeing their federal influence placed in serious jeopardy, cattlemen were confronted for the first time with a federal representative who was not their own man. The new Liberal MP for Alberta, Frank Oliver, had expressed himself strongly against the water reserve system and had been elected on the basis of a plurality in the now more heavily settled farming region from Calgary north.

Within six weeks of the election, Oliver was called to meet with the stockmen in Ft Macleod. The latter pressed upon Oliver the necessity of maintaining the status quo and elicited his verbal promise that 'some very grave cause for a change would have to be shown' for alteration of the reserve system, coupled with the reassurance that he did not consider that 'any good and sufficient cause could be given outside of the stock industry itself.'[72] Though the ranchers had voted against him almost to a man, Oliver recognized that they represented one of the most influential bodies in the west at the time and thus felt obliged to agree to their request that he meet with them a second time at the incorporation meeting of the new stockmen's association.

The purpose of this meeting in Calgary was twofold. The ranchers' first objective was to bring to fruition the work of nearly three years' internal reorganization that had commenced in 1892 with the notification by the federal government that the old 'closed' leases would be terminated in four years. Faced with increasing pressure on all sides, the larger stockmen sought to establish what had eluded the industry for over a decade: namely a strong central body that could claim the support of all ranchers in the southwest and speak with a single voice on their behalf. In December 1896, the entire ranch community, represented by delegates sent from the newly organized local associations at Bow River (Calgary), Maple Creek, Lethbridge, Pincher Creek, Willow Creek, High River, Sheep Creek, and Medicine Hat met at Calgary to ratify the proposed terms of incorporation for a new universal cattlemen's association.

The second, and possibly the more immediately pressing, reason for meeting was the ranchers' growing unease about Oliver's continued pro-settlement activities. Not long after their first meeting with him, the ranchers received information that led them to completely discount the assurances they had been given early in November. William Pearce had passed to ranch circles certain correspondence which had come to his official attention. The illuminating document involved was a letter written by Oliver to Acting Minister of the Interior R.W. Scott urging the Minister to investigate complaints of settlers who, he alleged, were being 'driven off their locations, on the plea of making stockwatering reserves.'[73] In his appended letter Pearce justified his forwarding of this confidential information, which he admitted was 'a little out of departmental usage,'[74] with the explanation that the future of the region's most valuable industry was at stake. He gravely warned: 'If Mr Oliver's wishes regarding these squatters are to be met, the stock interest will in a very short time be annihilated or at least largely so.' Pearce urged stockmen to act together with their influential friends within and outside Parliament to counter such agitation.

Given Pearce's warning, the cattlemen speeded up their incorporation proceedings. The first item on the agenda of this initial meeting of what came to be the Western Stock Growers' Association was preparation of a petition to the new federal government requesting continuation of protective quarantine regulations against American cattle, and maintenance of existing stock-watering and shelter reserves – the latter being the key to limited, or at least controlled, settlement in the southwest.[75] This accomplished, the chairman quickly temporarily put aside consideration of the terms of incorporation and election of officers and adjourned the meeting so that a separate gathering could be held with Oliver. The assembled cattlemen did their utmost collectively to impress upon him that they were unalterably opposed to cancellation of any existing stock-watering reservations and that, in fact, additional reservations were necessary.

While the subsequent election, after the regular meeting had reassembled, filled the executive with the directors or owners of large ranches in the traditional manner, and underlined the fact that local associations sent mainly large ranchers as delegates to the meeting, the most significant long-term result of this gathering was the fact of incorporation itself. This meant that members could be legally bound to the Association's collective will. Moreover, as the general association was dominated by the large ranchers, it gave their position of leadership legal strength and thus helped maintain their function as spokesmen for the entire ranch community.[76]

During this period, while the cattlemen were establishing a new general organization with affiliated locals, the *Macleod Gazette* was left to face the retribution of the community it had alienated. Wood's paper had never fully recovered from the economic consequences of its first altercation with the cattlemen in 1889, and the editor's subsequent attempt to bring the Dunbar dispute to national attention in 1891 made reconciliation impossible. The paper stagnated for want of subscriptions and advertisements, eventually forcing Wood to resign and the paper to be reduced in size a second time. By October 1893 the number of ranchers advertising in the *Gazette* had dropped to ten from an average of ninety in the mid-eighties. The new editors, not identified on the paper's masthead, assiduously avoided antagonizing the ranch community and finally in 1894 announced their total capitulation.

The years ... have proved that Southern Alberta is essentially a Stock Raising Country. Stock raising is its chief industry now, and ... we believe it will always be the foremost of its industries. It will be our aim therefore to make the Gazette a medium for advancing that interest; and if ... we neglect any opportunity of doing all in our power to make their industry even more successful and profitable than it has been; if we fail in fact to make the stockmen's interests identified with our own, we shall feel that we have failed in our duty to the country.[77]

The seal of approval was immediately given by the three most important corporate members of the ranch establishment, the Walrond Ranche Company Ltd, the Cochrane Ranch Company Ltd, and the New Oxley Ranche Company Ltd, who returned their long-absent advertisements to the paper. Thus by the mid-nineties the newly organized strength of the ranch community was accompanied by the decline of articulate opposition within the North-West Territories.

Much more significant than elimination of local press opposition was the additional support of the Department of the Interior which came at this point. As the department officially responsible for western settlement, its policy was singularly important to the ranching interest. Federal legislation as it applied to the stock-raising industry, such as the quarantine laws, the duty on American cattle, and the water reserve system, is not to be explained simply as the work of an extremely powerful ranch lobby. There was a strong inclination within the Department of the Interior to treat the south-west as a region different from the rest of the prairies. This they attempted for over twenty years, arguing in support of the ranchers that settlers were a nuisance, if not a menace, in a region best suited for grazing. Though the Department was on occasion prepared to make limited concessions to settlement in the name of political expediency, before 1900 it did not abandon its conviction that the south-west was 'cattle country.'

In keeping with this tradition, the department's 1896 report to Clifford Sifton, the newly appointed Liberal Minister of the Interior, presented a case for the ranchers that was equal to any statement that the Western Stock Growers' Association might have prepared. The report explained that most ranchers planned to continue operations and had purchased their ten per cent land option, and that it was now the government's duty to see that stock-watering and shelter reservations were not reduced. The report further implied that settlement was not advisable even near water reservations, as 'range cattle will not go near any place where dogs are kept and every settler keeps one or more.'[78] Nor should settlers' fences be allowed to block sheltered valleys, for in regions such as the Porcupine Hills it was alleged that a fence restricting a herd's movement could cause the loss of 250 to 1000 head of cattle during a severe storm. Members of Parliament were warned further that if the Department did not keep reservations, much grazing land too dry for farming would become useless. The question of water reservations was held to be the key to the settlement problem and only through recognition of this problem, the Department maintained, could one understand the much-maligned position of the cattlemen. It was claimed that: 'The larger stockmen [had] never objected to settlement, if the settler [would] only leave free access to all the winter grazing, shelter and water, for his stock, essential to their welfare, in fact, to the very existence of all.'[79] According to the ministry, the clamour against the reserve system could be silenced simply 'through the ejection of a few squatters and a firm attitude on the part of the department.'

The author of this section of the report was none other than William Pearce. Pearce's duties as Superintendent of Mines included recommending necessary regulations and legislation to protect and utilize the lands, forests, mineral resources, and waterways of the territorial west. Also included within this wide jurisdiction was the settlement of squatters' claims. The plenitude of power attached to this office was hardly overstated by the colleague who wrote that: 'William Pearce, with his office in Calgary, was regarded as the ruling power in the West. We regarded him with fear and trembling, and he was undoubtedly a Czar in all western affairs which came under the jurisdiction of the Department of the Interior.'[80] The seventeen-year supervision of this man, who was committed to protection of the region's 'vested interests,' and to what he sincerely believed was in the best interests of proper land use, was a trenchant factor in the assertion of ranch supremacy. Though Pearce was a founding member of the prestigious Ranchmen's Club and seems to have identified socially with the cattlemen, and though his decisions for the most part were favourable to the ranch interests, it seems evident that his action was motivated by his honest conviction that the south-west was too dry for successful farming.

This conclusion was widely held, and was certainly sustained by the technical experts within the Surveys Branch of the Department of the Interior, who urged in their report of 1897 that colonization in the dry region be controlled for the 'ultimate good of the country as a whole.'[81] This dry area was described as extending from the fourth meridian to a location just north of Provost, from which its boundary was drawn south-westerly to a short distance west of Three Hills, thence straight west to the mountains. Such boundaries were more extensive than even the most arrogant member of the cattle compact would have dared to suggest. Accumulated information by this branch of the department led them to insist in their section of the report that: 'as long as the large area at present open for settlement in the humid portions of Manitoba and the Territories remains available for settlement by the incoming immigrant, the government will not be justified in attempting to further, in any marked way, the colonization of arid lands ...' such lands possessed natural advantages for ranching or stock-raising that, according to these officials, had been demonstrated beyond doubt.

These convictions within the Department of the Interior were consistent from 1882 to 1896 and did not at first alter with the new Liberal government. A.M. Burgess and William Pearce retained their positions as Deputy Minister and Superintendent of Mines, respectively, and cattlemen thus continued to have the advantage of powerful friends engaged in the critical task of formulating policy within the government department that most concerned them. Consequently, ranchers had more influence on the policy-making process than most groups in the north-west. In addition, they had access to other efficient and productive channels of communication through which they might intervene. They possessed the multiple advantages to be gained from sitting members within the Commons and Senate, the sympathy of important eastern business-men, and paid parliamentary lobbyists. Special advantage was still to be gained through economic influence in the metropolitan centres. Many of these individuals found little difficulty adapting to Laurier's version of the National Policy. Duncan McEachran, for example, accompanied the Honourable Sydney Fisher, Minister of Agriculture (who just happened to be a neighbour and friend of Senator Cochrane at Compton, Quebec), to Washington for trade discussions and his voice on quarantine laws could be expected to reflect the larger ranchers' concern about American beef imports. The confusion and dismay of mid-1896 after the defeat of the Conservative government was ameliorated by urban associates who lost little time in opening new channels of communication with the government.

In the south-west itself, the compact was in firm economic control and bought local press support. Supplementary to this, a strong centralized organization had emerged from the intermittent fraternal altercations of the preceding decade to give the cattle kingdom an unprecedented degree of organized strength. Such effectual modes of intervention at the local and national levels meant that the ranch establishment was largely in control of its political environment and thus operated as an effective power élite.[82]

The dominant characteristic of this élite, as is apparent from the foregoing, was its intimate metropolitan associations. This relationship developed on two levels, each centred on a metropolis. On the national level, Montreal emerged before 1900 as the financial and political centre of the Canadian cattle kingdom. The cattlemen's second metropolis, Calgary, also occupied a special place in the ranchers' world and as such merits further consideration than heretofore afforded. In an economic and political capacity the city of Calgary played only a minor supporting role during the early years of the ranching frontier. In fact, for the first decades of its existence the traditional role of the metropolitan centre was reversed and the growing town was dominated by the economically and politically powerful ranchers in the hinterland. It was as a social centre that Calgary initially played a more important, and in the long term, a more lasting part.

Calgary was fundamentally a product of the CPR. It might be suggested further that Calgary owed its early existence as a railway centre to the influence of the eastern ranch establishment. It seems likely that the CPR's decision to select a more southerly route across the plains was partly influenced by the presence in the south-west of an industry already established by important members of the Montreal financial community who spoke confidently to their friends during the early 1880s of the further development of the rapidly growing beef export trade. The railway represented the metropolitan umbilical cord upon which the town's ambition to become a distribution centre for the surrounding hinterland was entirely dependent, as was the burgeoning beef-raising industry, upon which the newly arrived merchants cast their eye.

The cattlemen were a relatively affluent group and, as they represented by far the most important economic force in the south-west before the turn of the century, their business was sought aggressively. During the first years Ft Macleod, with its advantage of a central location within the grazing region, was an important rival for this trade but by the 1890s Calgary's transcontinental rail connection had tipped the scales in that city's favour.

Calgary's growth between 1884 and 1894 was intimately related to the rapid expansion of the cattle industry during this decade. The 1892 British embargo that compelled the slaughter of Canadian cattle within ten days of reaching port squeezed profit margins, but did not greatly depress the trade. (See Table 5.) Beef prices had risen continually throughout the period and by 1894 over 150 ranches around Calgary were annually shipping thousands of head of cattle to the British market.[83] Stock of lesser quality was shipped in quantity to the mining communities of British Columbia. Calgary's merchant community, alert to the prosperity of the south-western range, quickly provided the relevant services in the form of hotels, harness shops, livery stables, and assorted general stores. The dependence of the town's business community on cattlemen is suggested in part by church records which reveal that ranchers in the locality outnumbered farmers by a ratio of greater than five to one.[84]

The ranchers were especially important to Calgary's early economic development not only for the market they provided, but equally, if not more so, as one of the limited sources of investment capital available to finance the town's development. The small manufacturing base established by the early 1890s, which included stockyards, slaughtering works, tannery, pork packing plant, cold storage plant, and brewery, was wholly owned by local stockmen. Most of the large sandstone commercial blocks that appeared in the business section of the town after 1889 were financed by cattle intersts.[85] Local lumbermen and ranchers also owned the community's waterworks, electric light, telephone, and street railway companies.[86] Cattlemen therefore performed a critical dual function in Calgary's initial development by providing both the market and investment capital upon which its growth depended.

The political influence of the ranchers in early Calgary was equally remarkable, if less direct than their economic presence. Like certain other major investors whose main sources of revenue lay outside the town, cattlemen did not take an active personal part in civic politics. Not only was the rough-and-tumble life of town politics considered demeaning, it was largely unnecessary. The business élite was generally consulted upon important matters and often, as a precaution, made certain that they had supporters on council.[87] Beyond this, the ranching and investment interests in the hinterland had access to superior levels in the political structure. The Calgary district was represented in Ottawa before 1896 by the rancher D.W. Davis in the Commons, and by J.A. Lougheed in the Senate. The latter held substantial property interests in Calgary and headed the legal firm that looked after most of the larger ranchers' business. At the Territorial Assembly in Regina, Calgary and its environs were represented for most of the period by John Lineham, who complemented his stock-raising enterprise with substantial investments in town properties.[88] In short, local government was subservient to the upper echelons of the ranch and business class, which were of much greater political and economic consequence.

From the beginning Calgary was characterized by a distinctly stratified social and economic order that was dominated by a small group whose ranch and business interests were closely integrated. The stratum below, at the city council level, was also of basically the same mould. During the period discussed, city councils were comprised almost entirely of merchants, over twenty-five per cent of whom owned ranches outside the town.[89] This same class controlled both newspapers and dominated practically all local organizations, whether economic, social, or religious.

The foregoing observations bear witness to the degree to which cattlemen in the hinterland influenced the economic development and the political life of the city. But there is also another aspect to Calgary's intimate relationship with the cattle interests. It was a relationship that issued from city to hinterland in the traditional manner. Through the Western Stock Growers' Association located in the town, Calgary gradually became the administrative headquarters of the cattle industry. Its position was strengthened further by virtue of the fact that Calgary, with its railway connections, stockyards, meat-processing plants, and commission houses also became the financial centre through which most of the cattle country's business was transacted. Calgary bankers long regarded the cattlemen as their most important clients. In this respect Calgary exercised the traditional function of a dominant regional metropolitan centre. Within the broader context of economic and political relations between the town and the cattlemen, however, it is apparent that the interchange was very much a two-way exchange in which both benefited.

The remarkable integration of urban business and ranch interests in local affairs was complemented by the intimate social bonds between these two groups. The cattlemen made Calgary the centre of their social activities and in so doing gave the city a special character that endured long after their political and economic influence waned. Calgary's most exclusive congregation, the Ranchmen's Club, survives as a visible reminder of the cattlemen's social presence in early Calgary. Founded in 1891, the club was modelled on the St James Club of Montreal and was intended to provide the characteristic amenities of the Victorian gentleman's club. The ranchers required a 'respectable' place where they might wine, dine, and enjoy the congenial company of colleagues during a game of whist or poker and where they might lodge when on business in the city. The club's founders were quickly joined by other prominent ranchers, most members of the bench, and the more important representatives of the local professional and business class. The charter membership consequently reads as a 'who's who' in the region's social, economic, and political élite.[90] Provision for temporary or non-resident memebers was also provided to embrace officers of the army or navy as well as persons holding civil appointments under the imperial government and officers of the Canadian Active Militia or NWMP.[91] Though membership qualifications were meant to be vocationally broad, they were rather specific as to the type or class of people qualified. If applicants were members of the armed forces or police they had to be officers; if from the city, a profession or wealth was necessary; and within the ranch community, adequate social standing was essential. The extraterritorial and metropolitan interests of the club's membership are illustrated by the club's newspaper and journal subscriptions.[92] Through the London Times, members could feel the strong pulse of empire, just as the bust of Queen Victoria, prominently placed in the entranceway, vicariously reminded many members of their distant loyalties and of their 'civilizing mission' on the dominion's frontier.

More important than the congenial atmosphere that the club provided for its members, through its dining or game rooms, or through its support of polo, racing, and lawn tennis, was its influence in the subtle blending of the professional and business élites with the ranch establishment. The Ranchmen's Club acted as a vehicle through which intimate social and economic understandings were cultivated.

Beyond the confines of the club existed a much-travelled social circuit between the town and nearby ranches. 'Grande balls,' as they were inevitably called, held alternately in town and at a ranch, were well-attended and typically described as the 'event of the season.'[93] After the turn of the century, Glenbow, fifteen miles to the west in the Bow River valley, dominated the social scene. Glenbow boasted four great sandstone mansions of more than thirty rooms each as well as an excellent race-track and polo field to which the region's affluent thronged for various special events. The most popular form of social gathering among this group centred about sporting occasions, particularly polo and race-meets. Both were of high calibre and the polo teams of the south-west were known internationally. In addition to the formally organized public race-meets, some larger cattlemen held private race tourneys with attendant social convivialities at their ranches. Lady Cochrane, for example, contributed to social harmony at her race gatherings by providing a gayly decorated tent to protect the ladies from the sun while they took their tea or punch.[94] The society described was exclusive but not closed and the outsider with the proper credentials was hospitably welcomed. The sister of one rancher who came directly west from her Paris boarding school adjusted readily to the social setting, much to her brother's relief.[95]

This evident social congeniality was materially strengthened through intermarriage, which enabled ranchers to secure and further their economic and social ties with the judiciary as well as the professional and business community.[96] Thus by 1896, as external pressure on the compact began to increase, they had evolved into an even more closely knit social group. These kinship ties within the ranch community were a paramount factor in the preservation, until World War I, of the community's distinctive character.

The ease with which ranchers coalesced with the town's business establishment was quite predictable given the similar origins of both groups. These entrepreneurs from town and ranch came mainly from the same eastern background, and British ranchers found congenial entry into a society that displayed an especially strong attachment to things British. Many ranchers had never really left the urban business environment. The large stock-raisers, especially the company men, were businessmen in much the same sense as their town counterparts and many managed ranches and city businesses with equal success. On perhaps no other frontier were cattlemen so much a part of the urban environment at both the national and local levels. This helps to account for perpetuation of the cattlemen's influence long after their relative economic importance in the hinterland had declined.

The social and economic unity of the town and country élites led Calgary to interpret its position in the prairie west quite differently from other prairie communities. Calgarians, like the Department of the Interior, viewed the south-west as a region distinct from the prairie proper and were determined to ensure that this hinterland remained their preserve. Confident in the future of their region, Calgarians rejected the concept of a single western community[97] and have remained indifferent to this idea. The capital of the cattle kingdom has never bent to Winnipeg's guidance and early in its career came to see itself as the capital of what it hoped would become a new southern province.[98] Such economic pretensions were implicitly assisted by the social character of the region's élite who, when they looked beyond Calgary, did not identify with the rest of the prairie west. Extraregional ties were with Montreal, London, and the warmer climes of the British Columbia coast.

The mythology of the western 'cow town' which post-war city administrations have promoted for commercial advantage have obscured the true nature of the city-rancher relationship. This 'stampede ethos' has in turn imposed an ill-fitting American stereotype upon the ranch community at large. The city's intimate relationship with the dominant economic group in the hinterland did impart a special quality to the community, but it was of a quite different character. The cattlemen left a legacy of gentility and social exclusiveness that has persisted to the present. The cattlemen and the town business and professional community blended easily to create a stratified and cultivated society in imitation of the social structure they had formerly known in Canada's eastern cities and in Great Britain. The innovative spirit of exuberant democracy traditionally ascribed to frontier communities is noticeable by its absence.

PART II

THE CATTLE COMPACT AND THE PUBLIC DOMAIN
1896-11

4

The Western Stock Growers' Association
and the agrarian frontier 1896–1905

It was in the decade after 1896 that the cattlemen finally had to face the full impact of the farming frontier's westward movement. Heretofore they had lived more in fear of future settlement than with the actual fact. The newcomers after the turn of the century, the dry-land farmers, were convinced of their own destiny to occupy the entire plains region and were inclined to view the rancher and his herd as the symbol of an older order that would have to disperse in the face of 'progress.' The farmers were led into the south-west by a vanguard with a generation of experience on the dry western plains of the United States. There they had already forced cattlemen to fall back and so they were not prepared to accept the scepticism of 'old hands' within the Department of the Interior or the warnings of the Canadian rancher that the south-west grasslands were unfit for grain farming. The new Liberal government was similarly unconvinced and was prepared to assist the farmers' advance. It was some years before it became apparent to many legislators that aridity could not simply be legislated away. In the interval the ranchers faced the full political and economic thrust of commercial agriculture and by the end of the decade the struggle was reduced essentially to an economic contest between cattle and wheat. During the decade both groups contended that the south-west was best adapted to their particular economic interests, and by its end it was the farmers' voice that was most clearly heard. Against the growing farm community and a government dedicated to rapid western settlement stood the cattlemen. The national and local power of the cattle compact ensured that the struggle for control of the semi-arid region would not be resolved quickly.

In the early period cattlemen had relied upon well-placed individuals within their ranks to look after the industry's interests through their intimate connections within the eastern establishment. But following the 1896 Liberal victory, the success of such representation was less certain and ranchers were compelled to rely more heavily on their organized strength. The cattlemen's association had to be made into an effective political lobby. At the same time, the traditional role of range management did not become less important; if anything, the pressures of increasing settlement and market competition intensified the need for efficient and co-operative endeavour.

The central role played by the Western Stock Growers' Association in the cattle country during the two decades subsequent to its formation justifies a closer look at its initial composition and organizational structure. The forces prompting cattlemen to establish a new general association and their attempts to do so have already been discussed; it will suffice to re-emphasize that perhaps the single most important motivating force behind the formation of the WSGA was the government's 1892 decision to cancel the old closed leases after a four-year period of grace. This conclusion is suggested by the fact that all ranchers who submitted the articles of incorporation for ratification by the territorial assembly in the autumn of 1896 were large leaseholders.[1] The articles vested control of the association in a board of management consisting of a president, first and second vice-presidents, and a committee of eleven selected from each stock district into which the cattle country had been divided. The stock districts of Bow River, Sheep Creek, Lethbridge, Medicine Hat, and Maple Creek were each allowed one member, while the foothills districts of High River, Willow Creek, and Pincher Creek were each permitted two members in recognition of the much more heavily concentrated ranch population in that area. (In 1903 the board of management was increased to fifteen, each district except Sheep Creek being allowed two representatives.) Each committee member was required to be a resident of the district represented. Membership was restricted to 'stock-growers,' who were defined as 'any person, association, partnership or corporation owning or controlling horses or cattle and engaged in the business of breeding, growing or raising the same for profit within any of the stock districts [defined in the ordinance].'[2] Persons seeking membership were required to submit their application, along with a $5.00 entrance fee, to the board of managers for consideration. This meant that although the definition of 'stock-grower' was rather inclusive, the ranch establishment represented on the board of management, which was always very conscious of the social and economic distinctions that separated rancher and farmer, could exercise a membership veto to ensure that the organization would not be subverted by the grain-growers and remade into a farm organization. The incorporating ordinance also provided for the association to finance its operations through an assessment of not more than three cents per head per year on all horses and cattle owned by each member. The WSGA was also empowered to pass 'by-laws, rules and regulations ... for all purposes bearing upon or relating to the well-being of the association, including the regulation of round-ups and the suspension, expulsion and retirement of members,' and because this was an incorporated body, members were legally bound by such provisions. In return for the obligations assumed by its members, the association promised 'to protect and advance the interests of the stock-growers in the North-West Territories.'

The articles of incorporation gained assent in the Territorial Assembly on 30 October 1896 and were formally accepted by a large gathering of cattlemen in Calgary on 28 December. At this first meeting D.W. Marsh was elected president and W.F. Cochrane and F.W. Godsal were respectively chosen first and second vice-presidents. These men, along with most of those elected as district representatives, were big ranchers and company men. This ensured that the new association, like those before it, would act first as the guardian of the interests of the large stock-grower and second as a warden for the ranching industry as a whole.[3] In fairness to the large cattlemen it should be understood that this group produced nearly all the beef exported from the region, and that when one speaks of ranching in the south-west at this time the reference is to an industry in which volume beef production was confined to about 200 to 250 ranches. Beyond the obvious strong vested interest of the larger ranchers in the WSGA, it was at first a reasonably representative association that included many medium-sized producers and a number of smaller ranchers who distinguished themselves, at least in the social sense, from those who later became known as 'mixed farmers.' For the big cattle-raisers the incorporation of this new association was significant in that it enabled this dominant group to exercise legally a degree of control over how the industry was conducted locally, and, more important, it allowed the cattle compact to act as official spokesmen for the entire stock-raising industry.

The activities of the WSGA can be divided into two main categories, the first pertaining essentially to range management and the day-to-day operation of the industry, the second relating mainly to federal political affairs. At the first level the association fulfilled a varied and extremely useful function. Matters of a strictly local nature, the most important of which were the spring and fall round-ups, were left to the district associations with the understanding that members of the general association 'would be given every possible advantage over non-members.'[4] For those issues of operational concern to stockmen throughout the south-west, the WSGA assumed active leadership.

One such concern was the depredations of the grey (timber) wolf. In the early 1870s wolves were so numerous in the southwest that hunters from Montana known as 'wolfers' made annual forays into the region to collect pelts. Throughout the 1880s, 1890s, and the first decade of the twentieth century, wolves caused serious stock losses. The territorial government traditionally gave the stock associations a grant to pay bounty on wolves, but funds were always insufficient and ranchers were obliged to supplement the grant to make the bounty attractive. The seriousness of this problem in the mid-nineties is suggested by the declaration of a WSGA policy committee at the organization's first annual meeting in 1897 that 'the destruction of wolves is the most important question now before the Association.'[5] It was decided to raise the bounty to ten dollars per head for grown wolves and two dollars for pups. But despite the hundreds of wolves killed each year by bounty hunters and by ranch parties with their imported hounds, the menace did not seem to abate. In 1900 the bounty was raised to fifteen dollars per head for grown wolves and five dollars for pups and in some areas individual ranchers supplemented association bounties by as much as thirty dollars per head.[6] Faced with this continuing expense, the association tried unsuccessfully to gain the federal government's assistance in the form of a refund of a quarter of the grazing lease rental to supplement their hard-pressed bounty fund. Finally in 1903 the territorial government accepted the WSGA's plea that, while the financial burden was growing excessive, the wolf population did not seem to be declining, and agreed to meet the full cost of the bounty through refunds to the association.[7] From this date, with increasing settlement, the problem gradually diminished. In 1907 the province of Alberta assumed full administrative responsibility for the program and implemented it on a province-wide basis.[8]

Of all the association's activities, one of the most beneficial to the entire stock-raising industry in the south-west was its constant pressure on individuals and government to undertake greater preventive efforts in disease control. Large cattle exporters had always been fully aware that their continued entry to the British market was dependent on their ability to ship high-quality, disease-free animals. Through their association they made yearly requests to the territorial government to compel all breeding stock entering the south-west to be tuberculin-tested.[9] Similar attention was directed towards blackleg control.[10] An extended effort was also made to acquaint the membership and general public with the need to prevent mange (scabies), the most serious stock disease to threaten the Canadian range.[11]

Mange seems to have made its first appearance among range cattle in the southwest in 1898. In order to instruct its own membership the association brought the NWMP Veterinary Inspector Dr Wroughton, and then their fellow rancher and Chief Veterinary Inspector of the Dominion Department of Agriculture, Duncan McEachran, to address their meetings.[12] On 9 June 1899 a special meeting of the board of management, plus Dr McEachran, Police Commissioner Herchmer, and W.F. Cochrane decided to construct a 'dipping' station on the NWMP property at Kipp (near Ft Macleod) which the police would supervise and to which members could bring their cattle. The federal government assisted the association by imposing a quarantine on the portion of Alberta south of the CPR main line; it prohibited removal of cattle from the region without a certificate from a veterinarian showing that the cattle had been treated at a dipping station. This measure enforcing treatment of diseased cattle was well received by the large ranchers, who also requested that action be taken by the Department of Agriculture to restrict the indiscriminate drifting of American cattle across the Canadian boundary.[13] Canadian cattlemen were convinced that the mange outbreak originated with American 'tramp cattle' from Montana, where there existed an alarming prevalence of contagious diseases, especially among steers brought from Texas. The board of management also instructed round-up captains to herd all diseased cattle, regardless of ownership, to the nearest dipping vat.

This concerted action appeared to bring rapid results and in April 1901 the WSGA requested removal of the quarantine. Optimism proved unwarranted, however, and by 1904 compulsory dipping was again necessary. During this year 373,738 cattle were treated once and 228,451 head twice, but this represented only sixty-four per cent of the estimated 583,976 cattle in the quarantine area.[14] Many smaller ranchers, especially in areas where little or no mange was evident, were reluctant to co-operate. Others simply relaxed standards when the problem seemed to abate, with the result that mange remained a recurring curse on the south-western plains until well after World War I.

The constant concern of the WSGA for the health and general quality of western cattle reflects the preoccupation of the vast majority of the association's membership with export markets. This concern often separated members of the association from non-members who produced a few head of cattle each year for local consumption and who were generally opposed to the blanket measures requested by the WSGA, viewing them as expensive and unnecessary. During the 1880s and 1890s the Canadian range had gained an important export advantage from its reputation as a disease-free region. After the turn of the century, with increasing settlement, this reputation became more difficult to defend.

Another problem to which the association directed almost continuous attention was the standard of service offered by the CPR – this much the ranchers had in common with other western settlers. Shipping rates were a long-standing source of contention from 1880 to 1920. The essence of the problem was summed up succinctly by the territorial Department of Agriculture in its annual report for 1898. The department pointed to the growing competition facing Canadian cattle in the British market from the United States, Australia, and the Argentine Republic, and expressed particular concern regarding the latter country, where the quality of breeding stock was being improved and where the government had proposed to subsidize transportation costs. The report explained that as this competition increased the Canadian cattle industry laboured under the growing disadvantage of heavy transportation rates. It was estimated that it cost six dollars less per head to ship cattle from the western United States to Liverpool than from Ontario, and that the difference from western Canada was proportionately greater.[15] The WSGA continually pressed for reductions and was able from time to time to obtain concessions such as the reduced rates on all purebred stock imported into the south-west, which the association negotiated with the railway in 1897.[16]

A second long-standing issue between the cattlemen and the railway concerned compensation for cattle killed by trains. Railway officials, including Superintendent William Whyte, were invited to the association's first annual meeting in 1897 to initiate discussions regarding this problem. Whyte promised that he would personally attend to the matter and that compensation would be paid, but he differed with the association as to the amount. The association wanted a fixed schedule of half value, whereas the railway preferred to deal with each case separately.[17] The definite schedule requested by the stockmen was finally accepted by the railway in 1899, though the values were judged by the cattlemen to be too low and it was not until 1901, after the association executive and several of the most prominent stockmen visited Whyte, that the company agreed to meet ranchers' demands.[18] (See Table 8.) It seems that the threat made by the delegation at the second meeting to put the issue in the hands of two of the most influential western liberals, Frank Oliver and Walter Scott, had a telling effect on the company, whose relations with the Liberal party were already strained.

Noting that the WSGA had negotiated a successful settlement, the Department of Agriculture concluded that since the agreement applied to the whole range country it could be presumed that the provisions applied to all stockmen irrespective of whether they were WSGA members or not. In this regard the settlement remained unclear and in any case it was apparent to most ranchers that they were more likely to achieve satisfaction if their claims were made through the association than as individuals. For this and similar reasons many smaller stockmen quickly realized the advantages of association membership.

There were also many other aspects of the cattlemen's relationship with the railroad upon which the association kept watch. Prairie fires set by sparks from passing trains were an especially serious problem with which earlier stockmen's organizations had contended in the eighties and nineties. After 1896 the WSGA was charged with the responsibility of making certain that the railway's plowed fire guards were properly maintained.[19] As late as 1904 extensive range fires ignited by railway locomotives were still a serious problem.[20] The WSGA also paid close attention to the condition of CPR stock-loading yards, urging from

TABLE 8

Railway cattle compensation schedule 1901

Calves	$12.50
Yearlings: steers and heifers	17.50
2-year-old heifers	25.00
2-year-old steers	25.00
Cows	25.00
3-year-old steers	32.50
4-year-old steers	40.00
Bulls	40.00

SOURCE: North-West Territories, Department of Agriculture, *Annual Report* (1901) 68

time to time that new yards be constructed, old ones expanded, and others like the 'dangerous mudhole' at Moose Jaw be cleaned up.[21] The slow rate of travel and the often poor condition of stock cars, both detrimental to cattle, were other areas where the WSGA sought improvement.

One of the most important functions of a cattlemen's organization, at least as originally conceived in the days of the open range, was to protect the rancher from cattle theft. Rewards of up to $1000 were offered for information leading to conviction of thieves who had stolen cattle from any member rancher, and the association was prepared to undertake prosecution on a member's behalf. Association files list numerous legal proceedings in which the WSGA was involved.[22] As settlement increased after the turn of the century, stock-stealing cases became more numerous, leading the association in 1903 to hire P.J. Nolan, Calgary's most prominent criminal lawyer, to conduct all such cases initiated by the association.[23] Nolan was in turn succeeded as the cattlemen's solicitor by R.B. Bennett; the association thus enjoyed the best legal talent available in the North-West Territories during this period. The ranchers were rewarded in 1904 with a great number of successful prosecutions. In Calgary there were nine convictions with terms ranging from six months to seven years[24] and in Ft Macleod twenty cattle thieves received sentences ranging from one to ten years. The Superintendent of Police at Ft Macleod, P.C.H. Primrose, expressed satisfaction that such sentences 'surely ought to act as a deterrent to crime in this district.'[25] The success of the association in this regard presented another reason for the medium or smaller operator, who did not generally have access to such impressive legal counsel, to retain or acquire membership.

Despite its success in court, the main emphasis of the association's protective endeavours was directed towards preventive measures rather than prosecution after the fact. Of the WSGA's many contributions to the development of the Canadian cattle industry – perhaps the most important – was its long campaign to persuade the territorial and federal governments to implement a proper system of stock inspection.

Any practical system of stock inspection is first dependent upon some system of marking by which the ownership of each animal can be determined. Range cattlemen had long agreed that the age-old practice of burning a mark on the animal's hide was the simplest method and had the great advantage of being highly visible. Given the rangemen's universal agreement as to the superiority of the brand system, it remained for someone to act as recorder and distributor of suitable markings. This function was first assumed in the 1870s by the police at Ft Macleod and subsequently by the cattlemen's associations. With the rapid increase in the number of stock-growers during the 1890s this became, apart from the growing administrative expense, an increasingly complicated and time-consuming task requiring the full-time attention of the association's secretary. At the same time the brand system could not function efficiently until it was binding upon stockmen over the entire region rather than only those belonging to or consenting to the association's administration.

In 1898 the WSGA solved both problems by persuading the territorial government to assume responsibility for brand registry and to pass an ordinance requiring all users of brands to register their marks with the territorial Department of Agriculture.[26] In consultation with the executive committee of the WSGA, department officials revised and updated the approximately 4000 brands registered at Ft Macleod and transferred the files to Regina.[27] While anxious to relinquish their administrative control, cattlemen were insistent that their secretary remain an official brand recorder.[28] From their point of view it was critically important that brands be distributed by a trusted individual with intimate knowledge of the cattle industry in order to prevent, among other things, the old practice of unscrupulous ranchers registering brands very similar to ones owned by their larger neighbours, so that with the deft stroke of a 'running iron' their own herds might be artificially increased at a neighbour's expense.[29]

Even after the association relinquished control, it was largely through the interest and initiative of this organization that functional brand laws were enacted and brand books up-dated, printed, and distributed. In 1899, for example, when the Territorial Assembly decided to revise the brand ordinance, it did so on the basis of an agreement negotiated with the WSGA.[30] In only one aspect of brand legislation did it have difficulty securing the legislation required by their industry. Despite repeated requests by the association and the full support of the NWMP Commissioner, the cattlemen were unable until 1900 to persuade the territorial government to amend the brand ordinance so that the presence of a recorded brand could be accepted as *prima facie* evidence of ownership.[31]

Beyond bringing order to the brand system, which was the prerequisite for any viable means of stock inspection, the WSGA campaigned to have the government establish the necessary supporting structure to ensure that the basic problems of disease control and stock theft could be dealt with more effectively. When the association initiated its campaign in 1896, the limited legislation that did exist in this area was much too rudimentary to accommodate the vastly expanded export industry that the large cattlemen had developed. The main point of concern was the absence of regulations regarding the loading and shipping of stock. Cattle were generally accepted at railway stockyards from whatever source on good faith and without a bill of sale or other proof of ownership. The laxity of the system greatly eased disposal of stolen stock and was therefore an open encouragement to cattle rustling. A similar problem existed with regard to the large shipments of the big ranches. Some ranchers made little effort to sort out cattle belonging to others that had become mixed with their own large herds. The NWMP were aware of the problems and the Commissioner recommended in his 1896 report that 'the interests of the ranchers require the appointment of stock inspectors who should be detailed to inspect all cattle when being loaded, and see that only those properly sold are shipped, and no cattle should be loaded after dark.'[32] In response to repeated requests from the police and stockmen, the North-West Council eventually did appoint 'hide inspectors' whose duties were to inspect and mark all hides before beef could be sold. The WSGA was not impressed by the qualifications of some initial appointees and quickly persuaded the government to make certain cancellations in favour of those acceptable to the WSGA.[33] Inspectors of the cattlemen's choice were paid an additional sum and required to submit monthly reports to the board of management.

The system of stock inspection that gradually evolved was one of joint administration by the government of the North-West Territories and the WSGA, with the initiative for formulation of required legislation being left to the association. This authority demonstrates its dominant role in determining the manner in which the entire stock industry was administered. Perhaps the most important legislation in this regard initiated by the stockmen was that making it compulsory for 'all stock to be inspected by a Hide Inspector before they [could be] shipped or driven out of the country.'[34] When this provision became law in July 1899, the railway immediately notified its agents not to issue contracts for shipping livestock without production of the statutory stock inspection certificate, thereby rendering it much more difficult to ship stolen or stray cattle out of the country.[35] Despite such legislation, irregularities were still frequent enough to lead the association in 1901 to engage a well-paid travelling stock detective to guard the interests of members at the Calgary and Winnipeg stockyards or wherever special problems arose.[36]

The WSGA's inspection system was financed through a government grant supplemented by a levy on each member of a few cents per head for every animal shipped. The charge after 1902 was five cents for every animal shipped to another point within the North-West Territories and twenty-five cents for cattle shipped outside.[37] From 1903 the association was empowered to collect twenty-five cents on *all* cattle shipped from the southwest with the proceeds placed in a fund jointly controlled by the territorial government and the WSGA.[38] In this manner the association gradually acquired pre-eminent administrative control of cattle exports and, though the association was responsible for inspection of all stock, it was apparent that the interests of members would receive closest attention. Consequently, for any rancher who proposed to export cattle, even in small numbers, the advantage to be gained through membership was obvious. None the less, while the WSGA's primary and quite natural concern for its own membership cannot be denied, the association must be given full credit for bringing a degree of administrative order to the western cattle export trade that had hitherto been lacking.

There was really only one area where the cattlemen and their association were unable to secure desired legislation. The maverick issue, which had traditionally plagued earlier stockmen's organizations, was taken up at the first annual meeting of the WSGA, where it was resolved to petition the North-West Territories government to vest ownership of all mavericks in the association so as to give range custom the full legal authority so far denied.[39] The traditional objection of the small stockmen is epitomized in the urgent conter-appeal of one such individual outside the association who warned of the 'endless trouble and gross injustice' of such a measure, with the explanation that:

Settlers with small bunches of cattle and rangers who look after their cattle closely, do not belong to this Association and consequently, any calf missed by them or temporarily separated from its cow, accidentally or otherwise, will be scooped up by this Association, many members of which are noted for a keen eye for mavericks. In the spring and fall round-ups they drive their herd of range cattle thro' a bunch of gentle stock, picking up everything as they go along and if one does not look out sharply his calves are likely to become mavericks, and if he does not belong to this Association and this proposal becomes law, are hopelessly lost to him.[40]

Though repeated requests for legal authority to do so were refused, the WSGA continued, as had been the custom for nearly twenty years, to sell mavericks by auction with the proceeds going to the organization's general revenue, and to direct stockmen's activities on the range as it saw fit. As one regional police officer observed, 'there is no greater autocrat on the continent than the captain of a round-up,' and round-up parties under his command did not usually go to much trouble to establish ownership of non-members' cattle.[41] Opposition to the practice grew as settlement increased and eventually in 1903 a round-up captain of the Medicine Hat Stock Growers' Association was brought to trial on a charge of theft.[42] On this occasion the cattlemen could not ignore the judge's verdict of guilty, as they had done in 1895 when a similar decision was handed down by the presiding magistrate. Moreover, by this time the problem was well on the way to solving itself as each year the open range was further restricted and the general round-up gradually became a thing of the past. In this sense the 1903 decision symbolizes the end of an era.

While activities relating to the administration and supervision of the stock-growing industry occupied much of the association's energies, pressing political matters at the federal level also required close attention. Many cattlemen feared the worst from the new Liberal government, particularly from Frank Oliver, and all waited anxiously for government policy statements regarding stock-watering reserves, leases, and western settlement.

Even more immediately concerned than the cattlemen were two key officials within the Department of the Interior, who in the minds of many had long been associated with the ranchers' hegemony in the south-west. The major force directing the agitation for the removal of Deputy Minister A.M. Burgess and Superintendent of Mines William Pearce was of course the editor of the *Edmonton Bulletin*, Frank Oliver. He had vigorously opposed federal land policy in the south-west since the early 1880s but with a singular lack of success, and in his frustration his campaign gradually acquired all the unhappy qualities of a bitter personal feud. With the Liberals in power at last, Oliver was determined to rid the department of the two officials he considered the main obstacles to open settlement and western development. In a scathing editorial shortly after the election, Oliver reported the rumour that Burgess was soon to be suspended, and announced that such an event would be greeted with enthusiasm through-out the west. Burgess's main fault, he alleged, was that: 'he saw the Northwest through the narrow spectacles of one who considered himself essentially an official, a servant and a bailiff of the government – and of those friends of the government, the land sharks and speculators and monopolists of every grade from the CPR down.' He charged further that to Burgess 'the settler was an unpleasant incident whom unavoidable circumstances required should be toler-ated, [and] who required to be constantly watched, as a menace to the interests of the government and its friends.'[43] Appeals for Burgess's removal also came from within the cattle country itself, where certain smaller stockmen thought that he was responsible for holding the district 'under the control of a few foreign cattle companies, and [for] harassing settlers.'[44] The agitation was not without result, for early in 1897 Burgess was demoted to the position of Commissioner of Dominion Lands and J.S. Smart, a close political friend of the new Minister and fellow citizen of Brandon, assumed the deputy ministership.[45]

The second official facing Oliver's censure, William Pearce, proved more difficult to dispatch. In anticipation of Oliver's campaign to restaff the upper echelons of the Department of the Interior, Pearce immediately after the election began a carefully conducted defence of his well-known policy against settlement in the semi-arid region. His prompt request to meet with his new Minister, Clifford Sifton, in order to discuss land policy included the earnest and rather unpolitic admonition that conditions in the dry south-west were 'not at all similar to the conditions existing in the Province of Manitoba [Sifton's home province] and the remaining parts of the Territories.'[46] This was the beginning of a series of letters, reports, and pamphlets sent by Pearce to Sifton regarding what he deemed to be the special characteristics of the grazing region. At the same time Oliver was pressing Sifton for Pearce's removal. The new Liberal MP urged that the Land Department be completely reorganized, starting at the top.

The officer with whom we are most concerned in this part of the country is Mr Pearce, nominally superintendent of mines, actually agent general, secret service man and go between for the Government and its friends who are opposed to the settlers of the country. I may say that as long as Mr Pearce retains his present position the settlers of this country will have no confidence in even the good intentions of the Department.[47]

Pearce's position remained tenuous throughout 1897. In February he was informed by a friend of Sifton's comment that though he considered the Superintendent 'a valuable government servant' he had been 'so deluged with complaints' that he feared a change would have to be made.[48] It seems that the new administration at first hoped that by ignoring Pearce they might persuade him to resign. Pearce was left alone in his Calgary office without secretarial staff and in November was compelled to hire on his own account a stenographer and typewriter in order to complete his annual report.

Pearce was not to be forced out so easily and continued to defend himself vigorously. He explained at length to Sifton that as the federal official responsible for the disagreeable task of adjudicating conflicting land claims he had naturally made enemies of many who believed that they had been unjustly treated, and that perhaps his refusal of Oliver's land claim in Edmonton in 1884 was a factor in the latter's animosity. He argued further that his 'sympathy for the struggling settler or any legitimate enterprise' was second to none, though he did admit that when it came 'to those who attempted to obtain what should not be granted, or in other words, a straight steal, my indignation gets the better of me and I frequently express myself more forcibly than diplomatic.'[49] Pearce also expressed confidence that if the evidence was reviewed regarding each charge against him, he would not be found to have acted in a partisan or unjust manner and he requested that an official inquiry be made. He insisted that he had been a loyal and honest servant of the government since 1872 and that, to ensure public trust, he had never cast a vote for any federal, territorial, or municipal candidate or attended a political meeting since the date of his entry into public service. Such direct appeals and strong support within the department eventually persuaded Sifton to retain Pearce's services despite Oliver's persistent opposition.[50] Moreover, Oliver had been somewhat overzealous in his attack upon Pearce and at one point had proceeded to press legal charges on behalf of an allegedly wronged settler, only to find in the end that the plaintiff had falsified his circumstances. Annoyed by this fiasco as well as by Oliver's persistent interference in matters of party patronage in the west, Sifton requested Oliver to submit an apology.[51] Though none was forthcoming, the Alberta MP was compelled to wait for a more auspicious moment to renew his attack. Pearce himself never regained the power he had formerly enjoyed, and was no longer the most important official voice in the formulation of western land policy.

In retrospect there seems little doubt that Pearce's sincerity and knowledge of the south-west more than compensated for his lack of tact and diplomacy. What appeared to the pro-settlement group to be partisanship was in reality an unwavering conviction that full and open settlement could not be morally or economically justified in all parts of the prairies, and the drought-driven refugees of later years are witness to the validity of his assessment. Unfortunately, officials, politicians, newly arrived homesteaders, and would-be settlers living outside the southwest never believed or accepted the cautions of western officials and long-term residents.

Aware of the uncertainty of his position and conscious that compromise might ease his situation, Pearce none the less chose to defend to the letter the water reserve system which Oliver and others repeatedly cited as evidence of his and the previous government's determination to exclude settlement in the south. In the spring of 1897 Oliver forwarded to Sifton a letter from one of his southern constituents urging the government to ignore the recent motion of the WSGA calling for an expansion of existing reserves.[52] The writer maintained that the Association was naturally anxious to preserve the system 'that has served so well in the purpose of preventing settlement in Southern Alberta,' but the 'much cherished "range business" ' could survive well enough without such assistance. He observed that members of the association by virtue of their early arrival had all availed themselves of the privilege of selecting the best-watered locations for ranches and the association's request seemed to suggest that the established ranchers wanted to prevent the small settler doing what they had done themselves. If the WSGA was successful in inducing the government to continue the policy he warned that 'there will continue to be a lack of settlement and development in southern Alberta.'[53] Oliver's correspondent specifically singled out Pearce as the main obstacle to open settlement and suggested that the Superintendent, who had allegedly denied his claim for a nearby water reserve and suggested a windpump instead, 'be granted a long leave of absence with a recommendation to go to Holland where he could study the windmill system to his heart's content.'

The cure recommended for the 'water reserve evil' was that no reserves should be made in a township without the consent of at least two-thirds of the resident landholders. This, it was maintained, would prevent any association or company from withholding such lands from settlement on the pretext that they were required for public use. The foregoing complaints summed up the sentiments of many small stockmen and farmers newly arrived in the south-west and gained almost universal sympathy outside the region. Consequently, when Oliver expressed his hope in the summer of 1897 that the policy formerly in vogue, which he explained was 'to wait until a settler takes up a spring and then fire him off and reserve it,' be discontinued, and that all existing reserves be inspected, he received a close if not entirely sympathetic hearing.[54]

Pearce in turn spent the summer of 1897 and 1898 attempting to convince Sifton of the necessity of retaining the water reserve system. In June Pearce urged that additional lands recommended for reservation be approved by order-in-council before squatting became a serious problem.[55] His concern had been aroused when he learned that a settler had squatted on a key location on the old Walrond lease, which had been reserved pending approval of the department, and that officials in Ottawa under pressure from Oliver were about to allow the entry to stand on the grounds that the reservation had not yet received official approval.[56] Despite Pearce's charge that the squatter had knowingly located on an intended reserve that controlled an entire creek valley in which several thousand cattle normally grazed, and the testimony of the WSGA that not only was this 'one of the most important springs on the whole range' but that the individual concerned was currently before the Crown on a charge of cattle theft, the request for cancellation was denied.[57] Though the new Minister, for obvious political reasons, was prepared to let the outcome of this case be determined according to the wishes of his fellow Liberal, who had chosen to make the matter one of personal concern, he did come to accept the general principle of the water reserve system as presented and defended by Pearce. On 21 September 1897 a large number of new reserves were set aside by order-in-council[58] and in

November Sifton met with a delegation of the WSGA in Calgary to assure the ranchers that it was not the government's policy to open the reserves for settlement.[59]

Even with Sifton's verbal commitment to retain the reserve system, Pearce and the cattlemen were called upon repeatedly to defend their creation. In the spring of 1898, for example, A.M. Nanton, managing director of the Alberta Railway and Coal Company, who had just returned from a meeting with the London bondholders of the Calgary and Edmonton Railway Company, complained to Sifton that his company was not being 'fairly treated in the matter of stock water and irrigation reserves.'[60] He explained that the company 'would never have thought of taking thousands of acres of the dry lands had it not understood that it would also receive with it the water fronts.' Nanton's request that the reserves be cancelled underlines both the ranchers' hold on the country and the degree to which water was the key to their control. This, and the growing number of individual requests that certain reserves be withdrawn, were skilfully countered by the tireless efforts of Pearce and the WSGA, who continued for several more years to hold the Minister and his department to their point of view. Pearce insisted that uncertainty regarding government policy was the cause of many individual requests for reserve cancellation, as those who became alarmed that the system or a particular reserve in their vicinity was likely to be done away with applied for entry to protect their interests. In the autumn of 1898 Pearce forwarded to Ottawa a current list of applications for certain reserves with detailed reasons why each should be refused.[61]

In this manner the system was defended and maintained until after 1900. In the interval, however, pressure mounted apace with increasing immigration, and though the scheme had much merit in a dry region known to be afflicted with even dryer cycles, the water reserve program became an ever-increasing political liability almost impossible to defend outside the region among a public uninterested in the annual precipitation statistics that had been accumulated for almost two decades. The federal department's south-western policy was particularly undermined by the pronouncements of certain territorial officials. The Commissioner of Agriculture, G.H.V. Bulyea, in his 1898 *Annual Report* charged that the government's policy of discouraging settlement in the arid portion of the prairies while vacant lands remained elsewhere displayed 'but a very narrow view of the situation.' He went on to cite how successfully settlement had been undertaken in the arid American west.[62]

Coupled with this hostile view outside was a growing inclination on the part of many newer Department of the Interior officials in Ottawa to view the south-west as an integral part of the western prairie to be administered in the same manner as the other districts, in contrast to their predecessors, who had tended to accept the premise that the grazing country should be considered a special region. The 'special region' philosophy and its concomitant water reserve system was identified mainly with William Pearce, and it was upon him that opposition to the policy had naturally focused since 1886. Despite the logic of his analysis, his position was undermined by the often tactless and arbitrary manner in which he dealt with settlers and others who differed with his view of the south-west. Moreover, department officials and elected representatives had learned through experience over the years that Pearce was completely uncompromising in his attitude. Consequently when the government decided that its south-western policy would have to be reassessed, it thought first of the Superintendent of Mines. In deference to Pearce's long-standing and generally competent service, the Department of the Interior first attempted to get him out of the way by redefining the function of his office, namely by relating the duties more closely to those inferred from its title. Sifton proposed to move the office of the Superintendent of Mines to Ottawa, where Pearce could superintend the growing mining activity in the Canadian Shield. Pearce's refusal to leave Calgary and his subsequent demotion to Inspector of Surveys in 1901 marks the end of an era in southwestern land policy.[63]

The Department's shift in attitude is clearly illustrated in Deputy Minister James Smart's response to a letter from a recently arrived American settler a few months after Pearce's departure. This would-be homesteader had complained that he had been motivated to come to the territory through pamphlets disributed by the department, only to find that 'the Stockmen had all the creeks and springs reserved,' making it impossible to find a place to settle.[64] He further alleged that the land office in Calgary was known by settlers to be in league with the cattlemen, that many Americans had already returned to the States, and that he had written to intending immigrants in his home state of Nebraska to remain there until the water reserves were cancelled. In a subsequent internal memorandum Smart agreed that there was substance to the charges, and personally informed the complainant that it had been decided 'to send an officer of the Department this summer to make a thorough investigation of the various reserves with a view to re-adjusting them in the interests of the settlers.'[65]

Aware of the mounting pressure to cancel the reserves, cattlemen viewed the investigation with much apprehension. While the study was under way, the WSGA reminded the government that stockmen considered the reserves of critical importance and urged that the current influx of squatters be removed.[66] The association argued that the outcry against the reservations was mainly from new arrivals who wanted these desirable locations for homesteads, and that many had squatted in anticipation of government withdrawal and with the expectation that they would gain the land as a free homestead. While the association insisted that cancellation was ill advised, it requested that if the government was determined to proceed the lands be disposed of by public auction, as was the practice with school lands, rather than allowing them to be simply open to free entry. Stockmen held that it was only just that those who had previously come to settle in the vicinity should have a chance to obtain lands that were preferred but heretofore denied.

The Department's investigation was completed in the summer of 1901 and the conclusions outlined in a confidential memorandum to the Minister. The memorandum stated that much of the land withdrawn was no longer required for water reserves and should therefore be sold. In cases where settlers had established squatters' residence before the land was reserved by order-in-council, free homestead entry was recommended. In all other cases it was suggested that withdrawn lands be opened to public competition at an upset price of $5.00 per acre. In order to prevent domination of a valley by a single individual, the report also recommended that no one be allowed to purchase more than one quarter section, and where land was divided by a river or stream that ownership of both sides be refused.[67]

The new policy also reflected the growing political strength of Frank Oliver, whose mandate had been renewed by Albertans in the federal election of the previous year. His opinion regarding the sale of the water reserves was accordingly solicited. Having campaigned for cancellation for over a decade, Oliver was pleased with the proposed sales, but objected to the $5.00 upset price as being too high. Oliver feared that it would discriminate in favour of the wealthy stockmen and in effect maintain the system. He recommended an upset price of $3.00 per acre and stressed that special care should be taken to see that the land sales were carefully advertised so as to forestall 'collusion between interested parties to prevent the public generally from getting notice of the facts.'[68] After further thought he became convinced that the proposed auction method would have to be abandoned altogether if the settlers' welfare was to be protected from the region's vested interests and thus he persuaded the Department to undertake sales by sealed tender.

The gradual sale of reserves in this manner throughout the spring of 1902 and during 1903 caused general dissatisfaction in the ranching country among both settlers and stockmen, who found that this approach provided no means of determining how high to bid for a much-desired adjoining property. In 1904 the Department finally yielded to the warning of the WSGA that the entire ranching industry faced extinction unless certain concessions were immediately forthcoming, and agreed to the ranchers' second request that reserves be sold by public auction.[69] In June the first big disposal of Crown water reserves commenced at special auctions throughout the grazing country. At Ft Macleod, High

River, and Calgary, for example, 234 parcels were sold.[70] This modification eased the concern which had grown following Pearce's demotion. If ranchers were forced to accept reduction of their prized water reserves, public auction at least permitted them to use their economic superiority to advantage. However, the amendment proved to be a short-lived victory, for the following year Clifford Sifton resigned from the Laurier cabinet and the appointment of Frank Oliver as his successor caused general despair among cattlemen.

Closely related to their preoccupation with the water reserve issue during this period was the matter of grazing leases. At first, before 1900, concern regarding the latter was definitely secondary, as the cattlemen placed their confidence in the water reserve system which they had negotiated with the government in 1892. Lease acreage rapidly declined after 1896 as ranchers purchased what choice lands they could and assumed de facto control of adjoining properties through the reserve system. As pressure to eliminate the reserves mounted after 1900, cattlemen were compelled to shift their attention again to the tenuous security provided by leases. The renewed interest in this direction marks the decline of the cattlemen's reliance upon collective action in favour of a more individualistic approach to security such as that provided by a lease.

In the interval before 1900, however, the practice of taking leases fell into general disuse. When the old 'closed' leases were cancelled in 1896 many ranchers declined to renew their leases in the new form. Given the one-tenth purchase allowance and reserved springs and stream fronts, there seemed little reason to be burdened with a yearly rental for lands where the water was already controlled. The former leaseholders simply elected to follow the practice of free grazing, as many smaller stockmen had always done. It was not long before the government realized the extent to which cattlemen were grazing their herds freely on public lands. Consequently, between 1896 and 1900 the department of the Interior sought to devise a new system that would ensure that the government was properly remunerated. The responsibility for finding a new formula at first devolved upon William Pearce, who had actually begun to assess the problem during the summer of 1895. The solution proposed was that a per capita charge be levied on all stock grazing outside of land leased or owned by the rancher. Pearce admitted that such a regulation would 'raise an awful howl' but argued that there was no policy more equitable.[71] He warned also that certain portions of the country were in danger of being 'eaten out' unless immediate action was taken and thus recommended that the per capita charge be coupled with the provision that a licence be required to graze stock so that the number of ranchers grazing cattle in an area could be controlled. Canadian officials were aware that though the American government made no assessment for grazing on federal lands, most states in the ranching country did impose a tax based on a percentage of the average value of cattle, horses, and sheep. Pearce's subsequent detailed investigations of these systems, however, did not produce satisfactory answers to the obvious administrative difficulties inherent in such a policy and the whole problem remained unsolved.[72]

At the same time Ottawa was reluctant to return to the former emphasis on the lease system. Not only was a lease structure that did not provide for uninterrupted tenure for at least ten years of little interest to cattlemen, such a policy had been consistently opposed by the advocates of open settlement on the grounds that it gave control of the region to the big operators. Faced with this dilemma the government was unable to decide upon any policy until well after the turn of the century. The absence of regulations further exacerbated the tension between rancher and settler and for the first time portions of the ranching country became overgrazed. The resultant situation soon confirmed Pearce's initial prophetic warning: 'It is only when there are no regulations governing the matter that the argument is: "If I do not take advantage of this somebody else will".'[73]

In the ensuing struggle for control of the foothill region, each side used all tactics short of open violence and each made repeated appeals to the government to protect their interests against the other. Shortly after the 1896 election, settlers in the High River and Sheep Creek districts pressed the new Liberal government to act on its pro-settlement platform. In a petition to Frank Oliver, sixty-six settlers joined farmer Robert Findlay to protest that the cattlemen were driving them from their lands. The memorial stated that each spring the cattle companies and large individual owners living south of High River drove their herds, estimated to be in excess of 12,000 head, northwards from their accustomed winter range and across the High River where they were held from returning by line riders stationed along the river. The petitioners alleged that while there was sufficient grazing land south of the river the northern region was so overgrazed that starvation threatened their stock, and that this was all part of a deliberate plan to 'discourage new settlers from coming in and [was] calculated to drive present settlers out.'[74] The settlers explained that they were actively engaged in improving the country through cultivation of land and construction of irrigation ditches but were continually harassed by large bands of range cattle that destroyed their fences and caused their tame cattle to run off. The farmers' cattle were sometimes unbranded and thus were often lost for good, as such animals were sold by the stock association after the general round-up with the proceeds going to the association. The supplicants concluded with the hope that the stock association, which had been 'a ruling power in this country in the past' would be a lesser force in the future and requested that government act to force cattlemen to keep their range cattle south of High River lest settlers be forced to move away from the region.

Uncertain as to how this complex problem might be solved, the government allowed the matter to drift. In November a settler complained to Oliver that settlers had received no word from the government, that the stockmen mocked them with the query, 'what has become of the "Findlay Bill",' and that those who had signed the petition were being abused.[75] He charged that the cattlemen and their association were doing 'all in their power to prevent settlement' and reminded Oliver of where his political support resided: 'at the last election you will remember how much these very men helped us – F. Stimson [Manager of the North West Cattle Company] in particular ... said he would fire every man he had that did not vote right.' Oliver responded by bringing the matter before the Department of the Interior with the personal endorsement that he 'fully believed that the complaint of the settlers is well founded and that the ranchmen do herd their cattle in the vicinity of the settlers' farms for the express purpose of injuring those settlers by eating out the grass.' Though he announced that the problem required the quickest possible adjustment he was unable to suggest a solution, and in September 1898 the Department informed Oliver that the only action the government could take, until the entire question of ranching in the south-west could be fully investigated, was to advise settlers to lease lands near their homesteads and thus secure the right to charge trespassers.[76]

While ranchers and settlers waited for the government to establish some means of regulating use of the range country the situation continued to deteriorate. Early in 1899 Sifton was informed by a close political friend, James H. Ross, Commissioner of Public Works for the North-West Territories, that:

in the Pincher Creek district, which was at one time looked upon as one of the best grazing areas in the Territories, the range has become so eaten out owing to want of any regulations regarding the grazing of cattle at large, that some of the Ranchers there have had to move their cattle away to other and less crowded portions of Alberta. This same condition is being rapidly approached in other districts, notably in the vicinity of High River and some parts of the Maple Creek district, and the public domain in certain districts is being practically rendered worthless owing to lack of regulations to restrain those who are grazing their cattle thereon free of any charge.[77]

Ross warned also that large stockmen in Montana were making preparations to put large herds of cattle on the Canadian side of the boundary where they could run their cattle without payment of any tax. Like others long resident on the dry southern plains he was convinced that much of the area could never be farmed and was thus sympathetic to the cattle interests. His personal influence with the Minister was enough to balance that of Oliver and other advocates of unrestricted settlement, but the balance of logic and political expediency was so evenly divided that the government continued to do nothing. Ross's suggestions that all ranchers intending to graze stock on public lands be required to obtain grazing permits from the Minister and that the government drill deep wells to increase the grazing area on the open plains were not acted upon.

The slight incentive for cattlemen to take leases was further undermined in 1899 by an act of the territorial legislature which made lands leased from the federal government assessable and liable to taxation by municipalities for local improvements. Leaseholders quickly protested to Ottawa. As one rancher grumbled, the present rental was as much as a limited five-year lease was worth and given the additional cost of fencing an added municipal assessment would make the cost of grass more than the possible return.[78] The Department immediately sought an opinion from the Deputy Minister of Justice on the constitutionality of the territorial government's action, noting that such a measure would 'certainly have the effect of lessening the number of leases of Dominion Lands for grazing purposes.'[79] The reply that the territorial government did have such jurisdiction seemed to complicate further what was already a confused situation. The state of flux continued for the next five years. As settlement pressure threatened the water reserve system the cattlemen expressed renewed interest in leases. At the same time the Department began to have doubts that any kind of a lease system was politically tenable in view of the rapid increase in settlement.

Petitions in 1901 from the WSGA and from ranchers of south-eastern Alberta and Assiniboia for greater security of tenure were ignored.[80] Finally in the late spring of 1901 Deputy Minister of the Interior J.S. Smart departed for the grazing country with a special assistant in order to assess matters at first hand. Smart and his assistant were particularly impressed by the initial success of many small stockmen and squatters. 'The gardens seen at the homes of the squatters in the valley of the Milk River,' they reported, 'could not be surpassed anywhere. Corn, tomatoes and melons were noticed amongst the other things grown, which we were informed, grew to perfection. Any grain we saw was of excellent quality and was ready for harvesting.' The memorandum prepared for the Minister on their return was consequently inclined towards the settlers and small stockmen. They admitted that while there were extensive tracts of country in the dry belt that could be utilized only for pasture, they could report from their personal observation that much of the 'so-termed grazing land is admirably adapted for the growing of grain and root crops when it is brought under irrigation.'[81] Until such time as the boundaries of these two classes of land could be accurately defined, the memorandum recommended that permanent regulations should not be considered. Smart also suggested that the lease system be discontinued or at least curtailed on the grounds that it allowed a few large operators to control the region's limited water supply, and more important, would subject the government to endless difficulties as growing numbers of settlers squatted on the leaseholds. As a temporary solution the Deputy Minister urged that all grazing lands be open to the public on the payment of a fee of so much a head.

The report did not end the government's indecision. Others within the Department, particularly J.G. Turriff, the Commissioner of Dominion Lands, who happened to be from the dry country of Assiniboia, did not concur with Smart's evaluation of the situation in the south-west or with the proposed recommendations.[82] Confusion and uncertainty, which by this date had become almost a fact of life in the cattle country, continued for the next two years. The opinion current in some government circles seems to have been that if left alone the matter would be solved in a short time through rapidly increasing settlement; by not taking a stand the government would offend no one.

Yet along with this expedient attitude was another factor of political gamesmanship that pulled in the other direction. As the demand for leases continued, it was inevitable that certain applicants were counted as influential friends of the government. By the end of 1902 the phenomenon of the large grazing lease had reappeared in the Canadian west, though the concentration was now on the plains of southern Alberta and western Assiniboia rather than in the foothills country of the Rockies. The new leaseholders differed from the lessee establishment of the previous decade in that, with few exceptions, they were westerners from the United States and Canada. The latter were often Manitobans, particularly from Brandon, which was in Sifton's constituency. The Minister's Brandon friend, James D. McGregor, and the well-known Assiniboia Liberal, James H. Ross, for example, obtained a lease of 46,114 acres, and a group headed by the prominent New Mexican rancher, H.W. Cresswell, acquired leases totalling 196,960 acres.[83] Sifton had actually granted the first few big leases in 1899 and each year a few more were given to meritorious candidates. Moreover, though it was not generally known at the time, a select few had been given 'closed' leases by special order-in-council. Such attractive leases had not been granted since the generous awards made by the Conservative government to its friends in the early 1880s.[84]

Though the leased acreage in the southwest by 1903, as shown in Table 9, began to approach the level of the previous decade, it did not come close to meeting the demand. In August 1903 Sifton attempted to stem the flow of lease applications by ordering the Department to dismiss all applications currently

TABLE 9

Grazing leases 1897–1905

Year	No. of leases in force	Acres	Size of largest lease
1897	375	248,219.89	7,500
1898	448	333,469.68	7,500
1899	567	510,226.68	69,120
1900	715	605,794.75	69,120
1901	908	1,272,849.66	69,120
1902	978	2,147,567.69	69,120
1903	889	2,292,504.60	69,120*
1904	745	2,328,113.00	
1905	748	2,773,453.99	

SOURCE: Canada, Department of the Interior, *Annual Reports* (1897–1905), reports of the Timber, Mineral, and Grazing Lands Branch
* Individual holdings after 1903 are no longer listed.

being considered. Once the door had been opened, however, it proved impossible to reclose. The WSGA warned the government that settlement was being encouraged on lands unsuitable for farming and unless some privileges in the way of obtaining extra land or more satisfactory leases could be granted the larger ranches would be forced out of business with heavy financial loss. The association recommended that right of homestead entry be withdrawn from lease lands until in each case the suitability for agriculture was determined by federal inspection.[85] Other ranchers forwarded their protests individually to Sifton. One frustrated pioneer rancher complained that he had expanded his ranch from a 160-acre homestead and a few head of cattle to a section and a quarter and 200 animals, and was now being forced out of business because he could not buy or lease any government land in his vicinity. With undisguised bitterness, he informed Sifton:

I must sell and go to Argentina where I can continue in the business for which I am best fitted. Farming I do not intend to try as this country is not fitted for it. There are years in which hot winds dry up all vegetation and bring nothing but vexation and debts to the inexperienced that try to farm on the strength of two or three wet seasons in succession.[86]

Despite Sifton's refusal to approve additional leases the Department was deluged throughout 1903 and 1904 with applications ranging from requests by small stockmen for adjoining sections to very large requisitions from cattle companies such as the giant Scottish-owned Matador Land and Cattle Company of Alamositas, Texas. George Lane, the new owner of the big North-West Cattle Company, even managed to persuade the cattlemen's old antagonist Frank Oliver to recommend to the Minister on his behalf that ranchers with cattle currently on the range be allowed to lease twenty acres of land for each head of stock.[87] While Oliver understood that the land desired by Lane and his friends was in the westernmost foothills country, where the high elevation precluded farming, the exigencies of the impending federal election perhaps partly account for Oliver's uncharacteristic action, for the discreet support of the powerful was not without its reward.

The big ranchers' anxiety to obtain lands deep in the foothills was occasioned by the dense settlement along the railway between Calgary and Ft Macleod. As this strip of land was put to the plow and fenced, the big herds were cut off from the plains. Formerly cattle owned in the foothills drifted out onto the plains for the summer and the grass in the hills was thus saved for the winter months. Now, confined to the eastern edge of the foothills, big cattlemen were faced with the necessity of drastically reducing their herds unless additional lands could be secured further west. Lane even went so far as to suggest to Ottawa that small stockmen be permitted to choose their lands first so as to 'prevent the old cry of "the big man squeezing out the small man".'[88] He cannot, however, have been unmindful that an allowance of twenty acres per head would still give the lion's share to large operators.

In the frustration of being unable to procure the lands required to range their cattle, many cattlemen resorted to fencing desired properties illegally and holding them through the presence of their large herds and hired cowhands. By 1903 the prevalence of this practice caused alarm among some Department of the Interior officials in the west. It was learned, for example, that Crown land along the entire length of the north side of the South Saskatchewan River from Medicine Hat to the forks of the Bow River was enclosed by a continuation of illegal fences. Advantage was most frequently taken of a bend in the river where a single line of fence could enclose a large area. In one such case a recently arrived rancher from Mexico, Lord Beresford, took advantage of such a bend in the Red Deer River and enclosed nearly four townships and controlled about thirty-five miles of river front.[89] Such fencing could result in serious loss for neighbouring ranchers, as did the Beresford fence during the winter of 1903-4. A series of bad storms in the latter part of February and March drove some ten to twelve thousand head of cattle from points further east down the river in a westerly direction until they struck the Beresford fence, which held them on the high windswept bench lands where they perished by the hundreds. An inspector who rode the length of the fence in May reported dead cattle, twelve or fifteen to a pile, at short intervals all along the fence. He pointed out to his superiors in Ottawa that since the grazing regulations had been withdrawn there was no lawful way, except for the few who had obtained leases before the cut-off, to obtain control of grazing lands and in consequence extralegal means would flourish. The great demand for grazing land was confirmed by the backlog of applications for some 3,172,100 acres that had accumulated by the spring of 1904.[90]

Confronted with such growing complications and demands, the Minister finally was compelled to establish a definite administrative policy for the grazing country. To assist Sifton in his deliberations, the Department of the Interior's Timber and Grazing Branch forwarded to him a detailed report on the grazing question prepared by one of its officials the previous autumn. The Department had been without an impartial and knowledgeable assessment of grazing regulations since the decline of Pearce's influence in the mid-1890s. The author of this review, R.H. Campbell, was, like Pearce, convinced that without irrigation much of the south-west was unsuitable for agriculture. The problem therefore was to devise regulations that would permit the most equitable and efficient use of grazing lands. Campbell outlined the evolution of grazing regulations in Canada, the workings of the lease system in the various colonies in Australia, from which the original Canadian system had been borrowed, as well as the free-range experience in the United States, and concluded that the lease system was vastly superior. Evidence was presented in the form of statements from reputable American sources. The comments of Professor R.H. Forbes of the Arizona Agricultural Experimental Station were quoted.

A striking instance of this process of ruin [the free range system] is offered by the San Simon Valley. This once beautiful district has been despoiled and hopelessly ruined within the short space of some fifteen years … The ruinous methods which seem inevitable upon a public range, which, being everybody's property, is nobody's care, have so destroyed its value, and have so changed the original condition of the country that in many cases, in spite of the present high prices of cattle, the ranges now carry but a tithe of what they once did. In the San Simon Valley alone it is judged that within the past decade the number of cattle has fallen off from 75 to 90 per cent. This one district, at least 2500 square miles in extent, would at the extremely low rate of four animals to the square mile per year yield an annual revenue of $150,000 in a region where now it would take hard riding and a sharp eye to gather a single train load.[91]

It was alleged that nearly all those practically and professionally acquainted with the problem in the United States favoured a system of leasing but that popular opinion was still opposed. A bill to provide for a system of leasing grazing lands had been introduced into Congress in 1902, but strong opposition developed on the ground that the object of the bill was to establish the large landholders firmly in their position and prevent homesteading, and the legislation was consequently defeated. It was a similar Canadian attachment to the myth that the nation's progress could be measured by the expansion of plowed acres and the number of homesteads taken each year, with little or no thought to climate or soil type, that caused many unfortunate settlers to learn at excessive cost that the valid but unpopular arguments of informed men like William Pearce should not have been ignored.

Campbell insisted that there was still a place for large ranches and recommended that they be assisted to continue through provisions for increased security of tenure. Sifton's decision, formalized by an order-in-council of 30 December 1904, provided for the continuation of the grazing lease system along the lines Campbell suggested. The basic provisions repeated those enacted in the past. Grazing leases of up to 100,000 acres were made available for periods not exceeding twenty-one years at an annual rental of two cents per acre. The lessee was obligated to stock the tract with one head of cattle for every twenty acres within three years and afterwards not to exceed this maximum. In return, the leaseholder was permitted to purchase up to ten per cent of the leased area for a home ranch. From the cattlemen's point of view the most important provisions were those relating to the right of homestead entry, and in this regard the government made an important concession. The terms decreed that the whole or any part of the lands leased were open to homestead and pre-emption entry, *unless otherwise provided.* This key qualification permitted the Minister of the Interior, on receipt of an application for a lease for grazing purposes of lands claimed to be unfit for agricultural purposes, to have such lands inspected and, if agricultural unsuitability was confirmed, to withdraw such lands from homestead entry or sale for the duration of the lease.[92] Approval to proceed with the numerous applications for closed leases and to purchase under the ten per cent option was given by the Minister in February 1905.[93]

After almost a decade of indecision and confusion the cattlemen had finally convinced the Minister of the Interior that agricultural settlement was inadvisable in large areas of the south-west, and that special legislation was required to give some sense of permanency to the cattle export industry. Throughout the spring of 1905 ranchers applied for, and a few received, the closed leases that had been largely absent from the grazing country since 1896, but their triumph was short-lived. On 28 February 1905 Clifford Sifton resigned from the Laurier government in protest against the initial separate school clause in the autonomy bills that created the new provinces of Alberta and Saskatchewan. As noted earlier, the new minister was none other than the cattlemen's oldest bête noir,

Frank Oliver. Within two months of assuming office, Oliver informed his staff that a review of all legislation relating to the grazing industry would be undertaken. For an industry which had been plagued for a decade with reviews instead of policy the future looked bleak indeed.

The ranchers' sense of urgency about obtaining leaseholds and their great alarm at the threatened dismantling of the water reserve system were but manifestations of the basic fact that they now faced what they had struggled so hard to contain and deflect – the full onslaught of the prairie homesteader. The magnitude of the homesteaders' rush into the south-west after 1900 was unprecedented. That the full thrust of settlement into the foothills region was about to begin was suggested in the remarks of the Dominion Land Agent at Lethbridge. In the 1898 annual report of the Department of the Interior he noted that a number of homestead entries had been made in the heart of the ranching country near Pincher Creek and that cultivation had demonstrated that these lands would yield abundant cereal crops.[94] The following year about 100 new homesteads were taken up near Pincher Creek.[95] This pattern was duplicated along the entire eastern edge of the foothills from the American boundary to Calgary. During the 1900–1 season an estimated 4000 immigrants settled along the railway line running south from Calgary.[96] Around Pincher Creek, where the inflow was most concentrated, few large range herds remained after 1900.

The pace of colonization continued to increase throughout 1901–2, when an estimated 12,600 settlers arrived in Calgary and 1495 homesteads were granted in that area.[97] Immigrant arrivals and homestead entries around Calgary increased each year to 1905 and the town's population doubled to 10,000 within the short space of four years.[98] From this date the rate of settlement near Calgary began a decline which the local land agent attributed to the fact that nearly all available land along the Calgary and Edmonton railway was homesteaded, thus forcing would-be settlers arriving after 1905 to go up to forty miles from the railway to obtain entry.[99] During 1904 the last gaps were filled in the band of settlement that stretched from Calgary south to Ft Macleod along the old cattle trail that marked the division between the western foothills and the open eastern range. In the neighbourhood of the ranching community of High River, 300 homestead entries were granted; a little further south at Nanton, 400 new arrivals were situated and six new school districts opened; and at Claresholm about 500 new homesteads were established.[100] Still further south near the once vast holdings of the Oxley Ranche, where two years before there was not a settler within forty miles, the little town of Staveley had blossomed forth from the prairie complete with two general stores, a hardware store, two meat markets, two hotels, three livery stables, three blacksmith shops, a lumber yard,

7 Settlement along the Calgary and Edmonton Railway 1905. This railway became part of the Canadian Pacific Railway on 1 July 1903.

two elevators, a schoolhouse, a church, and the dwellings of several hundred inhabitants.[101] This one hundred mile barrier of fields and fences pushed the ranchers deeper into the foothills and cut them off from their accustomed summer range on the plains, thus forcing a fundamental alteration in the ranching practice of the two previous decades.

Immigration into the grazing lands south of Medicine Hat and in the Lethbridge region was equally rapid. Nowhere was the growth more marked than near the Mormon communities of Stirling, Cardston, Taber, and Spring Coulee. As these settlements straddled the main route northwards for thousands of immigrants from the western American states, the visible success of the Mormon pioneers was sufficient to influence the majority of those entering from the United States to remain in the south. Such settlers locating in the Lethbridge region numbered 2456 for the year ending 31 March 1902, 2313 in 1903, 1778 in 1904, and 1329 in 1905.[102] With immigrants numbering in the thousands each year, Crown lands swiftly diminished. Around Lethbridge alone land sales exceeded 300,000 acres in 1905. Similarly, by the same date, all land within a fifteen to twenty-mile radius of nearby Pincher Creek was homesteaded, causing the immigration agent there to predict that within a few years the cattle industry would largely disappear. Acreage sown to grain increased by thirty to fifty per cent annually in the environs of nearly every community in the south, so that as early as 1903 southern Alberta was already being described by government officials as a 'mixed farming country.'[103] The colonists who had wrought this fundamental shift in the region's economic base were almost entirely American, which meant also that the social and cultural structure of the south was equally affected.[104]

Even the last stronghold of cattlemen, the dry plains about Medicine Hat, seemed destined to fall before the farmers' onslaught. With the undisguised optimism engendered by five years of unparalleled western settlement, the Commissioner of Immigration reported in 1905 that 244 new homesteads had been granted during the year in the Medicine Hat district and that an 'abundance of moisture has continued the desirable change of making what was considered a grazing district admirably suited for farming operations.'[105]

The Commissioner's judgment of the farmers' advance into the Medicine Hat region as a 'desirable change' is significant in that it is representative of the confident attitude that had gained dominance, that progressive farming methods rendered the entire prairie region habitable and for the sake of the nation's moral and economic well-being such settlement should be pushed into all areas with all haste. 'Too optimistic an estimate can scarcely be made of the agricultural wealth of western Canada,' the Deputy Minister of the Interior William Cory assured the nation in 1905 and he counselled that since the 'opening to the plough of these western lands had been one of the most potent factors in the ever increasing prosperity of the country during the last decade, [this] should be considered as the strongest possible ground for prosecuting with increased vigour the land and immigration policy to which the satisfactory results now reported are chiefly attributed.'[106] The great outburst of national feeling engendered by the vision of countless thousands turning the western sod and building towns and cities on the plains completely smothered the discordant voices of the few doubters.

This tremendous growth of western settlement coincided with almost a decade of above average precipitation. The two settlements at either end of the hypotenuse of the ranching triangle, Calgary and Medicine Hat, seldom enjoyed more than ten inches annual precipitation between 1885 and 1895; from 1896 to 1903 the average never dropped below fifteen inches.[107] With such encouragement settlers, and government officials who should have known better, were not inclined to listen to those who had lived in the region during the previous dry decade. The voice of caution, coming as it did mainly from the cattlemen, was dismissed as simply the anti-settlement propaganda of a reactionary vested interest. The warnings of William Pearce in his annual reports for 1899 and 1900 that normal dry conditions would in due course return were similarly ignored.[108] In 1902 Pearce forwarded a special confidential appeal to the Minister of the Interior regarding what he considered to be the questionable activities of immigration agents in the south-west. Commenting on a recent trip from Calgary to Ft Macleod, he explained that he had noticed considerable settlement on tracts of land that he had earlier reported, in his capacity as Superintendent of Mines, as unsuitable for agriculture unless combined with irrigation, and predicted that a large number of these homesteaders would be forced to move elsewhere as soon as there was a return to average seasons. Pearce suggested that the honesty and reliability of many immigration agents was compromised by the temptation to secure a commission, and he singled out the agents at Omaha, Nebraska, and Duluth, Minnesota, for particular blame. Some agents, Pearce charged, had even gone so far as to assure prospective homesteaders that the climate was changing and that plenty of moisture was assured in the future.[109] But his appeals were of no avail and each year settlers pushed into more marginal areas, in the end to experience disaster and heartbreak.

Against the farmers' advance the cattlemen put up determined opposition. Motivation for this spirited defence, the political side of which has already been discussed, came from the cattle industry's unprecedented economic buoyancy. The opening of the Crowsnest Pass Railway in 1897 provided access to a sizeable market in the south Kootenay mining towns for cattle that were not of sufficient size or quality to warrant export to England. Prices obtained for choice four-year-old steers reached $40-$45 in 1897 and remained at this price or better until 1905.[110] Reports from all parts of the cattle country in 1898 described the ranching industry as in a flourishing condition and during the following year the demand for beef exceeded the ready supply, with some 30,000 head being purchased by buyers in the Calgary region alone.[111] The assertion of the Superintendent of Police at Calgary that there 'has never been a time in the history of the cattle industry in Alberta when the prospects were brighter or more promising' was confirmed by the comments of ranchers the next year who declared that the season had been the best in the history of ranching.[112] As the ranching industry from the beginning had been predicated upon the mass production of beef for export, the condition of this market provides a reasonably good index of the economic health of the cattle business. From 1899 to 1904, as shown in Table 10, beef exports from the ranching country maintained a steady and profitable volume. These statistics, the first reasonably accurate ones available, show the domination by the ranch country of the cattle export industry. Two-thirds to three-quarters of the total cattle exports from the North-West Territories each year were from the grazing districts of West Assiniboia and South Alberta. The latter district, which comprised mainly the foothills region, accounted for almost half the yearly exports. Given the 3½-4½ cents a pound live weight, or the $45-$55 a head that choice four-year-old export steers brought during this period, cattle exports remained a vital contributor to the regional economy.[113]

The destination of these cattle exports cannot be precisely determined and what they represent relevant to national economy is hard to define. Enough statistics are available, however, to help provide a general picture. First, the live cattle trade still counted as a first-rank item on Canada's list of export staples; between 1895 and 1905 the value to the Canadian economy of live cattle exports and grain and grain product exports were nearly the same.[114] Though the United States market began to grow again after 1897, this important export sector remained centred on British demand. The western contribution to this trade grew from about ten per cent in 1893 to thirty-three per cent in 1895 and fifty per cent by 1900.[115] As the western percentage, or more specifically as the foothill region's percentage of the trade grew, the western grazing country increasingly became the destination for thousands of eastern and American stocker cattle that two years later would be shipped to Great Britain.

From 1900 to 1914 the breeding and sale of horses also contributed substantially to many ranchers' income. Raising horses required more specialized attention than raising cattle but the return per animal was two to five times as great, which led some stockmen to concentrate their activities entirely in this area.

TABLE 10

Stock shipments from the North-West Territories 1899–1904

| Districts* | Year | Exports from the region | | | | | |
| | | East | | West | | Total | |
		Cattle	Horses	Cattle	Horses	Cattle	Horses
West	1899	10,929	453	170	10	11,099	463
Assiniboia	1900	10,942	127	172	6	11,114	133
	1901	9,322	537	227	8	9,549	535
	1902	17,158	868	280	15	17,438	883
	1903	6,168	1,458	3	25	6,171	1,488
	1904	9,640	1,247	58	29	9,698	1,276
South Alberta	1899	13,095	1,251	5,906	202	19,001	1,453
	1900	18,549	1,865	5,875	131	24,424	1,996
	1901	13,631	3,518	6,627	297	20,258	3,815
	1902	21,557	3,270	7,505	418	29,062	3,688
	1903	16,937	3,148	6,447	353	23,384	3,501
	1904	25,631	1,446	8,093	402	33,727	1,848
Territories	1899	35,330	1,730	6,141	213	41,471	1,943
as a whole	1900	48,114	2,010	7,015	137	55,129	2,147
	1901	31,573	4,139	8,190	313	32,763	4,452
	1902	50,490	4,416	9,568	444	60,058	4,860
	1903	31,462	4,658	7,373	453	38,835	5,111
	1904	40,238	2,823	9,150	453	49,388	3,276

SOURCE: North-West Territories, Department of Agriculture, *Annual Report* (1901) 82–3;
(1904) 45
* Shipping points included in each district:
West Assiniboia: Moose Jaw, Maple Creek, Regina, Medicine Hat, Swift Current, Dundurn
South Alberta: Okotoks, Morley, Lethbridge, Coutts, Ft Macleod, High River, Gleichen, Cayley,
  Cochrane, Pincher Creek, Calgary
Territories as a whole: East Assiniboia, Saskatchewan, North Alberta, West Assiniboia,
  South Alberta

Given the industry's economic success, cattlemen were not inclined to allow themselves to be pushed out of business and were prepared, in addition to taking political action, to make necessary economic adjustments. Consequently, from 1896 to 1905 there was a fundamental shift in the basis of the western cattle industry. The change began in 1896 as cattlemen began to alter the capital basis of the industry from cattle to land after the old closed leases were cancelled. It was already apparent that the only real security was derived from outright ownership. Consequently, cattlemen began to purchase home ranch sites and key properties along streams and rivers, which, with the water reserve system, they hoped would allow them to control surrounding grazing lands.

By 1900, however, a new frontier figure had entered the region and greatly complicated the system. The arrival in force of the dry-land farmer extended the competition of former years between rancher and farmer for the same habitat from the creek and river bottoms on to the plains beyond. Assisted by a government that was prepared to mark out 160-acre parcels in parts of the country where in dry years it took twenty to forty acres to furnish enough grass for a single steer, and a confidence born of improved farming techniques and a series of wet summers, the dry-lander was determined to occupy the entire region. The settlers' rapid purchase of public land after 1900 hastened the stock-growers' retreat behind the defences of privately owned pastures. The situation was summed up concisely by the Superintendent of Police in Calgary in his 1902 report. 'The days of the big rancher are numbered,' he wrote, 'and unless he purchases enough land out-right to run his large herds on, he will have to seek pasturage elsewhere.'[116] The problem was that this was the cattlemen's last frontier; there were no new lands further north or west to which they might go. This left only that part of the existing region hitherto used mainly for summer pasture. Moreover, the stockman moving onto the eastern plains south of the Bow River and the lower reaches of the Red Deer River or south of Medicine Hat faced not only a more severe winter climate but also growing competition from retreating Montana stockmen for use of the open range. As well, in the river valleys and more sheltered regions was the now ubiquitous farmer. For most stockmen there was little alternative but to remain where they were and attempt to buy and lease the land required. But even this alternative was tentative, for few could afford to buy outright the large acreages needed and leases which were difficult to obtain did not in any case preclude homesteading within the boundaries of the leaseholds. Repeated attempts to persuade the government to alter land laws to suit the demands of the range industry were frustrated and eventually led to overgrazing, illegal fencing, and harassment of settlers.

The growing emphasis on direct and individual land control brought renewed interest in the lease system. When the old lease system was terminated in 1896 most cattlemen were prepared to place their trust in the vast system of water reserves created during the preceding decade. Control of the region's water promised control of the surrounding grazing land. But after 1900, as the water reserve system came under increasing attack, ranchers again considered grazing leases more favourably.

The shift from public grazing to leased acreages and direct ownership precipitated a number of important short- and long-term changes in the economic and political structure of the cattle industry. It brought a certain and swift end to the old range system that had been in decline for a decade. With reduced acreages, ranchers herded their cattle closely, cattle were still ranged if possible during the summer, but forage crops were planted to provide for winter feed and some stockmen even provided limited winter shelter. While many ranchers had decided long before that it was undesirable simply to turn cattle loose to fend for themselves, it now became physically impossible in many areas. Though the large companies out on the plains and near Medicine Hat were able to continue this practice for some years, the big cattle companies in the foothills were forced to move, sell out, or adapt. For those operators who chose the latter alternative it usually meant restricting the herd to a size that could be accommodated on land directly controlled by the company.

This process of adaptation was accompanied by a gradual decline in the influence and power of the big companies, particularly those with headquarters in the east or Great Britain. The relative decline of the managers in turn occasioned the rise of new men in the ranchers' fraternity. These men were inevitably stock-raisers long resident in the ranching country, many of whom had arrived just before or during the early company period. Many had started out as managers or foremen of the big companies and later branched out on their own or in a partnership. By 1900 a number of these individuals had acquired holdings and herds of respectable size ranking not far behind some of the old companies. The influence and importance of such stockmen came naturally to the fore during the trying decade after 1905.

The changes occurring within the cattle kingdom between 1896 and 1905 are mirrored clearly in the stockmen's association. The WSGA, founded at the beginning of this decade, was really the child of earlier organizations structured to meet the demands of a cattle industry based on the open range. During this period the WSGA's main concern, apart from settlement and stock theft, shifted gradually. Attention moved from such matters as round-up organization, adjudication of ownership, branding regulations, prairie fire prevention, herd and bull control, and wolf bounties – all of which were of significance during the range period – to subjects like disease control and quarantine regulations, compulsory stock inspection, railway shipping procedures and facilities, and market information. This shift in emphasis reflects the growing maturity of a basic export industry. Whether as a body providing for internal administrative control or as a political lobby seeking desired legislation, the WSGA was perhaps the major contributor in the development of a viable cattle export industry in the west.

Though the association's administrative and economic function enabled it to remain a strong regional body, its political influence had begun to wane by 1905 because of the rapid settlement after the turn of the century which reduced the cattlemen to a minority within the region. The WSGA could no longer pretend to speak for the population in the south-west; the new federal government, not having the same close links as its predecessor with the cattle compact, was less inclined to listen. Moreover, the new men of the ranching community who had begun to replace the eastern ranch company directors as spokesmen did not yet possess the advantage of national economic or political stature. Though the new leaders of the stock association in some ways enjoyed greater acceptance within the ranch country, which made for a more cohesive organization at the local level, they found it difficult to exert decisive collective influence upon the government. The issue of most critical concern to stockmen as they faced the advancing tide of settlement was the question of a lease system and in this regard, despite the persistent efforts of the association and individual ranchers, the government remained unmoved. For a decade, Ottawa refused to commit itself to an official policy regarding the cattle industry in the south-west. While federal officials seemed to hope that the problem would solve itself as they persisted with their interminable reviews, the future of the western ranching industry remained uncertain, and settlement changed forever the face of the grazing country.

5

The struggle for survival: the dark years 1905-11

After 1905 the rancher was compelled, however unwillingly, to accept general settlement of the south-west as an accomplished fact. Western colonization had proceeded at such a pace over the preceding five years as to warrant creation of two new prairie provinces. The cattlemen had traditionally maintained a circumspect attitude towards provincial autonomy as it was fitfully debated in the press and Territorial Assembly. They understood that whatever autonomy might mean to the rest of the population, it would thrust them into a minority position in a province dominated by the farm community. Coupled with their fear that this dominance might be translated into legislation on such matters as herd and pound laws, branding regulations, stock inspection, and school and municipal taxation, and other issues where rancher and farmer did not see eye to eye, was their specific apprehension that the grant of autonomy might also include federal surrender of Crown lands to the new western provinces. Stockmen generally preferred control of western lands to remain in a more distant quarter. They were used to dealing directly with Ottawa and had the advantage of solid connections within the metropolitan business and political community. Although their influence had diminished since 1896 and although Frank Oliver's antagonism was a growing threat, friends were still to be found within the Department of the Interior and, in addition to longstanding Conservative supporters in Parliament, there was a growing number of prominent Liberals who had obtained leases in the border country and hence had a vested interest in ranching. It was evident, moreover, that the federal government was unlikely to be controlled by western farmers.

When provincehood became inevitable the cattlemen naturally sympathized with the endeavours of their Calgary business friends who were trying to promote an east-west boundary that would create northern and southern provinces rather than eastern and western jurisdictions.[1] Calgarians saw in this plan the opportunity to become the predominant community, if not the capital of the region. To the ranchers, a division which included Alberta and Assiniboia promised to maintain the geographic unity of the ranching country. Stockmen on the plains of western Assiniboia and in the Alberta foothills were used to political co-operation through their common membership in the Western Stock Growers' Association. The formation of a southern province which excluded the northern agricultural population and retained the entire ranch community within its bounds would ensure a much more acceptable power balance. At the ninth annual meeting of the WSGA at Medicine Hat in May 1905, cattlemen officially announced their opposition to the north-south boundary. Led by ranchers from West Assiniboia, the stock-growers adopted the resolution that 'it would be advisable from a stockman's point of view to extend the eastern boundary of Alberta to the 107th parallel of west longitude, as far north as the northern boundary of Assiniboia.'[2]

In the end this minority opinion regarding provincial boundaries did not prevail and stockmen were confronted with eastern and western provinces, in both of which they were a minority economic group, particularly in Saskatchewan. However, the new provinces were not given control of Crown lands and ranchers were permitted to adjust to these new political entities more gradually than would otherwise have been the case.

With the question of land policy their always paramount concern, apart from markets, ranchers returned to their traditional preoccupation, the Department of the Interior. The longstanding antagonism of the new Minister, Frank Oliver, made stockmen even more sensitive and uncertain about the future of their industry than they had been during the first half of the decade. Oliver spoke for those who were inclined to view the west in terms of what had come to be popularly known as the 'mixed farm.' It was alleged that such farms would supply both the needs of the nation and export requirements for grain and cattle, and at the same time create a populous and independent citizenry that would comprise the matrix of a growing and progressive nation. This vision was accompanied by the parallel stereotype of the monopolistic cattle baron, member of a landed and reactionary establishment standing in the way of settlement and 'progress.' Few people understood the beef export industry and fewer appreciated the region's climatic or physiographic characteristics. The tradition of small farm homes for poor men lived on among politicians, who did not trouble themselves to learn that not all prairie lands were identical with the farm country of Ontario, Manitoba, or the Qu'Appelle valley. Yet distance from the southwest was not the sole reason for error. Within the region itself there were thousands of newly arrived settlers who expressed their confidence that modern agriculture could surmount climatic deficiencies. This confidence

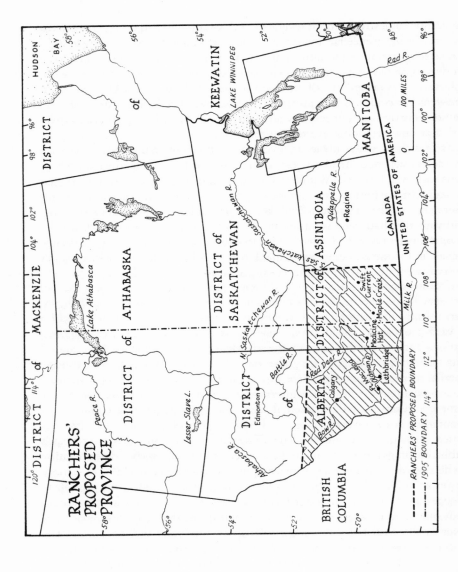

8 Ranchers' proposed province 1905

would not be destroyed until several periods of drought had been experienced. The aridity experienced in some parts of southern Alberta was so severe in 1907 that settlers attempting to farm near Coutts on the American border had to be supplied with hay, oats, and even chicken-feed. Yet as one government official observed, 'the great bulk of the new settlement [during 1907] is going on non-irrigable lands ... There appears to be a growing belief that "dry farming" may make irrigation unnecessary altogether, and through widespread cultivation, not only retain but attract precipitation.'[3]

The ranchers, who had faced Oliver's pro-settlement arguments for over two decades, anticipated the worst, and his actions soon proved that their apprehensions were well founded. Within two months of taking office, Oliver instructed his staff to make the necessary arrangements for the withdrawal and sale of water reserve lands.[4] Department officials began by withdrawing all shelter reserves or driftways that had been set aside in the foothills country and which usually adjoined water reserves. It was decided that these lands would be made available for sale in the same manner as regular Crown lands.[5] As far as the stock water reserves were concerned Oliver was determined to get rid of most of those in settled areas and by December 1905 approximately 200 parcels of what had formerly been considered key strategic locations, totalling over 100,000 acres, were selected for disposal.[6] When the Minister was informed that an inspection of each property would delay the sale nearly a year, he directed that the sale proceed without inspection, with the advertised provision that any parcel listed might be withdrawn from sale. The reason for this proviso, as an interesting internal memorandum explained, was to protect 'the rights and improvements of any person who has placed improvements thereon.'[7] This represented a complete reversal of departmental land policy in the grazing country. For twenty-five years the government had refused to recognize squatters' rights on closed leases or water reserves. The numerous squatter evictions and repeated public warnings are testimony to the Conservative government's determination in this regard. Though closed leases no longer existed when the Liberals came to power in 1896, Clifford Sifton had maintained the policy and refused to countenance squatting on stock-watering reserves during his administration.

While Oliver had been unable to convince Sifton otherwise, his attitude towards the reserve system and to squatters was none the less made plain whenever possible. In a letter to Sifton during the government's first year in office, Oliver wrote: 'I hope there is no likelihood of the policy formerly in vogue being continued, namely, to wait until a settler takes up a spring and then fire him off and reserve it.'[8] In Oliver's mind such squatters were legitimate settlers who had been persecuted unfairly by wealthy ranchers opposed to settlement. At the same time he knew that most big cattlemen were stalwart supporters of the Conservative party. Once in office, Oliver was determined to assist squatters who had sought his assistance over the preceding decade. Where illegal improvements had been made on water reserves by squatters, Oliver insisted that they be given the opportunity to purchase the property at a private sale where they would not be outbid by those with more capital.[9]

At the first auctions held during June 1906 at Calgary, High River, Pincher Creek, Ft Macleod, Lethbridge, and Medicine Hat, over 25,000 acres were sold.[10] During 1907 and 1908 the remaining reserves were inspected and those located in what was still mainly ranching country were retained while the others were listed for withdrawal. A second sale in June 1910 disposed of sixty parcels, and at a third auction the following year an additional 10,000 acres were transferred from public to private ownership.[11] By this time the sales caused little dissent among the ranch community. Cattlemen had decided that the only reliable security was that provided by actual ownership and as long as the sales of water reserves were by auction they had the opportunity to purchase those essential to their operations. Second to outright ownership, stockmen were prepared to put their trust in closed leases, and it was over this issue that they clashed most sharply with Oliver.

In early 1905 they had finally gained from Sifton what they had been after for five years. The new lease regulations presented on 15 February provided for the issue of both open and closed leases. The open lease provided for the withdrawal of lands for homestead entry and sale, whereas the closed leases did not. Neither form of lease provided for complete cancellation on two years' notice, as had been the case with all previous leases. The only qualification was that before a closed lease could be granted the Minister had to be satisfied that lands included in the lease were not fit for agricultural purposes. The ranchers' satisfaction was short-lived; Sifton resigned later the same month and Oliver took office in April. In the interval only six closed leases were granted under the new regulations. The fortunate six included the Milk River Cattle Company (60,000 acres), the Glengarry Ranche Company (13,794 acres), George Lane (43,736 acres), Messrs Brown, Bedingfield, et al. (55,747 acres), and the Grand Forks Cattle Company (two leases of 47,218 and 47,615 acres respectively).[12] The fact that the two major shareholders of the latter company, J.H. Ross and J.D. McGregor, were important western Liberals and close political friends of the former Minister might explain the government's largesse in this instance.

Oliver's amended regulations which followed in July prevented others from obtaining such prized closed and irrevocable leases. Under the new provisions leases of up to sixty acres for every head of cattle owned, to a maximum of 100,000 acres, could be granted for up to twenty-one years, but the Minister could, for any reason, cancel the lease on giving the lessee two years' notice. The

TABLE 11

Grazing leases 1906–11

| Year | No. of leases | Acres | | | | |
		Man.	Sask.	Alta.	BC Rail- way Belt	Total
1906	787	6,688	899,765	1,651,397	444,655	3,022,505
1907	939	12,642	632,493	2,132,218	481,418	3,259,271
1908	990	6,174	605,159	2,088,736	491,532	3,601,700
1909	971	4,814	570,551	1,737,874	456,825	2,770,064
1910	1,166	1,105	848,283	2,023,169	420,982	3,293,539
1911	1,424	945	1,145,966	2,001,234	406,152	3,554,297

SOURCE: Canada, Department of the Interior, *Annual Reports* (1906–12), Report on Timber, Grazing, and Irrigation. Oliver preferred to assign small leases of several sections to mixed farmers or small stock-raisers, which partly accounts for the growing number of leaseholders during this period.

new leases were not open to withdrawal for homestead entry, but lands were not to be granted without confirmation from the Inspector of Ranches that they were unfit for agricultural purposes.[13] The official regulations were further tightened by the explicit instructions given by Oliver to his staff. In keeping with his view of the squatter as the virtuous underdog, the Minister ordered that if there were any homesteaders or squatters within the tract applied for who owned stock, sixty acres per head was to be reserved for them around their holdings. If stock was not owned, a reserve of 640 acres adjoining the settler's 160 acres was to be held.[14] The Inspector of Ranches was informed that: 'In inspecting and reporting upon applications for grazing leases you will hereafter *not recognize climatic conditions* as deciding whether or not the land is suitable for agricultural purposes. Only land that is *too gravelly, stony, sandy*, or of *too rough a surface* for agriculture, is to be classed as not fit for that purpose, and as being suitable to be covered by grazing leases' (my italics).[15] It is obvious that Oliver did not intend any significant expansion of leased acreage and during his administration the area under lease remained relatively constant, as shown in Table 11. The intrinsic merit of the lease system made no impression on him and it was only because of the political pressure that big ranchers exerted that a token system, which never offered cattlemen more than two years' security, was maintained. Specific instructions like the foregoing underline Oliver's preference, more so than any previous Minister, to undertake direct personal supervision of the department's Timber and Grazing Branch.

Apart from the difficulty of convincing the Department that the land applied for was totally unfit for agricultural purposes, the rancher never knew once the lease was obtained whether or not he would still have it two years hence. For this reason the main thrust of the stockmen's political activities for the next five years was directed towards improving the terms of leasehold tenure. To this end the WSGA sent many memorials to Ottawa urging that the two-year clause be withdrawn and that irrevocable tenure of at least ten years be granted.[16] It was pointed out that the cattle export industry was in serious difficulty and that with only two years' security cattlemen could not justify the expense of properly fencing the tract, constructing adequate shelter, or building a herd of costly breeding stock. While the Association received courteous replies from Oliver or the Deputy Minister, William Cory, that the matter would be given 'careful consideration,' the Department's true attitude is reflected in the memorandum to Oliver that accompanied a stockgrower's petition, wherein the official in charge of the Timber and Grazing Branch surmised: 'As I presume you have no intention of meeting the request of the Association I would suggest that an acknowledgement be sent to the Secretary and that no further action be taken.'[17]

Oliver's position remained fixed despite increasing support for the ranchers' position even among important Liberals. In April 1910 the *Calgary Albertan*, the leading Liberal paper in the south, warned that the ranching industry was in a critical state and that unless changes were made in the lease regulations it would soon disappear. The *Albertan* insisted that there were large areas unfit for agriculture but suitable for cattle-raising and pointedly remarked that 'this is no reflection upon the country and is a fact.'[18] The editor caught the essence of the problem when he observed that the authorities seemed to have assumed that stockmen were restricting settlers and that 'the rancher in some way [was] keeping back the progress of the country.' The *Albertan* argued that this was not the case, that it was senseless to destroy so important an industry, and that longer-term irrevocable leases should be granted so that ranching could be conducted in a businesslike manner. It took four or five years to stock a ranch properly and as long as the two-year cancellation clause hung over their heads most cattlemen could not contemplate improvements to the property or the herd. The government was also pressed for amendment by the Calgary Board of Trade, where the ranchers' influence was very strong.[19] Through its support a resolution in favour of improving lease tenure was adopted at the annual convention of the Western Board of Trade. Support also came from parts of the recently settled foothills country, where many farmers had already begun to transfer their interest to stock-raising.[20] But the Minister remained adamant. In his view there were few sections of the country where agriculture could not be practised and for this reason he was not prepared to see extensive areas withdrawn from settlement through long-term irrevocable leases. As he replied to one group from the Alberta foothills who had petitioned for a closed-lease policy:

the Government is faced with the fact, that during the past ten years vast areas of the country which had been considered unsuited for grain growing and permanently devoted to grazing, have actually been brought under profitable cultivation. Judged by the records [sic] of the past, it is a most difficult matter to decide where possible cultivation ends and where permanent grazing rights should begin.[21]

Oliver was determined not to err on the side of the latter.

While 1905 was the year that brought Oliver to stewardship of the Department of the Interior, it was also a year that aroused another of the industry's traditional concerns. With the formation of Saskatchewan and Alberta, the ranching community became increasingly apprehensive about the impending fate of the police (as of 1904 renamed the Royal North-West Mounted Police) now that the region was no longer a federal territory. Though the question did not rank in importance with the lease question or land matters and did not occupy the ranchers' attention for the entire period, the close and longstanding relationship between policeman and rancher in the south-west made this issue, as suggested earlier, one of sentiment as well as economics.

It appeared for a time in 1905 that responsibility for law enforcement would be turned over to the governments of Saskatchewan and Alberta and the jurisdiction of the RNWMP confined to the remaining northern territories. The ranchers were certain that they would not receive the same consideration and extensive protection from the new provincial government as they had from the federal police for the past quarter of a century. In December 1905 the WSGA forwarded to Ottawa a memorial outlining the vital necessity of the continued presence of the RNWMP in the south.

We desire to point out that without the protection of this body of men, the ranching industry would suffer in many ways. Amongst the many now settling in the North West are some of the worst criminals that the country has known, as the records of the courts for the past two or three years will show. Another phase of the matter is this: that the small farmers will persist in burning around their places and the fires frequently get out of control and burn large tracts of country, which is most ruinous to the stock growing industry, and it is only through the vigilance of the Police that we can carry on our business. We realize more and more that without the Police the stock industry would be in a very critical condition. We therefore strongly urge upon your Government the necessity there is for the continuance and if possible the increase of the RNWMP.[22]

The stockmen's interest was further advanced a short time later through a personal visit to Ottawa by George Lane, a leading member of the association and one of the region's largest ranchers. After his interview with Prime Minister Sir Wilfrid Laurier, and Fred White, Comptroller of the RNWMP, Lane informed his fellow rancher, A.E. Cross, who was also a prominent Calgary businessman: 'Now I am satisfied if the ranchmen and businessmen do not take this matter up, there will be changes; in fact I am told this. The Controller will be in Calgary in a short time and be sure and get a few of the good solid men together to meet him.'[23] Lane's comment that White was on his way to Edmonton to meet provincial officials and that 'if the local government should take this out of the hands of the North-West Mounted Police, you know what that will mean,' was well understood. While Cross solicited the support of his fellow businessmen, the campaign in Ottawa was continued by M.S. McCarthy, newly elected Conservative MP for Calgary, and the wealthy meat-packer and rancher, Pat Burns. At meetings with the Comptroller, the Minister of Justice, the Honourable Charles Fitzpatrick, and Sir Wilfrid the cattlemen gained the 'emphatic' assurance that it was 'not the intention of the government to withdraw the force from the Southern or central parts of Alberta, and that the government [would] keep up and continue to maintain the first line at the boundary, and second line along the main line of the CPR'[24]

While conceding this, the ministers were not prepared to abandon their plan to press the provincial administration to take responsibility for regular police duties in the northern region, despite the caution tendered by the ranchers' spokesman that such a concession might be 'the thin end of the wedge, and the force would be abolished by reason of the fact that the greater power in the provinces is located where there is perhaps none too good feeling towards the police.'

In the end, the provinces' reluctance to face the expense of establishing their own police force resulted in the continued presence of the RNWMP over the entire region. Had the provincial governments been less economy-minded the cattlemen might have persuaded Ottawa to make their region an exception. The ranchers' success in this regard manifests the growing prominence of the new men, Lane, Cross, and Burns, who, along with A.J. Maclean, who had initiated the police campaign within the WSGA, were already known in Calgary and the cattle country as 'The Big Four.'

As the police issue suggests, the ranchers' relations with the new provincial government were cautious at best. The cattlemen, who had voted mainly Conservative in Alberta's first election and who had helped elect one of the two successful Conservative candidates, were confronted with a Liberal government whose support rested securely in the farming country from Calgary north and in the capital city of Edmonton. The new administration was basically a farmers' government and the larger cattlemen apprehensively awaited legislation regarding herd and pound laws that would confine stock to enclosed pastures, fencing, and road allowances, and especially school and improvement district taxation. While waiting to learn the government's direction and expecting the worst, the cattlemen were dealt a staggering blow from another quarter.

The winter of 1906–7 was the worst ever experienced in the ranching country. This seemingly unending winter began with a heavy snow storm the third week in November and the weather became progressively more vicious, so that by 8 December temperatures had descended to –28°, –35°, –30°, and –25° F at Calgary, Gleichen, Ft Macleod, and Medicine Hat respectively.[25] Apart from a short break near Christmas, temperatures remained frigid. January was even more severe. At Gleichen, about fifty miles east of Calgary, where many large foothills ranchers had taken leases to counter declining acreages in the west, the average temperature for the month was –15⁹ with the minimum reaching –51°. Temperatures elsewhere in the ranch country were only fractionally better as the indispensable chinook failed to make its accustomed appearance. During February there was some moderation after the middle of the month but not before all centres in the south had recorded temperatures of –40° or lower. In March temperatures continued to improve gradually but not enough to melt the heavy snowfall; thus ranchers, their supplies of feed exhausted, were unable to turn their cattle out to graze, and starving animals that had so far managed to survive the desperate winter perished.

The stockmen's plight is presented vividly in a series of letters exchanged during the winter between A.E. Cross and C.L. Douglass. During the summer of 1906 Cross had made an arrangement to bring excess 'A7' stock from his ranch in the foothills to a lease held by Douglass along the Red Deer River north-east of Bassano. The first hint of difficulty came about the middle of December when Douglass informed Cross that the winter to this point had been by far the worst he had experienced in the country and that the cattle were difficult to drive from the sheltered river valley to feed on the benchland above.[26] By early January the feeling of impending tragedy mounted. After passing by train along the CPR between Bassano and Brooks, Cross reported about 1000 head of starving and dying cattle along the tracks and inquired of Douglass if any A7 cattle were that far south.[27] In his next letter of 20 January Douglass explained that for the previous ten days the temperature had stayed between –30° and –50°, yet he and the men, even the cook, had been compelled to ride every day to feed the 300 or so head they had gathered close to the ranch and to drive others out to feed. He confided that enough feed existed for another month and that the cattle were still strong. He added optimistically 'it can't last forever.' In the next report, a week later, the optimism had vanished and the tone was one of despair; it seemed that this most vicious of winters would indeed last forever. Douglass informed Cross that they were doing their best to keep strays from drifting to the south but it was becoming more difficult for man or beast to endure. 'The hardest part,' Douglass wrote,

is hauling [feed], I have got two teams going every day two loads each, and there is hardly a day passes without a blizzard or wind to fill up the trails. One can hardly imagine the drifts, stacks are buried in snow and a crust on the level ground, all the flats have been belly deep to a horse since November, so that the cattle are and have been living on brush. It has been [so] cold with winds when one breaks trails and puts them out on the banks to patches of sage or grass the poor brutes fight you right back to shelter. I am astonished sometimes how well some of them look yet.

By this point stored feed was getting very low and attempts were made to plow the snow and expose the grass underneath, but as Douglass reported, 'one can drive them to death now before they will stay out' on the range to feed. Douglass had ridden every day of the month collecting yearlings, taking as long as three days to move those along the river back to the ranch, until they were feeding all that could be managed. From this point, as he informed Cross, there was no use looking for the weak and the dying. Cross agreed that there was no use feeding those that were going to die anyway and suggested that 'it would be advisable to knock them on the head, so as not to waste any hay.' The long-awaited chinook finally came in the middle of February but the deep snow that remained well into March aggravated losses already incurred.

Elsewhere on the plains the situation was much the same. In temperatures of −20° to −50° cowboys rode daily trying to drive cattle to feed and to hold them on their home ranges. Despite such adverse conditions cattlemen spared no effort, even life itself, to save their herds. The desperate struggle for survival in the Cypress Hills country south-east of Medicine Hat was recorded by one rancher:

Every morning the cattle would leave their shelter and head out on the wind swept ridges where they could find some grazing. They would stay until the wind became unbearable and then they would file back to shelter. Their trails became hard and frozen and they were all footsore. Many of them would bed down at night and turn their heads around on their sides, trying to keep what warmth they could in their poor freezing bodies. In the morning we would ride and find them in this position yet. They would be floundering around trying to get up, their necks so cold they were unable to straighten them out. We would have to dismount, take hold of the animal's head and help straighten out its neck. Then, after a few moments, the animal would flop around and eventually manage to come to a stand on sore, half frozen feet.[28]

Cattle in the sheltered foothills country did not fare as badly. Though the manager of Cross's home ranch reported in January that the weather was worse than that experienced during the famous winter of 1886-7, losses were relatively small.[29] The decimation suffered on the plains east of the Calgary-Macleod Trail seemed to confirm what most foothills ranchers had always feared about the open prairie and many reappraised their plans to sell smaller western holdings to move to less crowded lands in the east, as many had done in the preceding half decade.

In March, stockmen began to assess their losses and to look for the scattered remnants of herds that had drifted miles from their home ranches. Northern cattle moved south in the thousands where, if they did not perish along fence lines, they collected in the sheltered valleys of southern rivers. When the final reckoning had been made many big ranches had losses in the thousands. The winter claimed about 5000 of the 20,000 head Walrond herd.[30] It was alleged that the Two Bar Ranch of Gordon, Ironside, and Fares Ltd near Gleichen lost 11,000 head from a total herd of 13,000.[31] The big cattle companies in the south-east, the Texas-owned Turkey Track Ranch, the Bloom Cattle Company, the Matador Land and Cattle Company, and the 76 Ranch all suffered equally. 'It is a terrible thing,' wrote one embittered rancher who gathered only five head on the spring round-up, 'to see one's "bunch," practically representing one's worldly wealth on four legs, diminishing day by day, and to stand by powerless to stem the ebb. To come upon four year old steers so thin and poor that they are unable to stand. To see a cow's horns protruding from some snow bank and dig down to find your brand on her ribs ...'[32]

While the Dominion Livestock Commissioner estimated the total loss of range cattle at fifty per cent, the losses suffered by individual ranchers ranged from five per cent for many of the smaller stock-raisers to over eighty per cent for some of the large cattlemen.[33] Perhaps the best measure of the havoc visited upon the ranching community during the 1906-7 winter is the number of ranch sales during the summer and autumn of 1907.[34] For some, the winter simply took what little enthusiasm was left to continue in face of difficulties which seemed to press from all sides; for others, cattle losses represented such a reduction in working capital that there was no alternative but bankruptcy and sale.

In some quarters, however, the disaster was unlamented. In his section of the Department of Agriculture's 1908 *Annual Report* the Recorder of Brands was sure there should be no cause for alarm. 'At first sight so many men going out of the cattle business might appear to mean a serious loss to the southern part of the province, but it must be borne in mind that the advent of winter wheat, grown for the past few years, has virtually displaced the rancher in a number of districts, and the transition from a ranching to a farming district was thus made easy.'[35] From the ranchers' point of view the transition imposed by a winter of such destruction would never be remembered as easy. Even the CPR was not quite so callous, and in recognition of the magnitude of ranchers' losses cancelled the unpaid rentals due from those who held leases of railway lands in the irrigation block.

While the big cattlemen seemed threatened with extinction, the government and farmers in the south were convinced that they had discovered a crop that, with their dryland farming techniques, would bring assured prosperity. The crop, as the Recorder of Brands observed, was winter wheat. Its initial success was used by the new provincial government in a campaign to encourage further settlement in the south. Cattlemen thus faced the continued pressure of colonization in the few remaining unsettled areas into which they had been pushed. The main focus of this last agrarian advance was the Medicine Hat region. Indicative of the fundamental change occurring in this area was the tone of an article that appeared in the *Medicine Hat News* in May 1906, entitled 'Bad for Ranchers' and subtitled 'But Their Loss Is the Country's Gain and They Must Retreat.'

Reports received here from the country lying south of the CPR, Swift Current, Saskatchewan and Alberta, show that the ranchers there are gradually being driven out by the increasing line of settlement. Germans coming in from the north are fast filling up the country, closing the water holes, and gridironing the district with barbed wire fences. These conditions are rendering things desperate. Many are going northward, and there starting ranching again undisturbed by the newcomers. This whole district, which includes Walsh and other former prosperious ranching country, comprises some 6,000 square miles, and has long been regarded by Canadian farmers as unusually good for ranching on account of its drinking places. The German-Americans are, however, demonstrating that it is as good wheat land as any in the provinces, and it is fast filling up.[36]

In another section subtitled 'Americans Purchased Almost 10,000 Acres at Medicine Hat This Week,' the paper reported that a party from Ohio, Indiana, Minnesota, and Nebraska had purchased fifteen sections and applied for a large number of homesteads within a ten-mile radius of the town. It was noted that the Americans planned to go into 'extensive wheat raising' and it was predicted that Medicine Hat would at last 'get its share of the great incoming tide of immigration.' The town's rival paper, the *Medicine Hat Times*, added enthusiastically the following year that the area had been judged particularly suitable for winter wheat by farmers who were arriving by the hundreds and that Medicine Hat was 'the Coming District.' The area had always been known as the centre of the ranching industry, the paper editorialized, and 'naturally, the rancher had striven to retain it. It took years for the outsider to discover that the vast prairies over which roamed thousands of cattle, and had never felt the plow, were only waiting for the touch of the farmer to blossom forth into great tracts of wheat fields.'[37]

Ironically, or perhaps fittingly, the American cattlemen who had retreated into the region during the previous decade had been followed by the people who had driven them from their previous homes. In this part of the Canadian west the competitors for control of the grazing lands were basically part of the same group that had started the struggle a generation earlier along a line extending from Texas to Montana. Thus it was on the Canadian range that the American ranchers and farmers enacted the last chapter in the struggle for control of the North American semi-arid region. As a large rancher from Texas bitterly lamented in Medicine Hat in 1907, the farmers who had driven him north from Old Mexico and eventually across the Canadian border were, with the winter of 1906-7, about to force him out for good.[38]

In the heart of the old ranching country in Pincher Creek the talk was the same – of farming and winter wheat. The editor of the *Pincher Creek Echo* proclaimed that not only did the honour of first growing this popular cereal belong to his town, but the Pincher Creek country was also the best place in the province to grow such wheat, as was confirmed by that community's capture of the top awards for winter wheat at the recent Chicago World's Fair.[39] The victory of 'wheat ranching,' as the *Echo* phrased it, over cattle ranching seemed confirmed during the summer of 1907 with the announcement that the directors of the Walrond Ranche had decided to terminate their ranching operations after twenty-five years as the dominant power in the Porcupine Hills north of the town. The cattle herd was sold for approximately $250,000, and the 38,000 deeded acres were retained to be sold as market conditions warranted.[40] The sale of the Walrond, along with disposal of the 63,000-acre Cochrane Ranch for six dollars an acre to the Mormon Church the year before seemed in the minds of most southerners to mark the end of an era. Larger ranches remained, but these two, the oldest and most prominent of the big company ranches that had established their herds as the buffalo departed, by 1905 had become, like the police, an intimate part of the region's historical experience. When people thought of ranching in either negative or positive terms they thought particularly of these and several other original ranches. Thus the demise of these two old companies had a definite psychological impact and many accepted this as a sign that the day of the rancher had definitely passed, though others with more insight realized that it was really the day of the old cattle kingdom that had ended.

As with the towns of Medicine Hat and Pincher Creek, the vision in the mind of the provincial government that bespoke progress and development was that of the wheat field rather than of the cowboy on the open range. The Alberta Department of Agriculture even went so far as to give this vision substance in the form of a three-dimensional display erected at the Dominion Exhibition at Calgary and the Canadian National Exhibition at Toronto in 1908. In the Department's words:

the main feature of [the exhibit] is a field of standing grain with a cowboy in the distance. The title of the scene is 'Another trail cut off.' The idea was to represent the rapid development of the province from a ranching country to that of a grain-growing one. The cowboy is following a familiar trail which again appears in the foreground on the other side of the wheat field but is suddenly stopped by a wire fence and a field of grain.[41]

In addition to advertising in leading American magazines and newspapers throughout the United States, the government promoted agricultural settlement in the south by sponsoring 'Dry-Farming Meetings' in southern communities. In 1908 Professor H.W. Campbell of Lincoln, Nebraska, was brought to Medicine Hat, Cardston, Lethbridge, Pincher Creek, and Gleichen to instruct farmers how best to grow cereal crops in the dry season.[42] In subsequent years delegates from the south were sent each year to the annual 'Dry-Farming Congress' in various American centres. The dramatic increase in wheat acreage in five seasons, as shown in Table 12, is testimony to the region's popularity and the government's success in encouraging cereal agriculture during this period, and incidentally, to the pressure on the declining range.

The homesteaders' push onto federal lands in the dry country was also the product of a unique scheme of the indefatigable champion of unrestricted settlement, Frank Oliver. In 1908 he presented a new Dominion Land Act, the essential purpose of which was to provide funds to build a western railway to Hudson Bay through the special sale of crown lands on the south-central prairie between Moose Jaw and Calgary. The odd-numbered sections in this area of some 28,000,000 acres were set aside to be offered for sale in the form of 'pre-emptions' for existing homesteaders or as 'purchased' homesteads, at three dollars per acre.[43] Ranchers who had managed to hang on after the winter of 1907 were soon receiving notices that the odd-numbered sections in their leases

TABLE 12

Wheat acreage 1906–10

Crop district	Year	Winter wheat acreage	Spring wheat acreage
Medicine Hat	1906	6	6,820
	1910	1,829	12,098
Lethbridge	1906	7,758	9,225
	1910	4,580	29,603
Cardston	1906	7,438	2,855
	1910	32,189	11,044
Ft Macleod	1906	762	2,194
	1910	5,580	10,874
Pincher Creek	1906	9,704	3,599
	1910	15,942	559
Claresholm	1906	11,593	20,230
	1910	7,054	58,134
Nanton	1906	4,038	3,072
	1910	4,819	22,444
High River	1906	2,738	1,157
	1910	12,840	10,013
Okotoks	1906	565	1,213
	1910	3,336	4,961
Gleichen	1906	588	484
	1910	8,682	21,804

SOURCE: Alberta, Department of Agriculture, *Annual Report* (1910) 45, 52–3

were being withdrawn and an immense area of former grazing land was thus opened for settlement.[44]

This rapid agrarian advance after the turn of the century forced ranchers who wished to remain in business to retreat to deeded holdings or move into more marginal areas. While much ill-feeling towards the farmer remained throughout the southwest, it was on the periphery of farm settlement that the traditional acrimony between rancher and farmer remained strongest. On the defensive and without the support of William Pearce and his water reserves or an acceptable lease system, some cattlemen resorted to other tactics to hold the advancing line of farm settlement. The usual weapon was the rancher's cattle.

Cowboys would graze a large herd immediately outside a settler's fence. When the herd finally moved elsewhere the ground was left, as one farmer described it, 'about as bare as an asphalt pavement,'[45] thus denying the settler the use of nearby grazing land. At worst, the presence of the cattlemen's great herds could be even more damaging, for with encouragement and sometimes by accident range cattle could destroy fences, trample crops, and eat the farmer's stored feed supply. The method was old and its effectiveness is attested to by the numerous pleas for protection in Department of the Interior files.[46] Others appealed, usually anonymously, in the columns of the public press. One such entreaty posed the rhetorical question, 'Will the ranchers succeed in their attempt to starve out the settlers?' and then answered: 'It is this question alone that is causing a number of settlers along the Milk River to desert their homes, and a larger number contemplating [sic] the same movement.'[47] The writer argued that as long as the locality was overrun by thousands of cattle settlers had no chance. 'To see the great numbers of horses, cattle, and sheep,' he wrote, 'reminds one of the olden times and the buffalo instead of a country settled up [since] 1908.' He charged that ranchers deliberately drove cattle on to the settlers' premises at night and related how men had stayed up every night for a month guarding a green patch of oats or a garden only to succumb in the end to exhaustion and be eaten out when their vigilance ended. Though the ranchers did not try to keep their cattle away it was probably the severe drought of 1910 as much as the cattlemen that forced certain of these deluded settlers from the region.

Farmers retaliated in some measure through herd or pound ordinances. Such ordinances allowed farmers to petition the provincial government to have their township declared a pound district and thus prevent the running of animals at large. Provisions of the ordinance permitted damages to be assessed when a legal fence was broken through. Range animals found grazing in the township were impounded and the owner fined and charged a fee by the pound-keeper for quartering the animal. If after public advertisement the owner was not found, the animal was sold and the proceeds deposited in the public treasury.[48]

Petitions to apply the ordinance came not from fully settled areas where cattle were kept on private fenced properties, or from areas that were mainly open range, but from regions where the rancher and the farmer were in competition. Thus whatever the government's response, one group bitterly objected. Cattlemen complained that when such a district was established, all stock running at large, singly or in bunches, that unknowingly corssed the township's imaginary boundary line 'immediately become legal prey, and during slack times it is considered in many districts quite justifiable to assist them in crossing.'[49] It was also alleged that pound-keepers often advertised the brands of impounded animals incorrectly so that the animal was sold before the rancher realized it was missing. In fighting the establishment of such districts stockmen argued that the creation of one such closed township rendered the eight adjoining townships unsafe for normal grazing purposes because cattle inevitably strayed over the unfenced boundaries of such a district. In localities where farmers and ranchers were numerically balanced, where the pressure for the creation of such districts was most acute, the government was plagued with heated petitions from both sides.[50]

The most serious issue between cattlemen and the provincial government after 1905 was the question of school and municipal taxation. Like the pound and herd law problem, this issue grew directly out of general agricultural settlement. The new farm population was anxious to undertake numerous local improvements, particularly building roads and bridges which they, unlike stock-men, deemed essential. Not only was the rancher reluctant to help pay for roads he did not want, but he also found the local improvement tax when added to the school tax and the lease rental to amount to more per acre than he felt could be justified by his per acre return. Ranchers interpreted the provincial govern-ment's intention to tax leased lands as a calculated plot to exterminate their industry. In 1908 the federal Inspector of Ranches reported that many ranchers were relinquishing their holdings. This he attributed partly to two causes, the winter losses of 1906-7 and the dread of a tax on leased lands.[51] The ranchers' attitude is clearly revealed in a letter from A.E. Cross to his partner relating his decision to cancel their eastern lease. 'I find this lease will be subject to local improvement taxes of 1¼ cents per acre, and school tax of 1¼ cents per acre, so I do not think I should be warranted in keeping it on subject to such heavy taxes.'[52] Cross suggested that they consider running their cattle without a lease, as he assumed many others would be or were already doing.

Cross's decision, like that of many of his fellow ranchers, was based on the premise that at the end of the season he would greatly reduce his herd size. In the view of most ranchers the future did not warrant expansion, and for some it did not even warrant continuation. Not only were settlers crowding them out, but both the federal and the provincial governments seemed anxious to hasten their departure. Equally important was the less favourable market faced by the cattle industry. During the previous decade returns were sufficient to encourage cattlemen to initiate a vigorous defence of their enterprise. Now the incentive had diminished and some stockmen began to shift their economic basis in the hope of cashing in on what the press popularly described as 'the wheat bonanza.'

The beef market decline actually began in the 1906 season and like all the ranchers' problems it was in part related to settlement. As many of the big company ranches began to reduce their herds or, like the Cochrane Ranche Company in 1905, sell them in their entirety on account of insufficient range, a beef surplus and declining prices resulted.[53] Unfortunately, much of the stock sold in the fall of 1906 had to be turned back on the range because of a shortage of railway cars for shipping, which in turn added to the winter losses of 1906-7. These direct losses incurred through exposure were only part of the disaster and the long-term effects were equally serious. The calf crop was much reduced,

TABLE 13

Cattle export and local shipments 1905–11

	Exports*			Local	
Year	East	West	Total	shipments	Total
1905	45,266	8,838	54,104	11,401	65,505
1906	73,889	8,941	82,830	8,398	91,228
1907	79,807	13,924	93,731	9,162	102,893
1908	73,888	16,453	90,341	15,076	105,417
1909	79,329	23,684	103,013	38,806	141,724
1910	85,388	37,895	123,283	60,986	184,269
1911	25,862	31,188	57,050	93,253	150,303

SOURCE: Alberta, Department of Agriculture, *Annual Report* (1905–11), section entitled
'Stock Inspection.' Statistics from Saskatchewan were gathered and compiled according to a
different system and are therefore not directly suitable for comparison.
* ie, exports outside Alberta

many that survived were deformed, and the weakened and thin state of all young
stock in the spring meant that they did not make the growth they otherwise
would have done.

Still, as Table 13 shows, exports increased. However, these figures are deceptive, for included in the export shipments over the subsequent three years were
thousands of head of breeding stock that would have been retained under more
favourable circumstances.[54] Consequently the output from western ranches
tended to remain constant while farm shipments, though a small percentage of
the total, gradually increased. As it became apparent that range production was
being maintained through the sale of female and breeding stock and that farm
production would be unable to fill the gap, either in terms of quality or quantity,
it was predicted in some quarters that within a few years there would be no cattle
for export. In 1909 the Deputy Minister of Agriculture took issue with this
widespread view and claimed that a much more optimistic outlook was justified.
He insisted that central and northern Alberta were admirably adapted to mixed
farming and in a few years would be sending as many cattle to market as were
formerly sent from the older ranching districts. It would, he admitted in his
1909 annual report, take several years to make the adjustment from ranching to
mixed farming, but once this transition period had passed, he predicted the
number of animals available for export would steadily increase.[55] The relatively
static export level which caused this concern is shown in Table 13.

The following statistics, however, should be taken as only a general measure
of western stock production, for by the Department of Agriculture's own

admission the figures are often widely misleading. The dramatic increase in shipments during 1910, for example, is explained by the severe drought which occurred in the south that year and forced ranchers to send large numbers of stocker or feeder cattle to more favourable locations both within and outside the province to be finished.[56] As the local shipments column includes sales to local meat-packers as well as the type of shipments just mentioned, the most meaningful comparisons can be drawn from the total exports column. It should also be noted that these statistics do not include exports from that part of the range country east of the Alberta boundary.

Prices continued moderate to low from 1907 to 1910. While prices were often a little higher in the spring and early summer, 1908 and 1909 returns were 3–4½¢ per pound live weight for export steers ($40–50 per head), 2¾–3½¢ for butcher steers and 2½¢ for export cows.[57] In 1911, beef prices began to improve as fewer cattle were offered. The reduced exports of 1911 suggested also that the transition period, envisaged by the Deputy Minister of Agriculture in 1909, might be somewhat longer than he had anticipated.

The industry's disappointing price performance from 1905 to 1911, and the consequent decline in the ranchers' incentive to remain in business, had much to do with cattlemen's longstanding disadvantage in the market-place. They were burdened not only with high freight rates to eastern markets, but were also at a disadvantage because the large cattle-buyers in the west were too few for satisfactory competition. The thirty per cent customs levy on imported cattle denied Canadian cattlemen the alternative of the generally higher Chicago market. As the local market therefore grew in relative importance after 1900, complaints by ranchers about regional marketing became more pronounced. In 1902 William Pearce transmitted their grievance in this regard to the Minister of the Interior, Clifford Sifton. 'It would appear,' he wrote, 'that we are at the mercy of a combination of dealers and the result is that there is a feeling throughout the country that not sufficient is received for beef.'[58] A number of cattlemen attempted the following year to establish a sellers' combination against the buyers, agreeing not to sell their cattle to any buyer below a set minimum.[59] Small ranchers, however, did not possess the capital resources to withhold their cattle from market for a season and the very large stock growers who marketed several thousand head were less inclined to make an issue of ½–¾¢. This tended to isolate the medium-sized producers who initiated the combination and hence prevented the plan from becoming effective. Charges against the buyers continued to accumulate none the less, and in 1906 the Alberta government announced that a 'Beef Commission' would investigate 'the general belief of the farmers and ranchers that prices were unduly depressed through a combine of buyers.'[60]

Between 10 June and 20 July 1907 the commission conducted hearings at every important cattle shipping point in the province. At the sessions, scores of stockmen denounced their inferior position relative to the buyers. It was alleged that the firms of Pat Burns of Calgary and Gordon, Ironside and Fares of Winnipeg had divided the market between them, the Winnipeg firm buying for the export market and Burns confining himself to the slaughter market. Export cattle purchased by Burns were always sold to Gordon and Ironside. Ranchers unanimously insisted that competition was not noticeable among buyers. As a rule only one buyer would come around to an area and at shipment centres where two or three agents were present they would never compete with one another. If the rancher was not prepared to take the price offered by one, no other purchaser stepped forward; he either accepted or took his cattle home. Bigger stockmen did not have quite the same disadvantage. With larger herds they could ship their export cattle by the trainload direct to Winnipeg, Montreal, or on to Liverpool. They remained none the less subject to the price set by Burns for slaughter cattle. Buyers were also accused of often failing to honour previous contracts if the market price happened to drop.

Equally strong charges were made against the CPR, whose negligence the ranchers claimed cost them thousands of dollars. Cattle were sometimes loaded onto boxcars rather than cattlecars, animals were sometimes left days without food or water, and travel times, especially for small shipments, were often incredibly slow. Stockmen complained of trips taking as long as ninety hours to go from Lethbridge to Winnipeg when the normal running time was less than half this. As a result, cattle arrived at Winnipeg or Montreal reduced in weight and often badly bruised, with considerable loss to the shipper. Ranchers often arrived at loading points with their herds on a date previously arranged with the railway only to be compelled to wait as much as ten days before the promised cars arrived. In the interval the stockman who had been planning his shipment all season could miss the most favourable market. Though large stockmen were equally bitter in their indictments of the railway, they generally received better service than the small stockman or farmer as they were able to ship entire trainloads and thus usually gained through service and booking preference.[61]

For its part the CPR was not especially sympathetic. The company's livestock agent pointed out to the commission that the season for shipping cattle was very short, lasting from about 10 July to mid-October. This meant that everyone wanted to use the limited number of cars at once. He admitted that the normal run from Calgary to Winnipeg took forty-two hours, but that it had on occasion taken ninety hours and 'small shippers had to take their chance,' and he did not see why the company should assist in watering, feeding, and unloading the cattle.[62]

The buyers' rebuttal naturally focused on two individuals, Pat Burns and J.T. Gordon. In what the *Calgary Herald* described as an 'emotional' and sometimes 'excited' defence, Burns testified under oath that a cattle combine had never existed. He explained that he fixed his price by his own judgment and claimed that the price he paid was the highest in the west and that during the previous winter he had overpaid $150,000. 'There are three concerns which the people of this western country have made up their minds to knock for some reason or other,' Burns charged, 'these three concerns are the CPR, Gordon and Ironside and Pat Burns. Men like Gordon and Ironside have been the making of the west. Through adversity they have persevered and have done the country priceless good by the fact of their existence.' Burns went on to say that he never experienced any trouble with CPR shipping and in fact took a rousing stand diametrically opposed to all the stock-growers' allegations. In his view the cattle industry was in fine condition.

I have never had an understanding with no outfit in America, I care for nobody. I stand on my own bottom. There is nothing the matter with the cattle business. It is all right. Men can get from $40 upwards for a four-year-old steer, and I have very seldom seen one sold for less. Is not this a free country? I have fed 10,000 to 17,000 cattle during the past winter, and I find shipping very profitable. I have never squeezed anybody. Opposition, I love opposition. The more the merrier.[63]

Burns further informed the commissioners that he paid the biggest wages in the country and cautioned that 'without Pat Burns the western country would starve in ten days.' When a commissioner asked whether he did not think that someone would take his place if he went out of business he answered defiantly, 'they could not do it.' Gordon's appearance before the Commission in Winnipeg was equally unrestrained and all charges of collusion with Burns and the CPR were categorically denied. Gordon's rebuttal even roused some of those assembled to invite him to step outside to settle the matter in Marquis of Queensbury fashion.[64]

The Commission's findings were presented in the Department of Agriculture's 1907 *Annual Report*. From the stock-growers' point of view the conclusions were generally disappointing. The Commission reported that although the producers furnished much circumstantial evidence of an agreement among buyers allotting districts in which other buyers would not compete, and though there were repeated assertions that buyers set prices, 'on no occasion have we been able to elicit information which would substantiate the charges.' With respect to the known agreement between Burns and Ironside regarding export and slaughter cattle, the commissioners explained:

we would like to mention that although Burns and Co. are very extensive buyers of all classes of cattle in this province, of late they have done no exporting, their export cattle being turned over principally to Gordon and Ironside of Winnipeg. We know that Mr. Gordon has selected Mr. Burns' cattle at the shipping point, taking the exports to Winnipeg, while Mr. Burns took the remainder or butcher's stuff to Calgary. Some of the producers objected to this method, claiming that it was proof that there was an agreement between the two companies. We have to say that we are of the opinion that it is a method which has proved of direct benefit to the stock raisers of the province in that Mr. Burns when purchasing does not cull the bunch as most of the buyers are obliged to do.[65]

This conclusion, that the ranchers derived direct benefit, could hardly have been drawn from ranchers' testimonials, for a number had asserted that they were forced to sell to Burns because he was the only buyer that would accept any number of culls, and he would do so only if he was allowed to have the entire lot for sale, including the export steers. At the same time the Commission did admit, on the basis of Burns's own statement that were he to close the country would be starving in ten days, that Burns and Company had a monopoly on the retail meat trade of the province. As to that company's practices, the commissioners stated that accusations against the company could not be substantiated. The depth of the Commission's findings is suggested by the rather lame observation, that 'for some reason there is a lack of healthy competition in the buying of cattle in this province.' The only change it was prepared to urge upon the buyers was that the practice of universally deducting five per cent of the animals' live weight to allow for shrinkage be discontinued.

Against a more distant target, the railway, the Commission was prepared to take a stronger stand. 'We consider,' the commissioners reported, 'that the time occupied in shipping cattle from Alberta to Winnipeg and Montreal, and the treatment the rancher receives at the hands of the CPR, must be expressed in no milder terms than outrageous. The delays in transit occasioned by neglect on the part of the CPR ... in many cases bring ruin and disaster to the western rancher.'[66] It was accordingly recommended that the railway commission be asked to compel the CPR to run a weekly scheduled stock train that would have right of way after passenger trains and maintain a speed of at least twenty miles an hour. The Commission also asked that it be made unlawful to carry stock longer than forty-two hours without unloading them for feeding and watering.

The commissioners concluded that the decision of British Columbia and Saskatchewan not to participate greatly reduced the scope of the investigation. They admitted that their knowledge of the workings of the export industry was deficient and recommended the appointment of a livestock commissioner to be paid by the province whose chief business would be to assist the marketing of Alberta export cattle.

The Department of Agriculture acted quickly upon this suggestion with the appointment of W.F. Stevens, and his first report in 1908 reveals both the need for and the success of such an officer.

In a number of cases when farmers refused to sell to buyers at ridiculously low prices and the cattle buyers threatened to leave their animals untaken if their prices were not accepted, and in other cases where the animals were actually left on the feeder's hands, the livestock commissioner has been able to find a market for these animals, frequently at better prices than were originally offered.[67]

While a formal combine among buyers may not have existed, there was no doubt that the lack of competition placed stockmen at a severe disadvantage and throughout the period cattlemen continued to complain that the 'big packers' had the power to determine day-to-day livestock prices.[68] The livestock commissioner, however, gradually shifted the balance; he organized trainload shipments for small stockmen, pressured the CPR to deliver cars promptly, and prepared detailed marketing reports.[69] Stevens's knowledge of the industry and success in the stockmen's interest was such that he was eventually persuaded to leave government service and work directly for the WSGA.

The picture that emerges during this period is one of an industry in decline. Market conditions, as outlined above, were unsatisfactory. Continuing settlement in the semi-arid region was forcing fundamental economic adjustment. Relations with both levels of government were unfavourable to the rancher; from the one he faced increased taxation, from the other a refusal to adopt a lease policy that permitted economic security. Under these circumstances many ranchers, large and small, left the region or devoted themselves to other pursuits. But the majority remained to fight for limited concessions and to adjust the nature of their enterprise where it seemed necessary. Out of these trying years emerged the second generation of the stock industry's leadership. One individual stands out, both because of the role he was later to play, and in terms of his response to the problems faced by the cattle industry, a response which represents in microcosm the stratagem attempted with less success by the industry at large.

Alfred Ernest Cross came west from Montreal in 1884 as bookkeeper and veterinarian for the Cochrane Ranche Company. A year later he established his own ranch on Mosquito Creek in the foothills fifty-five miles south of Calgary. By 1900 he was a well-established cattleman and as founder and majority shareholder of the Calgary Brewing and Malting Company he was also one of that city's more prominent businessmen. Despite this latter enterprise and his residence in Calgary, he always considered himself a rancher first.[70] As a rancher of experience and as an astute businessman, Cross was convinced that the production of quality beef cattle could offer attractive returns.

He recognized with others after 1900 that the key to remaining in business was to retain control of sufficient land. To this end Cross and neighbouring ranchers first consulted as to the strategic locations which controlled water and driftways as well as the entrances to valleys or other such places, ownership of which prevented easy access to lands beyond, and endeavoured to ensure that as many such locations as possible were individually or collectively purchased.[71] Cross then commenced to make yearly purchases of available adjacent or nearby Crown and railway lands.[72] Even with an outside source of capital, funds were initially insufficient to purchase all the lands required, thus necessitating the addition of leased property. While Cross worked as an executive member with the WSGA to secure a more satisfactory lease policy, he also went to additional lengths on his own behalf. When his first application to lease adjoining property was turned down by officials within the Department of the Interior, he prevailed upon his brother, Selkirk Cross, senior member of a well-known Montreal legal firm, to call personally upon the Minister of the Interior. This visit, along with the drafted support of the Minister of Marine, Joseph-Raymond Préfontaine, was sufficient to have the Department change its mind, withdraw the land in question from homestead entry, and grant a lease.[73] When Oliver took office, however, the Department's withdrawal agreement was rescinded without notice and several choice sections were taken by homesteaders. Appeals that the Department had violated a drawn agreement were ignored in face of Oliver's determination to see the region settled.[74] Unable to come to any understanding with him, cattlemen endeavoured to intercede with two other key officials in the department, William Cory, Deputy Minister, and William Stuart, Inspector of Ranches. Before Oliver was prepared to grant a lease, the land had to be declared unfit for agricultural purposes; it was thus imperative to ensure that Cory order an inspection and that Stuart declare the desired lands unfit. To this end Cross was advised by a fellow rancher who had just been to Ottawa regarding such matters, to see Stuart as soon as he returned from Ottawa and 'hand him a cheque for his trouble, it may have a good effect – he is in poor health and his salary is not large.'[75] In this atmosphere trips to Ottawa became even more frequent and no doubt the Inspector of Ranches found new interest on the part of those who could augment his salary.

In the struggle for lands in the foothills region ranchers did enjoy some initial advantages, but after 1900 they were clearly on the defensive. Settlers had the advantage of numbers and official government support at both levels. Through democratic majorities and government legislation they could turn such normally prosaic acts as those providing for school and improvement districts into useful weapons against the ranch interests. That many settlers were not adverse to using such grounds to further their own interests in the ranch country is suggested by the actions of several of Cross's farm neighbours. Two seasons after making homestead entry on part of the lease that Oliver had recently opened, two settlers offered to sell their land to Cross. To establish the attractiveness of their offer they informed Cross:

As you are undoubtedly aware, we have formed a School District, Trustees has [sic] been appointed, and the site for school house decided upon, which is at present before the department for their approval ...

You will at once realize that if 'Mr. Parks' and myself leaves [sic] the district, the school question will at once drop. I need not point out what this means to you.[76]

Cross agreed to purchase when assured that the school question would be dropped. The settlers made a handsome profit and may typify many who settled in the vicinity of larger ranches mainly for speculative reasons.

By 1911 many homesteaders were offering to sell their quarter sections to Cross, motivated no doubt by the drought of 1910, the first very dry year that most newcomers had experienced since settlement in the southwest. A few also had begun to realize that 160 acres was not viable for growing grain or cattle.[77] Up to 1910 most of Cross's land purchases had been from the government and the railway; after that they were mainly from homesteaders desiring to move elsewhere.

Coupled with land as an anxious concern of cattlemen was the question of markets. In this regard Cross seems to have done reasonably well. Though often disappointed with the return gained by his well-bred animals, he was able, by stressing quality and producing several hundred head per year for the export market, to justify remaining in business. The winter of 1906–7 persuaded him to abandon the idea of ranging cattle on the eastern plains and confirmed his general practice of keeping his herd down to a size that could be grazed near his home ranch and for which adequate winter feed could be prepared. Failure to adopt such methods cost many larger ranchers reduced profits and in some cases resulted in bankruptcy. While Cross generally received top regional prices for his cattle, he also found it difficult, like the small stock-grower, to escape the Burns-Gordon and Ironside network. His plans for direct shipment to the British market in 1905, for example, were confounded by the report from his Montreal commission agent that Gordon and Ironside had booked up most of the available shipping space for the summer months. 'I don't know if it is this firm's intention to try and secure a monopoly on space for the following months,' the agent wrote, 'but it looks a little that way.'[78] While the bigger operators could press for better terms, it seems that they too were often stuck with Burns or Gordon and Ironside. Ocean shipping rates grew progressively more prohibitive and by 1911 Cross displayed a growing interest in the Chicago market despite the steep tariff.

Cross's activities show that, despite the industry's decline, some cattlemen were still powerful. While the application of influence at the federal level grew more difficult, they still possessed a strong regional power base. Cross, for example, directed the Calgary Board of Trade to petition the government on the ranchers' behalf to establish no more herd districts.[80] Of more direct personal concern, he similarly persuaded the Department of Public Works to turn down the petition of residents who wanted the government to designate as local improvement districts, the two townships in which his ranch was located.[81] But not many cattlemen were as well served as Cross. Those who were able, at least in part, to duplicate his management skill and influence seem to have survived this half decade of decline most effectively.

Apart from a few big ranches, the survival rate seems to have been highest among medium-sized operators like Cross. It was the small ranchers who were in the most desperate position. The situation they faced in the foothills country was accurately summed up by one of their number, John Bratton, who complained to the Department of the Interior in 1905 that homesteaders had filed on his small bit of grazing land without even bothering to come to look at it first:

these parts of the Porcupine Hills are not suitable for agriculture but for stock ranching we are unable to by [sic] land at present hy [sic] prices and people are coming in and taken [sic] the land many have not enough cash to carry them over the first year they may be able by working out to stay long enough to acquire a title to ther [sic] land but by that time they will have destroyed the stock industry and they will find it hard to realize enough on there [sic] land to take them out of the countrey [sic].[82]

Many small ranchers sold out, or if they decided to remain kept only a few head of cattle, grew small crops and waited for better days. Bratton's prediction that if he could wait the period out the country would revert back to the small rancher for which it was naturally adapted, proved prophetic, for by 1911, though it was not yet discernible to foothills residents, a gradual movement of farmers out of the region had begun.

6

Transition and the American presence
1900–11

It is apparent that the Canadian cattle kingdom had undergone important changes by 1911 and that these changes were, in essence, the result of settlement. The impact of the homesteader was immediate and far-reaching; his presence changed forever the economic, political, and social structure of the south-west. While it is obvious that these three factors are intimately related, a clearer picture of the Canadian ranching community as it existed during the first decade of the twentieth century can be drawn by focusing separately on each factor.

The cattlemen's empire was built upon a tremendous demand for beef in rapidly growing urban centres and the availability of vast unsettled grasslands where thousands of head of cattle could be efficiently and cheaply grazed. The formation of numerous cattle companies during the 1880s was the natural consequence of a ready market and the accessibility of extensive unsettled grasslands in the Canadian west. The great company ranches that were established were the product of the economic rationale which held that large size was essential to profit maximization. During the period of the big leases the main expense after capital investment in stock was labour, and company directors quickly realized that the more cattle on the ranch, the less labour needed per animal. On the small ranch one or two men might look after 100 to 300 animals, whereas on the big ranch the ratio was closer to one man per 1000 animals. Since the cost per head, in terms of land and labour, declined as the number of head increased, it followed that the rate of return on a given ranch investment increased proportionately to the number of livestock the operation carried, or so it was assumed would be the case under ideal conditions.

The large ranch, which made more extensive use of land and labour per head, also had another advantage in its potential ability to survive price fluctuations. Larger returns during normal years enabled the big rancher, unlike the small stockman with more limited resources, to sell for less or even to withhold some of his marketable cattle during periods of falling prices rather than sell at too great a disadvantage.[1] With unfavourable climatic conditions or a market decline, it was the small producer who usually suffered most. The exceptionally severe winter of 1906–7, for instance, was not the direct cause for the closure of the big *foothills* ranches. Though closures do seem to follow in quick succession after 1907, the unfortunate effect of this one winter was not the critical factor that motivated big operators to quit. When the final reckoning was established, losses in the western part of the foothills country seem to have varied between ten and twenty-five per cent and could be sustained more easily by the big than the small stockman.

Most big cattle companies of the early period were economically viable. Once they adjusted their grazing methods to fit the region's climatic characteristics, particularly through provision of feed supplies and shelter for unseasonable winters, big companies that were properly financed and had good local management were very successful, as is confirmed by their yearly returns. There were certainly a number of companies that experienced disaster in the south-west and the strange manner of their operation and subsequent decline has become part of the cattle country's folklore. The Quorn ranch, owned by members of the Quorn Hunt Club of Market Harborough, Leicestershire, did produce quality horses for the English market, but the financial burden imposed by the summer visits of numerous titled stockholders and their friends hardly allowed the ranch to function normally and did little to enhance the company's profits. But this or other such colourful failures should not obscure the fact that companies like the Cochrane Ranche Company, the North-West Cattle Company, the Glengarry Ranche Company, and the Walrond Ranche Company survived for over a quarter of a century, displaying a tenacity not typical of unprofitable undertakings.[2]

Despite the current myth in the cattle country that the disappearance of the big foothills cattle companies was due to disastrous mismanagement, their decline or removal to the southeast was entirely the result of the advance of commercial agriculture. In the early period the big ranchers contended with the small stockmen and mixed farmers of the river bottoms; after 1900 their main adversary was the wheat-grower, who seemed to have mastered the techniques of dry-land agriculture. Shortly after 1900 the point was reached where profits to be realized from well-situated land in the grazing country were greater from farming than from ranching. Because the per acre return for wheat was greater, the immediate result was a rapid escalation in land values. Assertions by some officials and ranchers that the region could not consistently produce satisfactory wheat crops were another matter; what was important was that new homesteaders had full confidence in the country and their ability to grow wheat successfully. Most ranchers had begun a gradual shift of their capital base from cattle to land in the mid-nineties, but by the early 1900s the competition and the price of land reached a level where the cattlemen could no longer compete. Ranchers who had based their enterprise on one head of cattle per ten to thirty acres, or five to sixteen head per quarter section, were now confronted with the homesteader who was prepared to base his entire enterprise on 160–320 acres, and who would pay five to ten dollars per acre for the land required. Unable to afford or to justify the expenditure of such sums for the remaining portions of their former leaseholds, cattlemen were forced to reduce the size of their herds, thus losing an important advantage.

There was consequently a strong motivation from two directions for the big rancher to dispose of his holdings. On the one hand he was no longer able to conduct his business on the scale he preferred or on the scale which to him seemed to offer the best return, and on the other hand the appreciated value of his deeded property offered the possibility of attractive capital gains. Some companies had acquired considerable land and at this point disposal of the property seemed to offer an immediate gain that raising beef would take years to equal. It was this latter motive, not poor management or a loss of faith in the beef industry, that led two of the oldest and most successful foothill ranches to end their operations. In 1905 the Cochrane Ranche Company sold its 63,000 acres to the Mormon Church for six dollars an acre, which, with the several hundred thousand dollars received for the cattle, permitted James Cochrane to enjoy a comfortable retirement. The decision of the Walrond Ranche to cease business several years later was also predicated upon Duncan McEachran's business-like judgment that the company's lands had become too valuable for ranching.[3] McEachran proposed gradual sales by which he hoped to capitalize on increasing yearly values.

Some big ranchers chose to sell their more valuable foothills land and move to the southeast to continue ranching in a less crowded region, and still others elected to remain and to supplement their deeded holdings with smaller leases deeper in the foothills. While two of the larger old companies, the Glengarry and the North West Cattle Company (under new ownership), continued operations in the foothills, most of those remaining were medium-sized stockmen who owned from five to fifteen sections and herds of one to two thousand head.

The practical alternatives of the small stockman were much more limited. As settlers homesteaded on the land around him, his section or half section could no longer support a herd of any size. This was especially so given the declining beef prices faced by the industry after 1906. He could not afford to withhold his marketable cattle and in a market not noted for competition among buyers he was at an even greater disadvantage than the larger rancher. With the promise of a much greater return per acre to be gained from wheat, many small ranchers sold their cattle and tried to save their investments by putting what land they could to crop.

In the minds of most federal and provincial government officials during the first decade of the twentieth century, the dislodging of the big cattle companies was an inevitable mark of progress. Legislation formerly enacted in the cattlemen's favour was amended or repealed. Both governments, in the best democratic tradition, were prepared to let the settler choose his homestead freely; it was decreed that the homesteader should have the right to try to farm any piece of land he deemed worthy of his attention. What lands the farmer did not want, and these seemed few, were left for the rancher.

The actions of the provincial government were in part motivated by the belief that thousands of farmers each producing a few head of cattle would soon produce more cattle for market than the ranchers had ever done. Though the Alberta government persisted in this belief, it did admit by the end of the decade that the transition to the point at which the demand for beef could be met by the small farm producer would take longer than previously anticipated.[4] The void left by the decline of the cattle companies was not filled by the mixed farmer as the government had hoped. While there was increased farm participation in the local butcher market, the export market that the companies had developed was maintained by medium-sized stock-growers with herds from 1000 to 3000 head. Such herds were small enough to be fed over part of the winter and large enough to prevent inbreeding and warrant the expense of quality bulls. While it should be emphasized that there were at least two herds in the foothills country over 10,000 in size and a number of these large operations in the south and southeast, as well as a number of high-quality herds numbering only several hundred, it was the 'new man,' the middle-sized operator, who now dominated the WSGA and who saved the western cattle export industry from threatened collapse after 1905.

The decline of the cattle companies marked a fundamental change in the economic structure of the south-west. The regional economic control that the stock industry had exercised over the territories of Alberta and West Assiniboia for two decades shifted in the first years of the new century to the grain-grower. At the same time the company withdrawal brought a shrinkage in metropolitan and particularly Montreal financial domination of the beef industry. As the decisions of eastern boards of directors came to apply to a diminishing sector of the industry, there was a corresponding increase in local control that improved the industry's ability to adjust and adapt. In the long term this meant that henceforth most of the capital accumulated by the stockmen would remain in the region that produced the wealth and be reinvested in ranch improvements or in the growing towns and cities of the south-west. The severance of the links with the Montreal financial community resulted in the loss of an important source of influence at the national level, but this was partly balanced by the greater political acceptability of the industry's new leaders among those smaller stockmen who had been inclined in the past to view the managers of eastern and British companies as alien. The ranchers' newly emerging power base was much more regional in character and the longstanding bond between the cattlemen and Calgary's business élite became even more important as the decade advanced.

The shifting economic and political balance within the region was also accompanied by considerable social tension. By 1900 the animosity engendered by the struggle between rancher and farmer for control of the southwest was part of a tradition that was already a generation old, so that the economic and political responses of either group were supported by firmly established social attitudes. To this point the cattlemen, while on the defensive, had faced their adversary from a position of strength and their attitude towards the farmer and his vocation was one of open condescension. The rancher's feeling of superiority and distaste is confirmed in the standard epithet 'sod-buster' which he applied to the farming class. From the outset the cowboy was reluctant to perform what was known as farm work. This attitude was frequently commented upon by inhabitants of the foothills region throughout the 1880s and 1890s. In his annual report for 1888 the NWMP Commissioner observed that 'the ranchers live well and are hospitable to a degree, but everything, even butter, is generally purchased. They all say ... that the cow-boys will not work on foot.'[5] Writing of his experience in the south-west before 1900, Colonel S.B. Steele explained that until the Mormon settlement was well established in the late 1890s, butter, eggs, and vegetables were not readily available. 'Even the large ranchers who owned thousands of cows used tinned milk, and even tinned vegetables.'[6] Most of the hay put up on the larger ranches before World War I was done on contract by neighbouring farmers. While there was obviously some economic advantage to be gained by this procedure, it was also clearly understood that the independent-minded cowboy did not like such work. Though ranchhands were gradually compelled to undertake such 'menial' tasks, old attitudes died hard. As late as 1921 an experienced ranch foreman seeking employment on the Cross ranch felt obliged to state in his letter of application that although he had been 'punching cows' in the region for over twenty years he had changed with the times and was prepared to handle all kinds of ranch work.[7]

Disparagement of the sedentary farmer was an ingrained part of the super-masculine cowboy subculture that was fully developed in the cattle country by the turn of the century. The feeling is well portrayed in a mock last will and testament prepared in 1919 by a cowboy employed by the Matador Land and Cattle Company. The executors of the will were instructed

to immediately sell by public auction the whole of my real estate situated in the City of Swift Current, Saskatchewan. And with the monies thus procured to create a fund, to be ultimately used for the extermination of that class of Vermin, commonly known as farmers, who are at present polluting by their presence, the country adjacent to the *South Saskatchewan River*.

In 1922 a codicil was added.

I give, devise and bequeath to *George Windsor*, my navajo saddle-blanket; to *William Vincent Smith* my rope; to *Pete LaPlante* my rifle; in recognition of the fact that they are respectively the best rider, the best foot-roper, and the best shot, in the Hills. Finally, I leave to each and every *Mossback* my perpetual curse as some reward to them for their labors in destroying the *Open Range*, by means of that most pernicious of all implements, the plow.[8]

In this regard the cowboy's attitude towards the settler reinforced that of his employer and tended to ensure his reliability when given orders in the early period to pull down a squatter's house or, later, to graze the herd close to a farmer's fence line.

The feelings of the ranch owner towards the farmer had a somewhat more obvious basis than those of the cowboy. The differences separating the two grew basically from a straightforward contest between two competing economic systems of land use. From this foundation grew a definite set of values and attitudes as each contestant endeavoured to assert or defend his position. Those who argued for open settlement were prone to refer to the ranchers as the 'cattle barons,' the 'vested interests,' the 'monopolists,' or most frequently, 'the big men,' and they proposed to replace the former with those described as 'yeoman farmers,' 'homesteaders,' and 'poor, common or small men.' For their part the cattlemen attempted to identify southern settlers as 'speculators,' 'misguided agriculturalists,' 'foreigners,' and 'squatters.'

Almost from the outset, however, the farmer gained the support of the national press and acquired the advantage of the underdog. The stereotyped picture of cattle baron versus yeoman farmer that quickly achieved dominance put the ranchers at a disadvantage in any public defence of their interests throughout the subsequent two decades. Thus, when the cattlemen argued strenuously with those from outside the region that vast sections of the southwest were unsuitable for agriculture, they found the weight of their statements destroyed by the accusation that their motive was simply to protect their own vast empire. While the extravagant claims of aridity, poor soil, and early frost made by some cattle companies in the early period no doubt hindered ranchers' later appeals from being taken seriously, and their insistence that the region was best suited to grazing was admittedly spoken with a vested interest at heart, it was none the less asserted with conviction, sincerity, and in some cases with a deep-felt belief that this was ordained by the Creator.

Some cattlemen adopted the romantic notion that they, as well as their vocation, were part of the region's natural environment. Newcomers who desired change were branded as misinformed interlopers who would eventually face retribution in the form of drought. The feeling of some ranchers that their calling had a definite moral sanction is suggested by the recorded sentiments of one long-time rancher who wrote, after witnessing the breaking of the prairie sod near his ranch in 1904, that it was 'heartbreaking to see these awful wounds appearing on this beautiful prairie.'[9] Another old stockman who strongly resented his farm neighbours consoled himself with the belief that when he was 'called to the "Last Great Groundup" ' and the land became worn out and useless, it would not be recorded that he 'was the one who turned it upside down.'[10]

The farmers appealed to a morality that was much more in step with the buoyant enthusiasm of nation-building gripping the country during the first decade of the twentieth century. It was generally accepted that every man had the right to gain his independence and prosperity on 160 acres in the nation's great western estate. Not only was it implicitly believed that this vast expansion of independent freehold farmers strengthened the country's democratic and moral fibre, but the settlement of millions on the western prairies was considered essential to Canada's economic development. There was also general confidence that 'modern' farming methods, that is, new dryland farming methods, permitted colonization of almost the entire area, particularly the open southern plains, and for a decade the weather conspired to lend credence to such optimism. 'Progress' and 'settlement' came to be synonymous terms. In this atmosphere the cattlemen who argued for restricted settlement, or predicted drought and spoke gloomily of disaster, were entirely out of harmony with national feeling and therefore received little attention and even less understanding.

Evidence of the frustration consequently felt by the ranch community at being unable to respond effectively and of the general animosity towards the settler who was destroying the range is revealed repeatedly in ranchers' correspondence. With undisguised rancour one rancher wrote of his unwanted neighbours: 'men of this class are not worth much' and unfortunately 'birds of his [the squatter's] feather flock together, and if he does not bring them he may breed them.'[11] The correspondence between William Cochrane, part owner of the Little Bow Cattle Company near High River, and A.E. Cross spans the period of most intense settlement from 1901 to 1906 and offer revealing comment. In June 1901 Cochrane concluded a letter devoted mainly to the purchase of additional brewery shares with the information that: 'It does nothing but rain here. It is drowning the settlers. There are five shacks below me on the creek and two just above me, all with dogs. We must pray for a drought.'[12] Several weeks later he reported to Cross the success of their invocations. 'My farmers in Squaw Coulee are sick, two have pulled out and one is left with his woman and seven months old kid. [The weather] is dry and the cattle have skinned out with the range cattle – his heart is on the ground.' Cochrane's relief was short-lived and the next summer he reported that there were more settlers than ever. In the summer of 1904 he was again encouraged by the dry weather. 'The country is drying up very fast, settlers tongues [are] hanging out for want of water.'[13] At the same time he reported that his cattle were in 'great shape' and that he expected the year's calf brand to equal 600 head. But the tenacious settlers managed through the drought, eventually to elicit Cochrane's frustrated oath: 'these b-d sod-busters have driven me to drink.'[14]

On occasion the ranchers' hostility burst forth in caustic prose in the local press. In one such instance an irate rancher in the Pincher Creek area protested against being obliged to help pay for roads far back into the hills so that farmers could haul their supplies and produce more easily: 'if settlers were mad enough to live up in the mountains they had only themselves to blame for their travelling difficulties.'[15] As the debate continued in the *Pincher Creek Echo* the same rancher questioned the general intelligence of the offending district councillor who defended such settlement.

For many years Mr. [S.] has been to me a physiological and psychological curiosity, but I often wonder that he has not discovered long ere this, that his vapid and vacuous vaporings are always in vain, inasmuch as they are powerless to remove or obliterate plain hard facts, have no force with the things that count, and are generally charitably attributed to the well known malign effects and influence of a disordered digestion.[16]

With this the debate terminated. In this district, the original home of the Canadian ranching industry, emotions regarding the farm-ranch question were always easily aroused. As late as 1911 the main speaker at an 'Old Timers' banquet in Pincher Creek felt constrained to call upon his audience to abandon the suspicion and distrust of the farmer and businessman characteristic of former years, and expressed his hope that the latter had won the confidence of the old ranchers with the success of their undertakings.[17]

The phenomenal settlement of the grazing country between 1900 and 1910 completely changed the region's social and cultural structure. Not only did the economic pursuits of most newcomers set many of them aside from the original inhabitants, but their mainly American origin gave them a political and social background that contrasted sharply with the British and Canadian ranch establishment. This new population was not prepared for the most part to become British Canadian, or even Canadian unless on their own terms. They were proud of their democratic tradition and republican institutions and viewed themselves as the agents of progress, and in some cases of manifest destiny, in the Canadian west. Their preferred model was, in short, the 'American' and not the 'British' way. As the noted student of North American migration, Marcus Lee Hansen, has observed, the people who found their way north were used to moving where opportunity seemed to beckon; they 'viewed the continent as a whole' and for them the border held no real meaning.[18] The confident attitude of this new population is well illustrated in the tone of an article that appeared in *The Cosmopolitan* in 1903 entitled 'The Americanization of the Canadian Northwest.' The author spoke of the great changes wrought by American enterprise and predicted eventual annexation to the United States as the American population continued to expand:

since 1890 it is estimated that there has grown up in Western Canada a community of one hundred and thirty-five thousand American farmers, growers of wheat, corn and flax – settlers inbred with not only the American spirit of enterprise, but with American ideals of government and American aspirations for the future of the country which they have made their home.

With the coming of the Americans the lethargic first dwellers of Manitoba and the Territories have been awakened as from a dream. The busy sound of hammers has become heard throughout the land, marking the erection of new buildings and of barns to store the grain, and the splutter of machinery in the wheat fields has told of new methods in harvestry.[19]

In the foothills country this 'American' presence added another dimension to the rancher-settler relationship. Some cattlemen feared the danger of cultural assimilation as a menace second only to the economic threat posed by the arrival of thousands of American farmers. Duncan McEachran expressed the feeling of many original ranchers in the foothills when he informed his fellow shareholders: 'I would prefer when we go out of business that British people reap the benefits of our struggles and anxieties instead of as may happen it be given over to the Mormon Church [as was the case with the Cochrane Ranch] as American speculators.'[20] A.E. Cross was also concerned about Americans acquiring the ranches of departing Britons and announced his preference 'to have good British people as neighbors much rather than inferior, moving Americans.'[21] While all ranchers found it distressing that the farmers seemed to receive government preference, the vexation of some was intensified by the fact the farmers were Americans, whom they often considered as foreigners rather than fellow North Americans.[22] In the words of the wife of one rancher regarding the period before farm settlement, 'the first families who came in were different from those who came after. They were a superior class of people who came first – no foreigners except an occasional Mexican.'[23] When the stockmen's solicitor, R.B. Bennett, warned the Canadian Club in Montreal of the threat to British institutions posed by this vast influx of Americans, he echoed the sentiments of many of his fellow members of the Ranchmen's Club.[24]

Such concern grew easily from the anti-American bias that had existed in the region for a full generation. The police who came west to establish Canadian claim to the region and to remove the scourings of the American frontier from Canadian soil remained apprehensive about mass American settlement from the beginning.[25] Like many of the original ranch population, they had always been instilled with the idea that they were building a British-Canadian west and on occasion wondered whether Americans should be excluded or restricted.[26] In 1912 the Ranch Inquiry Commission was confronted not only by demands that leases be made more permanent, but that they be restricted to British subjects. This provision was eventually included in the order-in-council that gave effect to the Commission's recommendations.[27] This thread of anti-Americanism within the ranch community is woven throughout the entire period and it coloured what was essentially a conflict of economic interests.[28]

Aware that they had become a minority within their own region and aware that their community had also suffered an absolute decline in its upper social echelon commencing with the South African War, some in the community endeavoured to redress the population imbalance through a scheme to increase the number of British ranchers. While ranch pupils from Great Britain had been accepted on some ranches since the early eighties, the idea of a proper 'Ranche School' for Englishmen originated in 1904. A draft proposal circulated among some more prominent ranchers described the main object of the non-profit school as the preparation of Englishmen from sixteen to eighteen years of age for a ranching life through a three-year program of instruction wherein 'they would be taught everything connected with a ranche, the value of land under different circumstances, the business of a ranche and the ordinary labor on a ranche.'[29] Any boy leaving the school to establish a ranch was to receive the assistance of the manager and the 'board of visitors' as well as an expert appointed at the expense of the school to evaluate and report on the chosen property. The proposal stated that 'the right kind of names on the board of visitors' was essential to the enterprise and suggested that, in addition to the five founders, the Anglican Bishop of Calgary, the Premier of the North-West Territories, the Chief Justice, and another prominent man be secured. It was believed that there were hundreds of young Englishmen of means who would be attracted to such a school. The type of young Englishmen the promoters had in mind was quite explicit.

The preliminary expenses would pay the cost of sending an agent to England, his salary there for three months, advertising during that time in 'The Field,' 'Land and Water,' 'The Country Gentleman,' and the Eton, Harrow, Winchester and Westminister school magazines. The printing and sending out to the landed interests of a prospectus which would show the objects of the school, the great advantages of climate, sport, etc.[30]

The ranch school for public school boys and the sons of the English landed gentry that was eventually established six years later by the Reverend H.B. Gray, DD, Warden of Bradfield College, Berkshire, was somewhat less pretentious than that envisaged by the promoters of the original scheme.[31] The Bradfield College Ranche for Bradfield Boys, situated near Calgary, restricted itself to the training of boys mainly from one public school and its curriculum was designed to provide the kind of training required for a smaller stock-raising enterprise combined with the growing of some crops. None the less, the emphasis was placed on ranching; as Dr Gray explained in his prospectus, his ranch was not in a wheat-growing district. 'The exclusively wheat-growing regions are generally situated in the monotonous and "prodigious plains," eastward of Calgary, and have often a depressing effect on the settler.'[32] He stressed that the Bradfield ranch was located 'in a high valley amid the scenery of an English park, with low trees and hills.'

The purpose of the ranch was described as twofold: to dispel the 'remittance man' image through the provision of a program of instruction to ensure the greatest likelihood of success for those Britishers embarking on a ranching or agricultural career and to help save the region from complete American dominance. 'Though no one ought to grudge our American cousins their enterprise, foresight, and progressive sagacity, yet it would appear the bounden duty to the British Empire of those in positions of trust and influence in England to act as pioneers in encouraging the best of our sons to people and control the immense tracts of our great Dominions.' The Bradfield College Ranche, however, proved unable to fulfil the desire of many cattlemen to stem the American agrarian advance through recruitment of more congenial British colonists. The first three pupils of 1909 were joined by four others the following year and the pattern was repeated with four or five students being added each year to 1913. The resources of only one public school proved insufficient to supply the twenty-five to thirty students yearly as originally intended and the project was abandoned. With the outbreak of the war nearly all those who had come out returned to enlist, and none returned.[33]

Nevertheless, despite their inability to maintain or improve their numerical position in face of the mass agrarian influx, the foothills ranching community remained a viable social group throughout this period. Though the established country squirarchy proposed by Professor W. Brown of the Ontario Agricultural College at Guelph[34] did not emerge in the western grazing country, a British core and a broader British façade were much in evidence. It seems that for some people the façade became increasingly important as social stress within the community mounted.[35] Visitors to the foothills ranching country near Calgary at the turn of the century observed that many cattlemen had 'established themselves in charming homesteads, surrounded by the same kind of comfort and refinement which Englishmen associate with the life of an English country house.'[36] Such comfortable surroundings were made possible by the special economic characteristics of the stock industry which, unlike farming, made the country estate ethic workable. First, the establishment or purchase of a cattle ranch required considerable capital and therefore, from the outset, attracted those with greater resources and relative social preferment. The second important factor setting the ranch apart from the farm was the matter of labour. The large old country farm with its overseer, labourers, and tenants could not be duplicated on the Canadian prairies, as the singular failure of all such attempts bears mute witness.[37] Those who wanted to farm were not inclined to take permanent employment on a gentleman's farm in a region where they might easily acquire land of their own. The ranching enterprise, on the other hand, was different; it was much more congenial to the establishment and maintenance of a country estate. Those who would not labour on farms would herd cattle on a ranch, for even in its own day there was a mystique about the cattle industry that ensured a ready supply of 'cowhands.' The retinues, including governess, cook, foreman, and cowboys, reached substantial proportions on some larger ranches. The medium-sized Quorn Ranch, for example, maintained a staff of fourteen people from May to October 1891, for a combined wage of $495 per month. Five employees were retained with pay throughout the winter and often several others were allowed to remain and work for their lodging.[38] Thus, as a gentleman rancher, the proprietor could maintain the large household he was accustomed to in Great Britain or the Eastern Townships of Quebec. Cattle-ranching permitted retention of the manager-employer relationship as well as a leisured life-style and actually assisted in perpetuation of an imported social system that set the ranch community apart from the general social development of the agrarian frontier. In their comfortable homes with a Chinese cook and a maid or governess to look after their children, members of the cattle compact lived in a manner that contrasted sharply with the agriculturist in his sod or frame house situated on the often treeless and windswept plain.

The leisured social pursuits of the ranch establishment continued throughout this decade as they had in the past. While cricket seems to have disappeared and riding to hounds was stopped because of farmers' barbed wire fences, horse racing continued to flourish and cattlemen's polo teams reached their greatest proficiency and acclaim. In the winter the trek to warmer climates, which by this time had the force of twenty years' tradition, was continued.[39] Other ranchers like A.E. Cross, whose business interests kept them closer to home, purchased homes in Victoria where their families might spend vacations on the Pacific coast.

During this decade Calgary consolidated its social and economic dominance of the southern hinterland and the cattlemen's influence within the regional metropolis became increasingly important as the cattle industry's Montreal connections became more tenuous. In the social context the ranch establishment remained pre-eminent. Already some of their number had gained the sanctity conferred by aspiring newcomers through the title 'Old Families.' The Ranchmen's Club continued to flourish as the club, at a time when its American equivalent, the Cheyenne Club in Cheyenne, Wyoming, had long been in decline. The club's continued acceptance is suggested in the financial statement for the year ending 30 April 1914 which shows 201 members on the rolls and a net profit of $7744.28 on revenues amounting to $23,650.09.[40] While those whose livelihood depended solely on the stock industry were a small minority of the membership by this time, there were many others who supplemented their city business endeavours with substantial investments in the cattle industry and who were thus both sympathetic to the stockmen and well acquainted with the problems faced by the industry. Consequently, while the club remained non-political by constitutional definition, it continued to function as a useful vehicle through which the close social and economic ties between the cattle compact and the region's business and professional élite were fostered and maintained.

Some ranchers who spent much of their time overseas and others whose ranches were too distant from the city to warrant membership in the Ranchmen's Club continued as they had done throughout the nineties to make the Alberta Hotel their city residence. Z.M. Hamilton, who was editor of the *Calgary Herald* for several years after 1900, in his reminiscences of the place of this hotel in Calgary and ranch society noted that the guests were mainly men from the range. 'There were tall lean Englishmen of the type supposed to denote

Norman ancestry, some in riding breeches, the cut of which indicated Bond Street, and others in the "chaps" and belled spurs of the cattle country.'[41] In all, whether observed at the Ranchmen's Club or at the Alberta Hotel, at the polo matches or in the confines of their sandstone homes in the foothills, the cattlemen's fraternity as it existed in the Canadian west before World War I seems neither to evoke the image generally associated with the American ranching frontier nor to fit the 'stampede' stereotype that has subsequently developed.[42]

In keeping with the Canadian ranch community's peculiar ethos was a strong imperial bias among both its British and Canadian components which remained undiminished, as shown in their response to the South African War and later to World War I. Rumours of impending war in the Transvaal brought forth the notice in the Macleod Gazette from R. Ryan, a cattleman and veteran of the Indian Mutiny: 'let all British subjects at home and abroad exclaim, with one voice, that we are ready to meet Boers, Metabeles and all other outsiders who are enemies of our gracious Queen.'[43] When war was officially declared, Lionel Brooke, Ryan's neighbour and one of the first to begin ranching in the area, immediately outfitted himself and proceeded directly on his own to South Africa. The enthusiasm of others followed more regular channels. Among former British military men in the foothills were many reservists who returned to their old units. Others with no direct military commitment like Harry Adams, a nephew of Lord Kitchener, were led to South Africa by strong feelings of imperial solidarity and family tradition.[44] Many of the much-maligned remittance men also answered the call of empire, most never to return to the Canadian west. Several hundred other Canadians and Britons joined the ranks of the Canadian Mounted Rifles and Lord Strathcona's Horse, both recruited in the region. The example of the eighteen volunteers who left Pincher Creek for South Africa was duplicated in all the foothills communities between Calgary and the American boundary. Enlistments greatly thinned the ranks of the police and to a lesser extent of the English ranching community and additional cowhands had to be recruited from among incoming farmers.

While subsequent memorial services in the town of Pincher Creek honoured the loss of three of its young men in a minor engagement near Heuning Spruit, a railway defence point on the main rail line south of Johannesburg, overall casualties among the foothills soldiers and cavalrymen were not enormous.[45] However, the loss suffered by the ranch community was greater than casualty figures indicate. Some of those who enlisted returned to Great Britain after the war and a number of ex-policemen, such as Colonel S.B. Steele, remained with the imperial forces, while a few prominent ranchers such as Herbert Samson, co-owner of the XY ranch, remained in South Africa, where they felt they could continue their ranching careers free from the nuisance of incoming farmers.[46]

The effect of the South African War on the ranching community foreshadowed the dramatic effect that the imperial call to arms had a decade and a half later with the outbreak of World War I. In the interval, the military tradition brought to the foothills country by the early settlers and carried forward with the formation of Captain Stewart's Rocky Mountain Rangers in 1885 and Lord Strathcona's Horse in 1899 was maintained within the region's reserve cavalry units. Military sports days like that sponsored by C Squadron of the 15th Light Horse of High River, in which one of their number offered to meet all comers in the bayonet and sword contest, were popular events.[47] In a letter written during the 1909 naval scare to the president of the Navy League in London requesting membership and organizational information, A.E. Cross asserted that though the region was far from the sea the people 'are very patriotic to the British Empire when an occasion arises...'[48] The military heritage of some ranch families was continued from their new homes in the Alberta foothills through sons returning to attend school in Great Britain or going to the Royal Military College at Kingston.[49]

While the economic contest between rancher and farmer in the foothills was coloured by the contrasting social values of the protagonists, the agrarian advance in the southern and southeastern portion of the grazing region resulted in an essentially straightforward economic contest. During the late 1890s, significant numbers of American cattlemen from Montana began to move into the region around Medicine Hat, the Cypress Hills, and Swift Current. The movement from the crowded southern ranges grew after the turn of the century and included both large companies and small stock-growers.[50] The British and Canadian group, always numerically smaller in the southeast, was completely submerged. (See Table 14.) There was a limited movement of ranchers from the foothills to the southeastern plains, but most foothills ranchers, confronted with only the choice of selling or moving east, chose the former rather than going to what they considered to be inferior and less pleasant country. With the rush of American farmers into the south after 1900 the farm-ranch competition that increased in tempo differed in one respect from the foothill contest in that the contending parties were both comprised mainly of Americans. It was thus on the dry southern plains of the Canadian cattle kingdom that the American grazier and dry-lander enacted in a somewhat less turbulent manner the last chapter in the struggle initiated a quarter of a century before far to the south. While there remained an underlying economic unity that bound together ranchers throughout the entire region as they sought redress for common problems, it is evident that the ranching community in the Canadian west after 1900 was composed of two dissimilar social groups. American ranchers had formed an important part of the Canadian ranching community from the

TABLE 14

Birthplace of population in ranch country other than native-born 1885-1911

		British Isles	United States	Ontario	Quebec	Maritimes	Manitoba	Europe
Alberta	1885	1,164	420	1,134	476	233	507	170
	1891	4,041	1,215	4,473	906	858	842	785
	1901	7,120	10,972	11,420	2,506	1,294	1,097	11,767
	1911*	23,685	22,856	16,707	1,973	3,183	1,285	14,483
Assiniboia	1885	5,635	481	6,967	717	615	1,013	365
	1891	7,714	110	8,209	725	554	1,201	2,970
	1901	9,446	1,887	15,241	1,229	894	2,076	16,855
	1911*	13,216	15,281	20,614	2,455	1,194	3,500	11,126

SOURCE: Census of the Three Provisional Districts of the North-West Territories (1884–5); Census of Canada (1891, 1901, 1911)

* The data for 1911 are based on the different boundaries that emerge from formation of Alberta and Saskatchewan in 1905. The census districts of Calgary, Ft Macleod, and Medicine Hat in Alberta and Moose Jaw and Assiniboia in Saskatchewan were selected for the 1911 statistics. This is an area that almost exactly covers the grazing area and as such represents more appropriate boundaries than the somewhat more extensive Provisional Districts of Alberta and Assiniboia, from which the earlier figures are drawn. The 1921 census does not identify 'American-born.'

beginning, but it was not until after 1900 that they became a numerous or socially and economically significant group. The growing American ranching community remained concentrated in the south while the once dominant British-Canadian cattlemen remained in the western foothills. From this time the evolution of two somewhat different ranching societies can be observed. In addition to the different social base there was also a minor variation in economic orientation between the two communities. In the south-east the range cattle industry remained dominant and ranchers looked more to the Chicago market, while in the foothills the cattlemen decreased the size of their operations but continued to concentrate on preparing quality cattle for the British market. This regional economic variation within the cattle country is reflected in the different emphasis within the minutes of the stock associations in the two areas.[51]

In all, the changes within the cattle empire during the decade 1900-10 were fundamentally the consequence of massive agrarian settlement. The dramatic increase in population which resulted in creation of two new provinces introduced a new political framework and at the same time changed the region's economic base. Similarly, the primacy of the old social order declined. The vast majority of the new settlers were American, making the rural areas of southern Alberta, apart from the political system, not much different from western farm states to the south. In the foothills and in Calgary the remnants of the old cattle kingdom survived with a strength still vastly greater than their numbers, but a gradual departure of the leading families to the west coast and to Great Britain was already apparent. Many smaller stockmen at lower levels on the social ladder had become mixed farmers and already the social distinctions between this group and their newer farm neighbours were beginning to blur. It was to be another two decades before the decline ran its full course.

Ironically, the old Canadian cattle kingdom, hitherto considered to have been simply an economic and social adjunct of the American west was, if anything, one of the main bulwarks of the British tradition in the southwestern prairie region. The society that the cattlemen established and maintained in the southwestern foothills until World War I diverged from the social and political norm of the general farm population, and it did not replicate the cultural tradition of the American ranching frontier.

PART III

THE CATTLEMEN AND THE NEW WEST 1911–22

7

A new government and a new policy
1911–13

The onset of the second decade of the twentieth century brought a new political dilemma to the cattle country. The main issue in the prairie west during the 1911 federal election campaign was reciprocity. The reciprocity proposals that the Liberals presented to Parliament in January 1911 provided for free trade between Canada and the United States in a long list of natural products and some selected manufactured goods. From the cattlemen's point of view the attraction of such an agreement was duty-free access to the immense Chicago beef market. Enticing though the proposal was, its proponents were of the wrong party – the party of the farmer and open settlement, and worst of all, of Frank Oliver. At first it seemed that the lure of the Chicago market might be strong enough to lead many ranchers to abandon their longstanding support of the Conservative party. Aware of the uncertain feeling in the cattle country, the Conservative incumbent, John Herron, a former policeman and one of the region's earliest ranchers, sought to hold the enthusiasts for reciprocity by announcing support for the principle in his nomination acceptance speech. 'I see a good many dangers in Reciprocity,' he declared, 'but I see enough good in it to influence my choice. The greatest advantage, in my opinion, is that if the people do not find it to work out well it can be cancelled by a stroke of the pen.'[1]

But as the debate progressed into the summer of 1911 there emerged another consideration that evoked deep concern by many ranchers. The opponents of reciprocity charged that the agreement would result in severance of the British tie as well as economic subordination and eventual annexation to the United States. At the same time, statistics began to appear that threw some doubt on the alleged advantage of the Chicago market. It was reported that cattle production in the United States during the decade 1900 to 1910 had increased fifty-seven per cent and that this increase, which was greatly in excess of the population increase, meant that Canadian producers could expect growing competition rather than a growing market. A much-quoted publication of the United States Senate (no. 862), which stated that 'the free listing of live-stock benefits farmers and stock raisers on both sides of the line, but probably those in the United States get the larger benefit,' confirmed the suspicion of many.[2] The fear of American competition and the threat to the British connection were the same concerns that had led cattlemen to oppose vigorously the Liberals' 1887 'Commercial Union' platform.[3]

The evolution of the ranchers' attitude towards reciprocity is well illustrated by A.E. Cross. In the early spring he informed the Chicago livestock commission firm of Clay, Robinson and Company: 'as a whole, I think that the reciprocity agreement will be a good thing, more especially over the western half of Canada. Speaking as a manufacturer, of course, we believe in protection on manufactured articles. The agreement so far has not materially altered the position of the manufacturer in Canada ...'[4] With regard to the cattle industry, Cross explained that the opening of the United States market would do away with the basic problem faced by the Canadian stockmen of too few buyers to ensure satisfactory competition. Yet by the summer of 1911 Cross had decided to vote against the agreement. A subsequent confidential assertion by W. Fares of Gordon, Ironside and Fares Co. Ltd that had the duty not existed, at any time in 1911 'we could have brought in beef from the U.S. much cheaper than the price current here,' may have led Cross to reappraise the economic value of the agreement to the cattle industry and thus bolstered the decision that he had already made on political grounds.[5]

It was soon evident to the farm press in the southwest that the cattlemen formed the only important group in the region that had misgivings about the proposed reciprocity arrangement. Throughout August, Liberal papers endeavoured to demonstrate to the stockmen that access to the Chicago market would mean better prices. In a leading editorial on 22 August the *Medicine Hat News* told the rancher that 'his loyalty, and his devotion to Britain and Canada, [would] not be minimized or dwarfed because of that extra $10 on each steer' which the agreement was alleged to assure. Cattlemen were urged to give the arrangement a try. Later in the month the Honourable C.R. Mitchell, Alberta Attorney General and Medicine Hat's elected representative in the provincial assembly, read to southern audiences letters from American commission firms to Canadian ranchers which outlined the advantages of the Chicago market and invited patronage, as evidence of the kind of competition and improved prices that reciprocity would bring.[6] Coupled with their economic arguments, Liberal politicians and their press supporters made persistent efforts to refute the charges of disloyalty that became more frequent as the campaign advanced.[7]

The Liberals approached the cattlemen in the Ft Macleod-Pincher Creek area with the same arguments and assurances, but in this constituency their task was compounded by the fact that the Conservative incumbent, one of the region's prominent ranchers, had declared himself in favour of reciprocity. Their consequent tactic was to declare that John Herron was at heart opposed to reciprocity and their assertions in this regard were assisted by the conflicting statements made by some ranchers on the Conservative Association's executive who stridently argued that the Liberal government's naval policy and free trade with the United States would lead to the break-up of the empire.[8] On election day the majority of electors in the Ft Macleod constituency registered their approval of the Liberal government and the reciprocity bill, as did the voters in all other Alberta constituencies except Calgary, which favoured R.B. Bennett and the Conservative party. Outside the prairies the Liberals fared less well and the Conservatives were returned to power for the first time since their defeat in 1896.

Although Herron lost the Ft Macleod riding to the Liberals, most ranchers remained firmly in the Conservative fold, as polling statistics demonstrate.[9] Though some cattlemen were prepared to concede the advantages of reciprocity, many, given their anti-American bias, felt that the potential economic advantage was more than offset by the close integration with the United States that reciprocity promised to bring. But above all, most ranchers were not prepared to support what they considered to be a farmers' party. Their enmity towards Frank Oliver and his pro-settlement policies had been consistently expressed at every federal election from the date of the first Liberal victory in 1896.[10]

In 1900, ranchers had attempted to unseat Oliver, with R.B. Bennett as their standard-bearer. In the words of Bennett's main organizer in the south, 'the ranching country was Conservative. The cattlemen and their retainers could be relied upon to support the candidature of Mr. Bennett'; the main task in the south was therefore to counter the Mormons' Liberal vote.[11] The latter task proved impossible and Oliver's strong plurality in the north again tipped the balance in his favour. Cattlemen fought the next contest in 1904 with renewed hope, for an electoral redistribution since the previous election made Calgary and southern Alberta separate constituencies. Aware of the ranchers' virtual unanimity, the Liberal party's main western strategist, Clifford Sifton, attempted to persuade one whom he thought was an important member of the cattlemen's fraternity to run as the Liberal candidate. Meat-packing magnate Pat Burns, however, declined Sifton's request with the explanation that to stand as a Liberal would be 'disastrous for my business.'[12] Burns's judgment proved sound, for both the Calgary and the southern Alberta riding went Conservative, the latter electing John Herron. The Conservative victory was repeated in both constituencies in 1908. The ability of the stockmen to win the Ft Macleod riding in the face of the more numerous farm population and the Mormons' solidly Liberal vote is explained by the fact that most new American farmers had not yet become Canadian citizens and in the 1908 election most of the Mormon population became part of the new oddly shaped Medicine Hat riding.[13] Having thus consistently voted Conservative since the first federal election in the Northwest Territories in 1887, cattlemen were not prepared in 1911 to break a voting tradition that went back a quarter of a century.[14] During the entire Liberal administration only two members of the ranch establishment, George Lane of the Bar U and A.B. Macdonald of the Glengarry Ranche Company, actively and openly assisted the Liberal cause, and both, as it happened, were recipients of the very rare closed leases that Sifton handed out with careful discrimination in 1905.[15]

Some months after the 1911 election the *Medicine Hat News* berated cattlemen for their economic short-sightedness, noting that George Lane, a firm believer in reciprocity, had just shipped a trainload of Alberta beef to Chicago, where it netted one dollar more per animal than he could have obtained in Canada despite the heavy duty.[16] The editor emphasized that without the duty the difference would have been at least $25. The ranchers were unrepentant, for at last after fifteen years the party of their choice was in power and they could anticipate important assistance to their beleaguered industry.

The cattle compact wasted little time in their endeavour to persuade the new Acting Minister of the Interior, Robert Rogers, to initiate a new government policy towards their industry. Early in the winter of 1912 a committee of stockmen waited upon the Prime Minister and the Minister of the Interior to indict the previous Liberal government's complete disregard of their business. They urged the new administration to establish a commission to investigate the ranching industry and to make recommendations as to the means by which the stock-raising business might be restored to its former favourable condition.[17] Though the cattlemen were confident that such a commission could be led to report favourably on their behalf, they none the less made private representations at the highest levels to ensure that they would get what they wanted. In February 1912 George Lane informed A.E. Cross from Ottawa:

I think I have done a good deal of good on this trip for the Ranchmen. I went to the Minister of the Interior last night, explained this situation to him and asked for a 21 year lease on the land, telling him the two year clause was what started the people disposing of their cattle. He told me he would do this. I want you to make application right away, and if necessary you should be ready to come down here not later than the fifth of

March. You want to force this right now. I have also held out that they should sell 10 percent of the lease at $1.00 [per acre].[18]

The ranchers' official request for redress was forwarded to the government through the Calgary senator, James Lougheed. In this memorial the WSGA charged that on the basis of a few wet seasons the previous government had adopted a policy of inducing settlement in all parts of the country regardless of whether they were suitable for agriculture or not, with the result that large-scale ranching enterprises were nearly all put out of business. There was now a great shortage of breeding cattle, a consequent shrinkage in the beef supply, and the highest consumer prices on record. In the association's view the situation could be remedied if those parts of the country most suitable for raising cattle were set apart from homestead lands and leased on a permanent basis to stock-growers. The WSGA also requested that their past president, Walter Huckvale, be named to the commission to be established to assess the situation.[19]

Cattlemen throughout the south-west expected a change in government land policy and the memorials of smaller local groups supplemented and lent strength to pressures being exerted by the Calgary ranch establishment and the WSGA. Ranchers around Pincher Creek, for example, urged the Department of the Interior to extend the forest reserve boundary south and eastward to meet the line of foothills settlement in order to prevent further settlement and so protect the remnants of the stock industry from being pushed from their last stronghold deep in the foothills. They requested quick attention to their situation and insisted, as cattlemen had done ritually for thirty years, that 'the land in question is only a stock country and totally unfit for farming in any shape or form.'[20]

Within the Department of the Interior a change of attitude was soon apparent. In March 1912 it was decided officially to discourage settlers' applications to invoke the two years' notice of cancellation in order to obtain properties within leaseholds.[21] From certain western officials came reports whose tone had not been duplicated since the days of William Pearce. The attitude of the new Inspector of Ranches, E.E. Taylor, is indicative. After a number of inspections during the spring and summer of 1912 he concluded: 'The stock business is fast going into decay and it is up to us to do everything we can to assist it.'[22] Taylor soundly condemned the policy of encouraging homesteading deep in the foothills. He informed Ottawa, with reference to the foothills region south and west of Pincher Creek, that he found the country to be a first-class stock-raising area, it being very rough and broken but with plenty of water and good grass. However, he noted that many homesteaders had gone into the hills, right up to the Rocky Mountains, and that none of them was making any success unless they went in for stock-raising. 'I am of the opinion,' he informed his superiors, 'that it is a crying shame that this country should be so broken up by homesteaders, they pick out the choice spot for grass and water and drive the cattle men to hills or out of business.'[23] Taylor described the would-be farmers, who had ruined the country's grazing potential and driven ranchers to desperation in their search for alternative range, as a 'miserable and worthless class of homesteaders who would starve to death if it were not for the stock men.' The implication was that the settlers made ends meet by stealing cattle from their ranch neighbours. Taylor recommended that all remaining lands in the western depths of the foothills be withdrawn from homestead entry and reserved for the ranchers through reasonable-sized leases.

The government seems to have been quite prepared to accede to such recommendations from within the Department of the Interior and from the cattlemen, but Conservative politicians were also conscious that the matter was one that could arouse sharp public controversy, especially if the government appeared to be acting in an arbitrary manner. To avoid the suspicion that Ottawa was simply acting at the ranchers' direction, it was decided to conduct an open public inquiry into the state of the ranching industry as the cattlemen had initially suggested, and then act upon the recommendations of this 'outside' body. The eventual recommendations of the three appointed commissioners, George H. Pope, Clarence F. Graham, and Walter Huckvale (the latter named at the request of the WSGA) were never in doubt. In addition to assessing the general condition of the ranching industry, the commissioners were specifically charged to report upon what tract, if any, should be withdrawn from homestead entry and held exclusively for grazing purposes, and the advisability of extending the permanency of leases.[24] Public hearings accordingly were held in the main centres throughout the ranching country from Willow Bunch, Saskatchewan, to Calgary, Alberta, during October and November 1912, and the cattlemen turned out in force to present their case.

The arguments and demands presented were hardly new; they had been announced with unfailing regularity to anyone who would listen since the 1890s. Ranchers condemned the government's unwise settlement policy, which they said encouraged homesteading on unfit lands, as well as the refusal to institute a satisfactory lease policy. Two essential remedies were demanded, first, that those areas in the south country where less than twenty-five per cent of the land was found fit for agriculture be withdrawn from settlement and held for the cattlemen, and second, that permanent leases of not less than fifteen years be granted within such districts so that required capital expenditures could be justified.[25]

The ranch establishment was aware that the government was sympathetic and predisposed to act in their favour, but understood that the hearings would have to demonstrate both widespread concern and unanimity within the ranch community itself. To this end the larger stockmen endeavoured to ensure representative attendance at the various meetings, to see that there was some degree of co-ordination among the various presentations and to make certain that sufficient complementary detail was included within the submissions. As A.E. Cross informed a smaller rancher: 'I think it is of great importance that you should be here to give evidence, as it will be the last chance as far as I can see to get leases put on a permanent basis, [as well as] anything else you want ...'[26] Cross further advised his friend to get together with his neighbours and come prepared with the necessary information. Of the details about which consensus emerged after subsequent meetings, several warrant mention. The cattlemen requested that leases be given only to naturalized British subjects, that lease size be limited to two townships (46,080 acres) for individuals and four townships (92,160 acres) for companies and partnerships, that the lessee have the right to purchase ten per cent of the land within the leasehold in the event that the lease was cancelled at the end of the period, and that where isolated settlement was found to occur in unquestionably grazing districts, the government endeavour to transfer the settlers to more suitable locations.[27]

Farmers at first seem to have taken little notice of the Commission's hearings and when full accounts of discussions at the meetings began to appear in the press, it was too late to organize counter-submissions. The ranchers' consensus was challenged from only two sources, and these registered differences of degree rather than kind. Sheepmen, the oldest and much-detested competitors for unsuitable agricultural lands, also sought to gain the favourable attention of the government. Stockmen endeavoured to maintain the absolute exclusion of this group and bitter debate raged between the two factions at the meetings throughout southern Alberta.[28] The second challenge came from the provincial government. While provincial authorities were prepared to concede assistance to the cattle industry, they were at the same time interested in maximum settlement, and in regions not wholly suited to agriculture they wanted to ensure a numerous ranch population rather than occupation by a few large companies. The Alberta Livestock Commissioner accordingly informed the Commission that closed fifteen-year leases should be granted but such leases should not exceed ten sections. The Livestock Commissioner presented the opinion that ordinarily six sections were sufficient to graze a herd large enough to support one family and the ten-section maximum would allow flexibility to account for varying topographic or other conditions. It was argued that leases of this size would ensure a sufficient number of families in a township to support a public school.[29] The Alberta government was still hoping to encourage what it defined as a 'mixed' farming community in such areas and remained convinced that beef production from such operations would eventually surpass that of the cattle ranches and at the same time be of much greater social benefit.

The report of the Ranch Inquiry Commission, published 11 January 1913, informed the government that the decline in the number of livestock in the grazing country during the preceding five years was at least seventy-five per cent, and that the reduction was particularly significant because it applied mainly to breeding stock.[30] The supply of beef had been maintained to some degree by importation of stocker cattle, making the Canadian grazing country increasingly dependent on outside sources of supply. The essence of the problem, though not explicitly stated in the Commission's report, was that most cattlemen were not prepared to invest the large sums required to build and maintain a breeding herd when range land was constantly diminishing and the lease system did not guarantee permanency beyond two years.[31] In recognition of these facts the commissioners presented the government with a number of recommendations that they thought would assist the industry's recovery. In keeping with the substance of the ranchers' requests they urged that areas where arable land did not exceed twenty per cent be set aside for grazing, that leases guarantee ten years' uninterrupted possession, that no applicant be granted a lease in excess of 24,000 acres, that the lessee be required to maintain a minimum of one animal for every thirty acres, that lease applicants owning adjoining lands be given preference to encourage the development of mixed farming, that leases be granted only to British subjects, and that present leaseholders be allowed to bring their existing leases under the new regulations. The commissioners also suggested that the dominion government communicate with the provinces with a view to the adoption of regulations more favourable to the ranching industry in the areas of taxation, herd and pound laws, and the fencing of road allowances. Accompanying the text was a map showing the areas throughout the south-west where it was proposed that no further settlement be permitted.[32]

Farmers in the grazing country suddenly began to feel that they had been outmanoeuvred. The hearings had no sooner concluded when the *Medicine Hat News* warned the government that it was 'playing with fire' when it proposed to grant long leases to ranchers, and expressed concern that the Borden government might not treat the farmer with the regard to which he was entitled.[33] As soon as farmers became generally aware of the Commission's proposals they began to petition the Department of the Interior against such measures. Those who discovered that they were in areas where further homesteading was not to be allowed were especially alarmed and feared they might be driven from their lands. One group of thirty-one recent homesteaders south-east of Medicine Hat appealed to the government not to declare their region a free range area. Explaining that they had already taken one or more satisfactory crops from the land, the petitioners added optimistically that they had advanced past the experimental stage and had proven the country's suitability for agriculture. On the basis of this success the homesteaders informed Ottawa that they

viewed with alarm any thought of the district being declared a free range country, as ... it would create conditions under which it would be impossible for us to follow the occupation of farming with success we therefore appeal to your Department to protect us, and our holdings by not granting the request of the ranchers, but to allow the district to remain as at present, with benefit to the Dominion and district, and help us to become loyal and prosperous subjects of his Majesty King George V.[34]

A letter from a local of the United Farmers of Alberta protested that the Ranch Inquiry Commission had listened only to the 'wealthy cattle owners.'[35] The secretary of another protesting farm group informed the Department of the Interior: 'In wording the petition I have endeavoured to temper with moderation the zeal exhibited at the mass meeting held to take some steps to stay the proposed action. The settlers feel very keenly on this subject, and many things said at the meeting are unprintable.'[36] Supplicants informed the government that their municipality, which had grown to 1000 inhabitants from forty or fifty just three years previous, was in danger of being engulfed in one of the large ranching areas if the recommendation that lands containing less than one-quarter arable acreage be set aside for ranching was approved. If this came to pass it would not only exclude settlement from the considerable area of good farmland that remained in the vicinity, but the population would decrease and a return to frontier conditions would ensue. Settled farming country could maintain many more head of stock than the open range, farmers argued, closed leases were desired only by 'selfish men.'[37]

While many farmers were naturally apprehensive, the ranchers' general assertion was valid, for large tracts of the south-west were not suitable for agriculture and much of this territory had been settled unwisely. In addition to unfavourable government legislation cattlemen had also had to contend with unscrupulous 'locators' who made it their business to locate desirable quarter sections within leaseholds and then, for a fee or sometimes simply to increase settlement to a point where a cattleman was forced to abandon the area, directed newcomers to such parcels.[38] The increase of this practice throughout the spring of 1913 caused ranchers to press the government for speedy action on the Ranch Inquiry Commission's proposals.[39]

Despite the merits of the ranchers' case and the government's general sympathy for their cause, the strong reaction against the Commission's recommendations caused some hesitation. This caution was reinforced by the attitude of certain officials within the Department of the Interior. B.L. York, head of the Department's Timber and Grazing Branch, thought the commissioners had been too generous. He argued that within the tract proposed to be set aside for grazing was a considerable quantity of agricultural land; the withdrawal of such land from homestead entry would isolate existing homesteaders and prevent them from maintaining schools and churches, and consequently would lead to continuous bitter opposition from settlers within the tract as well as those without who desired homestead entry. He also cautioned that the Commission had not personally examined the territory shown on their map to be set aside and had been guided in their selection by ranchers living in the localities affected, who were naturally interested in having reserved as large a tract as possible. York forwarded repeated memoranda to his superiors outlining his objections and suggesting that provision of closed leases after inspection was sufficient to safeguard the ranchers' interests without setting aside an entire region in which further homestead entry would not be permitted.[40]

Growing opposition to the Commission's report complicated what had originally been planned simply as a public formality and caused the Minister of the Interior, W.J. Roche, to seek additional advice.[41] Roche approached A.E. Cross for his personal assessment of the recommendations. In view of Cross's previous exertions on the ranchers' behalf before the Commission, it is not surprising that his reply to the Minister, after consulting with certain of his ranch friends, was in favour of the commissioner's report.[42] The other person of whom the Minister sought advice was none other than William Pearce, on whom previous Conservative governments had relied.[43] In keeping with past practice and his profound interest in efficient land use in the south, his reply was detailed and it reflected the insight of almost thirty years' experience in the region. Given such an opportunity, Pearce could not resist a gibe at the policy of the former Liberal government, which he characterized as being devoted to demonstrating that the lease system in force from 1882 to 1896 was erroneous. Pearce was pleased to note that the intervening decade had demonstrated the desirability of closed leases and expressed his support in principle of the Ranch Inquiry Commission's report:

when I review closely the meteorological conditions which have existed during the past 30 years I can come to but one conclusion, that ... for probably 40 percent of what is considered the grazing areas the conditions have for 75 percent of that period proved sufficiently favourable to furnish a fair return to the farmer in the way of grain and fodder cultivation providing of course the soil and topographical conditions were suitable. There are some districts which during that time have not had the meteorological conditions fitted to produce a crop 25 percent of the time. No mixed farming settlement should be planted in any district except where at least fair crops can be obtained for at least two-thirds of the time.

Starting from this premise, Pearce examined each recommendation. With regard to the map delineating the lands to be reserved for grazing purposes, he observed that considerable change could be made that would fortify the government against the adverse criticism that Pearce knew from experience would inevitably ensue. There was only one provision of real concern to the stockmen to which Pearce took exception. He viewed the proposed 24,000-acre maximum for leases as excessive and suggested that a 12,000- to 15,000-acre maximum would be more appropriate as this was sufficient for a herd of 500 head and would encourage ranching operations of a more desirable size. In all, Pearce's characteristic reply was more complete and showed greater political awareness than did the Commission's report.

The grazing regulations which were finally approved by order-in-council several months later show the mark of Pearce's appraisal as well as that of the vigorous protests of certain farm groups. Under the new provisions, leases of up to 12,000 acres of vacant dominion lands unsuitable for agriculture were made available to British subjects at a rental of two cents per acre per annum. The new leases were closed to settlement during the ten-year period for which they were in force and at the end of the lease period, if the government decided to re-lease the lands covered, the holder of the lease had prior right to a renewal. Those with leases granted under previous regulations were entitled to relinquish their old lease if it had ten or more years to run, and have the new regulations apply regardless of whether or not the old lease was over 12,000 acres. In other words, previous lessees were favoured and could have leases of more than 12,000 acres.

Other important provisions included the obligation of the lessee within three years to build and maintain a herd equal to one animal for every thirty acres, as well as the requirement that at least twenty-five per cent of the herd be breeding stock. The latter was intended to discourage the less desirable feeder operations that had recently appeared in the south, whose practice was to ship thousands of inexpensive Mexican steers north, feed them for the summer on Canadian grass, and then market the stock in the fall. In an obvious gesture towards the leaseholders' farm and other neighbours, the lessee was required to enclose his lease with a suitable fence, and was denied lake, river, or creek frontage in excess of one mile for every four miles in the depth of his lease. In areas where several parties desired the same tract of land and where it would be an injustice to give the lease to any one person, and where it was also impracticable to divide the lands, the Minister was permitted to withdraw the land from homestead entry and reserve it for public grazing. The lessee was permitted to cultivate any portion of his leasehold so long as the purpose was to grow feed and not crops for barter or sale. In a token effort to encourage homesteaders to leave unsuitable lands in the grazing country, the regulations provided that the holder of an unpatented homestead could, after the Inspector of Ranches declared the land unfit for agriculture, sell his improvements to the rancher and be granted the right to re-enter for land elsewhere.[44]

While this legislation was a long way from reserving large sections of the south-west for grazing purposes only and forbidding homestead entry, as recommended by the Ranch Inquiry Commission, the new grazing regulations promised a degree of security that the ranching industry had not known for a decade and a half. Though many cattlemen had hoped for more, all recognized the significance of the gain that had been achieved. The new regulations moved one stockman to send his personal compliments to the Department of the Interior. 'I see no reason that the livestock industry will not grow rapidly if given a chance,' he wrote. 'We have suffered hard and long but now comes our rejoicing ...'[45] In his annual report the Inspector of Ranches stated that practically all stockmen seemed satisfied with the new regulations and that renewed zeal and energy were everywhere evident since the ranchers were assured the permanency of their leases.[46] This encouraging assessment was seconded by the Dominion Land Agent in Calgary, who praised the new regulations and called attention to the expansion of the Calgary stockyards to keep pace with the sudden surge in the livestock market.[47]

Coupled with the incentive created by a satisfactory lease policy was a newly buoyant beef market. Between 1911 and 1913 the price of beef practically doubled. In the latter year steers sold for 8½ cents per pound live weight, or from $100 to $200 per head, the highest prices ever known in the west.[48] The cause of this dramatic increase in price was the scarcity of cattle following depletion of the ranchers' herds. The Ranch Inspector judged that cattle were so scarce that there was hardly enough beef in Saskatchewan and Alberta to feed the local population let alone supply foreign markets. The situation roused a Calgary paper to report:

for several years ... the amount of stock available for market purposes has been continually decreasing with the result that meat prices have soared out of all reach of the common people, while in a great many sections of the country the grain which has been grown in such preponderance, to the exclusion of livestock, has been a drag on the market so that the farmers have been heavy losers.[49]

The paper urged agriculturists to go into stock-raising for their own and the public's benefit.

Beyond the encouragement offered by the new lease regulations and the return of good markets, the ranchers' confidence was restored most by the renewed political influence that came with their party's election victory in 1911. The new government had met their collective request to alter the lease system, and at the individual level ranchers understood that their persuasive power had increased and that henceforth their appeals would receive serious consideration. The cattlemen's favoured solicitor, R.B. Bennett, was the director of party patronage for the southern half of the province[50] and stockmen individually or through A.E. Cross were soon using their advantage to good effect.[51] In all, with permanent leases, soaring prices, and a government in whom they had confidence, it appeared to those ranchers who had survived the settlers' onslaught that the corner had been turned and that the cattle kingdom would yet survive.

8

Resurgent cattlemen and the sod-busters' retreat 1914–19

Expansion or contraction of the cattle industry was essentially determined by the availability or deficiency of land and markets. In 1914, with the vast improvement in cattle prices and a suitable lease system, the industry was poised for a period of growth. Hundreds of ranchers obtained new leases or changed their old ones to the new form and began to establish or increase their breeding herds. The confidence and prosperity that the decade brought to the cattle industry contrasts sharply with the homesteader's scepticism about the new government and with the disaster they eventually faced when confronted with the long-predicted dry cycle.

While the Conservative government's grazing lands policy was viewed with alarm by many, the ranchers' horizons had suddenly expanded by 1914 as the Department of the Interior set about translating the provisions of the new policy into functional administrative procedures. In this task the heavy hand of the Minister characteristic of Frank Oliver's administration was absent and federal officials were left more or less to themselves to work out the details of interpretation, procedure, and administration. Aware of the political sensitivity of the farm-ranch question in the south-west that had plagued them for the past thirty years, and because of the rather loose construction of some of the act's provisions, department officials proceeded slowly and it was several years before the new legislation was functioning efficiently. In general, the Department's efforts to make the regulations workable show a desire, particularly on the part of officials in the west, to arrive at an interpretation and administrative routine that were acceptable to ranch interests.

It was initially decided to administer applications for, and granting of the new leases entirely from Ottawa. Ranchers immediately complained that this was much too time-consuming. The Department therefore altered the procedure so that applications could be accepted by local dominion land agents, who were authorized to reserve temporarily all available land covered by the application. Final approval then came later from Ottawa, pending assessment of the property by the Inspector of Ranches.[1] Senior officials in Ottawa were never prepared to abandon final authority in the granting of leases to western officials. From the Minister's point of view there was an obvious political advantage to be maintained, but it seems also that there was always reluctance on the part of the Deputy Minister, the Commission of Dominion Lands, and the head of the Timber and Grazing Branch to trust fully the judgment of an Inspector of Ranches who often seemed overly sympathetic to cattlemen's interests.

Interpretation of some of the provisions proved a more fundamental problem than that of devising administrative routine. The Department quickly learned, for example, that the 12,000-acre assignment clause could not be made legally binding on those holding leases under the former regulations.[2] The 'stock homestead' clause in the Dominion Land Act posed an even greater difficulty. This recent provision permitted a homesteader in the southern region to earn the patent for his homestead by the substitution of stock in lieu of breaking and seeding. This clause made implementation of the new grazing regulations especially difficult. The Inspector of Ranches, G.M. Cloakley, immediately asked what constituted the difference between a quarter section suitable for a stock homestead and one which was suitable only for a grazing lease. Cloakley was left to make a purely subjective judgment whether a piece of land applied for would be more suitably used as a grazing lease or for homesteading under the stock clause. Departmental guidance as to how the decision was to be made confused the matter further. The Inspector was reminded, lest he be inclined to favour the big rancher, that if in the tract applied for there was sufficient suitable land for stock homesteads the land should not be recommended for a grazing lease, 'the object being to avoid as far as possible, granting leases for lands which are fairly fit for stock homesteads.'[3] It was suggested further that in the southern region the Inspector interpret his instructions liberally on the side of the applicant for a grazing lease, while elsewhere he was told to exercise care 'not to tie up under grazing lease, lands which settlers could profitably homestead under the Stock Clause.' Anyone familiar with the stock industry could see that there was a basic conflict here. Finally, in desperation, after being advised that he was not pointing out in his reports to the department whether or not land was fit for homesteading under the stock clause, Cloakley pleaded that he could not make any sense of Ottawa's directives.

to allow a Homesteader to take a Homestead under the Stock Clause it would be necessary for him to have sufficient grass to run cattle enough to make a living for himself and family during the whole year, and I might honestly say that I do not think that there is a Homestead or a quarter section of land in the Province of Alberta at least none that I have seen, which will carry sufficient stock during the period of [a] year ...[4]

Cloakley pointed out that additional adjoining lands would have to be reserved for the homesteader's cattle, as he could not survive on a quarter section. He advised his superiors that he could make no recommendations regarding lands suitable for stock homesteads until they could provide him with a definition of what was meant by 'Stock Homesteads.' In the end Ottawa was unable to formulate such a definition and henceforth the 'stock clause' in the Dominion Land Act seems to have been ignored.

The difficulty faced by the Inspector of Ranches typifies a problem which had confronted stockmen for over a quarter of a century. Few eastern officials outside the Department of the Interior's Timber and Grazing Branch appreciated how different the south-west was climatically from the rest of the prairie region, and they seldom understood the economic structure of the western beef-raising business. While it was widely agreed that the revival of the ranching industry should be assisted through the issuance of more permanent leases, many still seemed to harbour the deep-seated feeling that the big ranchers' resurgence should be a temporary phenomenon. For this reason they preferred the ten rather than the fifteen or twenty-one-year lease. Ranchers might have the land for a decade, while the settlement frontier paused and farming techniques were refined, before the push into the dry region resumed. The cattlemen's successful adaptation was not preferred, for his economic enterprise precluded further population growth. If cereal agriculture could not suceed then the next preferable alternative in the minds of most was the small 'mixed' farm or the small 'stock' farm. It was believed that this was not only desirable but in the long run inevitable as late arriving settlers were forced to take up poorer land.[5] There was thus an underlying concern in some quarters that the prospects of future homesteaders not be compromised and the region locked into a perpetual lease system.

Such anxiety was traditionally strongest within the Department of the Interior's Lands Branch and on occasion set this section at odds with the Timber and Grazing Branch. Conflict between these two branches as to the procedure to be followed on the cancellation or termination of a grazing lease provides a case in point. The practice until the summer of 1915 was simply to post a notice in the Land Office that such lands were available for homestead entry in the usual way. In the view of B.L. York, head of the Timber and Grazing Branch this procedure was quite unsatisfactory.

If a rancher desires to lease a cancelled ranche, or a portion thereof, he is obliged to line up in the Land Office with intending homesteaders when the land is thrown open. The result, most likely, would be that if he were first in line and applied for the whole tract, that many intending homesteaders who might be present would be dissatisfied, and, on the other hand, if he were not first, the homesteaders ahead of him would take up homesteads at different points in the tract, and thus spoil the tract for grazing.[6]

Since, in the case of all closed leases, the land had been reported unfit for agriculture before they were granted, York argued that it was hardly logical to open the land on termination of the lease on a first-come basis. He suggested that before such lands were opened another inspection be made and unless reason was found to change the original assessment, the land be reserved for grazing applications only.

The Commissioner of Dominion Lands opposed this recommendation. He asserted that a more satisfactory policy, and one that would be subject to 'very much less criticism,' would be to throw the land open to all applicants for leases or homesteads with the onus of proof as to the character of the land left to the individual applying. Each person should then be left alone to complete the duties required under his class of entry. The Commissioner's view represents the traditional laissez-faire attitude, that each individual had the right to judge the land for himself as well as the right to use the land for the purpose he chose, his success or failure not being the direct concern of the government. The Commissioner warned that

numberless cases can be cited where land said to be unsuited for agricultural purposes have been included in forest reserves, grazing leases, irrigation reserves and afterwards have been withdrawn from such reserves because of pressure being brought on the Department and the matter being closely investigated it was found that the lands were fit for agriculture.[7]

The Commissioner's implication that most of the closed lands could be farmed was not, however, accepted by the Minister of the Interior when he was compelled to adjudicate this difference of opinion within his Department. In view of the fact that it was compelled to send relief to drought-stricken settlers in the south during 1915, the arguments of the Land Office seemed strangely out of place and the Commissioner was curtly informed that the Minister was 'adverse to opening up for homestead entry lands which we know to be unsuitable for farming especially in the Southern country.'[8] He was informed further that the policy advocated by the Timber and Grazing Branch would be followed and instructed to include, in the notices advertising the availability of terminated or cancelled grazing leases, the warning that squatting on such grazing lands would not be recognized.

Another provision of the new grazing regulations that troubled officials was the British subject clause.[9] Initially there was some uncertainty whether a lease taken by a British subject could afterwards legally be transferred or assigned by its new owner to an American citizen. Despite instructions sent to ranch inspectors that the government would not allow such assignments,[10] there remained a question as to the legality of the Department's position with regard to companies incorporated under dominion or provincial law. Uncertainty regarding the Department's insistence that companies furnish statutory declarations showing the president or chairman and the majority of directors to be British subjects caused officials at one point to consider the War Measures Act of 1917 as a vehicle to support their action if challenged.[11] Reliance on such an awkward expedient was ended by a subsequent government decision to allow all but companies incorporated in enemy countries equal rights in the development of Canadian natural resources. As grazing lands were included within the broad definition of natural resources, the question was settled. Individuals making applications for leases were, however, still required to submit a statutory declaration of British citizenship.[12]

Though the new lease regulations were of sound intent, they were poorly formulated. As a result the new policy from the outset was plagued by conflicting interpretations and it was not until 1917 that the new system began to work efficiently. Nevertheless, such difficulties were overshadowed by the new feeling of confidence which the policy engendered in the ranching country. Cattlemen abandoned ideas of going out of business and made capital commitments that could not have been considered when the permanence of leases could only be guaranteed for two years. The increase in the numbers of leaseholders from 1780 in 1912 to 6105 in 1920 and the addition of over 2,500,000 leased acres as shown in Table 15 is evidence of the ranchers' change in attitude and of the success of the government's new policy.

The vast expansion of leased acreage was predictably accompanied by renewed animosity between ranchers and settlers in many districts. Petitions, complaints, and appeals directed to the Department of the Interior during the second decade of the twentieth century, like those forwarded to the Department in the previous twenty-five years, followed a definite pattern and reflect, at each stage, the relative strength of the contending parties. During the 1880s and 1890s protests had come mainly from would-be settlers opposed to the hegemony of the cattlemen. In the first decade after the turn of the century the balance shifted and appeals to the Department for redress came mainly from ranchers who alleged that they were being driven from the region. After 1912 complaints again came mainly from farmers and as such are a measure of the cattlemen's renewed political favour.

TABLE 15

Grazing leases 1912–22

Year	No. of leases	Acres					
		Manitoba	Saskatchewan	Alberta	British Columbia	Total	Yearly increase
1912–13	1,780	818	1,450,077	2,099,912	412,063	3,962,870	
1913–14	1,916	818	1,696,898	2,402,622	380,553	4,480,802	517,932
1914–15	2,457	24,843	2,106,222	2,330,110	392,380	4,853,555	372,752
1915–16	3,352	34,596	2,313,437	2,500,589	366,445	5,215,067	461,512
1916–17	4,060	64,399	2,724,368	2,509,527	391,170	5,689,464	474,397
1917–18	4,796	66,563	2,723,217	2,563,145	393,253	5,746,178	56,714
1918–19	5,346	86,033	2,824,654	2,850,002	410,606	6,168,295	422,117
1920	6,105	126,679	2,869,084	3,095,955	407,030	6,498,748	330,453
1921	6,201	140,629	3,021,556	2,908,215	417,234	6,487,634	–11,114
1922	6,518	135,837	2,911,365	2,879,504	415,246	6,341,952	–145,682

SOURCE: Canada, Department of the Interior, Annual Reports (1912–22) reports of the Deputy Minister

The nature of the farmers' concern during this period was indicated in the initial protests against the new lease regulations. Small groups of homesteaders in predominantly grazing areas knew that unless their communities were allowed to expand they would be unable to acquire or maintain desirable social services. One group in the Manyberries area, fifty miles south of Medicine Hat, protested that they were surrounded by a large grazing lease which contained much arable land. Urging that the land be opened to settlement, one farmer explained: 'We want neighbors – farmers who will check the weeds, we want schools, churches, stores, post offices, wagon roads, railroads, [and] coal mines.'[13] The Department of the Interior in turn advised that the land in question had been inspected before the lease was granted and declared unfit for agriculture, but in response to repeated appeals finally agreed to order a second inspection. The homesteaders, however, received no support from Cloakley, who reported after his inspection that while much of the land in question could grow good grain, rainfall was too deficient to assure continued success and the region should therefore remain closed. The Inspector of Ranches also informed the Department that J.H. Wallace, the rancher whose lease enclosed the settlers, had agreed to build a schoolhouse and pay the salary of a teacher to be selected by the homesteaders. He also agreed to allow the settlers' stock to run on his lease as well as to purchase whatever grain, hay, or green feed they were prepared to sell at market prices.[14] In Cloakley's and the Department's view this was a very fair proposition and the farmers' petition was denied. At the same time, in order further to protect his interests, Wallace requested and was granted a new ten-year closed lease to replace his former lease, which was subject to two years' notice. Not satisfied with Wallace's offer, the settlers made repeated requests and received continued refusals from the government over the next four years. At one point the homesteaders appealed to the Governor General with the slogan 'a farmer on each quarter section' to assist the Empire in its hour of need.[15] Other appeals directed to Prime Minister Robert Borden, Sir Wilfrid Laurier, and the Minister of Agriculture proved of no avail. The Department remained adamant and became increasingly annoyed at the homesteaders' persistent claim that the land in question was suitable for farming.

The debate between the Department and irate farm petitioners naturally centred upon the government's definition of land 'unsuitable' for agriculture and it underlines the observation made by other students of prairie settlement, that nowhere are contrasting environmental images more apparent than in reference to the Great Plains.[16] Here, literally, what was garden to the eye of one man was desert to another. Farmers who wanted lands set aside were never prepared to accept the technical judgments of people like William Pearce or G.M. Cloakley, whom they saw as guardians of vested interests. One agitated homesteader, who took exception to the Department's claim that land leased to the Sarnia Ranch Company was unsuitable for agricultural purposes, protested: 'I can assure you, Sir, on my oath, that is [the land desired] – I may safely say – *the best land for farming* purposes in the whole township! I live only about 100 yards from said land ...'[17] In the Bassano area, seventy miles south-east of Calgary, 300 farmers requested that Ottawa cancel seventeen leases totalling about 90,000 acres in their vicinity. In addition to presenting the usual arguments about ranchers' cattle trampling their crops and the need for a greater population to warrant building of roads and construction of schools, the settlers insisted that the area in question was good farm land capable of supporting 300 additional families.[18] Questioning the integrity of the Inspector of Ranches, the editor of the town paper asserted, after conducting his own investigation, that

we do not blame the holders of the leases for clinging most tenaciously to such rich and productive leases. With grasses belly deep in every direction these leases make the most excellent ranch lands, but any intimation – expressed or implied – that they are not rich agricultural land at the same time, cannot be construed as anything more nor less than a biased opinion activated by purely selfish interests.[19]

To its credit the Department stuck firmly to its belief that not all lands could be farmed, the editor's picture of 'belly deep grass in every direction' was not accepted, and this and other petitions were ignored.[20] This attitude was vindicated over the next few years as the worst period of drought experienced in the south-west since the early 1890s drove beleaguered homesteaders from the land. The drought also temporarily halted petitions seeking cancellation of the grazing leases.

While drought and government policy stayed the advance of the agrarian frontier in the south-west after 1912 and relieved the pressure on remaining grazing lands, improved beef markets further assisted the ranchers' recovery. In 1913 the price paid for choice export steers reached 7¾¢ per pound, leading the Alberta Livestock Commissioner to explain that 'the high prices that have prevailed during the last two years for all kinds of livestock, together with the unsatisfactory conditions that have attended the marketing of grain, have combined to create a keen interest in the production of livestock.'[21] The principal export market for the gradually increasing beef surplus in the Canadian south-west was Chicago, to which Canadian cattlemen finally gained duty-free access in October 1913. It was largely the influence of this market along with increasing local demand that held beef prices at their highest levels in history, even in face of the collapse of the traditional British trade. (See Table 16.) During 1915 and 1916 there remained an active demand and firm prices for all classes of livestock

TABLE 16

Exports of live cattle 1901–24

Year ended 31 March	Great Britain		United States		All countries	
	Number	Value	Number	Value	Number	Value
1901						8,777,123
1902	148,924	9,742,588	21,619	663,367	174,145	10,538,520
1903	161,170	10,842,438	5,699	233,206	171,809	11,282,831
1904	148,301	10,046,651	1,991	98,353	155,651	10,401,537
1905	159,077	11,047,092	2,130	134,252	165,201	11,338,431
1906	163,904	11,044,248	2,783	182,591	173,656	11,622,012
1907	149,340	10,200,137	7,360	470,490	161,220	10,922,105
1908	124,015	8,584,806	18,938	530,743	146,187	9,245,389
1909	143,661	10,115,793	13,194	507,027	159,868	10,734,330
1910	140,424	9,979,918	10,413	618,995	155,327	10,767,622
1911	113,795	7,942,144	7,024	450,267	124,253	8,521,979
1912	47,868	3,343,625	9,654	612,559	61,285	4,095,063
1913	12,069	913,954	22,959	1,064,357	38,887	2,183,311
1914	9,778	697,807	185,761	6,792,039	198,147	7,654,716
1915	0	0	149,604	8,736,700	151,821	8,851,496
1916	1,752	105,120	170,775	10,523,073	185,105	11,998,755
1917	0	0	104,979	6,824,905	107,110	6,959,440
1918	0	0	144,021	13,304,396	146,036	13,449,150
1919	0	0	268,724	29,135,247	271,579	29,346,027
1920	479	70,200	415,956	41,226,445	431,128	43,214,685
1921	131	19,350	221,278	19,759,329	223,689	19,989,370
1922	35,418	4,139,391	121,060	3,299,633	161,483	7,852,111
1923	25,758	2,809,796	199,272	5,609,998	229,237	8,742,373
1924	59,486	6,287,815	98,322	3,683,836	164,063	10,398,367

SOURCE: *Canada Year Book* (1905, 1910, 1920, 1925)

and the increasing registration of new cattle brands (2838 in 1916) is indicative of the increased popularity of the beef-raising business.[22] As in the past, the export industry continued to be dominated by the large producers. The huge 76 Ranch, which began operations in the Powder River country in Wyoming in the late 1870s, moved to Canada in 1886, and was eventually acquired by Gordon, Ironside and Fares in 1917 possessed over 250,000 acres of deeded and leased land. The 76 herds, which were maintained at 10,000 to 12,000 head, produced several thousand head for export yearly.[23] Other big ranches owned by George Lane, Pat Burns, the Cresswell Cattle Company, and the Matador Land and Cattle Company produced on a similar scale.[24]

Cattle prices continued high in 1917, with choice steers ranging from 9½ to 9¾¢, and average butcher steers from 8¼ to 8¾¢ at Calgary during June.

Equivalent prices for the same month at Winnipeg were 10¼ to 11¼ and 8¼ to 9¼¢ and at Chicago steers ranged from 8½ to 13¾¢ depending on quality.[25] In 1918, with the cessation of hostilities in Europe, beef prices dropped slightly and in 1919 dropped further in response to decreasing demand and increased supply, the result of the third year of drought, which forced cattlemen to reduce their herds for want of sufficient feed and pasture.[26] The downward trend in prices came just as production from newly established herds reached its peak and smaller stock-raisers were forced to sell their cattle in a declining market, thus reducing their own profits and at the same time contributing an excess supply which held prices down after 1920.

This cyclical pattern of high returns followed by a period of lower prices demonstrates a problem inherent in the beef industry. As prices rise more producers are attracted, as was the case between 1911 and 1914. Once farmers and others decide to enter the cattle business or vastly expand existing herds, it requires from three to five years before this decision results in a greater supply of cattle reaching the market. As the increased numbers of cattle begin to reach the market the beef price peaks and begins to decline. Eventually prices decline to a point where smaller producers are driven out of business. Then as the numbers of cattle taken to market decline, prices begin to rise and the cycle begins again. The peaks of four such distinct cycles occurred in 1884, 1902, 1915, and 1928.[27] While this underlying pattern imposes a certain regularity on beef price trends, it must be emphasized that other outside forces, such as the selling pressure motivated by the decline of available grazing lands, the new government lease policy, and the impetus of a war economy directly influence the duration of upward and downward price movements. It is evident also that the incidence of hardship imposed by this cycle weighs most heavily on the small producer, who commences stock-raising too late to gain the best prices and is compelled to sell in a falling market.

Alberta cattle exports during the period as well as the phenomenon of continued growth during three years of a declining market are shown in Table 17. The growing significance of local demand also is apparent. The vast majority of the cattle marketed during these years came from the ranching region. It seems also that beef production in Alberta equalled or surpassed that of Manitoba and Saskatchewan combined, especially if one excludes the cattle produced in the ranching country of south-western Saskatchewan.[28] As mentioned, a critical factor in the improved health of the immediate pre-war beef market was the opening of the Chicago market to Canadian cattle in 1913. Canadian stockmen had endeavoured intermittently to gain duty-free entry since the 1890s and many had shipped their cattle to this market over the preceding twenty years despite a prohibitive customs duty of twenty to thirty

TABLE 17

Cattle exports and local shipments 1912–20

Year	Exports*	Local shipments	Total
1912	56,544	78,708	135,252
1913	46,966	84,668	131,634
1914	60,572	87,635	148,207
1915	28,585	56,994	85,579
1916	33,568	108,349	141,917
1917	59,319	138,971	198,290
1918	99,570	235,624	335,194
1919	213,419	329,998	543,417

SOURCE: Alberta, Department of Agriculture, *Annual Reports*, 1912–20
* Exports means shipments outside Alberta.

per cent. Once unrestricted entry was gained, the quality of cattle raised on the northern range assured their favourable reception, as demonstrated by the excellent prices paid for western cattle. But Canadian success in the Chicago market also proved to be a liability in the long run, as the cattle lobby in the south-western United States soon began to press for exclusion of Canadian beef. Consequently, for the next decade the main concern of Canadian cattlemen was retention of free access to this market.

The importance and effect of the Chicago market upon western cattle producers is shown clearly in the returns from A.E. Cross's A7 ranch. In the summer of 1912 Cross confided to a friend that while scarcity had pushed beef prices upward there was still no real competition among buyers and that prices paid were low compared to prices paid at markets outside the country.[29] The decision of the American government in October 1913 to open their markets to Canadian cattle completely changed the state of affairs and Canadian prices drifted upwards as the much more competitive Chicago market dictated beef prices thoughout North America. Cross was informed of the change by telegram from a large Chicago commission firm hours after President Wilson signed the Underwood Tariff. Though Cross's cattle were not among those being sold in Chicago several weeks later, the price he negotiated with Burns for his 1913 cattle was greatly improved by virtue of the Chicago alternative.[30] During 1914 Cross was approached by several Chicago commission houses seeking his business. The Clay, Robinson Company was particularly aggressive and sent an agent to visit all the larger centres in the cattle country during 1915. The company also began to forward weekly livestock reports to all the larger Canadian ranchers. The result was that the bargaining power of the Canadian cattleman greatly increased. As Cross informed a friend in the autumn of 1915 at the onset of the range market season: 'I am waiting for Mr. Burns to return from the East, and if I cannot get the proper price here, I intend to ship them to Chicago through Clay, Robinson and Company.'[31] When he was unable to get what he judged to be a satisfactory price, Cross sent his cattle to Chicago and was pleased with the results.[32] By 1916 all the large ranchers were shipping cattle to the Chicago market and on 13 November 1916 Cross's cattle topped the market to break the previous record for North American range cattle.[33]

Cross's success reflected his longstanding policy of stressing quality over quantity, as the plaudits extended by his fellow cattlemen acknowledged. When asked to account for his stock-raising accomplishments for the benefit of the readers of The North West Farmer, Cross stressed that quality made a vast difference in the net returns and urged stockmen to purchase the best bulls they could afford. He recommended the shorthorn breed as the proper foundation for a beef herd and expressed his opinion that the best range steer was the progeny of a shorthorn cow and a Hereford bull.[34]

Canadian cattle continued to do well in Chicago in 1917, 1918, and 1919. In September 1917 Alberta steers again topped the market at $15.50 per hundredweight and in October 1919 a shipment of Burns's cattle achieved similar distinction.[35] In the latter year Cross earned $15.25 for his top steers. The shipments by Pat Burns to Chicago during these years underline the attractiveness of the American market and at the same time point out that the more lucrative export market was dominated by big producers. Smaller stockmen selling less than several carloads found it easier to sell locally unless they were able to persuade bigger stockmen to include their cattle as part of a large consignment. Moreover, the quality of cattle produced by many of the lesser stock-raisers did not warrant the expense of shipping to the United States and thus, as with the earlier British market, they did not participate in the more lucrative export business. Most of the stock marketed by the growing numbers of small producers was sold in Calgary or Winnipeg, where the big cattlemen sold their inferior cattle.

While cattlemen prospered during these years, grain farmers in the southwest generally fared less well and the movement of small farmers out of the foothills country gained momentum.[36] The confidence that had abounded among farmers between 1896 and 1910 gradually evaporated as the fields that once produced bounteous harvests became increasingly poor and eventually barren. The drought that cattlemen had experienced during the 1880s reoccurred in the south-west during the second decade of the twentieth century to verify ranchers' persistent but unheeded warnings. Despite several severe drought years before 1917, it was not until 1919 and 1920, after three or four years of continuous crop failure, that many officials and farmers were prepared to admit that, unless irrigated, much of the south-west was unsuitable for cereal agriculture.

Unfavourable climatic conditions had resulted in crop failures throughout much of the region in 1907 and the Department of the Interior was required to assist needy settlers with advances of grain to enable them to seed their 1908 crop. However, on the strength of the satisfactory 1908 harvest the Deputy Minister dismissed the bad experience of the year previous with the assurance: 'It has [been] demonstrated beyond doubt that if the expectations of one season are not realized, those of the next may be safely relied upon ...'[37] In 1910 the government was again compelled to assist drought-stricken settlers. At the same time the Department of the Interior was actively settling newcomers in the most seriously affected regions, and while the Commissioner of Immigration admitted that the hardship weighed most heavily on recent homesteaders, he advised: 'It is unnecessary, just yet, to speak of the condition of these homesteaders, as they all, more or less, suffered by last year's drought. But they are a hopeful and energetic class, and not at all depressed over their prospects, especially owing to the abundant precipitation all winter.'[38] Continued settlement was further justified by the rather devious means of speaking of a 'good average crop.' It was stated that because of the ever-increasing acreage brought under cultivation, the same climatic conditions were unlikely to prevail in all regions and that therefore 'the day when there can be a total crop failure in western Canada may be said to have passed away entirely.'[39] In this manner, while drought was acknowledged in southern Alberta, it was held that the 1910 season produced a good average crop. With this device, the fact that some regions were especially prone to crop failure could be ignored.

By 1912 the high hopes that farmers had held for winter wheat had begun to wane and acreages sown to this crop began to decline. Furthermore, the 1912 crop was seriously damaged by the fine spring-like weather that the foothills country experienced during February which, ironically, was the very condition that made the region so attractive for stock-raising. In the Pincher Creek area, formerly hailed as the centre of the winter wheat region, homesteaders began to leave the westernmost parts of the foothill region.[40] Near Medicine Hat, drought conditions were reported in some parts which, with the low price of grain, prevented many farmers from meeting their pre-emption payments.[41] The following year the Dominion Land Agent at Medicine Hat reported that many settlers had abandoned the region and that many of those remaining were beginning to recognize that 'it [was] not advisable to depend wholly on the production of wheat and oats, and have reached the conclusion that it is more profitable to have some stock.'[42] The Alberta Department of Agriculture was also concerned about the conditions on southern farms in 1913 and was pleased to note that 'mixed' farming was on the increase. The department observed that: 'a few successful years of growing grain crops turned the heads of many with the result that a serious attempt was made in many localities to engage exclusively in growing grain. The drought of 1910, unfavourable conditions in 1911 and again in 1912, clearly demonstrated that it was not wise to stake all on one crop.'[43]

Drought conditions continued throughout 1914 in some parts of the south-west, thus accelerating the movement from marginal areas and the growing interest in stock-raising.[44] This trend was temporarily arrested with the return of favourable climatic conditions in 1915 and 1916.[45] Resultant high crop yields coupled with excellent prices restored farmers' optimism and led many in the south to continue their dependence upon grain production. In 1917, however, the south again received below-average rainfall, which motivated the Alberta government to pass the Livestock Encouragement Act in order to promote diversification.[46] The 'Cow Bill,' as was popularly known, established a fund from which farmers could borrow in order to purchase female breeding stock. The fact that the fund was oversubscribed within a few months points to the fact that most small farmers on 160 acres possessed insufficient capital, not to mention insufficient land, to begin raising livestock. The following year in the grazing country was the driest on record and crop yields were the lowest ever. At the same time in central Alberta first-class crops were harvested.[47] As the agricultural disaster in the south became more apparent, unfortunate settlers within the region began to press the federal government to undertake extensive irrigation works. In response, the Deputy Minister of the Interior counselled in his 1918 annual report that while projects were desirable in what was again being called the semi-arid region, 'unfortunately there is only sufficient water available to irrigate 10 percent of the land requiring irrigation and plans for development must be limited by a consideration of this fact.'[48]

By 1917, farmers who a few years before had urged the government to cancel the stock-watering reservations established by William Pearce after 1886 were requesting that such a program be implemented.[49] On the initiative of the Lethbridge Board of Trade, a water conference was held in that community on 22 June 1917. It was attended by officials of the federal and provincial governments as well as interested farm groups and CPR representatives. The consensus of the delegates was recorded in the motion that 'this conference respectfully requests that full inquiry be made by the Department of the Interior of the Dominion Government into the important question of reservation along the rivers, lake and coulee fronts for sanctuary for livestock in time of drought in the drier areas of Southern Alberta and Southern Saskatchewan, with a view to making such reservations.'[50] The Department of the Interior had been awaiting the outcome of the conference, and given the unanimous interest in a water reserve policy, formally abandoned the program of disposal that Oliver had begun in 1905. The reserves remaining in William Pearce's once extensive system became the base of an expanded system jointly administered by the Timber and Grazing and Irrigation branches.

The drought in the south continued throughout 1919 for the third consecutive year and by then even cattlemen began to suffer. Practically no crops were produced in what Department of the Interior officials were now calling the 'dry belt.'[51] Hay was almost impossible to obtain and larger ranchers were forced to import it from the Edmonton area and in some cases from as far away as Winnipeg. Ranchers began to sell some of their breeding stock and others shipped their cattle northward where, according to the Alberta Deputy Minister of Agriculture, 'many districts ... were favoured by heavy local showers ... in the Peace River country these were sufficiently frequent to meet requirements. In such areas good crops were harvested.'[52] The deficiency of rainfall continued during 1920 and 1921. In the latter year very little rain fell in April and May, June was extremely dry and newly sown crops were seriously damaged by the hot, desiccating winds characteristic of the region, so that in spite of the fact that July rainfall was near normal, it came too late to save most crops.[53] In 1922 there was some improvement and a satisfactory crop was obtained in the western half of the southern region, but in the Medicine Hat area the drought continued and the wheat crop averaged a meagre nine bushels per acre. Reporting that central and northern Alberta had also experienced a dry year, the Deputy Minister of Agriculture asserted that overall agricultural conditions in Alberta had not improved over previous years.[54]

The situation faced by farmers in the south-west was desperate; the last satisfactory crop harvested by most had been in 1915, property payments had long been discontinued and by 1920 many were without even basic necessities.[55] The critical moisture deficiency faced by the grain farmer in the south-west after 1915 can be inferred from Table 18. It should be noted also that the decade began with a very dry year. The annual rainfall for 1910 at Calgary, Lethbridge, Medicine Hat, and Edmonton equalled 12.0, 5.7, 6.5, and 14.4 inches respectively.[56]

The problem faced by the farmer in the south-west was not simply the fact of too few inches of rainfall during the growing season. Summers in southern Alberta are characterized by hot dry windy days, which mean not only a higher summer temperature than regions further north but also a significantly higher rate of evaporation. In short, the semi-arid region gets less rainfall to start with and loses more of what it does get. Recent studies show that the plains region south of the Red Deer River and east of the foothills is truly a water-deficient area. The amount of additional moisture that plants could use for optimum

TABLE 18

Precipitation and crop production 1911-20 (in inches and bushels resp.)

	Calgary district				Lethbridge district			
	Rainfall		Yield		Rainfall		Yield	
Year	Growing season	Yearly total	Wheat	Oats	Growing season	Yearly total	Wheat	Oats
1911	14.2	20.0	19.3	43.4	13.3	22.2	20.3	44.0
1912	13.7	20.1	20.6	38.5	6.6	13.2	17.8	35.2
1913	12.0	17.4	26.7	40.3	9.6	14.1	17.0	32.4
1914	7.9	17.7	17.5	29.6	7.3	17.6	8.7	14.6
1915	10.8	18.2	39.5	59.5	12.3	17.4	39.3	63.9
1916	9.0	13.9	28.1	45.2	13.6	25.9	29.4	49.3
1917	5.7	11.4	22.8	34.8	5.7	11.9	18.2	30.5
1918	5.7	9.1	10.2	20.3	3.5	8.9	8.0	13.0
1919	6.7	12.2	14.8	21.8	5.5	13.4	5.0	12.0
1920	7.3	14.4	30.8	42.6	4.9	14.1	16.3	23.4
	Medicine Hat district				Edmonton district			
1911	9.3	16.0	18.2	36.4	16.1	20.7	22.8	36.9
1912	5.3	9.8	15.6	26.8	14.5	20.2	22.9	36.7
1913	8.6	12.7	12.8	24.9	13.6	19.6	22.1	37.0
1914	3.6	12.2	5.4	13.4	16.1	25.3	24.6	34.8
1915	11.2	16.1	38.7	72.7	14.2	18.6	26.6	45.2
1916	13.2	17.9	27.3	49.0	11.4	20.9	23.5	39.8
1917	5.6	13.4	19.0	30.4	8.5	15.3	23.9	26.1
1918	5.2	10.2	4.3	8.7	10.6	17.9	10.2	27.7
1919	3.0	7.7	4.2	9.6	7.1	16.4	30.8	34.2
1920	4.8	10.7	11.0	14.5	11.2	18.2	35.5	40.2

SOURCE: Alberta, Department of Agriculture, Annual Report (1921), 'Graphic Presentation of Precipitation Data for Southern Alberta with Relation to Crop Production.' The statistics presented for each district are the averages of statistics collected at several points in each district: Calgary district–Calgary, Gleichen, Cochrane, Didsbury, Okotoks; Lethbridge district–Lethbridge, Warner, Cardston, Pincher Creek, Ft Macleod; Medicine Hat district–Medicine Hat, Redcliff, Taber, Edmonton district–Strathcona, Leduc, Stony Plain, St Albert, Victoria.

growth in average soil areas within this region varies from six to twelve inches.[57] The difficulty imposed by the high rate of evaporation in the region was actually compounded by the farmers' much-lauded dry-land farming techniques. As the director of the federal government's newly created reclamation service noted in 1920:

The success of dry farming as now practiced depends primarily upon a system of summer-fallowing and frequent stirring of the surface so as to produce a mulch or blanket of fine soil particles which will prevent losses of moisture by capillarity. But this constant cultivation soon pulverizes the fine soil of the dry belt to a light powder which the frequent high winds blow about at will, either burying the seed or young crop, or blowing them out entirely.[58]

It was this phenomenon that, ten years later, contributed the label 'dirty' to distinguish the thirties from more prosperous decades.

The migration that so drastically reduced the farm population in this region during the 1930s was actually preceded by a similar smaller-scale movement at the beginning of the previous decade. One recent study of the American farmer in the Canadian west estimates that as many as two-thirds of those who came to Canada between 1896 and 1913 had returned to the United States by the end of the next decade[59] and there is no doubt that the south-western drought was the major cause of this vast exodus. The tragedy was that much of the region should never have been settled in the first place. The dry cycles characteristic of this region were well documented by statistics collected since the late 1870s. Important officials within the Department of the Interior like William Pearce had argued consistently against the folly of unrestricted settlement. Yet the Liberal government and particularly Frank Oliver were not prepared to let climatic records stand in the way of unrestricted settlement. Between 1896 and 1912 thousands of settlers led by federal land policy, their own confidence in new farming techniques, and several years of above average rainfall, homesteaded throughout Palliser's Triangle and the foothill valleys. In the end, tens of thousands of misguided settlers learned to their cost that optimism, hard work, and 'modern' farming methods could not surmount severe moisture deficiency. Across the prairies before 1927 four out of every ten homesteaders failed to 'prove up' and secure title to their 160 acres. From 1905 to 1930 in Alberta, nearly forty-six per cent of all homesteaders failed and, if the focus is narrowed to the south-eastern plains, one finds that seven of every ten settlers abandoned their land before obtaining title, still others left later. The survivors were often those who had adjusted to this frequently hostile environment by becoming small-scale stock-raisers. The magnitude of this human tragedy must temper any tendency to idealize the free homestead system. 'Available evidence,' as Vernon Fowke has written, 'establishes the existence of one major failure in the over all Dominion lands policy, the failure to base settlement of the prairies on anything in the way of land or climatic surveys which would exclude from homestead entry those areas wholly unfitted for cultivation.'[60] The last major act of federal lands policy, the Prairie Farm Rehabilitation Act of 1935, was largely devoted to correcting the excesses of the homestead period.

While the agricultural frontier was in the process of withdrawal from the point of furthest advance deep in the foothills country and farmers were in full retreat on the open plains, thereby helping to shore up the economic foundation of the cattle industry, a revival of the old social order was not possible. In decline for a decade, the war seems to have dealt the coup de grâce to the distinctive society of the cattle country. The Canadian- and British-born in the ranching country responded to the call to arms much as they had done during the South African War. On 22 August 1914 the *Pincher Creek Echo* announced that when the call comes for 'our Rangers [23rd Alberta Rangers] to go and fight for the Mother Country, overseas or otherwise, they will go in full strength.'[61] Recruitment for the Rangers was undertaken at Pincher Creek, Claresholm, Cardston, Magrath, and Ft Macleod and by 4 September 350 volunteers had assembled.[62] Even the less popular infantry, which sought twenty-five enlistees in Pincher Creek two months later, attracted seventy recruits, most of whom had rendered previous service in the British Army.[63] The feeling characteristic of the foothills country is well illustrated in the lines of an anonymous would-be poet who wrote in the *Okotoks Review* in the autumn of 1914:

When Britain Goes to War
...
We raise our herds of cattle;
We tend our fields of corn;
...
But we send our men to battle,
When Britain goes to war,
O mother, mother, Homeland
We want you now to feel
The strength of our affection
In this your dire ordeal.
...
We offer you our manhood,
Our bravest of the brave.
For we Britons here in Canada
Would British honour save.
...
What tho' they fall in battle
And fill the soldier's grave?
They fall, as falls the Briton,
Toward, not from, the foe.[64]

The public school boys at the Bradfield Ranche near Okotoks all returned to do service.[65] The few remaining remittance men also departed and gained a rare compliment from Bob Edwards, editor of the *Calgary Eye-Opener*: 'they may have been green but they were not yellow.'[66] Many of the ranch establishment, such as C.D. Hardwick and O.A. Critchley, returned to Great Britain to take commissions in the British Army.[67] Others of the younger generation, such as the latter's son, who had attended the Royal Military College at Kingston, served with Lord Strathcona's Horse. With the male population of the grazing region so drastically thinned, experienced cowboys became extremely difficult to find and ranchers had to accept assistance from practically anyone who could ride.[68]

The ranks of those who left were decimated through the carnage on the Western Front, and many who were fortunate enough to survive sold their ranches and remained in Britain or moved to the Pacific coast. Many of the older generation who lost sons overseas also lost their incentive to continue ranching. British leadership within the ranch community was especially reduced. Prominent long-time executive members of the WSGA and the Saskatchewan Stock Growers' Association were lost to the ranching fraternity.[69] A.E. Cross drew attention to the decline of the old social order in his testimony in 1916 before the Royal Commission on Land Settlement and Irrigation:

We had another class of men that originally came up, that is, the public-school boy from England. I was at a public school in England myself, so I know them. They were very nice men and great sporting characters, ranch life appealed to them. They had money, more or less, but did not have the experience, wanted too much pleasure and not enough work, and nearly all of those chaps have gone back. A lot of them have gone to the war ... there are a few left in the country today. A few have buckled down, stuck to the thing, and took the opportunity and are fairly well off.[70]

The loss sustained through the war coupled with the attrition that had been underway for the previous decade ensured that the ethos of the old Canadian cattle kingdom would fade quickly during the 1920s. Onto the ranches of the retiring and departing members of the early cattle compact moved a new group which seems to have been composed largely of the native-born from western Canada and the United States. It is perhaps observation of this later group and the failure to note the demographic evolution of the ranching frontier in Canada that has led to 'popular' acceptance of the 'American' stereotype.

9

Organized cattlemen and the cattle trade embargoes 1919–22

The cattlemen's most pressing concern after 1919 was markets. After seven very profitable seasons, ranchers were suddenly faced with a precipitous decline in beef prices and a situation of oversupply as abnormal wartime demands terminated. Western stockmen thus were particularly sensitive to the state of the Chicago market, where they had shipped most of their cattle since unrestricted entry was gained in 1913. When it was rumoured in 1919 that the Americans were considering reimposing a customs levy on Canadian cattle there was near panic in ranch circles. In an attempt to counter such an eventuality Canadian ranchers acted on two fronts. First, they organized to take extreme measures to control the recent outbreak of mange in the southwest so as not to afford the Americans an ideal excuse to exclude Canadian cattle. Then they redoubled their efforts to gain removal of the British cattle embargo that, since 1892, required the slaughter of Canadian cattle at the port of entry. The long rail trip to Montreal plus the lengthy ocean voyage usually caused western cattle to arrive at British ports in an inferior condition, which resulted in a much lower price to the producer. If the British government could be persuaded to allow Canadian cattle inland to be fed for several months on English or Scottish farms before being sold, Canadian cattlemen were convinced that a profitable export trade could be renewed. This campaign became increasingly urgent as closure of the American market grew imminent.

Under duress, ranchers responded in the traditional manner – through creation of a new stock association. As in the past, the impetus and direction came from the big cattle exporters. The ranchers' first fear was that the mange outbreak would be used by American cattlemen as a lever to have Canadian cattle excluded from the Chicago market. In January 1918 the American government informed Ottawa that during the previous three months at least seven shipments of cattle infected with mange (scabies) had arrived at American stockyards from Canada, and inquired what measures were in operation to prevent repetition.[1] The Veterinary Director General in Ottawa, Dr F. Torrance, immediately warned some of the leading stockmen that 'our experience with the United States Bureau is, that [if], after receiving a letter of this kind, further shipments of diseased stock occur, drastic regulations will be put in force in that country limiting the importations of cattle from Canada.[2] He then imposed a blanket quarantine covering all southern Alberta and south-western Saskatchewan. All stock shipped from the 'mange area' had to be accompanied by a certificate of inspection. The problem was that this procedure also penalized the majority of ranchers with 'clean' herds and tended to label the entire region suspect. Foothills stockmen like A.E. Cross were particularly unhappy as mange had not been reported in their area for many years. While most of the foothills region remained outside the mange area, cattlemen there were prevented from moving their cattle to traditional summer pastures further east in the restricted zone, thus seriously hindering the operations of some big ranchers like George Lane who owned ranches both in and outside the quarantine area and who were accustomed to moving large numbers of cattle back and forth. Though in order to protect their market they supported rigorous measures such as compulsory treatment for all cattle known to be in contact with infected animals, they objected strongly to what they judged to be an unnecessary universal quarantine that depreciated the value of all stock.[3]

Cattlemen first attempted to deal with the mange problem through the established stock association. The Western Stock Growers' Association, however, had fallen on difficult times and its vitality was much reduced. With a buoyant beef market and the lease question in abeyance, interest lagged after 1914 and many cattlemen allowed their membership to lapse. In the interval, power within the association shifted in favour of the plains cattlemen and away from the foothills establishment that had always run the association in the past. Its headquarters were eventually moved to Medicine Hat to be closer to the majority of the members. The move in one sense is evidence of the fact that the need for an association of the traditional mould was still more widely felt on the plains, where the old range system still existed in some part, and where there was consequently the need for a body to organize round-ups and supervise various matters peculiar to range practice. In 1919 WSGA activities were almost at a standstill for want of funds[4] and when the old association proved unable to pull its membership together to act with the speed and force some of the big foothills ranchers judged necessary, they quickly established a new organization.

The driving force behind the movement was George Lane, owner of the vast Bar U ranch. On 22 November 1919, Lane met in his Calgary office with five other ranchers: Edward Kenny, L.L. Smith, John Currie, T. Jackson, T. Birt, and

William Wilson to found the Cattlemen's Protective Association of Western Canada (CPA).[5] Each signed a $5000 bond to cover organizational expenses and to pay for whatever services were required of R.B. Bennett, their solicitor. Notices were immediately forwarded to all large ranchers outlining the purposes of the new association and requesting their support in the form of a signed guarantee bond for $5000. The response was enthusiastic; within three weeks sixty-five ranchers in the Calgary area had signed pledges amounting to $325,000.[6] The CPA's appeal lay in the ranchers' urgent feeling that the beef market was about to deteriorate even further, and their conviction that only an organization that united all the big exporters and had the resources to pay for the best professional and legal talent available could command the political clout their industry required. The ranchers needed 'an organization that will command respect wherever its representatives go,' the CPA informed the Knight, Watson Ranching Company near Lethbridge. In its judgment, recruitment had lagged somewhat in the south and the CPA urged the company, one of the largest and most prominent in the south, to lend its influence to the cause. The Association's secretary warned the company that

the opportunity is now and now only, for the completion of such an organization and if the stockmen of southern Alberta are going to be indifferent towards it, it unquestionably will cost them a lot of money ... Look at the way the freight situation is being messed up. With proper handling there might be no hardship in this country at all, but it will be messed around by politicians ... I would ask you as [men] live to the situation to give the necessary time to take advantage of the present opportunity to complete one of the strongest organizations that has ever appeared in Western Canada. The cattlemen of this section have come behind it wholeheartedly and I know if you will take this in hand and explain it as it should be explained to your people, that they will not be in any way backward.[7]

The new organization was anxious to draw the few remaining large ranchers connected with the WSGA into their association so that they could legitimately claim to speak for the big producers. In the first months of organization there was even some question as to whether smaller stockmen should be invited to join.

By the first week in December enough support had been gathered to warrant calling a formal organizational meeting. The ranch establishment accordingly gathered at Calgary's Palliser Hotel on 12 December and named George Lane honorary president. Dorsey P. McDaniel, a prominent cattle broker, was elected president, along with two vice-presidents and six directors.[8] Preparation of a constitution and by-laws was left to Bennett, the ranchers turning their attention to the issue of first priority – the mange problem. Exactly a week later the new executive met again in the Palliser with Dr J.H. Grisdale the federal Deputy Minister of Agriculture and Dr Torrance and secured a promise that the blanket quarantine would be lifted. The government agreed that if the stockmen would co-operate to ensure that all cattle in the mange area would be gathered, dipped, and held for two weeks for a second treatment under veterinary supervision, the blanket quarantine would be removed and stockmen could then ship their cattle without any interference. Any cases of mange thereafter would be dealt with by individual quarantines.[9] Other stockmen who had not yet joined were quickly impressed by the new association's vigour and success, and by the end of the year the CPA boasted 110 members and bonded support of over $500,000.

Early in 1920 the CPA persuaded the Alberta Livestock Commissioner, W.F. Stevens, to leave government service to become their secretary-treasurer and manager of their affairs. With a well-paid permanent staff and the best legal counsel available, the cattlemen's new association was well on its way to becoming a modern professional lobby. Its activities during 1920 and early 1921 are indicative of its energy and superior techniques. Its major success during this period, and the one that convinced members that the association should be continued even though its main purpose had been accomplished, was the Department of Agriculture's abolition of the mange area in August 1920.

In addition to its main preoccupation with the mange problem and the Chicago market the CPA had been active in other areas. A delegation had been sent to Ottawa to discuss grazing lease matters and several deputations had journeyed to Edmonton to press for amendments to pound and stray animal laws. Another group had attended the annual meetings of the Maple Creek Stock Association and the Saskatchewan Stock Growers' Association in an attempt to persuade these groups to affiliate with the CPA so that the beef industry could present a united front. The association also challenged the CPR and successfully negotiated reduced freight rates for live cattle shipped east from Calgary. In a notable legal action, also directed against the CPR on behalf of the Knight, Watson Ranching Company, the CPA won a guilty verdict for railway negligence and the payment of damages. Whatever the association undertook during this period it handled with care and precision. All federal matters were directed through the parliamentary office of Major Lee Redman, Conservative MP for Calgary East and solicitor in the Bennett-Lougheed legal firm. Deputations were sent armed with detailed statistics to support well-prepared arguments that bore the mark of the knowledgeable former Livestock Commissioner. CPA activities were co-ordinated with timely press releases as well as weekly presentations in Calgary's *Market Examiner*.[10] Late in the year, in keeping with their new concern about public relations, the ranchers changed the name of their organization to the Stock Growers' Protective Association (SGPA) so that the association would appear less exclusive.

In face of the SGPA's aggressive campaign the WSGA seems to have abandoned the field. Its program dwindled to almost nothing and no directors' meetings were held during 1920. Initiative for amalgamation eventually came from the SGPA, which was anxious to acquire the charter of the old association so that it could assume the WSGA's part in the joint administration with the federal government of brand inspection outside Alberta.[11] A special meeting of the WSGA was thus called by the president, W. Huckvale, to discuss the SGPA's overtures. Most of the twenty-two who gathered on 4 March at the Medicine Hat city hall realized that there was no sensible alternative but acceptance. The condition of the WSGA is suggested by the fact that all those present to discuss the matter first had to pay their dues before they could vote legally. After limited debate southern ranchers agreed to put the matter before a special general meeting called for 1 April. Even those founding members with a strong sentimental attachment to the old association, like A.E. Cross, one of the few Calgary ranchers to retain membership, admitted that the SGPA was a much healthier organization. Convinced that two competing associations were undesirable, Cross urged the president of the WSGA to accept union, but advised that

the name of the former [be] retained if possible, as I feel its traditions are certainly a credit and [it] has done a great deal of good for the stockmen of this country, and I am sorry to say, has not been appreciated in recent years. It was unfortunate, as I said at the time, that the eradication of mange was not taken up under its name. There is certainly a necessity for a stockmen's Association in the Province of Alberta in order to protect the livestock interests, especially in taxing, leaseholds, and marketing of cattle, and I hope everything will be done to maintain such an Association.[12]

At their subsequent meeting, southern cattlemen followed the advice of Cross and their executive to dissolve the older association. The charter was turned over to the SGPA on the understanding that members in good standing in the old association would be accepted by the new group without additional entrance fees. Members of the old association were accorded a warm welcome at the SGPA's annual convention the following week and given strong representation on the newly elected executive.[13] The amalgamation signalled the end of the traditional rangemen's organization; henceforth the cattlemen's association existed much more on the model of the professional interest group typical of the business community.

With their strength consolidated, the ranchers devoted their main attention to the situation evolving in the United States, where it seemed protectionists were gaining the upper hand. Early in 1921 Chicago commission houses warned Canadian customers that a protective tariff seemed inevitable and suggested that northern producers organize to have Ottawa pressure the United States to ensure the continued duty free entry of Canadian live cattle.[14] In the ensuing struggle it seems that Canadian ranchers relied on the tacit support of most of the Chicago commission firms, who were prepared to advise how the campaign might best be conducted and to provide names of those sympathetic to the cause who could provide assistance.[15] Also backing the SGPA's cause were many American farmers in the corn belt, who preferred Canadian feeder cattle to those from the American south-west.[16] Thus dependent on the assistance of one group that could not afford to play an open political role and upon a second group with whom they lacked direct contact, the SGPA was, as one of the commission firms put it,

up against a tough proposition ... [opposition] from the Western states such as California, New Mexico, Texas and Wyoming who have plenty of stockers and feeders and want to push them in on the American corn belt at prohibitive prices and [it is established] that they are not as profitable to the corn belt feeder as the northern feeders that come from a climate that makes them more rugged and a class that stretch out and show a whole lot bigger gains than these southern bred animals.[17]

In addition to the pressure exerted from a powerful regional interest group, Canadian ranchers faced the general protectionist sentiment of the governing Republican party. It is a measure of their evaluation of the Chicago market that they were prepared to contend against such odds.

Western ranchers had hardly completed the union of their two organizations in preparation for the work ahead when the American Congress passed the Young Emergency Tariff on 27 May 1921. It imposed duties on a wide range of agricultural products and was broadly intended to meet undefined 'present emergencies, and to provide revenue; to regulate commerce with foreign countries; to prevent dumping of foreign merchandise on the markets of the United States; to regulate the value of foreign money; and for other purposes.'[18] But despite the thirty per cent *ad valorem* duty on imported cattle imposed by the tariff, Canadian ranchers continued to ship to the Chicago market during the 1921 season. Since the duty was computed on the basis of the significantly lower value prevailing on the Canadian market on the date of export and because sales returned more highly valued American dollars, superior profits were still to be gained on the southern market. The legislation intended to provide a permanent tariff to supplant the emergency tariff was, however, much more stringent. The provisions of the proposed tariff as outlined in the 'Fordney-McCumber Bill' included a levy of 1¢ per pound on imported cattle less than two years old and 1¼¢ per pound on cattle two years and older.

The Canadian ranchers' counter-campaign was naturally directed first towards Ottawa. In June the stockmen outlined their plans to the federal Minister of Agriculture, W.R. Motherwell, and requested the support of his department. They proposed that Ottawa open negotiations with Washington and be prepared to yield in all areas of the beef trade except the entry of feeder or grass-fed cattle. Western cattlemen thought that it would be politically inexpedient to attempt to fight the proposed duty on finished beef or grain-fed animals, as this threat of competition would alienate the one group that they hoped to rally to their cause, the mid-western cattle feeder. The stock farmers or cattle feeders whom the Canadians courted based their enterprise on the purchase of grass-fed animals, which they fed for one to three months and then sold, profiting about $50 per head on the basis of 1920 figures. At the same time the western stockman, unlike his eastern counterpart, did not believe he was giving up a great deal as according to statistics gathered by the SGPA an estimated ninety per cent of western exports were of the feeder type.[19] The SGPA candidly informed Motherwell that 'our object at home is to induce our Government at Ottawa to make these proposals to the United States Government at Washington. The object of our propaganda in the United States is to place the Senate at Washington in a proper mood to receive them favorably ...'[20]

With this object in view, the ranchers asked that the Commissioner of Agriculture and former Minister of Agriculture for Alberta, Duncan Marshall, travel through the corn belt and speak at the numerous fairs and stock meetings held throughout the summer advocating removal of the duty against Canadian feeder steers while praising the latter's quality. In recognition of the fact that the Alberta cattle export industry contributed an estimated $50 million to the Canadian economy, both levels of government were reasonably receptive to the ranchers' appeal.[21] It was decided Marshall would go to the United States and that while direct interference in American politics through speeches in opposition to the duty was quite out of the question, he could none the less undertake private discussions. 'I know a good many livestock men in the Corn Belt States,' Marshall informed the SGPA, and

my plan will be to get them to raise the agitation there for the removal of the duty, in order that they might get our cattle to feed. I do not know how successful we can be in this matter, but you may depend we will leave no stone unturned in securing markets for our livestock and farm products, which is the most serious question facing governments in Canada.[22]

A month later a delegation from the SGPA that included the former Alberta Minister of Finance gained the promise of financial assistance for their proposed publicity campaign from the Minister of the Interior, Charles Stewart.[23]

The association's plan was to reinforce Marshall's visit to the corn belt region through a circular to American farmers in the region pointing out the advantage that they were about to lose. For this endeavour the Chicago commission firms were of key assistance. Though these companies were not prepared to take a public stand, they were predisposed to provide the SGPA with much-needed mailing lists. We 'will send you tomorrow a list of addresses of our customers in the Corn Belt,' one firm wrote, but explained that while the SGPA was 'at liberty to use it in sending [farmers] a letter on the subject and asking them to urge their Representatives in Washington to accomplish [the association's] purpose ...' it did not wish the name of the firm revealed. The company also promised a second 'large list of Corn Belt stockmen ... obtained from another source that is friendly to you, but whose name we are not at liberty to mention.'[24] Eventually over 30,000 letters were mailed to American farmers reminding them of the quality of Canadian bred animals, that free access was sought for grass-fed steers only, and that if the American market was closed the displaced Canadian cattle would be sent to compete with American cattle on the British market. It was also implied that if such a contest came about, Canadian quality, not to mention political advantage, would soon place American exports in jeopardy.

In addition to the letters, the SGPA endeavoured to circulate press releases in both countries in support of the ranchers' cause. Support was also sought from all other organized western groups, including the United Farmers of Alberta, the Western Canada Livestock Union, the United Grain Growers, the stock-growers' associations in Saskatchewan and the British Columbia interior, and the various city boards of trade.[25] In the Canadian west their efforts met with almost unanimous success, but the attempt to influence American organizations, particularly the stock-growers' associations, made little or no progress. In a curt rebuff, the powerful American National Livestock Association informed Canadian ranchers that

Canada overlooked a golden opportunity when it failed to ratify the so-called reciprocity treaty. Conditions have somewhat changed in this country since that time and there is not the slightest doubt that the tariff bill before the Senate now will contain import duties on practically all agricultural products, including livestock and meats. So far as [we are] advised there will be no preferential rates to any country on these livestock commodities.[26]

The American association thought that there should be reciprocal relations between the two countries but Canada had had its chance and while a general

change in sentiment would in time occur and result in mutual tariff modifica-
tions, 'that time is not at present.' These feelings were shared by members of the
Montana Cattle Growers' Association, who were convinced that the sale of
Canadian cattle in the United States had caused their own sales to decline.[27]

As the strength of the cattle interest in the American Senate became increasingly apparent, the SGPA decided that they would have to expand the basis of
their support, centred in the Chicago area.[28] They consequently hired the
services of a well-known professional Washington lobbyist, Theodore M.
Knappen, to prepare a brief and present it before Congress.[29] Knappen lamented
that he had not been asked to act months before when the bill was in committee
in the Senate, but since the House of Representatives and the Senate had each
passed a different levy to be set on live cattle, a conference committee of the two
houses was due to be convened to iron out differences and while no new matter
could be introduced before the committee, Knappen proposed to present a brief
supporting the lower levy of the House of Representatives.[30] Alberta ranchers
were told that to achieve any significant change they would have to think further
ahead. If the Democrats took control of the House in the coming fall election the
picture would alter considerably; in the meantime Knappen advised that the
ground be prepared and contacts made so that they would be ready if the rising
tide of public opinion forced the Republicans to redraft the entire bill.

Knappen's program in the interval would have two general objectives: to
overcome the opposition of American farmers outside the corn belt by working
through their organizations, which Knappen explained would be assisted
through his close personal touch with J.R. Howard, president of the American
Farm Bureau Federation, and second, to show members of Congress that
although the cattle tariff did hurt the Canadian grower, it also did not help the
American.[31] The latter objective was to be based in part on statistical evidence
which showed that all Canadian cattle exports to the United States during 1919,
1920, and 1921 respectively supplied only 1/44th, 1/70th, and 1/110th of the
total receipts of cattle at American markets.[32] On the basis of this plan, Knappen
was hired by the SGPA for a retainer of $500 per month plus a monthly expense
allowance of an equal sum.[33] This agreed, Knappen wanted it clearly understood
that he would run the campaign from this point.

It would not help matters for the Canadian papers to have anything about me nor yet the
cause. That is the kind of publicity that is best conveyed by word of mouth. Let them say
all they want about getting a better Tariff deal – but don't let them say who it is they are
working through. I think this will be obvious to anybody. *Remember I know this game.*[34]

Perhaps, as Knappen had stated, the ranchers had waited too long before
bringing their case directly to Congress, for they were unsuccessful in their bid.

They were left to cultivate friends and hope that a Democratic victory in the autumn would lead to tariff amendments. In the meantime Canadian cattlemen had to seek a more hospitable market. In this regard the Alberta ranchers were not entirely unprepared. While they were disposed to go to great lengths to retain the Chicago market, they were realistic enough to recognize the considerable odds they faced, and, good businessmen that they were, endeavoured to prepare an alternative market should their fight prove unsuccessful. There was thus a simultaneous second part to the ranchers' campaign designed to reopen the vast British market to Canadian live cattle.

This part of the struggle, which grew in seriousness as the hope of holding the Chicago outlet dimmed, was really the continuation of an embittered controversy that already had a history of nearly thirty years. The British embargo on Canadian cattle was originally set in November 1892 after two cases of alleged contagious pleuropneumonia were discovered in two cattle shipments originating in Canada. The British Board of Agriculture immediately ordered that henceforth Canadian cattle be slaughtered at the port of arrival so that contamination would not be spread among British herds.[35] The Canadian government promptly organized a thorough investigation, found no evidence of the disease, and requested the order be rescinded. Getting no response, Ottawa continued the investigation and in 1894 presented to the British cabinet the Canadian government's strenuous disagreement with the Board of Agriculture's findings. Canadians thought that the Board's case for continuing the restrictions, based as it was on three alleged new cases found after special examination of sixty-seven cargoes comprising 30,561 head of cattle, demonstrated neither a significant incidence of the disease nor its contagious character. The weight of the government's submission was directed to refute the diagnosis of pleuro-pneumonia made by Professor Brown, Director of the Veterinary Branch of the British Board of Agriculture. In his report, Brown had insisted that he had found contagious pleuropneumonia and noted that while there seemed to be some deviations between the North American and European varieties 'the history of pleuro-pneumonia on the North American Continent proves beyond doubt that it is as contagious and fatal as the pleuro-pneumonia of Europe.'[36] In the Canadian view this was preposterous. In a stirring rebuttal, Canada's High Commissioner, Sir Charles Tupper, had argued:

If the special type of the disease in question is 'as contagious and fatal' as pleuro-pneumonia in England, and if such existed in Canada, it would be known by the fact of its spreading among animals, and causing many deaths. It would be something which could not be concealed and which could not remain unknown. But there has been no spreading of any such contagious disease in Canada nor deaths of animals arising therefrom. Not a single case has been discovered; and in so far as it is possible to prove a negative, the Minister submits that the report of the investigations of the Veterinary Officers of the Department of Agriculture, aided by numerous veterinary surgeons carried out ... in all those parts of the Dominion from which the animals shipped ... were traced, the findings ... established such proof. No trace of any contagious disease was found in any of the localities throughout the Dominion whence the animals in question came; and it is impossible that such a position could exist if there had been present in any of these localities a type of disease as contagious and fatal as pleuro-pneumonia is known to be in Europe and elsewhere where it has existed.[37]

To further support Canada's case, detailed evidence drawn from the investigation by Canada's Chief Veterinary Inspector, Dr Duncan McEachran, was included in Tupper's memorandum. McEachran went to great lengths to explain the procedures taken under the Animal Contagious Diseases Act to ensure the health of animals in Canada, particularly the compulsory ninety-day quarantine for all cattle entering from the United States. McEachran, who happened also to be president of the Walrond Ranche Company, noted in addition that from the summer of 1880 to November 1892, 909,828 live cattle were exported from Canada to Great Britain, that tens of thousands of these had mingled freely with herds of the United Kingdom, and that only a single case of the alleged contagious disease had come to light during the entire period, and even it was by no means satisfactorily proven. He also drew attention to the fact that some British veterinarians shared Canada's rejection of Brown's diagnoses.

Canada's evidence, along with its concomitant claim that since a serious error in diagnosis had been made no cause for continuing the restriction remained, failed to move the British Board of Agriculture. It announced with a tone of finality after assessing the document that 'the Veterinary Officers of the Department have fully considered these reports, but their views remain unaltered.'[38] When even the direct intervention of the Colonial Office on Canada's behalf failed to bring removal of the embargo, it gradually became apparent that to demonstrate the good health of Canadian cattle would continue to be of no avail because this was not the real issue.[39]

The situation even moved Senator Cochrane to address his fellow senators. 'I do not know that it has occurred more than once or twice in twenty years that I have risen to speak a word in debate here ...,' Cochrane informed the Chamber, and then he proceeded to accuse Great Britain of using an unfounded charge of pleuropneumonia as a guise to protect the English farmer. He urged his English friends to be honest, to state outright that their policy was one of protection and that Canadian animals must consequently be slaughtered at the port of entry 'instead of cursing us in the eyes of other nations and destroying potential markets for Canadian beef elsewhere.'[40] Cochrane's accusation was close to the mark. The scheduling of Canadian cattle which signalled the end of the foreign store cattle trade in Great Britain was the product of a thirty-year campaign that allied those who sought effective disease control with the powerful self-interest of those who were in direct competition with non-British imports. While all would gain from effective disease control, some stood to gain more directly.[41]

Senator Cochrane's anger was hardly surprising, for he and his fellow investors in the western beef industry had built their enterprises with an eye to the British market. The restriction was especially burdensome to western producers, who contributed about half the cattle exported to the United Kingdom,[42] the bulk of western export cattle being unfinished feeder stock unsuitable for marketing on arrival. Western ranchers were thus the heaviest losers, and consequently were more interested in the restrictions than beef producers in the east. The government faced persistent appeals from this quarter to take the matter up with the British government. At the founding meeting of the WSGA removal of the embargo was set as one of its major goals and this question was considered at nearly every subsequent annual convention. Though the Canadian government did respond to such appeals from time to time, they made no headway, even with the strong support of farmers in the north-eastern counties of England and Scotland who had developed a profitable feeder business based on Canadian imports. In 1900 when the Canadian Minister of Agriculture, Sidney Fisher, visited Great Britain to interview the President of the British Board of Agriculture, he was confronted with an emphatic refusal to open the question and the matter remained, at least as far as the British were concerned, a non-topic until World War I.[43]

The beef shortage and rising prices that came with World War I created a situation that seemed to favour renewal of the campaign, initiated this time from the British side. In late 1915, the Free Importation of Canadian Cattle Association of Great Britain (FICCA), formed earlier by northeastern farmers, again began to distribute pamphlets to promote importation of Canadian live cattle.[44] The moment was also judged auspicious on the eastern side of the Atlantic and the Canadian government was encouraged to reopen the matter with the British government.[45] Some form of common action or understanding between the two like-minded parties at once seemed obvious. Thus, having been briefed fully on the history of the issue by his Minister of Agriculture, the Canadian Prime Minister arranged to meet with representatives of the FICCA during his planned visit to Great Britain during March and April 1917.[46] In Edinburgh on 11 April 1917, both groups seem to have agreed that the Irish cattle interest was the main block in their path.[47] Armed with additional information supplied by the

Scottish farmers, Borden requested that the question of the admission of Canadian cattle into the United Kingdom be placed on the agenda of the Imperial War Conference then underway. Borden was then able, on 26 April, to present Canada's case at a special meeting chaired by the Colonial Secretary, W.H. Long, and attended by the President of the Board of Agriculture, R.E. Prothero.

In Borden's view, the meeting was a complete success and he believed that he had secured the promise that the restrictions on Canadian cattle would be lifted at war's end.[48] Borden informed his office in Ottawa of the good news, but added: 'Do not on any account make announcement as it might upset the whole arrangement. The matter is strictly confidential until the British Government makes the decision public.'[49] A short time later the Canadian Prime Minister was assured by the Colonial Secretary that an announcement regarding the embargo would be made in the British House of Commons on 17 May.[50] When the announcement finally was made and turned out to be noncommittal about lifting the restrictions, Borden was profoundly disappointed and felt that Britain had backed out of a definite agreement. A few weeks later he was informed by R. Rogers, his Minister of Public Works, who had attended the special meeting with the Prime Minister, that the minutes of the discussion regarding the cattle embargo had not been included in the official extracts of the 'Minutes of Proceedings of the Imperial War Conference.'[51] An indignant Borden requested the Canadian High Commissioner in London to see the Colonial Secretary regarding the omission and to find out why 'Prothero's statement in the House of Commons was not in accordance with the distinct understanding reached at the conference.'[52] The British government eventually agreed to issue a revised publication containing the proceedings but refused, despite Prothero's words at the conference, to make any further statement regarding the embargo.[53] For the next two years the question became, as it had been in the past as far as the British were concerned, a closed topic, while the Canadians were left with a bitter feeling of foul play.

When the issue was again broached in 1919 by a deputation from the Canadian Peace Conference Mission, they found that the President of the Board of Agriculture and Fisheries, R.E. Prothero (now Lord Ernle), had no intention of lifting the embargo. In statements to the public through the press and in the House of Lords, the British for the first time publicly admitted that the restriction could not be justified on the ground of protection from disease, but now stated that it had to be maintained to protect the breeder of cattle from the effects of overseas competition.[54]

Witnessing the Canadian government's continuing failure, though unaware of the full extent of Sir Robert's efforts on their behalf, and increasingly apprehensive about the rising protectionist tide in the United States, western ranchers decided for the first time to enter the contest directly. The co-ordination of ranchers' endeavours in this direction was left in the hands of SGPA's manager, W.F. Stevens, whose Scottish background and former experience as Alberta's Livestock Commissioner particularly suited him for the task.

Stevens's plans to achieve the association's objective were worked out during the summer of 1920 in co-operation with James Lennox, a prominent Scottish farmer and spokesman for the National Farmers' Union of Scotland, who had visited Alberta during the early part of summer, and a long-time friend of Stevens, W.T. Ritch. The latter was also a Scot and at the time was employed by a large American wool brokerage firm, but he had formerly worked for the Canadian Department of Agriculture. It was decided that the main part of the campaign would be directed towards the British public through the press. The idea, as Ritch explained to Stevens, was

to educate the favourably disposed but indifferently informed factory people in the large cities, who know nothing about agriculture but, want cheap food and free imports, but you do not require to educate the British farmers beyond getting the backing of the Liberals among them. The north of England and Scotch farmers are nearly all Liberals and free traders and always have been, while the south of England farmers are blind, bigoted tories and always will be. It is useless to waste time and energy where votes cannot be changed.[55]

In Ritch's view there were four main themes upon which the newspaper propaganda should rest, namely:

the unpopularity of protection in the British Isles, the dislike of the high cost of living among the laborites, the tory slogan of preferential trade within the Empire and the liberal policy of free trade and a closer bond ... of mutual interests with the Dominions, in addition to the Lloyd George promise [made at the Imperial War Conference].

It was thought that a persistent and well-organized propaganda campaign emphasizing these issues would catch either of the major parties in whatever direction they moved.

In essence the anti-embargo forces directed their efforts along these lines. At the end of September, Lennox reported to Stevens that the *Dundee Advertiser* had agreed to give the whole weight of its influence to the campaign, that the *London Daily Herald*, the most influential Labour paper, would use their material, and that he hoped to persuade the *Glasgow Herald* and *Manchester Guardian* also to assist. He added that the Scottish Cooperative Societies were behind them and that a meeting was set with the Master Butchers' Association.[56] The initial work of the SGPA was mainly to supply the necessary press material on the Canadian position, which would be distributed to the British papers by Lennox. The real burden of the campaign was left to Lennox and the Scottish farm associations. The FICCA, which had carried on the struggle for the preceding twenty years, at first did not become actively involved. Having failed for so long, the association had resigned itself to defeat and while prepared to distribute printed matter, the chairman frankly informed Stevens, 'I have no hope of success to our cause.'[57]

The corner in the struggle seems to have been turned in March 1921 with a notable bye-election success. Early in the year the SGPA, through R.B. Bennett, had made contact with a former Calgarian, the now-powerful newspaper publisher, Lord Beaverbrook.[58] The Beaverbrook press subsequently turned the cattle embargo question into the major issue in the Dudley bye-election where Sir Arthur Griffith-Boscawen, the newly appointed President of the Board of Agriculture, was facing the electorate. The message in Beaverbrook's *Daily Express* was simple: 'A vote for Boscawen is a vote for dear meat.'[59] Boscawen's rebuttal that the campaign was inspired by 'a prominent Canadian, who, with his friends, will profit by sending Canadian cattle here,' and that 'the first duty of the British minister of agriculture is to see that British herds are preserved and immune from disease' proved of no avail, and Boscawen lost the seat he had held since 1910 to the Labour candidate.[60]

From this point the pace quickened; the question had at last become, as the SGPA and the Scottish farmers had endeavoured to make it, a national issue. Impressed by their success in the working class constituency of Dudley in the Birmingham area, the Labour party adopted removal of the cattle embargo as a plank in their national platform.[61] Less than a week after the election, at a conference held at the London Guildhall, on the invitation of the Corporation of the City of London, and attended by representatives from a great number of urban councils and other public bodies, a resolution calling for removal of the restriction on importation of Canadian cattle was carried by seventy-two votes to forty-four.[62] The press campaign was intensified[63] and by April even the long-despairing chairman of the FICCA began to speculate that the embargo might be removed and proceeded to bestir his organization.[64] Finally, in May, in response to rising public pressure, the British government appointed a Commission to investigate the whole question.

At its hearings evidence was collected from all the vested interests, including the Canadian government. The commissioners noted that the balance of opinion among farmers in England appeared to be strongly against admission. Resolutions in favour of retaining the embargo were passed by all branches of the National Farmers' Union, with the exception of the Northumberland branch. Elsewhere in England, in London and the towns, sentiment favoured admission and was based on the expectation that this would lower the price of meat. The commission also reported that, with the exception of smaller farmers in the Scottish Highlands who feared Canadian competition, Scottish farmers favoured removal of the embargo. In Ireland the feeling favouring maintainance of the restriction was reportedly unanimous. There farmers thought Canadian competition would be disastrous and would drive them from the market. Opposition was also tendered by Lord Ernle, former President of the Board of Agriculture. Ernle attempted to make the case that the real question was 'what the farmer would think' if the embargo were removed. He explained that the farmer was very cautious and conservative and if he was at all apprehensive about Canadian importation he would not rear stock, which in turn would leave Great Britain ever more dependent on outside supply.[65]

After assessing the evidence, the commissioners presented their report on 30 August 1921. Lord Ernle's concern about what the farmer would think was, 'with most unfeigned respect,' dismissed. The true question, in the Commission's view, was 'what the facts really are.' On the basis of data collected, the conclusions drawn were that the cost of shipping cattle from western Canada would always ensure against undue competition, that the fear of disease was unfounded, and that, while the admission of Canadian cattle might to some extent deprive Irish farmers of their present market, it would in the long run tend to lower meat prices. It was therefore concluded that importation of Canadian store cattle was advisable.[66]

The issue now carried itself and Canadian ranchers watched closely as the matter moved gradually towards a parliamentary decision. In the interval, as the public grew impatient with the government's delay in acting on the Commission's recommendations, the matter was taken up by the London Times. Hoping finally to press the government to action, municipal authorities gathered in convention at the London Guildhall on 15 June 1922 and with one dissenting vote approved a resolution calling upon

his Majesty's Government forthwith to honour the unqualified undertaking given to the Prime Minister of the Dominion of Canada by the President of the Board of Agriculture and Fisheries at the Imperial War Conference in April 1917, and to act upon the unanimous conclusions of the Royal Commission on the Importation of Store Cattle in favour of the admission into this country of Canadian stores.[67]

The Times noted that delegates assembled at the convention represented nearly three-quarters of the population of Great Britain and, in an editorial directed to the government, warned that the people's will was clear: 'it now only remains for [their] representatives at Westminster to carry its expressed wishes into effect.' In the debate that soon followed in the Commons, the English squirarchy stood squarely opposed, as they had done before the Commission the year before, but although their parliamentary strength was still formidable the urban members and their northern allies were more numerous, and when the division was called the vote was 247 to 171 in favour of removal.[68] In the Lords the entrenched power of the landed interests was even greater, but under pressure from the anti-embargo forces to restore the government's integrity in the eyes of the senior dominion and honour the 1917 pledge, the Upper House also approved the measure.[69]

In the end the strategy of the SGPA and the Scottish National Farmers' Union had been sound. The battle was really won in the urban centres, and perhaps the key to the eventual success had been the ability of the Calgary ranchmen to recruit Lord Beaverbrook to their cause. Another factor that helped the anti-embargo forces was the declining influence of Irish landowners after World War I. The Anglo-Irish Treaty signed in London on 6 December 1921 and ratified a month later in Dublin greatly weakened the irish appeal for preferential treatment.

The access thus gained to the British market in the autumn of 1922 in part compensated for the loss of the American market suffered some months previous. But the new outlet, when at last obtained, was not as profitable as the one lost. While the big ranchers were saved from serious economic dislocation, margins were drastically trimmed.[70] For the small producer the distant British market was less accessible and he became even more dependent on the less competitive Calgary and Winnipeg markets. Though unrestricted access to a new market saved the big exporters from despair, the beef industry in the west remained on an uncertain economic footing for the next five years.

While the stock-growers' attention was mainly occupied after 1919 with the campaign to maintain a satisfactory market, the old lease question also returned to plague them. In July 1920 Senator James Lougheed, Minister of Soldiers' Civil Re-establishment, was assigned a second portfolio, the Department of the Interior. Almost immediately he sought to amend the lease legislation. Despite the warnings of the head of the Timber and Grazing Branch that permanency of leasehold was essential to the industry's well-being, Lougheed decided that all new leases would have a three-year cancellation clause and secured an order-in-council to this effect.[71] There had been no warning of such a move and ranchers were instantly alarmed. The ten-year closed leases that they had eventually secured several years after the Conservatives had come to power in 1911 were now half gone and the prospect of having to return to the old system added a new factor of uncertainty to a problem that cattlemen thought had been solved. Ranchers were especially puzzled that such a measure should be proposed by Senator Lougheed, who had been a political friend for many years and whose legal firm had traditionally handled most of the big ranchers' business.

A clue as to the government's intent was provided a short time later in a speech made by Prime Minister Arthur Meighen in Medicine Hat, in which he announced that the federal government was considering turning over to the prairie provinces the natural resources (including Crown lands) that the federal government had withheld in 1905. While the proposal could be expected to win western friends for the government in many quarters, their old supporters, the ranchers, were less than pleased.[72] The SPGA responded by sending a delegation to Ottawa to determine the government's full intent. On their return the delegation informed their fellow ranchers that nothing further had been said about the resource question but that they had encountered serious opposition from the Minister of the Interior, 'who was strongly in favour of cancelling all leases and utilizing them as public grazing lands or commons by farmers in the vicinity.'[73] Before the year was out Lougheed was being labelled by the ranchers a new 'Frank Oliver.'[74]

It was apparent that the Conservative government was anxiously casting about for policies that would improve its position among the farm population for the coming federal election. The community pasture idea was popular and was believed by many to be a necessary measure of assistance to drought-ridden farmers in the south. Since it had been proven that the area could not be relied upon to produce grain crops, unfortunate farmers who remained there were encouraged to improve their position through the purchase of a few head of cattle. However, the problem was that most farmers had insufficient land to keep more than a few head, especially in very dry years. The solution, according to a brief sent to the Department of the Interior by the United Farmers of Alberta, was community grazing. The UFA proposed that no leases be renewed until surrounding settlers had an opportunity to organize and make joint application.[75] The well-known and highly respected southern Conservative, C.A. Magrath, in a report of the Survey Board of Southern Alberta, also recommended that big leases should be allowed to lapse in favour of community pasture.[76] G. Hoadley, another prominent Conservative turned United Farmer, was also an outspoken champion of the idea.

In practice the community grazing idea differed little from the old 'free' range system that organized Canadian cattlemen had opposed at various times since the 1880s. In its counter-publicity against community grazing the SGPA therefore called attention to the dangers that cattlemen had identified in the past. Presenting their case in the farmers' journal, *The Grain Growers' Guide*, the SGPA informed farmers that the principal counts against the system were the inferior animals it produced and the inevitability of overgrazing. Beyond this the association insisted that there was the matter of morality and justice.

It involves the displacing of those who are now in possession of the lands ... This raises the question of justice and of public policy that does not [apply] to lands that have been unused and are now unproductive. It implies that land that is now yielding to the Dominion revenue in the form of rentals, and to the Province revenue in the form of taxes that is being utilized by men, who know their business, and who after years of experimenting have developed a class of animals that have reflected much credit and brought much wealth to the Province, is to be taken out of the hands of those who have been in possession of them in the past, and set aside for the use of another class of men who came to the Province without any intention of engaging in the cattle business; men who had so little knowledge of the business they did propose carrying on, namely, grain growing, that they took land unsuited to their purpose and failed in their undertaking ... In other words a body of men who have made a success of their business is to be dispossessed at the demand of another but larger body that has failed, and a system of cattle raising that has been identified with the growing of the best that Western Canada produces is asked to give way to a system that has been associated with the production of that which is common and in many instances inferior.[77]

While it is doubtful that the charge of replacing the successful with failures won many converts among the farm community, the essence of the ranchers' argument was sound. Cattlemen with quality herds did not look forward to having their farm neighbours grazing their inferior bulls in the same pasture. There was little question that if this came to pass the cattle export industry would suffer.[78] To ensure that this did not happen the SGPA passed a resolution calling on the federal government to guarantee renewal of ranchers' grazing privileges and then collected the traditional sources of support for their position. To this end they secured the favour of the Lethbridge, Calgary, and Edmonton Boards of Trade and the prestigious Canadian Bankers' Association.[79] The SGPA also coordinated the efforts of other like-minded associations, including the Interior Stock Association of British Columbia and the Saskatchewan Stock Growers' Association.[80] A special brief was sent by the association to the Prime Minister Meighen, and R.B. Bennett was directed to use what influence he could.[81]

At the same time a complementary operation was being conducted at the provincial level. During the previous several years the cattlemen's relations with the provincial government had improved greatly. Several stockmen, including D.E. Riley (later Senator Riley), president of the SGPA, had become prominent in provincial Liberal circles. Another, A.J. Maclean, had risen to cabinet rank, and the Minister of Finance, C.R. Mitchell, was considered by ranchers to be a friend of their interests. Most important of all was the good will of the new Premier, Charles Stewart. The ranchers' new party contacts turned out to be especially useful. In a complete reversal of the situation in past struggles, stockmen now turned to the provincial government to help them thwart the policy proposed by the federal authorities. Their immediate request to the Alberta government was that it refuse to be party to the commission Lougheed proposed to investigate the community grazing question.[82] Lougheed's commission was to include representatives from Alberta, Saskatchewan, and the federal government, and it appeared that only one rancher would be appointed, thereby assuring that the farm interest would prevail. Taking the easiest political response, the Alberta government simply put off a decision one way or the other, which stalled creation of the commission and satisfied the ranchers. Premier Stewart was later persuaded by the ranchers to take a definite stand on their behalf and inform Lougheed that he preferred renewal of the closed-lease system.[83]

The ranchers' influence within the Alberta government in 1921 was also enhanced by an impending provincial election and the fact that the Liberals were most apprehensive about the farm vote given the decision of the UFA to enter the political arena directly. The SGPA understood the situation perfectly. In the words of their secretary, W.F. Stevens, 'politically speaking they have not as much to gain by courting the farmers because the farmers are dead sure to oppose them in the next election,'[84] and consequently stockmen were not reticent about asking for favours. Ironically, while the ranchers' influence was ascendant in the provincial capital, where it always had been weak, their power was in decline in the seat of its traditional strength. Their influence in Ottawa declined somewhat as another shaky government tried to improve its popularity among western farmers. In the end, however, the results of the provincial and then the federal election turned the cattlemen's world back to its traditional form. In July 1921 Albertans called upon the UFA to form their new government, thus restoring the old relationship between the cattlemen and their provincial government. The victory of the federal Liberals in December completed the reversal. The prospect of a new Liberal government in Ottawa was well received in ranch circles for it meant they were finished with Senator Lougheed. Their satisfaction was even more complete when the new Prime Minister, William Lyon Mackenzie King, announced that the new Minister of the Interior would be none other than Charles Stewart, the stockmen's friend and recent Premier of Alberta. A short time later it was announced that Duncan Marshall, former Alberta Minister of Agriculture, would become the new federal Commissioner of Agriculture.

The ranchers' relief proved well founded. In the late winter Stewart sent his Deputy Minister to meet with the ranchmen in Medicine Hat.[85] The SGPA in turn sent to the Department of the Interior a list of the alterations it desired in the regulations governing grazing leases, and on 25 April 1922 was informed by the department that most of the alterations requested had been approved.[86] The new provisions essentially brought the system back to what it had been before Lougheed's amendments. The cancellation clause was dropped and provision was made for lessees with leases having less than five years to run to apply for renewal. The stockmen officially recorded their approval of the changes in a letter to the Minister thanking him for the prompt action his department had taken in revising the grazing lease regulations, and assuring him that the industry could return to a proper business basis.[87] The ranchers' gratitude was genuine, for they well understood that they had gained their end despite the fact that the governments of Saskatchewan and Alberta had made known their preference for lease cancellation and community grazing.[88] The SGPA's appraisal of the attitude of the Alberta government is suggested in its advice to members to act quickly now that lease renewal was possible:

not renewing them until [they] expire is more or less a gamble in view of the fact that the Province is likely to get its Natural Resources and if it does, the matter of leases will be taken over by it. The Provincial Government is none too friendly toward the matter of releasing this land, but desires rather to turn [it] over to Community Grazing ...[89]

As ranchers hurried to renew their leases they were further reminded that 'no publicity regarding these regulations is needed.'[90] With their lease problems again resolved they could devote their full energies to seeking means to relieve the depressed market situation that had faced the industry since 1920.

The SGPA had served the ranchers well since it was founded in 1919. Until 1922 it had fought simultaneously three major campaigns on the stockmen's behalf. Though it had failed in Chicago, it had succeeded in gaining access to the British market and at the same time protected the big ranchers' leases, which, after markets, were their major concern. The organized activities of the cattlemen during the first years of the third decade of the twentieth century reveal that the rancher still retained much of the influence and power that had marked his presence in the south-west since the arrival of the ranch companies forty years before. Though greatly reduced as a social unit, the ranch community remained an aggressive political force outside the farmers' political movement, as shown in their determined and increasingly sophisticated struggle to maintain their markets and lands. Careful attention to both factors was essential to the cattlemen's survival and both were problems they had faced since the 1880s. The

SGPA's confrontation with the community grazing idea in 1921 was but the latest episode in a continuing struggle for control of south-western land that had begun with the coming of settlement, and the ranchers' continued success in meeting this challenge is testimony to the effectiveness of their political and economic organization.

The ranchers' stubborn endurance and ultimate survival is testimony also to their important, if little understood, role and contribution in the opening and development of the prairie west. In the south-west almost three decades before the farmers arrived, the cattlemen invested in an isolated frontier, established lasting communities, contributed to the Canadian economy a key trade staple, and perhaps most important, pioneered and developed an enterprise especially suited to the region's semi-arid environment; it is a not insignificant legacy.

Epilogue

For western stockmen the 1920s were years of both promise and frustration. On the one hand, grain farmers no longer demanded the break-up of remaining leaseholds on the dry plains of south-eastern Alberta or in the remoter valleys of the western foothills. When the drought persisted through the early part of the decade, the Western Stock Growers' Association persuaded the Department of the Interior to reduce the lease rental by half, from 4¢ per acre to 2¢ and ultimately, in 1925, to restore the long-sought twenty-one-year closed lease. Outside of deeded title this provided a security of tenure unmatched since the terms of the original western grazing leases were altered in 1886. With this very important change the ranchers' traditional apprehension of federal transfer of lands and natural resources to the farmer-dominated governments of the prairie provinces was moderated, so that when the assignment was actually made in 1930 there was only limited and unorganized concern.

What stability the stock-raising industry gained through the new security of land tenure was compromised by the generally difficult market situation that prevailed during most of the 1920s. The newly gained access to Great Britain for live cattle never compensated for the loss of duty-free entry to the Chicago market. While Canadian live cattle exports to Great Britain climbed dramatically from a mere 320 head in 1920 to over 110,000 head in 1925,[1] profits to the western producer were few. The essential problem was the vast distance that separated the rancher from this market. Hence, reduction of rail and ocean shipping costs that cut so deeply into returns became a major goal of the WSGA after 1922.[2] Eventually successful in gaining a reduction in ocean rates, cattlemen made little headway in persuading the CNR and CPR to decrease shipping levies. Given the critical disadvantage of high transportation costs, western ranchers therefore continued, despite the thirty per cent duty, to ship about 100,000 head yearly to American markets and at the same time continued to press the Canadian government to discuss the tariff question with American authorities.

In seeking support from Ottawa, cattlemen in the 1920s, like their counterparts in previous decades, used high level political connections. In fact, during the immediate post-war period there seems to have been something of a political realignment within the upper ranks of the cattle compact that for the first time saw bonds forged between stockmen and the Liberal party at the provincial and federal levels. Underlining this new political linkage was the appointment to the Senate by the Liberals in 1926 of the long-time president of the WSGA, D.E. Riley. With the active support of the Liberal party by at least a few members of the ranch establishment came the advantage of an improved relationship with federal officials in the Department of the Interior, particularly in the Timber and Grazing Branch.

While the immediate post-war reorganization of the WSGA made it a much more effective instrument to deal with the marketing problems that were the industry's main concern through the twenties, its broad mandate to protect the stockman's interests moved it into new areas. Increasingly, the Association advised members on taxation and lobbied for desired changes in tax law. Also, it came to reflect the ranchers' interest in a new enterprise underway in the heart of the cattle country by the mid-1920s. The major oil discovery at Turner Valley in 1924 by the Royalite Oil Company set off a rush of exploration activity. Pioneer cattlemen often held mineral rights to their deeded holdings, unlike the homesteaders who came later and obtained their lands after the federal government had discontinued surrendering mineral rights with surface title. Not surprisingly, ranchers became intimately involved in the developing petroleum industry. Beyond this evolving link between the old and the new industry in the Alberta foothills, the physical proximity of the two enterprises demanded that there be some accommodation of competing land uses. Stockmen looked to their association to establish guidelines.

The attention directed by the WSGA to larger economic problems confronting the industry or to subjects new to ranchers' experience was not at the expense of the traditional concerns of the range cattle industry. In its day-to-day operation, western stock-raising had changed little. The WSGA throughout the twenties concerned itself with cattle-branding, stock-rustling, wolf bounties, range fires, cattle disease control, herd and pound laws, and municipal taxation. Along with these traditional issues the association's minutes reveal the concomitant and continuing pride of place and occupation that, in their own eyes at least, separated rancher from sod-buster. In 1926 at the WSGA's thirtieth annual convention, ranchers assembled in Calgary were informed that 'certain farmers' organizations' had expressed the formal views of those engaged in the livestock industry. In response, the convention warned the Canadian Council of Agriculture and other farm organizations that they were not entitled to speak on behalf of the livestock industry.[3] In the stockmen's view, farmers who raised small bunches of cattle were not now, nor had ever been bona fide stockmen.

This characteristic economic exclusiveness within the larger agrarian community, as has been argued, had a social dimension, aspects of which were still observable in the inter-war period. Indeed, in the early 1920s following the purchase of a foothills ranch by Edward, Prince of Wales, and with the prince occasionally in their midst, ranch society enjoyed a flurry of activity and displayed a certain quality that harked back to the old days before the turn of the century. But despite the initial promise, the war had taken a toll that precluded reconstruction of the old order.

Overall, cattlemen saw their industry progress modestly through the third decade of the century. If markets were difficult, cattlemen had at long last established their right to a permanent place in the western Canadian economy. The cautious optimism that grew in the ranch community throughout the 1920s, however, did not prepare cattlemen for the disaster that affected all prairie agriculture in the subsequent decade.

Notes

PREFACE

1 See, for example, L.V. Kelly, *The Rangemen* (Toronto: William Brigs 1913); C.M.
MacInnes, *In the Shadow of the Rockies* (London: Rivingtons 1930); J.F. Booth,
'Ranching in the Prairie Provinces' in R.W. Murchie, *Agricultural Progress on the
Prairie Frontier*, Vol. V of Canadian Frontiers of Settlement, ed. W.A. Mackintosh
and W.L.G. Joerg (Toronto: Macmillan Company of Canada Ltd 1936); A.S.
Morton and C. Martin, *History of Prairie Settlement and Dominion Lands Policy*, Vol.
II of Canadian Frontiers of Settlement (1938); C.A. Dawson and E.R. Young,
Pioneering in the Prairie Provinces: The Social Side of the Settlement Process, Vol. VIII of
Canadian Frontiers of Settlement (1940); Grant MacEwan, *Between the Red and the
Rockies* (Toronto: University of Toronto Press 1952); J.H. Warkenton, 'Western
Canada in 1886,' *Papers Read before the Historical and Scientific Society of Manitoba*,
Series III, no. 20 (1963-4); W.S. MacNutt, 'The 1880's' in J.M.S. Careless and
R.C. Brown, eds, *The Canadians 1867-1967* (Toronto: Macmillan Company of
Canada Ltd 1967). The work of Paul F. Sharp, *Whoop Up Country: The Canadian-
American West, 1865-1885* (Helena: Historical Society of Montana 1960) and
Lewis G. Thomas, 'The Rancher and the City: Calgary and the Cattlemen,
1883-1914,' *Transactions of the Royal Society of Canada*, VI, Series IV (June 1968),
are exceptions to this tradition.

CHAPTER ONE: THE RANCHING FRONTIER IN CANADA 1874–82

1 E.S. Osgood, *The Day of the Cattlemen* (Chicago: University of Chicago Press 1968) 23
2 P.F. Sharp, *Whoop-Up Country: The Canadian-American West, 1865–1885* (Helena: Historical Society of Montana 1960) 38–9
3 Henry Youle Hind, *Reports of Progress; Together with a Preliminary and General Report on the Assiniboine and Saskatchewan Exploring Expedition* (Toronto: John Lovell 1859) 31. Though Hind did not actually travel in what is now southern Alberta, with the information he had gained from other sources by 1860 he was writing and speaking of most of this southern territory as part of the 'Great American Desert.' See John Warkentin, 'The Desert Goes North,' *Images of the Plains*, ed. B.W. Blouet and M.P. Lawson (Lincoln: University of Nebraska Press 1975) 152–7.
4 Captain John Palliser, *Further Papers Relative to the Exploration under Captain Palliser* (London: George Edward Eyre and William Spottiswoode 1860) 8–91
5 Captain John Palliser, 'The General Report' in *The Papers of the Palliser Expedition 1857–60*, ed. Irene M. Spry (Toronto: The Champlain Society 1968) 19–20
6 W.F. Butler, *The Great Lone Land* (London: Sampson, Low Marston, Low and Searle 1872) 376
7 S.W. Horrall, 'The March West,' in *Men in Scarlet*, ed. Hugh A. Dempsey (Calgary: McClelland and Stewart West 1975) 17–20
8 UAA, Pearce Papers, Letter Book II, Schedule of Squatters to whom Entry Is to Be Granted Forthwith, 8 September 1885
9 Canada, *Sessional Papers* (Commons), 1877, X, Vol. 7, No. 9, 25
10 *Ibid.* 24. One former policeman, D.J. Whitney, has generally been singled out as the first constable to take up ranching. He is alleged to have purchased cattle in 1876 and turned them out on the range to fend for themselves until his term expired the following year. While Whitney's ingenuity cannot be disputed, there were a number of policemen who had left the force to begin ranching the previous year, though they may not have acquired cattle until 1877. See, for example, anon., 'Early Range History,' *Scarlet and Gold*, Vol. 46, 102.
11 GAI, Kenneth R. Coppock, Alberta Ranch Brands 1881–1900, *Brand Index*, 372. Canada, *Sessional Papers* (Commons), 1879, XII, Vol. 6, No. 7, 67
12 Canada, *Debates* (Commons) II (1880) 28 Apr. 1814–15. See also *Manitoba Daily Free Press*, 19 Sept. 1883.
13 That a number of police left the force to engage in stock raising is confirmed in police registers, early press reports, and Department of the Interior files. Possibly the best source of accurate information is the Pearce Papers. As the chief Department

of the Interior official in the North-West Territories, he was, among other things, responsible for settlement of conflicting land claims. The information for such adjudication has the advantage not only of being collected within several years of the original settlement, but also of being sworn under oath. There were particular problems concerning many individuals who settled prior to the original surveys of 1881–3 and resultant files kept by William Pearce are therefore one of the few sources of accurate information regarding the arrival of many of these original settlers. Some important early ranchers who came west with the first police contingents and who commenced ranching before 1882 include D.J. Whitney (1877), E.H. Maunsell (1877), J.W. Bell (1878), George Maunsell (1878), G. Ives (1879), D. Allison (1879), J.D. Murray (1879), Sgt W.F. Parker (1879), R. Patterson (1880), F.R. Morris (1880), D. Grier (1880), A.H. Lynch-Staunton (1880), Sgt-Maj. C. Bray (1881), A. Wilson (1881), C. Ryan (1881), Supt W. Winder (1881), Col. James Walker (1881). Others before 1882 to whom a precise date cannot be fixed are: C. Kettles, J. Brueneau, H.S. Smith, M.J. Gallegher, G. Genge, A.H. Henry, S. Sharpe, Capt. C.E. Denny, W. Pocklington, J. Hollies, F. Shaw, A. Shead, F. Pace, D. McAuley, R. Wilson, and D. Cochrane. In addition to the foregoing, who established long-term residence in the west, there were others who remained only a few years in the south-west of whom no precise record remains.

    See GAI, Southern Alberta Pioneers Association, nominal rolls, A.E. Freebairn, I.C. Lynch-Staunton, 5. *Macleod Gazette*, 18 May 1886. Pearce Papers, LB.II, pp 491, 499, 501, 14B12, 14B16, 14B2. Anon., 'Early Range History,' 101–11.

14 John McDougall, *Opening the Great West: Experiences of a Missionary in 1875–76*, ed. J. Ernest Nix (Occasional Paper No. 6; Calgary: Glenbow-Alberta Institute 1970) 26. The traditional date, 1871, ascribed to the arrival of McDougall's cattle is incorrect, being two years before the mission at Morleyville was established. This error is but one example of the countless inaccuracies in the literature on Canadian ranching and is possibly explained by the reminiscent nature of much of the source material commonly used, as well as the tendency to rely on secondary sources.

15 GAI, Richard Hardisty Papers, 1861–97, John Bunn (Bow River) to Richard Hardisty, Chief Factor HBC Edmonton, 14 Aug. 1875

16 G.E.G. Thomas, 'The British Columbia Ranching Frontier, 1858–1896' (MA thesis, University of British Columbia 1976) 86, 95–6

17 *Ibid.* 88

18 Alexander Begg, *History of the North-West* (Toronto: Hunter Rose and Co. 1894) II, Appendix 14, LXX

19 The scale of supply was two cows for every family under five, three cows for families of five to ten, four cows for families over ten, and one bull for every chief.

244 Notes pp 10–13

20 Canada, Department of the Interior, *Annual Report* (1879) Appendix D, 22

21 Canada, *Journals of the Council of the North-West Territories, from 1877 to 1887* (Regina: Printer to the Government of the North-West Territories 1886) 11

22 See, for example, L.V. Kelly, *The Rangemen: The Story of the Ranchers and Indians of Alberta* (Toronto: William Briggs 1913) 125.

23 Pearce Papers, 14B2, 14B12, and LB.II, 'Schedule of Squatters'

24 Canada, Department of the Interior, *Annual Report* (1880–1) Part II, North-West Mounted Police, Commissioner's Report, 1880, 25

25 *Ibid.*, 21–5

26 Of the thirty-nine men who took their discharge from the Ft Macleod detachment in 1880, twenty-five remained, for the most part to take up cattle-raising. For a discussion of the social background of members of the force, see R.C. Macleod, *The North-West Mounted Police and Law Enforcement 1873–1905* (Toronto: University of Toronto Press 1976) 73–88.

27 Pearce Papers, 14B12. One such person from Compton was G.S. Ives, whose father was a justice of the Quebec Superior Court.

28 Robert Sellar, *The Tragedy of Quebec: The Expulsion of Its Protestant Farmers* (Huntington, PQ: by author 1907; reprt Toronto: University of Toronto Press 1974)

29 L.S. Channell, *History of Compton County* (Cookshire, PQ: by author 1896) 33; J.L. Little, 'The Social and Economic Development in Two Quebec Townships, 1851–1870,' in *Canadian Papers in Rural History*, I, ed. Donald H. Akenson (Gananoque, Ontario: Langdale Press 1978) 89–94

30 J.D. Higinbotham, *When the West Was Young* (Toronto: Ryerson Press 1933) 203. Pearce Papers, 14B12

31 Some western ranchers who benefitted from such high-placed contacts included Cave-Brown-Cave (banking), R. Newbolt (military), Higginson, (military), D. McPherson (military), W. Gordon-Cumming (banking), D. Fraser (banking), the Hon. T.B.H. Cochrane (military), Recardo (banking), A. Samson (banking), G. Ross (banking), B. Hartford (banking), H. Eckford (military), A. Wyndham (military). In selecting the foregoing and following names (in n33) as examples, I have restricted the selection to those who came before 1890. The list is not inclusive. The names were selected on the basis of prominence within the ranch community and in terms of longer residence in the west. Each list could be expanded by the addition of similar social types who arrived after 1890 and on into the late 1920s.

32 Some more prominent representatives of the British squirarchy in the south-west included W. Skrine, O.A. Critchley, W. Bell-Irving, Wilmot, L. Brook, L. Garnet, G.E. Goddard, D.H. Andrews, W. Huckvale, and J. Deane-Freeman.

33 Captains Bryant, Wilson, Lyndon, Quin, Bedingfeld, and Scobie were among the more successful ranchers. For biographical information on the British population see the following: GAI, Southern Alberta Pioneers Association, nominal rolls; GAI,

Robert Newbolt, autobiography, 19–23; GAI, F. Ings, 'Tales from Midway Ranch' 4–40, 124–59; GAI, A.L. Freebairn, 'The Story of Pincher Creek and District' (1958) 1–8; A.E. Cross, 'Round-Up of 1887,' *Calgary Historical Society* (nd) 2–14; F.W. Godsal, 'Old Times,' *Alberta Historical Review* XII (Autumn 1964) 19–24; H. Frank Lawrence, 'Early Days in the Chinook Belt,' *Alberta Historical Review* XIII (Winter 1965) 9–19; C. Lynch-Staunton, 'A History of the Early Days of Pincher Creek,' *Women's Institute of Alberta* (nd) 4–54; Gerald L. Berry, *The Whoop-Up Trail* (Edmonton: Applied Arts Products 1953) 99–110; High River Pioneers' and Old Timers' Association, *Leaves from the Medicine Tree* (Lethbridge, Alberta: Lethbridge Herald 1960); Higinbotham, *When the West Was Young* 95–102, 202–4, 259; Pearce Papers 14B2, 14B12.

34 GAI, C. Inderwick, diary and personal letters from North Fork Ranch, 13 May 1884

35 James G. MacGregor, 'Lord Lorne in Alberta,' *Alberta Historical Review* XII (Autumn, 1964) 14; from original articles in the *Edinburgh Courant*, 18, 27, and 28 Oct. 1881

36 Canada, *Journals of the Council of the North West Territories* (13 Oct. 1886) 8

37 Moira O'Neill, 'A Lady's Life on a Ranche,' *Blackwood's Edinburgh Magazine 163* (Jan. 1898) 3–16. See also *The Emigrant*, 1 Sept. 1886, 95.

38 J.J. Young, 'Ranching in the Canadian North-West,' *Canada: An Encyclopedia of the Country*, ed. J. Castell Hopkins (Toronto: The Linscott Publishing Co. 1899) V, 62

39 Alexander Begg, 'Stock Raising in the Bow River District Compared with Montana,' in *Manitoba and the Great North West*, ed. J. Macoun (Guelph: The World Publishing Co. 1882) 273–7, quoting W. Brown

40 R. England, *The Colonization of Western Canada* (London: P.S. King and Son Ltd 1936) 57, quoting Canada, *Sessional Papers* (Commons) XIII, No. 4

41 Duncan McEachran, *Impressions of Pioneers of Alberta as a Ranching Country, Commencing 1881* (Ormstown, Quebec: by author, nd) 4

42 *Montreal Gazette*, 13 Aug. 1903 (obit.). See also W. Naftel, *The Cochrane Ranch*, Canadian Historic Sites, Occasional Papers in Archaeology and History, No. 16. (Ottawa: Parks Canada 1977) 87–90.

43 PAC, Department of the Interior, Timber and Grazing Branch, X, 142709 (Cochrane Ranch) Pt 1, M.H. Cochrane to Col. Dennis, Deputy Minister of the Interior, 26 Nov. 1880. Department of the Interior, Timber and Grazing Branch, hereafter cited as RG15, B2a

44 Canada, *Statutes* (1872) ch. 23, sec. 34

45 *Ibid.* (1876) ch. 19, sec. 15

46 RG15, B2a, 10, 142709 Pt 1, M.H. Cochrane to Sir John A. Macdonald, 17 Dec. 1880

47 *Ibid.*, M.H. Cochrane to the Minister of the Interior, 10 Feb. 1881

48 *Ibid.*, draft of memorandum to Privy Council, 21 Feb. 1881

49 *Ibid.*, copy of a note from Sir John A. Macdonald to J. Pope, Minister of Agriculture, 12 May 1881, as enclosed in letter of J.A. Gemmill to Minister of the Interior, 31 July 1882

50 *Ibid.*, M.H. Cochrane to Deputy Minister of the Interior, 31 May 1881

51 Alberta, Department of Lands and Forests, orders-in-council, Department of the Interior, 1864–1932, III, order-in-council No. 1710, 23 Dec. 1881, 805–12

52 *Ibid.*, IV, 159–61, text of the first grazing lease

53 RG15, B2a, 10, 142709, Pt 1, J.A. Gemmill, Solicitor for Cochrane Ranche Co., to Minister of the Interior, 31 July 1882, enclosing copy of letter from Sir John A. Macdonald to J.H. Pope

54 *Ibid.*, M.H. Cochrane to D.L. Macpherson, Minister of the Interior, 7 June 1883

55 RG15, B2a, 3, 11007. 'Statement Showing the Number of Horses, Cattle and Sheep, and the Name of the Importer, Entered in the District of Alberta from the First of June 1880'

56 RG15, B2a, Vol. 172, 145330, Pt 4, 'Grazing Regulations,' 6 Nov. 1903. The Imperial Wastelands Occupation Act of 1846 divided New South Wales into three areas: a settled region, where there was normal land sale, as well as intermediate and unsettled areas where leasehold was the standard form of tenure. See H.S. Robert, *History of Australian Land Settlement, 1788–1920* (Melbourne: Macmillan Co. of Australia 1968) 184, 194–5.

CHAPTER TWO: THE CATTLE COMPANIES AND THE 'BEEF BONANZA' 1882–91

1 Simon G. Hanson, *Argentine Meat and the British Market* (Stanford, CA: Stanford University Press 1937) 46

2 W. Turrentine Jackson, 'British Interests in the Range Cattle Industry,' *When Grass Was King*, ed. Maurice Frink (Boulder: University of Colorado Press 1956) Pt II, 139, citing Herbert O. Brayer, 'The Influence of British Capital on the Western Range Cattle Industry,' *Westerners' Brand Book* (Denver, May 1948) 3–4

3 *Ibid.*, citing Great Britain, Final Report on Her Majesty's Commissioners Appointed to Inquire in the Subject of the Agricultural Depression, 1897

4 J.R. Fisher, 'The Economic Effects of Cattle Disease in Great Britain and its Containment, 1850–1900,' *Agricultural History* LIV (Apr. 1980) 278–87

5 A. Bogue, 'The Progress of the Cattle Industry in Ontario during the Eighteen Eighties,' *Agricultural History* XXI (July 1947) 163

6 Jackson, 'British Interests in the Cattle Range Industry,' citing Clare Read and Albert Pell, 'Further Reports of Assistant Commissioners, Ministry of Agriculture and Fisheries,' *Royal Commission on Agriculture, 1879–1882* (Great Britain) 7–16

7 Cited in Mari Sandoz, *The Cattlemen* (New York: Hastings House 1958) 238

8 John Clay, *My Life on the Range* (Norman: University of Oklahoma Press 1962) vii
9 Sandoz, *The Cattlemen* 239. See also W.P. Webb, *The Great Plains* (Boston: Ginn and Company 1959) 235; W. Baillie, 'Cattle Ranches in the Far West,' *The Fortnightly Review* XXVIII New Series (July-Dec. 1880) 438-57.
10 Jackson, 'British Interests in the Cattle Range Industry' 160
11 W.D. Zimmerman, 'Live Cattle Export Trade between United States and Great Britain, 1868-1885,' *Agricultural History* XXXVI (Jan. 1962) 52. Feeder cattle were purchased on arrival by farmers who fattened or 'finished' the animal for several months and then marketed it, gaining substantial profit on its improved weight and quality.
12 GAI, C. Acton Burrows Papers, II (scrapbook) 93. *The Times* (Winnipeg) 30 Mar. 1881. See also *The Gazette* (Montreal), 4 Nov. 1881.
13 The Governor General was particularly impressed and remarked to F.W. Godsal, a friend who visited him at Rideau Hall the following year: 'If I were not Governor General of Canada, I would be a cattle rancher in Alberta.' F.W. Godsal, 'Old Times,' *Alberta Historical Review* XII (Autumn 1964) 19. Lorne's enthusiasm was shared by his staff, many of whom later established ranches in the west. Lorne himself, along with other titled friends, also became a shareholder in a western ranch.
14 J. Macoun, *Manitoba and the Great North-West* (Guelph: The World Publishing Co. 1882) 277-80. Author of the chapter entitled 'Stockraising in the Bow River District Compared with Montana' was the noted western booster, Alexander Begg.
15 See, for example, Sir Francis De Winton, 'Canada and the Great North-West,' *The Journal of the Manchester Geographical Society* VII, 4-6 (Apr.-June 1892) 91-3; *The Times* (London), 21 Oct. 1898; University of Alberta, Rutherford collection; anonymous, *A Stockman's Paradise* (Lethbridge: Alberta Railway and Coal Co. and Canadian North-West Irrigation Co. 189?).
16 Henry Youle Hind, leader of the Canadian government's expedition to the western interior in 1857-8, was convinced that meteorological records had been deliberately falsified by Macoun, and that negative assessments of settlement prospects were actively suppressed by government, railway, and colonization company interests. See Henry Youle Hind, *Manitoba and the North-West Frauds* (Windsor, NS: by author 1883) 17-18, 33.
17 Canada, Department of Consumer and Corporate Affairs, Companies Branch, Cochrane Ranche Company Ltd. According to the usage of the period most British and Canadian ranchers, unlike their American counterparts, spelled ranche with an 'e'.
18 *Ibid.*, North-West Cattle Company Ltd. Frederick S. Stimson was also the brother-in-law of Capt. W. Winder, who seems to have been a key person responsible for publicizing western ranching prospects in the Compton area.

19 PAC, RG15, B2a, Vol. 19, 175296 (Winder Ranche), George Barry to Lindsay Russell, 25 Aug. 1882

20 Ibid., C. Stimson to Lindsay Russell, 29 May 1882

21 Ibid., Vol. 20, 179180 (Chipman lease)

22 Canada, Department of Consumer and Corporate Affairs, Companies Branch; Stewart Ranch Company Ltd

23 PAC, Macdonald Papers, MG26, A1(e), Vol. 575. Letterbook Pt 1, Sir John A. Macdonald to C.S. Campbell, 22 June 1883

24 Canada, Department of Consumer and Corporate Affairs, Companies Branch, Glengarry Ranche Company file

25 See RG15, B2a, Vol. 170, 145330, Pt 1; Vol. 46, 43887, Vol. 19, 174372, and Vol. 3, 11007.

26 Ibid. Some MP's were active ranch promoters while others like D'Alton McCarthy, MP for Simcoe, Ontario, R.R. McLennan, MP for Glengarry, Ontario, A.T.H. Williams, MP for Port Hope, Ontario, J.C. Patterson, MP for Grenville, Ontario, T. Temple, MP for York, New Brunswick, the Hon. John Henry Pope, MP for Compton, PQ, E.T. Brooks, MP for Sherbrooke, PQ, L.H. Massue, MP for Richelieu, PQ, C.C. Colby, MP for Stansted, PQ, and D.O. Bourbeau, MP for Drummond-Athabaska, PQ were directors or investors in various ranch companies.

27 John R. Craig, Ranching with Lords and Commons (Toronto: William Briggs 1903) 108

28 GAI, 'Lord Lorne's Expedition to the North West,' clipping from Liverpool Journal of Commerce, 24 Oct. 1881

29 C.W. Buchanan, 'History of the Walrond Cattle Ranch Ltd,' Canadian Cattlemen VIII (March 1946) 171

30 GAI, C.E. Harris, 'Trip of Charles Edward Harris to the Canadian West: 1882,' mss, 1–3; Henry J. Morgan, ed., The Dominion Annual Register and Review (Toronto: Hunter, Rose and Co. 1882) 370; (1883) 340

31 H. Frank Lawrence, 'Early Days in the Chinook Belt,' Alberta Historical Review XIII, 1 (1965). Other sources of biographical information include Craig, Ranching with Lords and Commons 170; A.E. Cross, 'Round-Up of 1887,' Calgary Historical Society (1923) 2–14; A.L. Fairbairn, 'The Story of Pincher Creek and District' (Calgary: Glenbow Foundation 1958) 1–8; C. Lynch-Staunton, A History of the Early Days of Pincher Creek (Pincher Creek: Women's Institute of Alberta, nd) 4–54; Henry J. Morgan, ed., The Canadian Men and Women of the Time 1897 and 1912 (Toronto: William Briggs 1898 and 1912); and High River Pioneers' and Old Timers' Association, Leaves from the Medicine Tree (Lethbridge: Lethbridge Herald 1960).

32 W.S. Macnutt, 'The 1880's,' in The Canadians: 1867–1967, ed. J.M.S. Careless and R. Craig Brown (Toronto: Macmillan of Canada 1967) 83. 'Macleod could produce Canada's best version of a wild west. The famous Camoose House, kept by an

ex-trader, ex-preacher, and squawman, was the resort of all the whisky vendors, bull-whackers, and mule-skinners of the region who called themselves ranchers.'

33 Sandoz, *The Cattlemen* 63–83, 296–310
34 *Macleod Gazette*, 30 Nov. 1886, quoting *The Times* (London), autumn 1886
35 *Ft Macleod Gazette*, 3 Feb. 1883
36 *Ibid.*, 14 Nov. 1882
37 *Ibid.*, 2 May 1885
38 *Calgary Herald*, 16 Sept. 1885
39 *Macleod Gazette*, 12 Jan. 1886
40 *Ibid.*, 9 Mar. 1886, Supplement
41 *Ibid.*, 9 May 1886
42 *Ibid.*, 20 Apr. 1886
43 *Ibid.*, supplement
44 *Macleod Gazette*, 18 May 1886. Official delegates included W. Skrine, T. Lynch, and J.J. Barter from the High River district; J. Herron, F.C. Inderwick, and S. Sharpe from the Pincher Creek district; and W. Frields, E.H. Maunsell, and S. Pinhorne from the Willow Creek district. At the first annual meeting of the NWT Stock Association (4 May 1887), delegates changed the name of their organization to the Alberta Stock Growers Association.
45 *Ibid.*, 1 June 1886
46 *Ibid.*, 22 June 1886
47 *Ibid.*, 20 Apr. 1886, supplement
48 Macdonald Papers, MG26, A1(a), Vol. 420, J.L. Evans to Sir John A. Macdonald, 8 Oct. 1885, and T. White (Minister of Interior) to Sir John A. Macdonald, 20 Nov. 1885
49 *Calgary Herald*, 9 Apr. 1885
50 Macdonald Papers, MG26, A1(d), Vol. 420, William Carter to Sir John A. Macdonald, 2 Mar. 1887; C. Drinkwater to Sir John A. Macdonald, 18 Dec. 1886. This was a special plea from the CPR to exempt Sir John Lister Kaye from the newly imposed duty.
51 UAA, Pearce Papers, IB 6, William Pearce to the Minister of the Interior, 10 Nov. 1886
52 PAC, Canada, Department of the Interior, correspondence of the Deputy Minister, Vol. 131, 142083 (Powder River Cattle Co.)
53 RG15, B2, Vol. 159, Pt 1, 141376, H.S. Pinhorne, Mgr, New Oxley Ranche Co., to Minister of the Interior, 14 Oct. 1886; W.E. Cochrane to Minister of the Interior, 21 Oct. 1886
54 *Ibid.*, D. McEachran, Mgr, Walrond Ranche, to Minister of the Interior, 5 Aug. 1887; F.S. Stimson, Mgr, North-West Cattle Co., to Minister of the Interior, 1 Sept. 1887

55 Pearce Papers, IB 6, Pearce to Minister of the Interior, 8 Mar. 1888; Minister of the Interior to Pearce, 16 Mar. 1888; *Gazette*, 11 Oct. 1888. Possible use of the quarantine as a device to restrict American competition did not go unnoticed in the US. See *Macleod Gazette*, 15 Nov. 1888 citing the *River Press* (Ft Benton, Montana), 18 Apr. 1888.

56 Pearce Papers, IB 6, Department of the Interior to W. Pearce, 20 Feb. 1893

57 *Ibid.*, W. Pearce to A.M. Burgess, Deputy Minister of the Interior, 14 Dec. 1892; A.M. Burgess to W. Pearce, 29 Dec. 1892

58 *Ibid.*, W. Pearce to A.M. Burgess, 3 Jan. 1896

59 *Ibid.*, 4B12, A.M. Morden to W. Pearce, 21 Mar. 1888; Department of the Interior to W. Pearce, 27 June 1889; A.M. Burgess to W. Pearce, 7 Aug. 1890

60 *Ibid.*, A. McLennan, Mgr Stewart Ranch Co., to W. Pearce, 13 Sept. 1890

61 *Ibid.*, Secretary to Minister of the Interior to W. Pearce, 18 Feb. 1896

62 RG15, B2a, Vol. 170, 145330 Pt 1, memo regarding amendment to the draft lease form, 26 Apr. 1882. RG21, Vol. 228, PC 892, 11 May 1882. The original order-in-council would have prohibited sheep-raising altogether had it not been for the caution of the Governor General, who withheld the original. MG 26, A1(a), Vol. 82, Lorne to Macdonald, 23 Apr. 1882

63 Macdonald Papers, MG 26, A1(d), Vol. 249, C. Colby, Conservative MP for Stansted, PO, to D.L. Macpherson, Minister of the Interior, 21 Mar. 1883; D.L. Macpherson to Sir John A. Macdonald, 22 Mar. 1883; M.H. Cochrane to J.H. Pope, Minister of Agriculture, 18 June 1883

64 *Ft Macleod Gazette*, 12 Sept. 1884

65 *Ibid.*, citing *Winnipeg Times*, nd

66 Pearce Papers, letterbook, P, p 315, W. Pearce to A.M. Burgess, 20 Sept. 1884

67 RG15, B1a, Vol. 114, 108068, petition of Morley settlers to W. Pearce, 19 Feb. 1886

68 RG15, B2a, Vol. 173, 96831, J. Hargrave to Minister of the Interior, 11 Jan. 1901; petition to restrict sheep ranchers and related correspondence. *Ibid.*, Vol. 103, 476534

69 Canada, Sessional Papers (Commons), 1885, No. 53, pp 2–9. Canada, Department of the Interior, *Annual Report* (1885) 33

70 *Ft Macleod Gazette*, 24 Aug. 1882; 23 Sept. 1882

71 *Ibid.*, 14 Nov. 1882

72 RG15, B1a, Vol. 59, 52928, 12 Oct. 1882, petition

73 *Ibid.*, A.M. Burgess to J. Trotier, 5 Dec. 1882

74 *Globe* (Toronto), 11 Dec. 1882, report of 11 Oct. meeting in Ft Calgary

75 *Calgary Herald*, 25 June 1884, quoting Toronto *News*

76 *Ft Macleod Gazette*, 24 Mar. 1883

77 RG15, B1a, Vol. 77, 65793, petition – settlers in Porcupine Hills, 10 Sept. 1883

78 *Ibid.* Department of the Interior to A. Shead, 5 Mar. 1884
79 *Ibid.*, F. Oliver to J. Smart, Deputy Minister of the Interior, 11 Nov. 1899
80 Macdonald Papers, MG 26, A1(b), Vol. 409, F. Girard to Sir Hector Langevin, 18 Nov. 1884
81 See, for example, *Gallagher* v *John B. Smith* and *Stewart Ranch Co.* v *Robert Auld*, as cited in *Ft Macleod Gazette*, 14 Aug. 1884 and Sept. 1884.
82 *Calgary Herald*, 9 Apr. 1885
83 *Ibid.*
84 Macdonald Papers, MG 26, A1(d), Vol. 414, pp 200489–98
85 RG15, B1a Vol. 101, 87193, C.B. Elliott to Sir David Macpherson, Minister of the Interior, telegram, 3 Apr. 1885
86 *Ibid.*, C.B. Elliott to Sir David Macpherson, telegram, 10 Apr. 1885
87 *Ibid.*, G.F. Clark to Sir David Macpherson, 10 Apr. 1885. Several of those 'watched' were Calgary lawyers with suspected Grit or Fenian leanings. Another, Ramsay, was an agent of the North-West Land Company, which had an obvious interest in seeing leases cancelled. See Macdonald Papers, MG 26, A1(b), Vol. 193, p 80356, G.F. Clarke to A.M. Burgess, 8 May 1885.
88 *Ibid.*, RG15, B1a, Vol. 102, 87776, Sir John A. Macdonald to Sir David Macpherson, 20 Apr. 1885
89 Macdonald Papers, MG26, A1(b), Vol. 525, Letterbook, Macdonald to the Hon. Alexander Campbell, Minister of Justice, 23 June 1883
90 Canada, Department of the Interior, *Annual Report* (1885) 11
91 GAI, W.F. Cochrane, diary and letterbook, Cochrane Ranch 1884–5, 103, 21 Mar. 1885
92 *Ibid.* 107, W.F. Cochrane to W.D. Kerfoot, 22 Mar. 1885
93 *Ibid.* 138, W.F. Cochrane to J.M. Browning, 26 Apr. 1885
94 Later the Earl of Shannon
95 *Macleod Gazette*, 21 July 1885
96 RG15, B2a, Vol. 159, 141376, Pt 1, W. Pearce to A.M. Burgess regarding Macpherson's instructions of 7 Jan. 1885, 10 Mar. 1886
97 *Ibid.*, W. Pearce to H.H. Smith, Commissioner of Dominion Lands, Winnipeg, 10 Sept. 1884
98 *Ibid.*
99 Pearce Papers, Letterbook 11, Pearce to Black, Secretary, Stock Association at Ft Macleod, 30 Nov. 1885; W. Pearce to F. Stimson, Vice-Pres North-Wes Stock Association, High River, 30 Nov. 1885
100 RG15, B2a, Vol. 159, no. 141376 Pt 1, North-West Stock Association to Minister of the Interior, 1 Mar. 1886
101 *Ibid.*, A.M. Burgess to T. White, 12 Mar. 1886
102 *Ibid.*, W. Pearce to T. White, 6 Mar. 1886

103 *Macleod Gazette*, 27 July 1886

104 *Ibid.* Cochrane's promise turned out to have a number of strings attached and it took another year for a compromise to be reached. See RG15, B2a, Vol. 5, 137261, Pt 1, memo. Additional lands were gained in the south in lieu of lands given up along the Bow River, 23 Aug. 1887.

105 RG15, B2a, Vol. 159, no. 141376, Pt 1, Cochrane, Allan *et al.* to White, 9 Oct. 1886; Canadian North-West Territories Stock Association to T. White, 3 December 1886

106 *Ibid.*, W. Pearce to T. White, 11 Nov. 1886

107 *Ibid.*, A.M. Burgess to T. White, 9 Jan. 1887

108 *Ibid.*, A.M. Burgess to T. White, 12 Mar. 1886

109 *Ibid.*, W. Pearce to T. White, 11 Nov. 1886

110 *Ibid.*, W. Pearce to H.S. Pinham [Pinhorn], Manager, Oxley Ranch, 27 Sept. 1886, enclosure in W. Pearce to T. White, 11 Nov. 1886

111 *Macleod Gazette*, 21 Mar. 1886

112 *Ibid.*, 22 mar. 1887

113 *Ibid.*, 2 Jan. 1885

114 RG15, B2a, Vol. 5, no. 137261, Pt 1, *Calgary Herald*, 16 Mar. 1887, clipping

115 RG15, B2a, Vol. 5, no. 137261, Pt 1, official notice, 23 May 1887

116 *Ibid.*, J.M. Browning to F. White, quoting manager's report, 26 May 1887

117 *Ibid.*, F. White to J.M. Browning, 28 May 1887

118 *Calgary Herald*, advertisement, 26 Aug. 1887

119 RG15, B2a, Vol. 5, no. 137261, Pt 1, *Calgary Herald*, clipping, 23 Aug. 1887

120 RG15, B2a, Vol. 5, no. 137261, Pt 1, W. Pearce to Commissioner of Dominion Lands, 19 Dec. 1888; petition to E. Dewdney, Minister of the Interior (269 names), 12 Jan. 1889; G. Goddard to E. Dewdney, 15 Mar. 1889

121 *Ibid.*, J. Cowan to E. Dewdney, 18 Jan. 1889

122 *Ibid.*, A.M. Burgess to E. Dewdney, 26 Jan. 1889

123 *Macleod Gazette*, 23 May 1888

124 *Ibid.*, 4 July 1888, and 11 July 1888

125 GAI, J.D. Higinbotham Papers, J.D. Higinbotham to Ed and Harry, 23 Mar. 1885

126 *Debates* (Commons) 1, 28 Feb. 1889, 372–4

127 *Calgary Herald*, 4 Apr. 1888; *Calgary Herald Magazine*, 31 Aug. 1963

128 *Ibid.*, 2 Jan. 1889

129 Later a member of Conservative McBride government in British Columbia

130 *Calgary Herald*, 25 Dec. 1889

131 *Ibid.*, 12 Dec. 1888

132 *Macleod Gazette*, 4 July 1889

133 RG15, B2a, Vol. 3, no. 1007, 'Statement Showing the number of Horses, Cattle, and Sheep, and the Name of the Importer, Entered in the District of Alberta, from the First of June 1880'

134 RG15, B2a, Vol. 23, 192192, 'Stock Returns,' 15 Jan. 1890; W. Pearce to Secretary, Department of the Interior, 25 Jan. 1890
135 *Ibid.*
136 This is an average value subject to great qualification. A herd with superior blood lines was worth considerably more, and there were a number of such quality herds, particularly within the 300–500 range. Below 400 head, cattle herds tended to be grouped at two levels, about 200 or less than 100, with non-leaseholders predominating in the latter category.
137 *Calgary Herald*, 26 June 1886
138 Canada, Department of Consumer and Corporate Affairs, Companies Branch, North West Cattle Co. Ltd
139 Craig, *Ranching with Lords and Commons* 234
140 *Calgary Herald*, 27 June 1888
141 Canada, Department of the Interior, *Annual Report* (1891) RG15, B2a, Vol. 123, 192192, Pearce to Secretary, Department of the Interior, 26 Jan. 1891
142 Calgary Herald, 16 Sept. 1891. By 1890 the big western ranches had an established reputation in Great Britain. See Canada, *Sessional Papers 1891* XXIV Vol. 6 no. 6E, 'Appendix to the Report of the Minister of Agriculture,' 'Report of the Liverpool Agent' 26–31, 40.
143 W.L. Marr and D.G. Paterson, *Canada: An Economic History* (Toronto: Macmillan of Canada 1980) 343
144 Canada, *Sessional Papers*, 1884 XVIII Vol. 8 no. 14 'Report of the Minister of Agriculture' vii

CHAPTER THREE: GRAZING LEASES TO STOCK-WATERING RESERVES: THE CATTLE KINGDOM 1892–6

1 *Macleod Gazette*, 15 Jan. 1891
2 *Debates* (Commons) XXIII (1891), 6466, 25 Sept. 1891, citing a letter of 8 Apr. 1891 from R. Dunbar to Sir John A. Macdonald
3 PAC, Department of the Interior, RG15, B1a, Vol. 184, 255938, D. McEachran to F. White, Comptroller, NWMP, 27 Jan. 1891
4 *Ibid.*, J. Royal to Department of the Interior, 25 Apr. 1891; R. Sedgewick, Deputy Minister of Justice to Department of the Interior, 6 May 1891
5 *Macleod Gazette*, 26 Mar. 1891
6 *Ibid.*, 30 July 1891
7 *Ibid.*, 3 Sept. 1891. See also *Debates* (Commons) XXIII (1891) 6469; Pearce Papers 14B5; 'Claims to Land, Fort Macleod.' Correspondence in this file indicates that Dunbar's claim was legitimate; he had settled three months before the area was first leased.
8 GAI, Dewdney Papers, enclosure in D. McEachran to the Hon. E. Dewdney, 13 Aug. 1891

9 PAC, RCMP Records, Comptroller's Office, Official Correspondence, RG18, A1, Vol. 56, F.695, report from Supt S.B. Steele to Commissioner L.W. Herchmer, 17 Oct. 1891

10 *Debates* (Commons) XXIII (1891) 6470

11 *Ibid.* 6473

12 *Ibid.* 6464–76

13 *Ibid.* 4676; Dewdney Papers, McEachran to Dewdney, 29 Mar. 1892, 1–2

14 Dewdney Papers, E. Dewdney to A.M. Burgess, 30 Mar. 1892

15 *Macleod Gazette*, 10 Mar. 1892

16 Dewdney Papers, A.M. Burgess to E. Dewdney, 6 Apr. 1892

17 *Macleod Gazette*, 21 Apr. 1892

18 RG15, B2a, Vol. 10, no. 142709, Pt 4, Circular, 15 Jan. 1892. Those present were Dr McEachran of the Walrond Ranche, H.M. Allan of the North West Cattle Company, A.E. Cross of the A7 Ranch, Messrs Holt and D. Mann of the Glengarry Ranche Company, A.M. Nanton of the Cypress Cattle Company, H. McLennan of the Stewart Ranche Company, and P.S. Ross of the Cochrane Ranche Company.

19 *Calgary Herald*, 9 Mar. 1892; RG15, B2a, Vol. 10, no. 142709, Pt 4

20 PAC, RG18, A1, Vol. 63, 'Macleod Monthly Report,' Supt S.B. Steele to Commissioner L.W. Herchmer, 1 Apr. 1892

21 *Ibid.*, S.B. Steele to L.W. Herchmer, 1 May 1892

22 *Macleod Gazette*, 10 Mar. 1892

23 *Calgary Herald*, 9 Mar. 1892

24 Order-in-council, 22 Apr. 1893. See also *Macleod Gazette*, 21 Mar. 1888.

25 C.M. MacInnis, *In the Shadow of the Rockies* (London: Rivingtons 1930) 242. A.S. Morton and C. Martin, *History of Prairie Settlement and 'Dominion Lands' Policy* Vol. II of *Canadian Frontiers of Settlement*

26 John Blue, *Alberta Past and Present* 1 (Chicago: Pioneer Historical Publishing Co. 1924) 323

27 Canada, Department of the Interior, *Annual Reports* (1884–96). Between 1884 and 1894 the large ranches had from time to time raised and lowered their acreages as the land and market situation warranted. Other important companies such as the Glengarry, Stewart, Brown, and Alberta ranches also experienced only minor lease reduction.

28 J.R. Craig, *Ranching with Lords and Commons or Twenty Years on the Range* (Toronto: William Briggs 1908) 236. Morton and Martin, *History of Prairie Settlement and Dominion Lands Policy* 323. RG15, B2a, Vol. 10, no. 142709, Pt 4, W. Pearce to Secretary, Department of the Interior, 28 Sept. 1894

29 *Calgary Herald*, 5 July 1957; see also *Calgary Family Herald* (GAI, clipping file).

30 *Calgary Herald*, 2–3 Sept. 1955; 24 Nov. 1956; *Lethbridge Herald*, 24 Oct. 1911

31 *Calgary Herald*, 8 Dec. 1956

32 RG15, B2, Vol. 159, no. 141376, Pt 2, W. Pearce to the Secretary, Department of the Interior, 24 June 1893, 29 Aug. 1893

33 *Ibid.*, F.W. Godsal to W. Pearce, 29 June 1893

34 See, for example, *ibid.*, A.E. Cross to Minister of Interior, 9 Jan. 1894; D. McEachran to Pearce, 23 July 1894; Pearce to J.H.G. Bray, Secretary, Medicine Hat Stock Association, 19 May 1896; W.F. Cochrane to Pearce, 22 Aug. 1896. RG15, B2a, Vol. 50, no. 22852, Pearce to A. Mclennan, Secretary, Pincher Creek Stock Association, 6 Oct. 1893.

35 *Macleod Gazette*, 18 Aug. 1893

36 RG18, A1, Vol. 116, no. 72, memo from Office of the Superintendent of Mines, 22 Mar. 1894. Correspondence from the Department of the Interior relating to the evictions and eviction proceedings does not seem to be present in existing Department of the Interior files.

37 *Ibid.*, Department of the Interior to M. Max Hebert and Levite Cyr, Pincher Creek, 1 June 1894

38 RG15, B2, Vol. 159, no. 141376, Pt 2, W. Pearce to Secretary, Department of the Interior, 29 Nov. 1893

39 UAA Pearce Papers, 14D3, Pearce to Secretary, Department of the Interior, 27 July 1894

40 *Ibid.*

41 RG18, A1, Vol. 116, no. 72, W. Pearce to Secretary, Department of the Interior, 27 July 1894

42 See for example, *ibid.*, memo to comptroller NWMP, 11 Oct. 1895; Department of the Interior to Comptroller, 7 Nov. 1895; Pearce to Comptroller, 5 Dec. 1895; Pearce to Department of the Interior, 5 Dec. 1895; RG15, B2, Vol. 159, Pt 2, no. 141376, Pearce to.W.E. Smith, 13 Apr. 1895.

43 RG18, A1, Vol. 116, no. 72, Department of the Interior to Comptroller, 19 Sept. 1895

44 Pearce Papers, 14D3, W. Pearce to S.B. Steele, 11 May 1896

45 RG15, B2, Vol. 159, no. 141376, Pt 2, W.M. Gunn to Department of the Interior, 21 Apr. 1895

46 *Ibid.*, C. Elton to Minister of the Interior, 27 Apr. 1895

47 *Ibid.*, D.W. Davis to J.M. Daly, 8 May 1895

48 *Ibid.*, W. Pearce to Gentlemen, 17 June 1895

49 *Ibid.*, W. Pearce to A.M. Nanton, 17 Aug. 1895

50 Ibid., Stock Growers' Association of Medicine Hat to W. Pearce, 9 May 1896; W. Pearce to Department of the Interior, 10 June 1896

51 GAI, H.M. Hatfield, 'Letters to Alberta Provincial Librarian from Yarrow, Alberta, 1908'

52 Craig, *Ranching with Lords and Commons* 293

53 Pearce Papers, 22–139, F.S. Stimson, Manager, North West Cattle Company to W. Pearce, 11 Mar. 1899. Pearce judiciously declined the gift. W. Pearce to F.S. Stimson, 13 Mar. 1899

54 *Calgary Herald*, 9 Apr. 1885; Macleod Gazette, 18 Apr. 1885

55 GAI, W.F. Cochrane, diary and letter book, Cochrane Ranche 1884–5, 4 Jan. 1885, 20

56 *Macleod Gazette*, 21 May 1885

57 John P. Turner, *The North-West Mounted Police, 1873–1893* (Ottawa: King's Printer 1950) II, 425–9

58 *Pincher Creek Echo*, 17 June 1909; article based on an interview with John Herron, ex-policeman, one of the first ranchers in the district and, at the time, Conservative MP for the district

59 E.C. Morgan, 'The North West Mounted Police, 1873–1888' (MA thesis, University of Saskatchewan 1970) 174. There is no evidence to suggest that murder was dealt with in any other manner than through the courts.

60 *Macleod Gazette*, 6 Dec. 1895. Some cowboys, particularly Americans, wore six-guns. The practice continued in the Cypress Hills country until well after the turn of the century. The carrying of side-arms, however, was frowned upon by the police and their use remained confined to a small minority in the foothills region and by the late 1890s was almost unknown in this area.

61 *Macleod Gazette*, 12 Oct. 1886

62 *Ibid.*, 22 Oct. 1891

63 *Calgary Herald*, 12 Nov. 1884

64 See, for example, *Macleod Gazette*, 21 Feb. 1885 and 11 Apr. 1885.

65 *Macleod Gazette*, 18 August 1893

66 See, for example, Turner, II, 531; *Medicine Hat News*, 23 August 1906.

67 R.C. Macleod, 'Crime and Class: Some Aspects of Law Enforcement in the Canadian North-West, *1885–1905*,' paper delivered to the Eleventh Annual Conference of the Western History Association, Santa Fe (Oct. 1971) 5

68 *Ibid.* 10

69 GAI, F. Ings, 'Tales from Midway Ranch' 42

70 See, for example, Canada, NWMP *Annual Report*, 1896, Report of the Commissioner, 11–12, 102; *Annual Report*, 1904, Report of the Commissioner, 91.

71 See, for example, *Gazette*, 3 Feb. 1883, 9 Mar. 1886, 20 Apr. 1886, Supplement; GAI, 'Western Stock Growers' Association Papers 1896–1963,' B1, F3.

72 *Macleod Gazette*, 14 Aug. 1896

73 Pearce Papers, File 1–B–9, Frank Oliver to R.W. Scott, 29 Oct. 1896

74 *Ibid.*, W. Pearce to A.B. Macdonald, 17 Nov. 1896

75 GAI, Western Stock Growers' Association Papers, B1, F3, minutes, 2, 28 Dec. 1896
76 The Western Stock Growers' Association was established on a firm basis and has maintained its protective function for stock-growers to the present day. It is still regarded by some stock-raisers as an association for large ranchers.
77 *Macleod Gazette*, 6 July 1894
78 Canada, Department of the Interior, *Annual Report* (1896) 33
79 *Ibid.* 34
80 *Calgary Herald*, 19 Apr. 1930; 3 Sept. 1955
81 GAI, R.E. English, 'A Synopsis of the Annual Report of the Dominion Land and Immigration Agents at Lethbridge,' 12, quoting J.S. Dennis, Inspector, Surveys Branch, Department of the Interior, 1897
82 Carl Beck and James M. Malloy, 'Political Elites: A Mode of Analysis,' Occasional Paper, University of Pittsburg, 1–44; W.G. Runciman, *Social Science and Political Theory* (London: Cambridge University Press 1965) 66–81
83 Canada, NWMP, *Annual Report* (1894) 9. See also Maxwell L. Foran, 'The Calgary Town Council, 1884–1895: A Study of Local Government in a Frontier Environment' (MA thesis, University of Calgary 1970) 33–6. Cattle shipments from the south-west to Great Britain began during the autumn of 1886. *Macleod Gazette*, 7 Dec. 1886
84 Foran, 'The Calgary Town Council, 1884–95' 34. The portion of this chapter on Calgary relies heavily on this penetrating study of the first decade of Calgary's corporate development.
85 For example, Lineham Block, Alexander Block, Alberta Hotel
86 Foran, 'The Calgary Town Council, 1884–95'
87 *Ibid.* 96
88 Other district representatives were J. Bannerman, H. Cayley, and O.A. Critchley. Though the first two individuals were not ranchers, they were reliable supporters of the ranch-business establishment. See L.G. Thomas, 'The Rancher and the City: Calgary and the Cattlemen, 1883–1914,' *Transactions of the Royal Society of Canada*, VI, Ser. 4 (June 1968) 207.
89 Foran, 'The Calgary Town Council, 1884–95,' 36–46
90 GAI, Ranchmen's Club Calgary, minute book, 1891–1904 (photocopy). See also *The Ranchmen's Club* (Calgary: Rous and Mann Press 1953). This is an outline history prepared for the club. Prominent original members included: H.B. Alexander, D.H. Andrews, A.D. Braithwaite, E.C.B. Cave, T.B.H. Cochrane, W.F. Cochrane, R.W. Cowan, O.A. Critchely, A.E. Cross, W.F.C. Gordon-Cumming, H. Hartford, Col. A.G. Irvine, J.A. Lougheed, D.D. Mann, C.C. McCaul, W.R. Newbolt, Wm Pearce, W.C. Recardo, Judge Rouleau, and F.S. Stimson.

91 Ranchmen's Club Calgary, minute book, 1891–1904, 5
92 *Ibid.* 93. The 1893 subscription list included *Illustrated London News, World, Scribner's, Graphic, Scientific American, Nineteenth Century, Punch, Saturday Review, Life, The Field, Illustrated Sporting and Dramatic, Pall Mall Budget, Harpers, Review of Reviews,* and the weekly edition of the *London Times.*
93 See, for example, *Calgary Herald,* 29 Jan. 1885.
94 *Daily Colonist* (Victoria), 28 Oct. 1962
95 Ings, 'Tales from the Midway Ranch' 43
96 Some family chaines in the compact include: (1) Macleod-Cross-Pinkham; (2) Galt-Magrath-Springett; (3) Sharples-Macdonald; (4) Bell-Irving-Kerfoot-Critchley-Cochrane-Newbolt
97 P.F.W. Rutherford, 'The Western Press and Regionalism, 1870–96,' *Canadian Historical Review* LII (Sept. 1971) 290
98 *Calgary Herald,* 29 June, 1891; *Tribune* (Calgary), 6 Feb. 1891

CHAPTER FOUR: THE WESTERN STOCK GROWERS' ASSOCIATION AND THE
AGRARIAN FRONTIER 1896–1905

1 North-West Territories, *Journal of the Legislative Assembly of the North-West Territories,* 3rd Leg., 2nd Sess., 1896, 201. The names listed are D. McEachran (part owner and mgr, Walrond Ranche), A.R. Springett (mgr, Oxley Ranche), F.S. Stimson (part owner and mgr, North West Cattle Co.), Leslie [Staveley] Hill (major owner, Oxley Ranche), as well as F.W. Godsal, E.H. Maunsell, and D.W. Marsh, who were large private operators.
2 *Ibid.* 205
3 GAI, WSGA Papers, B1, F3, minute book, 3. District representatives elected: Bow River, R.W. Cowan; Sheep Creek, E.J. Swan; Lethbridge, T. Curry; Medicine Hat, J. Ellis; Maple Creek, W.H. Andrews; High River, F.S. Stimson and G. Emerson; Willow Creek, A.B. Macdonald and D.J. Grier; Pincher Creek, C. Kettles and R. Duthie
4 *Ibid.* 24, 9 Apr. 1897
5 *Ibid.* 23, 9 Apr. 1897
6 North-West Territories, Department of Agriculture, *Annual Report* (1901) 107
7 *Ibid.* (1903) 76
8 Wolf bounty claims: 1899–454; 1900–391; 1901–374; 1902–365; 1903–330; 1904–326; 1905–224; 1906–221; 1907–164. Alberta, Department of Agriculture, *Annual Report* (1907) 24–5. The yearly totals include dogs, bitches, and pups for which bounty was claimed and excludes large numbers of wolves killed and poisoned by the ranchers themselves.
9 WSGA Papers, B1, F3, minute book, 50, 14 Apr. 1898; 85, 13 Apr. 1900

10 *Ibid.* 117, 12 Apr. 1901. Blackleg is a generally fatal disease striking young cattle and is characterized by high fever and crackling discoloured swellings under the skin. It is usually contracted from toxins entering through minor wounds and abrasions.

11 Mange is a contagious parasitic disease generally more prevalent among closely herded domestic animals. The eggs of the parasite implanted under the skin of the infected animal cause irritation which leads to constant rubbing. In the end the skin develops sores and sheds its hair, and the animal becomes emaciated and unlikely to survive the winter.

12 WSGA Papers, B1, F3, minute book, 63, 19 Apr. 1899; 73, 31 May 1899

13 North-West Territories, Department of Agriculture, *Annual Report* (1899) 51

14 Canada, RNWMP, *Annual Report 1904*, Report of the Commissioner, 10

15 Northwest Territories, Department of Agriculture, *Annual Report* (1898) 41

16 WSGA Papers, B1, F3, Minute Book, 12, 8 Apr. 1897

17 *Ibid.* 11–12, 8 Apr. 1897

18 *Ibid.* 96, 14 Sept. 1900; 98, 9 Jan. 1901

19 WSGA Papers, B1, F3, minute book, 12, 8 Apr. 1897

20 Canada, RNWMP, *Annual Report* 1904, Report of the Commissioner, 9

21 WSGA Papers, B1, F3, minute book, 120, 25 Oct. 1901

22 See, for example, *ibid.* 52–3, 15 Apr. 1898; 100, 9 Jan. 1901; 118, 25 Oct. 1901; 130, 8 Apr. 1903; 141, 25 June 1903.

23 *Ibid.* 142, 29 Sept. 1903

24 Canada, RNWMP, *Annual Report* 1904, 36, 45

25 *Ibid.* 49, Report of Supt P.C.H. Primrose, Ft Macleod

26 North-West Territories, Department of Agriculture, *Annual Report*, 1898, 71–4

27 WSGA Papers, B1, F3, minute book, 17, 8 Apr. 1897

28 *Ibid.* 35, 19 Aug. 1897

29 The term 'running iron' refers to the straight iron rod used by cattle thieves to alter the brand on stolen cattle. The iron was heated in a campfire till red-hot and then used to deface the original brand.

30 WSGA Papers, B1, F3, minute book, 61, 19 Apr. 1899

31 North-West Territories, *Ordinances of the North-West Territories of Canada, 1905* (Edmonton: Government Printer 1907) Ch. 76, 1900, c. 22, s. 5; WSGA Papers, B1, F3, minute book, 49, 14 Apr. 1898; Canada, NWMP, Annual Report 1896, Report of the Commissioner, 12, 'an amendment is required to the Criminal Code that a brand on an animal is *prima facie* evidence of ownership in order to ensure conviction.'

32 *Ibid.* 1906, Report of the Commissioner, 11

33 WSGA Papers, B1, F3, minute book, 20, 22, 9 Apr. 1897

34 *Ibid.* 37, 11 Oct. 1897

35 North-West Territories, Department of Agriculture, *Annual Report* (1899) 60
36 WSGA Papers, B1, F3, minute book, 116, 12 Apr. 1901. The individual hired was J.C. Patterson.
37 *Ibid.* 33, 25 Oct. 1902
38 *Ibid.* 148, 3 May 1904
39 *Ibid.* 19, 9 Apr. 1897
40 PAC, Sifton Papers, MG 27, II, D15, Vol. 29, A.E. Cox to F. Oliver, 10 May 1897, enclosed in F. Oliver to C. Sifton, 20 May 1897
41 Canada, RNWMP, Annual Report 1904, 17–19
42 *Ibid.*
43 UAA, Pearce Papers, 22–15, clipping enclosed in W. Pearce to A.M. Burgess, 17 Aug. 1896
44 Sifton Papers, MG 27, II, D15, Vol. 15, J.R. Craig to the Hon. W. Mulock, Post-master General, 17 Feb. 1897
45 J.S. Smart came to Manitoba in 1880 from Ontario. He was elected mayor of Brandon in 1885 and 1895. Between 1888 and 1892 he served as Minister of Public Works and Provincial Secretary in the Liberal Greenway government. Smart's term as Deputy Minister of the Interior lasted until his resignation in 1904.
46 Pearce Papers, 22–126, W. Pearce to C. Sifton, 23 Nov. 1893
47 Sifton Papers, MG 27, II, D15, Vol. 29, F. Oliver to C. Sifton, 4 Jan. 1897
48 Pearce Papers, 22–116, J.S. Dennis to W. Pearce, 18 Feb. 1897
49 Sifton Papers MG 27, II, D15, Vol. 30, W. Pearce to C. Sifton, 8 Mar. 1897
50 *Ibid.*, F. Oliver to C. Sifton, 25 Jan. 1897, quoting Sifton's letter of 13 Jan. 1897; Pearce Papers, 22–126, J.S. Dennis to Pearce, 18 Feb. 1897. See also E.A. Mitchner, 'William Pearce and Federal Government Activity in Western Canada 1882–1904' (PHD thesis, University of Alberta 1971) 298.
51 *Ibid.*, Mitchner 296
52 Sifton Papers, MG 27, II, D15, Vol. 29, D.O. Mott to F. Oliver, 28 Apr. 18978, enclosed in F. Oliver to C. Sifton, 6 May 1897. See also *ibid.*, F. Oliver to C. Sifton, 4 Jan. 1897 and WSGA Papers, B1, F3, Minute Book, 2, 28 Dec. 1896.
53 Sifton Papers, MG 27, II, D15, Vol. 29, D.O. Mott to F. Oliver, 28 Apr. 1897
54 *Ibid.*, F. Oliver to C. Sifton, 18 Aug. 1897
55 PAC, RG15, B2a, Vol. 160, 141376, W. Pearce to C. Sifton, 26 June 1897
56 *Ibid.*, F. Oliver to J. Smart, 16 June 1897; Department of the Interior to W. Pearce, 19 June 1897
57 *Ibid.*, W. Pearce to Department of the Interior, 26 June 1897; G.W. Riley to J. Smart, 6 July 1897; R.G. Matthews, Secretary, WSA to F. Oliver, 29 July 1897; F. Oliver to C. Sifton, 6 August 1897; J. Smart to F. Oliver, 21 Aug. 1897
58 *Ibid.*, Minister of the Interior to Governor General in Council, 13 Sept. 1897

59 *Ibid.*, A.B. Macdonald to W. Pearce, 25 July 1898; D.W. Marsh, President, WSGA to C. Sifton, 18 Nov. 1897; D.W. Marsh to W. Pearce, 12 July 1898
60 Sifton Papers, MG 27, II, D15, Vol. 49, A.M. Nanton to C. Sifton, 2 Mar. 1898
61 RG15, B2a, Vol. 160, 141376, W. Pearce to Department of the Interior, 7 Sept. 1898
62 North-West Territories, Department of Agriculture, *Annual Report* 1898, 18–20
63 Sifton Papers, MG 27, II, D15, Vol. 108, W. Pearce to C. Sifton, 31 January 1901; W. Pearce to C. Sifton, 1 June 1901. Pearce remained as Inspector of Surveys until 1 April 1904, when he joined the Canadian Pacific Railway to act as an adviser for that company's extensive irrigation and settlement project in southern Alberta. He remained with the railway as a development officer until retirement in 1926.
64 RG15, B1a, Vol. 260, 578835, L.E. Lish to C. Sifton, 5 July 1900
65 *Ibid.*, memorandum J. Smart to Ryley, 20 July 1900; J. Smart to L.E. Lish, 25 July 1900
66 WSGA Papers, B1, F3, minute book, 109–12, 11 Apr. 1901
67 RG15, B2a, Vol. 161, 141376, memorandum; J.S. Smart and E.F. Stephenson to C. Sifton, 14 Aug. 1901
68 *Ibid.*, F. Oliver to Dominion Land Commissioner, 26 Mar. 1902 and 8 Apr. 1902
69 WSGA Papers, B1, F3, minute book, 144–6, 18 Dec. 1903. RG15, B2a, Vol. 161, 141376, W.W. Stuart, Inspector of Ranches to J.G. Turriff, Commissioner of Dominion Lands, 13 Jan. 1904
70 RG15, B2a, Vol. 161, 141376, sales report
71 Pearce Papers, 14–H, W. Pearce to A.M. Burgess, 16 Jan. 1895. The High River referred to here is today known as the High Wood River.
72 *Ibid.* See the extensive correspondence in this file.
73 *Ibid.*, W. Pearce to R.A. Ruttan, Dominion Land Agent, Edmonton, 28 Nov. 1896
74 RG15, B2a, Vol. 171, 145330, Pt 3, petition to F. Oliver, [?] Feb. 1897
75 *Ibid.*, R.A. Wallace to F. Oliver, 30 Nov. 1897
76 *Ibid.*, Secretary, Department of the Interior to F. Oliver, 13 Sept. 1898
77 Sifton Papers, MG 27, II, D15, Vol. 70, J.H. Ross to C. Sifton, 22 Feb. 1899
78 RG15, B2a, Vol. 171, 145330, Pt 3, J. Kemmis to Minister of the Interior, 11 Apr. 1899
79 *Ibid.*, J.A. Smart to E.L. Newcombe, Deputy Minister of Justice, 28 Apr. 1899
80 *Ibid.*, WSGA to Minister of the Interior, 22 Apr. 1901; J.M. Riley to J.G. Turriff, Commissioner of Dominion Lands, 1 May 1901, petition to Minister of the Interior from residents and ranchers of the Districts of Assiniboia and Alberta; WSGA Papers, B1, F3, minute book, p 105, 11 Apr. 1901
81 RG15, B2a, Vol. 171, 145330, Pt 3, memorandum for the Hon. Clifford Sifton, re grazing lands, 14 Aug. 1901

82 *Ibid.* See Turriff's pencilled comments on the Sifton memorandum re grazing lands, 27 Aug. 1901. Turriff had been a resident of the west since 1878 and had served on the North-West Council and territorial assembly from 1884 to 1891. He was appointed Commissioner of Dominion Lands in 1898 and retained his position until 1904 when he was elected to the House of Commons as the Liberal member for Assiniboia East. He remained in the House until his appointment to the Senate in 1918.

83 *Ibid.*, 'List of Ranches.' J.H. Ross, a rancher from Moose Jaw, was elected to the North-West Council in 1883 and continued to sit as a Liberal in the North-West Assembly from 1888 to 1901 when he was appointed Commissioner of the Yukon Territory by Sifton. He was later elected to represent the Yukon in the House of Commons and was called to the Senate in 1904. Sifton's fellow Brandonite, J.D. McGregor, was a prominent Liberal worker in Sifton's constituency and had also been a Yukon appointee. See GAI, Southern Alberta Land Co., Grand Forks Cattle Co. Division.

Such avenues were also open to other Liberals with good connections. Before proceeding west to commence his ranching enterprise, J. Riddle of Dannville, Quebec, was able to secure good offices of Sir Wilfrid Laurier himself. See PAC, Laurier Papers, Microfilm, reel 790, pp 61676-7, John Riddle to Sir Wilfrid Laurier, 20 Jan. 1902; Sir Wilfrid Laurier to John Riddle, 21 Jan. 1902.

84 RG15, B2a, Vol. 172, 145330, Pt 4, memorandum, J.W. Riley to F. Oliver; and list entitled 'Closed Leases'

85 WSGA Papers, B1, F3, minute book, 144-6, 18 Dec. 1903

86 RG15, B2a, Vol. 171, 145330, Pt 3, E. Peachy to C. Sifton, 4 Dec. 1903

87 *Ibid.*, F. Oliver to C. Sifton, 4 June 1904

88 *Ibid.*, G. Lane to J.W. Greenway, Commissioner of Dominion Lands, 1 June 1904

89 *Ibid.*, R.H. Campbell to H.H. Rowatt, 13 Aug. 1904

90 *Ibid.*, J.W. Riley to J.S. Smart, 25 Mar. 1904

91 *Ibid.*, Grazing Regulations, 6 Nov. 1903

92 *Ibid.*, C. Sifton to His Excellency the Governor General, 30 Dec. 1904

93 *Ibid.*, memorandum, W.W. Cory to C. Sifton, 27 Feb. 1905

94 Canada, Department of the Interior, *Annual Report* 1898, Report of Dominion Land Commissioner 15-16

95 *Ibid.* 1899, Report of Commissioner of Immigration 156

96 *Ibid.* (1900-1) 109; (1899) 160-1

97 *Ibid.* 1901-2, Report of Commissioner of Dominion Lands 19

98 *Ibid.* (1903-4) 15

99 *Ibid.* (1904-5) 14

100 *Ibid.* 108-9

101 *Ibid.*
102 *Ibid.* 1901–2, Report of the Commissioner of Immigration, 115–6; (1903–4) 77–81; (1904–5) 108–9; (1905–6) 94
103 *Ibid.* (1903–4) 81
104 Of the 2456 newcomers registered at Cardston, Ft Macleod, Maple Creek, and Wood Mountain during 1902, for example, 1839 were American, 119 returned Canadians, 138 English, and 66 Scottish. Canada, Department of the Interior *Annual Report* 1901–2, Report of the Commissioner of Immigration 81
105 *Ibid.* (1904–5) 108
106 *Ibid.* 1905–6, Report of Deputy Minister ix
107 Alberta, Department of Agriculture, *Annual Report* 1922, precipitation averages 1885–1922, 107
108 Canada, Department of the Interior, *Annual Report* 1899, Report of Superintendent of Mines 27; (1900) xxvi
109 Pearce Papers, 22–126, W. Pearce to C. Sifton, 1 Sept. 1902
110 Canada, Department of the Interior, *Annual Report* 1897 Report of Superintendent of Mines 30
111 *Ibid.* 1898, Report of Superintendent of Immigration 254, 264; (1899) 160
112 Canada, NWMP, *Annual Report* (1899) 84; Canada, Department of the Interior, *Annual Report* 1900, Report of the Commissioner of Dominion Lands 13
113 North-West Territories, Department of Agriculture, *Annual Reports* 1900–4. The Chicago market during this period generally averaged two cents per pound more, but because Canadian sellers assumed shipping costs the difference was cancelled out.
114 Marr and Patterson, *Canada: An Economic History* 112
115 Of the 115,000 head exported to Great Britain from Canada in 1900, over 48,000 head were from the Territories. North-West Territories, Department of Agriculture, *Annual Report* (1901) 72. For a more thorough assessment see S.M. Evans, 'The Passing of a Frontier: Ranching in the Canadian West, 1882–1912' (PHD dissertation, University of Calgary 1976) 212–26.
116 Canada, RNWMP, *Annual Report* 1902, Report of the Commissioner 37

CHAPTER FIVE: THE STRUGGLE FOR SURVIVAL: THE DARK YEARS 1905–11

1 See, for example, *Calgary Herald*, 29 June 1891 and *Tribune* (Calgary), 6 Feb. 1891.
2 GAI, WSGA Papers, B1, F3, minute book, 161, 11 May 1905. The cattlemen's opposition is also reported in, North-West Territories, Department of Agriculture, *Annual Report* 1904, Appendix A, Territorial Cattle Breeders' Association 138.

3 Canada, Department of the Interior, *Annual Report* 1906–7, Report of the Commissioner of Immigration 97

4 RG15, B2a, Vol. 161, 141376, F. Oliver to G.W. Ryley, 6 June 1905

5 *Ibid.*, memorandum, W.W. Cory, Deputy Minister, 21 Oct. 1905

6 *Ibid.*, Department of the Interior to W.W. Stuart, Inspector of Ranches, 5 Dec. 1905

7 *Ibid.*, memorandum, W.W. Cory to R.H. Campbell, 9 Jan. 1906

8 PAC, Sifton Papers, Microfilm C465, F. Oliver to C. Sifton, 18 Aug. 1897

9 RG15, B2a, Vol. 161, 141376, circular to Dominion Land Agents, 12 Dec. 1905

10 *Ibid.*, Vol. 162, 141376, W.W. Stuart to R.H. Campbell, 27 July 1906. Parcels remaining unsold were held available to the first applicant at $3.00 per acre.

11 *Ibid.*, Vol. 163, 141376, sales, June 1911

12 RG15, B2a, Vol. 172, 145330, Pt 4. The two major shareholders of the Grand Forks Cattle Company, J.H. Ross and J.D. McGregor, were stalwart Sifton Liberals. For biographical information see note 98, chapter 4. Earlier they had received an open lease of 46,114 acres. The political background of the new leaseholders did not go undetected by the Conservatives and these examples were used widely to substantiate the charges of graft and corruption levied against the Liberals by the Conservatives in the 1908 election campaign. See, for example, PAC, pamphlet, library, anon., 'Facts for the People: Pages from the Record of the Laurier Administration, from 1906 to 1908' 11–13; Herbert B. Ames, MP, 'Western Heritage and How It is Being Squandered by the Laurier Government' (1908) 18–21; anon., 'A Session's Disclosures, Second Series: Some Transactions of the Laurier Administration Exposed in the Session of 1907' 58–71.

13 RG15, B2a, Vol. 172, 145330, Pt 4, F. Oliver to His Excellency, the Governor General-in-Council, 27 July 1905

14 *Ibid.*, F. Oliver to G.W. Ryley, 5 Aug. 1905

15 *Ibid.*, F. Oliver to W.W. Stuart, 9 Feb. 1906, my italics

16 RG15, B2a, Vol. 172, 145330, Pt 4, WSGA to F. Oliver, 22 May 1909; memorandum, B. York to F. Oliver, 1 June 1909; B. York to Fetherston, 14 Sept. 1910; Department to WSGA, 22 Sept. 1910; WSGA Papers B1, F3, minute book, 189, 14 May 1890, 200, 1 May 1910

17 RG15, B2a, Vol. 172, 145330, Pt 4, memorandum, B. York to F. Oliver, 1 June 1909

18 *Calgary Albertan*, 28 May 1910

19 RG15, B2a, Vol. 172, 145330, Pt 4, clipping, *Prince Albert Times*, 20 May 1910

20 *Ibid.*, resolution, High River Branch No. 157 of the United Farmers of Alberta, 5 Oct. 1910

21 *Ibid.*, F. Oliver to D.E. Riley, 12 Dec. 1910

22 WSGA Papers, B1, F3, minute book, 163, 7 Dec. 1905

23 GAI, Cross Papers, B58, F463, G. Lane to A.E. Cross, 5 Feb. 1906

24 *Ibid.*, B58, F464, M.S. McCarthy to A.E. Cross, 19 Mar. 1906

25 Alberta, Department of Agriculture, *Annual Report* (1906) 92–3; (1907) 48–9, 54

26 Cross Papers, B59, F467, C.L. Douglass to A.E. Cross, 16 Dec. 1906

27 *Ibid.*, A.E. Cross to C.L. Douglass, 5 Jan. 1907

28 P.S. Long, *Seventy Years a Cowboy* (Saskatoon: Freeman Publishing Co. Ltd 1965) 58

29 Cross Papers, B59, F468, A. McCallum to A.E. Cross, 19 Jan. 1907; B59, F472, A. McCallum to A.E. Cross, 6 Feb. 1907

30 C.W. Buchanan, 'History of the Walrond Cattle Ranch Ltd,' *Canadian Cattleman* VIII (Mar. 1946) 261

31 GAI, J. Martin, 'Notes on R.A. "Dick" Allen, Gordon Ironside and Fares Ltd, Two Bar Ranch'

32 R. Stock, *Confessions of a Tenderfoot* (New York: Henry Holt 1913) 60

33 J.G. Rutherford, *The Cattle Trade of Western Canada* (Ottawa: King's Printer 1909) 8

34 Alberta, Department of Agriculture, *Annual Report* 1907, Report of the Deputy Minister 6–7. 'The unusually severe winter caused the death of thousands of cattle and, it is feared, put out of business many of the small ranchers.' See also Alberta, Department of Agriculture, *Annual Report* 1908, Appendix B, 229–30. The Alberta Cattle Breeders' Association noted that many cattlemen had decided to sell out and urged those considering such a move to reconsider, assuring them that better days lay ahead.

35 *Ibid.*, 1908, Report of the Recorder of Brands 132

36 *Medicine Hat News*, 10 May 1906, quoting a Regina source of 8 May

37 *Medicine Hat Times*, 20 Aug. 1907

38 Long, *Seventy Years a Cowboy* 70

39 *Pincher Creek Echo*, 23 Aug. 1907

40 *Ibid.*, 21 June 1907

41 Alberta, Department of Agriculture, *Annual Report* 1908, 'Immigration and Colonization' 58–9

42 *Ibid.* 137

43 Martin, 'Dominion Lands Policy' 332–4

44 *Calgary Herald*, 18 Aug. 1949, 'Pre-emption Policy of 1908 Ruined Many Small Ranchers'

45 *Lethbridge Herald*, 27 Aug. 1910

46 RG15, B2a, Vol. 126, 544923, A.A. Thompson to Department of the Interior, 11 Dec. 1907; Vol. 131, 552704, F. Settle to F. Oliver, 23 May 1908; G.J. Elliott to Department of the Interior, 19 May 1908

47 *Lethbridge Herald*, 22 Aug. 1910

48 Alberta, Department of Agriculture, *Annual Report* 1910, 82-3; Alberta, *Ordinances of the North-West Territories of Canada, 1905* (Edmonton: Government Printer 1907) chapters 77, 79, 81

49 *Gleichen Call*, 22 July 1910

50 See, for example, PAS, Motherwell Papers, M12m F74.

51 Canada, Department of the Interior, *Annual Report* 1907-8, Report of Inspector of Ranches 74

52 Cross Papers, B59, F471, A.E. Cross to C.L. Douglass, 4 May 1907

53 Canada, Department of the Interior, *Annual Report* 1905-6, Report of Commissioner of Dominion Lands, 14

54 Alberta, Department of Agriculture, *Annual Report* 1907, Report of Deputy Minister, 6

55 *Ibid.* (1909) 22-3

56 *Ibid.* (1910) 26-8

57 Alberta, Department of Agriculture, *Annual Report* 1908, 152-3; 1909, 144

58 PAC, Sifton Papers, MG27, II, D15, W. Pearce to C. Sifton, 10 Jan. 1902

59 Cross Papers, B58, F451, memorandum of agreement, 19 June 1903. Parties to the combination were A.H. Eckford, E. Hills, H. Smith, P. Muirhead, A.E. Cross, W.R. Hull, and W.E. Cochrane. Minimum prices were: 4 years old and upwards, 4¢ per pound from 15 July to 15 Oct., 3¼¢ per pound after 15 Oct.; the buyer was allowed to take any three-year-old steers he wanted at these prices; all dry cows four years old and upwards, 3½¢ per pound from 15 July to 15 Oct. and 3¼¢ per pound after 15 Oct.

60 Alberta, Department of Agriculture, *Annual Report* (1906) 69

61 The ranchers' allegations are reported at length in: *Medicine Hat News*, 13 June 1907, 1 Aug. 1907, 31 Oct. 1907; *Lethbridge Herald*, 13 June 1907, 20 June 1907; *High River Times*, 27 June 1907; *Calgary Herald*, 22 June 1907, 24 June 1907, 25 June 1907.

62 *Calgary Herald*, 24 June 1907

63 *Ibid.*

64 *Medicine Hat Times*, 27 Aug. 1907

65 Alberta, Department of Agriculture, *Annual Report* 1907, 'The Beef Commission' 43

66 *Ibid.* 39

67 Alberta, Department of Agriculture, *Annual Report* 1908, Report of the Livestock Commissioner 7

68 See, for example, *Pincher Creek Echo*, 15 Aug. 1919.

69 See, for example, Alberta, Department of Agriculture, *Annual Report* 1910, Report of Livestock Commissioner 185-9.

70 In forms requiring identification by occupation Cross always put the designation 'rancher.'

71 Cross Papers, B56, F442, H.B. Alexander to A.E. Cross, 19 June 1901; J.S. Blake to A.E. Cross, 21 Apr. 1902

72 *Ibid.*, B57, F455; 1904 purchases, for example, included 320 acres from the Crown and 2720 from the railway.

73 *Ibid.*, B57, F453, Selkirk Cross to A.E. Cross, 1 Feb. 1904; F454, Selkirk Cross to A.E. Cross, 12 Feb. 1904; Selkirk Cross to A.E. Cross, 7 Mar. 1904; F455, Department of the Interior to Cross, 19 Feb. 1904

74 *Ibid.*, B59, F473. See letters Jan.-May 1907.

75 *Ibid.*, B58, F459, A.B. Macdonald to A.E. Cross, 24 Mar. 1905; A.B. Macdonald to A.E. Cross, 27 Mar. 1905; W.W. Cory, Deputy Minister to A.B. Macdonald, 10 Mar. 1905

76 *Ibid.*, B63, F497, T. Duggan to A.E. Cross, 17 Jan. 1910

77 *Ibid.*, B64, F505. See letters in file, B66, F526, F. Price to Cross, 18 June 1912. The author pleads with Cross to purchase his quarter so that he might move north to better grain country.

78 *Ibid.*, B58, F458, W.W. Craig to A.E. Cross, 6 July 1905 and 11 July 1905.

79 *Ibid.*, B65, F512, C.H. Webster, Secretary, Calgary Board of Trade, to A.E. Cross, 26 July 1911

80 *Ibid.*, B65, F509, J. Stocks, Deputy Minister of Public Works to A.E. Cross, 3 Apr. 1911

81 RG15, B2a, Vol. 79, 416960, J.W. Bratton to Department of the Interior, 12 Apr. 1905

CHAPTER SIX: TRANSITION AND THE AMERICAN PRESENCE 1900-11

1 In actual practice, the big rancher with several hundred export steers to sell was usually able to negotiate a better price than the small producer. It seems that the competition for large lots was greater than for smaller bunches. C.W. Vrooman, G.D. Chattaway, and Andrew Stewart, *Cattle Ranching in Western Canada* (Ottawa: Department of Agriculture 1946) 59-63. The findings of this detailed study confirm the superior investment return of the large operation.

2 Records of herd size and composition on the Walrond Ranche are sufficient to confirm that company's long-term success. Herd size between 1885 and 1905 seems to have varied between 7500 and 9500 head (calves not included). Records of the spring and fall calf-branding suggest an average increase of 1800 to 2000 head, while yearly sales can be estimated at 1100 to 1500 prime steers plus a number of hundred butcher cattle. Through most of these two decades export steers seldom netted less than $40 per head, and on the basis of 1200 head

exported per year, the annual return would have equalled $48,000. With the sales of slaughter cattle included the ranch probably returned at least $50,000 per year. Given the staff required for a ranch of this size and the wage rates of the period it can be estimated that $5000–$6000 was required to meet this expense and perhaps an equal sum to meet other operational costs. While precise figures of expenses are not available and herd accounts are missing for some years, the general situation is clearly profitable. See GAI, Walrond Ranche, Cattle Record and Beef Account Books, 1885–1901; Walrond Ranche Papers, D. McEachran to Sir John Walrond-Walrond, 21 Oct. 1905.

3 GAI, Walrond Ranche Papers, D. McEachran to Sir John Walrond-Walrond, 21 Oct. 1905; GAI, New Walrond Ranche Company Limited, reports, prospectus, and reports of Canada North West Land Company Ltd 1911–23

4 Alberta, Department of Agriculture, *Annual Report* 1909, Report of the Deputy Minister, 22–3; Canada, Department of the Interior, *Annual Report* 1912–13, Report of Inspector of Ranches 144–5

5 Canada, NWMP, *Annual Report* 1909, 20 *Macleod Gazette*, 10 Nov. 1893

6 S.B. Steele, *Forty Years in Canada* (Toronto: McClelland, Goodchild and Stewart 1915) 268. For further discussion of this problem see *Macleod Gazette*, 10 Nov. 1893 and J.D. Higginbotham, *When the West Was Young* (Toronto: Ryerson Press 1933) 132.

7 GAI, Cross Papers, B113, F.R. Pike to A.E. Cross, 25 Feb. 1921

8 GAI, will of J.B. Henson of Saskatchewan Landing, 28 Dec. 1919

9 Anon., *Lachlin McKinnon, Pioneer 1865–1948* (Calgary: J.D. McAra 1956) 177

10 GAI, Robert Newbolt, autobiography, ms p 22. See also Evelyn C. Springett, *For My Children's Children* (Montreal: Unity Press 1937) 155.

11 GAI, H.M. Hatfield, letter to Alberta Provincial Librarian from Yarrow, Alberta (1908) 4

12 Cross Papers, B56, F442, W.E. Cochrane to A.E. Cross, 10 June 1901

13 *Ibid.*, B57, F454, W.E. Cochrane to A.E. Cross, 28 June 1904

14 *Ibid.*, B58, F462, W.E. Cochrane to A.E. Cross, 28 Jan. 1906

15 *Pincher Creek Echo*, 20 Mar. 1908

16 *Ibid.*, letter to the editor, 1 May 1908. See also 24 Apr. 1908.

17 *Ibid.*, 19 Jan. 1911

18 Marcus Lee Hansen, *The Immigrant in American History* (Cambridge: Harvard University Press 1948) 190

19 William R. Stewart, 'The Americanization of the Canadian Northwest,' *The Cosmopolitan* XXXIV (April 1903) 603–4

20 Walrond Ranche papers, D. McEachran to Sir John Walrond-Walrond, 21 Oct. 1905

21 Cross Papers, B113, F909, A.E. Cross to Captain Balfour, 12 Apr. 1911. Cross was anxious to encourage the Prince of Wales to establish a ranch near his own in the Porcupine Hills. Before the letter was sent, however, the prince announced his intention to purchase another property in the same area.

22 UAA, Pearce Papers, 14B12, Louis and John Garnett. The file contains the records of a ten-year dispute between the Garnetts, who settled in the Pincher Creek area, and the Department of the Interior regarding homestead rights. See especially L.O. Garnett to W. Pearce, 14 Mar. 1899. For another example of this kind of sentiment, see Lathrop E. Roberts, ed., *Alberta Homestead: Chronicle of a Pioneer Family* (Austin: University of Texas Press 1968) 25–6.

23 GAI, Edna Kells, pioneer interviews, ms, 1935, 157. The comment is that of Miss Abigail Sexsmith, whose father came to ranch in the High River area from Hull, Quebec, in 1883.

24 *Lethbridge Herald*, 12 Mar. 1912; *Pincher Creek Echo*, 22 Mar. 1912. Both papers took issue with Bennett. The regional press, which was invariably pro-settlement, was traditionally quick to counter charges of Americanization. See, for example, *Lethbridge News*, 11 Sept. 1908.

25 See commissioner's annual reports. Police officers expressed even stronger concern about immigration from eastern Europe.

26 See, for example, PAC, RG15, B2a, 141376, Vol. 159, Pt 1, F. Stimson to Department of the Interior, 1 Sept. 1887.

27 Cross Papers, B66, F532, 'Resolutions Presented to the Ranch Inquiry Commission by the Ranchers of Gleichen District,' 20 November 1912; 'Suggestions Presented to the Ranch Commission at their Session in Calgary,' 22 Nov. 1912. Canada, Department of the Interior, *Ranching and Grazing Investigation Commission 7*; order-in-council, 16 Feb. 1914

28 The general economic objection to farm settlement which was peculiarized by a measure of anti-American sentiment among the ranch population was further characterized by a general feeling of Anglo-Saxon racial superiority which led cattlemen to consistently oppose 'pauper immigration' from eastern Europe to the prairie west. See, for example, C.E. Denny, *Riders of the Plains* (Calgary: The Herald Co. Ltd 1905) 218; *Calgary Herald*, 16 Sept. 1891, 5 July 1893, 22 Nov. 1900; *Macleod Gazette*, 10 Dec. 1891, 23 June 1893.

29 Cross Papers, B56, F457, 'General Idea of Proposed Ranche School'

30 *Ibid.* The names of the intended founders of the school remain unknown but the draft in the Cross papers suggests that Cross was one.

31 Library of the Royal Commonwealth Society, London; H.B. Gray, *The Bradfield College Ranch for Bradfield Boys near Calgary* (Reading: Blackwell and Gutch 1909)

32 *Ibid.* 12

33 GAI, G. Park, 'History of Bradfield Ranch near Millarville, Alberta,' ms

34 A. Begg, 'Stock Raising in the Bow River District compared with Montana,' *Manitoba and the Great North West*, ed. J. Macoun (Guelph: World Publishing Co. 1882) 273–7

35 Such reaction among 'better'-class British immigrants has been noted several times in Canadian history. See S.D. Clark, *Movements of Social Protest* (Toronto: University of Toronto Press 1959) 484 and Aileen Dunham, *Political Unrest in Upper Canada 1815–1836* (Carleton Library, Toronto: McClelland and Stewart Ltd 1963) 28.

36 J.J. Young, 'Ranching in the Canadian North-West,' *Canadian Encyclopaedia of the Country*, V, ed. J. Castell Hopkins (Toronto: The Linscott Publishing Company 1899) 62

37 See, for example, *Calgary Herald*, 10 Sept. 1895, quoting the *Toronto Globe*, 4 Sept. 1895: 'Farming in the west has not been able to support the great houses and the lavish equipment of an English estate. But in many cases expensive houses were built and the manners, customs, and expenditures of an English estate attempted.' The attempt at Cannington Manor in south-eastern Saskatchewan is probably the best known of such ambitious undertakings.

38 GAI, Quorn Ranch Company, account books, 1891–2. A cowboy's wages varied for most of this period between $30 and $100 per month, depending on experience. In addition to his wage he also received board and lodging and in some cases a horse and related equipment such as a saddle and rope.

39 The Cross Papers contain numerous reports of the winter activities of fellow ranchers in Bermuda, Tahiti, Hawaii, and more often in Britain. The letter from W.E. Cochrane to A.E. Cross dated 31 Jan. 1905 is representative. 'We had a pleasant trip down on the "Baltic." Cowan was with us and their friends. I had ten days in London painting the town. Walter Gordon-Cumming was there also Waldy and H.B. Alexander who was in great form.' The letter went on to mention the great shooting in the north, the availability of capital if Cross wanted it to expand the brewery, and his plan to return in the spring by way of Old Mexico. B58, F458

40 Cross Papers, B68, F544, Ranchmen's Club, Calgary. The club's bank balance for 1914 of $300,806.72 reflected the benefits of the sale of their choice downtown property the previous year. In 1914 the membership authorized expenditure of $120,000 for the construction of elegant new quarters.

41 Zachary MacCaulay Hamilton and Marie Albina Hamilton, *These Are the Prairies* (Regina: School Aids Text Book Publishing Co. Ltd 1948) 184

42 This is not to imply that 'the image associated with the American ranching frontier' necessarily fits the reality of the American experience.

43 *Macleod Gazette*, 15 May 1896
44 PMAA, Harry Long, pioneer cowboy and rancher, taped interview, 1957
45 *Pincher Creek Echo*, 27 June 1913, memorial service on 13th anniversary of battle in which the loss occurred
46 Cross Papers, B56, F445, H. Samson to A.E. Cross, 22 Aug. 1901.
47 *Pincher Creek Echo*, 14 June 1907
48 Cross Papers, B67, F495, A.E. Cross to R. Yerburgh, 30 Oct. 1909
49 A.C. Critchley, *Critch! The Memoirs of Brigadier-General A.C. Critchley C.M.G., C.B.E., D.S.O.* (London: Hutchinson of London 1961); see chapter 1 regarding his youth on his father's ranch near Calgary. GAI, Kerfoot papers, J. Kerfoot to J. Barman, 20 October 1979
50 To evaluate the nature and magnitude of the movement of American ranchers into the southeast see the following: Pearce Papers, 14–D–14, 'Settlement in Southern Alberta, 1898–1901; S.M. Evans, 'The Passing of a Frontier: Ranching in the Canadian West, 1882–1912' (PHD dissertation, University of Calgary 1976) 336; P.S. Long, *Seventy Years a Cowboy* (Saskatoon: Freeman Publishing Co. Ltd 1965); PAC, RG18, A1, Vol. 242, 25, Pt 1, Superintendent J.V. Begin to Inspector McEllre, 19 October 1903; RG15, B2a, Vol. 172, 145330, Pt 4, R.H. Campbell to Ryley, 17 Apr. 1905; Canada, Department of the Interior, *Annual Reports* 1896–1910. Some of the large American companies included the Conrad-Price Cattle Co., the Cresswell Cattle Co., the Bloom Cattle Co., the Matador Cattle Co., the Spencer Brothers Cattle Co., Kohn Kohr and Co., and the Floweree Brothers Cattle Co.
51 GAI, Stock Growers' Association of Medicine Hat, minutes, 1896–1901. These minutes in contrast to the WSGA minutes, display preoccupation with the traditional problems of the 'range' cattle industry.

CHAPTER SEVEN: A NEW GOVERNMENT AND A NEW POLICY 1911–13

1 J. Castell Hopkins, *The Canadian Annual Review* 1911 (Toronto: The Annual Review Publishing Co. Ltd 1912) 246
2 *Ibid.* 214–15
3 *Macleod Gazette*, 25 Oct. 1887
4 GAI, Cross Papers, B64, F508, A.E. Cross to Clay, Robinson and Co., 10 Mar. 1911
5 *Ibid.*, F513, W. Fares to A.E. Cross, 31 Aug. 1911
6 *Medicine Hat News*, 30 Aug. 1911
7 *Ibid.*, 13 Sept. 1911, 21 Sept. 1911. See, for example, *Calgary Herald*, 'Reciprocity Means the End of Canada's Independence,' 31 Aug. 1911, 'Every Patriotic Canadian Should Swat Reciprocity,' 14 Sept. 1911.

8 *Pincher Creek Echo*, 17 Aug. 1911, 24 Aug. 1911, 14 Sept. 1911, 19 Sept. 1911

9 *Ibid.*, 22 Sept. 1911. In addition to their strong showing in those parts of the foothills country where ranching predominated, the Conservatives also won majorities, in some Crowsnest mining towns where there existed fear of American competition under the reciprocity plan. The Conservatives also gained majorities in the old cattle towns of Ft Macleod, High River, and Okotoks. In Pincher Creek the vote was split almost evenly. In contrast to their rural hinterlands, the towns of Medicine Hat and Lethbridge also voted for the Conservative candidate (*Medicine Hat News*, 22 Sept 1911). While the tendency of many townsmen to vote against the Liberals in this election might be explained in part by economic factors, there is evidence that seems to suggest another factor that merits consideration and further investigation. Many prairie towns in the south during this period, unlike the surrounding countryside, had a majority British-Canadian population receptive to the pro-imperial arguments used by the Conservatives in their campaigns. This group in the towns seems to have been composed of many who had come to the west during the first wave of immigration before 1896. By virtue of their earlier arrival these settlers were able to take advantage of commercial opportunities. Moreover, great numbers of these first homesteaders from the wooded lands of Ontario and Great Britain found the prairies an especially harsh and unrewarding land. They were thus not reluctant to sell their holdings to the next group of in-coming settlers and go seek their fortune in the new towns.

10 The ranchers' feeling towards Oliver is exemplified in a letter written by A.E. Cross to an eastern friend some months after the election. 'The late Minister of the Interior always seemed to be hostile towards the cattle man and cut off all the lease[s] and range as much as he possibly could.' Cross Papers, B56, F525, A.E. Cross to W.R. MacInnes, Freight Traffic Manager, CPR, 13 July 1912

11 Zachary Macaulay Hamilton and Marie Albina Hamilton, *These are the Prairies* (Regina: School Aids Text Book Publishing Co. Ltd 1948) 146, 155

12 Sifton Papers, microfilm C555, P. Burns to C. Sifton, 28 Dec. 1903

13 The Conservatives also won the Medicine Hat riding in 1908 on the personal strength of their candidate, C.A. Magrath, who was held in high esteem by the Mormon community, and who captured much of the Mormon vote. The new Ft Macleod constituency comprised the entire foothills region from just south of Ft Macleod to Calgary, thus greatly enhancing the ranchers' voting power.

14 Canada, *Sessional Papers*, No. 29, Vol. XXXI, 1897, 'Return of the Eighth General Election, 1896,' 308–15; No. 36, Vol. XXXV, 1901, 'Return of the Ninth General Election, 1900,' 2–5, 8–11; No. 37, Vol. XXXIX, 1905, 'Return of the Tenth General Election, 1904,' 354–63; No. 18, Vol. XLIII, 1909, 'Return of the Eleventh General Election, 1908,' 394–401; No. 18, Vol. XLVI, 1912, 'Return of the

Twelfth General Election, 1911,' 473–83. The different southern Alberta voting pattern at the provincial level has been assessed by Thomas Flanagan in 'Political Geography and the United Farmers of Alberta,' a paper delivered to the Third Annual Western Canadian History Conference at Calgary, Mar. 1972. Flanagan notes the tendency of the foothills population to vote differently from their fellow Albertans in the prairie and parkland regions.

15 *Pincher Creek Echo*, 17 Aug. 1911, re Lane's support of the Liberal candidate in the 1911 election. A.B. Macdonald ran unsuccessfully as the Liberal candidate for Ft Macleod in the 1908 election.

16 *Medicine Hat News*, 5 Dec. 1912

17 Cross Papers, B66, F521, A.E. Cross to George Lane, Vice-President, WSGA, 6 Feb. 1912

18 *Ibid.*, G. Lane to A.E. Cross, 15 Feb. 1912; G. Lane to A.E. Cross, 17 Feb. 1912

19 *Ibid.*, F526, A.E. Cross to P. Burns, President, WSGA, 24 June 1912; enclosure, WSGA to the Hon. J.A. Lougheed, 'Live Stock Grazing Leases'. The Burns referred to here is not the Calgary meat-packer.

20 RG15, B2a, Vol. 172, 145330, Pt 4, Petition of Pincher Creek Stockmen, 6 July 1912

21 *Ibid.*, B. York to Deputy Minister, 8 Mar. 1912; proposal approved 13 Mar. 1912

22 *Ibid.*, E.E. Taylor to Department of the Interior, 22 Oct. 1912

23 *Ibid.*, second letter, E.E. Taylor to Department of the Interior, 22 Oct. 1912

24 Canada, Department of the Interior, *Ranching and Grazing Investigation Commission* (1913) 3

25 *Medicine Hat News*, 2 Nov. 1912, 7 Nov. 1912; *Pincher Creek Echo*, 8 Nov. 1912, 15 Nov. 1912

26 Cross Papers, B66, F532, A.E. Cross to G. Porter, 9 Nov. 1912

27 *Ibid.*, 'Resolutions Presented to the Ranch Inquiry Commission by the Ranchers of the Gleichen District,' 20 November 1912; 'Suggestions Presented to the Ranch Commission at their Session in Calgary,' 22 Nov. 1912

28 *Pincher Creek Echo*, 8 Nov. 1912, 15 Nov. 1912

29 Alberta, Department of Agriculture, *Annual Report* (1912) 202–4

30 Canada, Department of the Interior, *Ranching and Grazing Investigation Commission* (1913) 5–7

31 The capital invested in an average-sized breeding herd of medium quality is suggested by sales returns of the herd belonging to the Two Bar Ranch of Gordon, Ironside and Fares of Winnipeg. Between 28 Feb. and 14 Nov. 1906 the entire herd was marketed and the sum returned equalled $109,230. GAI, Gordon, Ironside and Fares; Statements of Cattle Sales, Wintering Hills, 1906

32 Canada, Department of the Interior, *Ranching and Grazing Investigation Commission* (1913) 5–7

33 *Medicine Hat News*, 28 Nov. 1912

34 RG15, B2a, Vol. 172, 145330, petition to Department of the Interior, 30 Dec. 1912

35 *Ibid.*, W.A. Lind to Minister of the Interior, 1 Feb. 1913

36 *Ibid.*, E.E. Brown to Department of the Interior, 28 Mar. 1913, enclosing petition dated 25 March 1913 signed by fifty-six residents of the Russthorn District of south-western Saskatchewan.

37 *Ibid.* For additional opposition to the Commission's proposals see *ibid.*, petition to Minister of the Interior, 8 Apr. 1913, from farmers and small stockmen in the Cypress Hills.

38 *Ibid.*, R. Sexsmith, Asst. Ranch Inspector, to Department of the Interior, 14 May 1913, urging the Department, in fairness to the stockmen, to withdraw all leases from homestead entry until the new lease policy was decided in order to prevent this widespread practice.

39 *Ibid.*, H. Butcher, Secretary, Twin Butte Cattle and Horse Association to Minister of the Interior, 29 July 1913

40 *Ibid.*, memorandum, B.L. York to J.G. Mitchell, Secretary to the Minister, 16 Apr. 1913; memorandum, B.L. York to J.G. Mitchell, 8 May 1913; memorandum, B.L. York to W.J. Roche, Minister of the Interior, 25 Sept. 1913

41 The Ranch Inquiry Commission had been appointed by Roche's predecessor, Robert Rogers.

42 Cross Papers, B69, F542, W.J. Roche to A.E. Cross, 20 Nov. 1913; A.E. Cross to D. Hardwick, 29 Nov. 1913; A.E. Cross to W.J. Roche, 29 Nov. 1913; A.E. Cross to W.J. Roche, 3 Dec. 1913. Cross's reply was followed by a visit to Ottawa by an official delegation from the WSGA, who in turn urged quick action on the terms recommended by the commission. See GAI, WSGA Papers, B1, F3, minutes, 2 Jan. 1914, 220–1, Special General Meeting.

43 Pearce Papers, 14–H, W.J. Roche to W. Pearce, 17 Nov. 1913

44 RG15, B2a, Vol. 172, 145330, Pt 5, order-in-council, 16 Feb. 1914

45 *Ibid.*, H.A. Noble to B.L. York, 17 Mar. 1914. See also W.H. Ogle, President, Saskatchewan Stock Growers' Association, to Secretary, Minister of the Interior, 3 Mar. 1914.

46 Canada, Department of the Interior, *Annual Report* 1913–14, Report of the Inspector of Ranches 139

47 *Ibid.*, Report of the Agent of Dominion Lands, Calgary 14

48 Canada, Department of the Interior, *Annual Report* 1912–13, Report of the Inspector of Ranches 144

49 *Ibid.*, 145, quoting a Calgary paper

50 Cross Papers, B68, F534, A.E. Cross to A. Kerfoot, 25 Feb. 1913
51 *Ibid*. See Cross-Kerfoot and Cross-Bennett correspondence on files 533, 534, 538. See also F537, A.E. Cross to R.B. Bennett, 14 Oct. 1913; R.B. Bennett to A.E. Cross, 28 Oct. 1913.

CHAPTER EIGHT: RESURGENT CATTLEMEN AND THE SODBUSTERS' RETREAT 1914–19

1 PAC, RG15, B2a, Vol. 173, 145330, Pt 6, B.L. York to Dominion Land Agent, Calgary, 8 Apr. 1914, 19 July 1914; B.L. York to Deputy Minister, 2 Nov. 1914
2 *Ibid*., B.L. York to Deputy Minister, 17 June 1914
3 *Ibid*., W.W. Cory, Deputy Minister to J.W. Greenway, Commissioner of Dominion Lands, 22 February 1915
4 *Ibid*., G.M. Cloakley, Inspector of Ranches, to B.L. York, 26 Apr. 1915
5 *Ibid*., memorandum, H.E. Hume to B.L. York, 12 Apr. 1915
6 *Ibid*., memorandum, B.L. York to Minister of the Interior, 20 Apr. 1915
7 RG15, B2a, Vol. 173, 145330, Pt 7, J.W. Greenway, Commissioner of Dominion Lands to W.W. Cory, 25 Aug. 1915
8 *Ibid*., W.W. Cory, Deputy Minister, to J.W. Greenway, 27 Sept. 1915
9 RG15, B2a, Vol. 172, 145330, Pt 5, Inspector of Ranches to Department of the Interior, 19 Mar. 1914
10 RG15, B2a, Vol. 173, 145330, Pt 6, B.L. York to Inspector of Ranches, 13 May 1914
11 *Ibid*., 145330, Pt 7, E. Rayan to B.L. York, 29 Jan. 1917; memorandum, B.L. York to Deputy Minister, 14 May 1914
12 *Ibid*., B.L. York to Dominion Land agents, 13 June 1917
13 RG15, B2a, Vol. 146, 581514, T.L. Duncan to the Minister of the Interior, 23 Aug. 1913. See also T.L. Duncan to Minister of the Interior, 5 Apr. 1913, petition enclosed.
14 *Ibid*., G.H. Cloakley to B.L. York, 24 Apr. 1914
15 *Ibid*., T.L. Duncan to the Duke of Connaught, 21 Jan. 1915
16 David M. Emmons, 'The Influence of Ideology on Changing Environmental Images,' *Images of the Plains: The Role of Human Nature in Settlement*, eds B.W. Blouet and M.P. Lawson (Lincoln: University of Nebraska Press 1975) 125–36
17 PAS, P142, Department of Agriculture, Lands Branch, 52992, W. Guenthner to Department of the Interior, 23 Feb. 1912. This file was originally part of the Department of the Interior records.
18 RG15, B2a, Vol. 147, 591130, A.T. Connolly, Chairman, Special Leases Committee of Bassano Board of Trade to W.J. Roche, Minister of the Interior, 10 June 1916

19 *Ibid.*, clipping from *Bassano Mail*, 10 Aug. 1916
20 *Ibid.*, B.L. York to A.T. Connolly, 26 Sept. 1916. See also RG15, B2a, Vol. 147, 590712, petition concerning grazing lands in southern Saskatchewan; Vol. 148, 592184, petition concerning grazing lands near Jenner, Alberta; RG15, B2a, Vol. 173, 145330, Pt 6, G.H. Fawcett to Department of the Interior, 27 Apr. 1914
21 Alberta, Department of Agriculture, *Annual Report* 1913, Report of the Livestock Commissioner, 136
22 *Ibid.* 1916, Report of the Recorder of Brands, 122. After 1913 the allocation of new cattle brands averaged over 2000 per year. While some registrations represented routine changes that came with changes in ownership and so on, it is probably safe to say that at least half the registrations resulted from establishment of new cattle herds and as such are a rough measure of the industry's growth in the south. It should be noted also that many farmers who kept a few head of cattle on fenced pastures did not bother to obtain registered brands, so that most of the new registrations were for herds in excess of fifty cattle and were from the south, where cattle still ran freely on the open range in some areas. See also, Alberta Department of Agriculture, *Annual Report* 1915, Report of Livestock Commissioner 74; (1916) 63.
23 T.B. Long, *Seventy Years a Cowboy: A Biography* (Regina: Western Printers Association 1959) 97–9
24 PAS, the Matador Land and Cattle Co. 1905–16. In October 1913 Matador shipped 2057 head from southern Saskatchewan to Chicago and netted $147,228. In November 1914 the 1179 steers sent to Chicago averaged $93.40 net each and earned the manager of the Canadian operation praise from the company's general manager. 'This means right at $17.00 a head more than what we were offered for the cattle in Canada and everybody connected with the Company are glad to hear of the splendid sales made by you.' MacBain to J.R. Lair, 6 Nov. 1914. Sales in 1915 consisted of four trainloads totalling 2237 head (averaging 1204 pounds each), which netted an average of $85.58 each.
25 GAI, Cross Papers, B110, F883, WSGA Bulletin No. 5, July 1917
26 Alberta, Department of Agriculture, *Annual Report* 1918, Report of the Livestock Commissioner 64–5; (1919) 13
27 F.A. Rudd, 'Production and Marketing of Beef Cattle from the Short Grass Plains Area of Canada' (MA thesis, University of Alberta 1935) 119
28 Canada, Department of the Interior, *Annual Report* 1914–15, Report of the Deputy Minister, xxxi
29 Cross Papers, B68, F525, A.E. Cross to W.R. MacInnes, 13 July 1912
30 *Ibid.*, B69, F541, A.E. Cross to Clay, Robinson and Co., 14 November 1913. A large shipment of cattle from the Maunsell Ranch near Pincher Creek to Chicago in late Oct. 1913 sold between $8.15 and $7.40 a hundredweight. B69, F437, Clay, Robinson and Co. to A.E. Cross, 22 October 1913

31 *Ibid.*, B109, F873, A.E. Cross to G. Porter, 20 Oct. 1915

32 *Ibid.*, B109, F876, Clay, Robinson and Co., to A.E. Cross, 17 Nov. 1915. The 185 head that Cross marketed returned between $7.60 and $8.80 per hundredweight for steers and $5.25 and $7.00 for cows. After all expenses were deducted net proceeds equalled $17,409.98.

33 *Ibid.*, B109, F879, Clay, Robinson and Co. to A.E. Cross, 13 Nov. 1916, sales receipt

Sale

	Cattle	Class	Weight	Price	Amount
	35	steers	50,120	$10.75	$ 5,387.90
	68	"	96,150	10.40	9,999.60
	22	"	31,000	9.75	3,022.50
	17	"	23,160	9.25	2,142.30
	38	"	50,000	9.75	4,875.00
	37	cows	41,740	8.00	3,339.20
	23	"	25,500	7.35	1,874.25
Total	240		317,670		$30,640.75

Charges

Freight charges	$2,600.96 (13 cars)	
Yardage 240 [cattle]	60.00	
Hay 5400 lb	54.00	
Commission	139.35	
Total	$2,854.31	
	Net proceeds	$27,786.44
	Shipping	114.48
		$27,671.96

34 *Ibid.*, B109, F878, A.E. Cross to *The North West Farmer* (Winnipeg), 31 Jan. 1916

35 *Ibid.*, B109, F880, Clay, Robinson and Co. to A.E. Cross, 17 Sept. 1917; B111, F893, P. Burns to A.E. Cross, 3 Oct. 1919

36 See, for example, *ibid.*, B108, F870, correspondence Nov. 1914–Dec. 1915. The Cross papers contain letters during this period from numerous individuals anxious to sell their homesteads to Cross so that they might move elsewhere.

37 Canada, Department of the Interior, *Annual Report* 1907–8, Report of Deputy Minister i

38 *Ibid.*, 1910–11, Report of the Commissioner of Immigration 95; Report of Agent of Dominion Lands at Medicine Hat 36.

39 *Ibid.*, Report of Commissioner of Immigration 95

40 *Pincher Creek Echo*, 5 Apr. 1912
41 Canada, Department of the Interior, *Annual Report* 1912–13, Report of the Commissioner of Dominion Lands 15, 33
42 *Ibid.* 1913–14, Report of Agent of Dominion Lands at Medicine Hat 34
43 Alberta, Department of Agriculture, *Annual Report* 1913, Report of Deputy Minister 6
44 *Ibid.* 1914, Report of Deputy Minister 8; *Pincher Creek Echo*, 1 May 1914; Canada, Department of the Interior, *Annual Report* 1914–15, Report of Deputy Minister ix; Report of Inspector of Ranches, Maple Creek 142
45 *Ibid.* 1915–16, Report of the Deputy Minister 1; Report of Inspector of Ranches, Maple Creek 139
46 Alberta, Department of Agriculture, *Annual Report* 1917, Report of Livestock Commissioner 56–9
47 *Ibid.* 1918, Report of Deputy Minister, 9–11
48 Canada, Department of the Interior, *Annual Report* 1918–19, Report of Deputy Minister, 23. See also Report of Director of the Reclamation Service 6.
49 See correspondence in RG15, B2, Vol. 164, 141376.
50 RG15, B2, Vol. 164, 141376, 'Conference on Farm Water Supply'
51 Canada, Department of the Interior, *Annual Report* 1920, Report of Director of the Reclamation Service 1
52 Alberta, Department of Agriculture, *Annual Report* 1919, Report of Deputy Minister, 9–11; *Pincher Creek Echo*, 28 Nov. 1919, 12 Dec. 1919
53 Canada, Department of the Interior, *Annual Report* 1922, Report of Director of the Reclamation Service 175; (1921) 1–4
54 Alberta, Department of Agriculture, *Annual Report* 1922, Report of Deputy Minister 7, 95
55 *Ibid.* (1920) 10. 'During the year it was found necessary in a few cases where families had suffered from repeated lightness of crops to give relief in household necessaries such as fuel and flour.'
56 *Ibid.* 1922, 'Precipitation Averages 1885–1922' 107
57 W.C. Wonders et al., *Atlas of Alberta* (Edmonton: University of Alberta Press in association with University of Toronto Press 1969), 'Water Demand, Surplus, and Deficiency' 19
58 Canada, Department of the Interior, *Annual Report* 1920, Report of Director of Reclamation Service 3
59 Karel D. Bicha, *The American Farmer and the Canadian West, 1896–1914* (Lawrence, Kansas: Coronado Press 1968) 137–44. Between 1898 and 1914, 591,996 American emigrants declared their destinations to be Saskatchewan and Alberta, but according to the 1916 census there were only 179,581 American-born residents in Saskatchewan and Alberta. Americans who left the prairies did not locate elsewhere in Canada; thus, some 400,000 would-be homesteaders seem to

have returned to the United States after short residence in Canada.

60 V.C. Fowke, *The National Policy and the Wheat Economy* (Toronto: University of Toronto Press 1973) 285

61 *Pincher Creek Echo*, 22 Aug. 1914

62 *Ibid.*, 28 Aug. 1914, 4 Sept. 1914

63 *Ibid.*, 27 Nov. 1914

64 Quoted in E. Ference, 'Literature Associated with Ranching in Southern Alberta' (MA thesis, University of Alberta 1971) 40

65 GAI, E. Park, 'History of Bradfield Ranch near Millarville, Alberta'

66 K. Liddell, 'The Remittance Man,' *Western Producer*, 4 June 1959

67 RG15, B2a, Vol. 103, 476534, J.R. Watt to Controller, Timber and Grazing Branch, 16 Oct. 1916, A.C. Critchley, *Critch! The Memoirs of Brigadier-General A.C. Critchley CMG, GBE, DSO* (London: Hutchinson of London 1961)

68 See, for example, Cross Papers, B108, F870, A.E. Cross to C.B. Waddell, Manager of A7 Ranch, 22 June 1915. Cross instructed his foreman to get the haying done quickly as so many had gone to war there would soon be few left. *Ibid.*, B109, F875. See correspondence with C.B. Waddell, Dec. 1915–Dec. 1916 and Long, *Seventy Years a Cowboy* 102.

69 W. Huckvale, D. Hardwick, Eckford, and O.A. Critchley were missed by the WSGA. 'Lord' Ogle, founding president of the SSGA, also retired from the country and spent his declining years at his country home in Sussex and on the French and Italian Riviera. PAS, Ogle Reminiscences

70 Cross Papers, B109, F880, minutes of evidence 125. Cross's cultural bias shows clearly in his judgment of the other major group, the American farm settlers. 'When the country was thrown open for settlement there was a large emigration into the country of Americans from the south, and there were a good many came up here of what we call a sort of hobo class, that is, people that come into a country for a time and then drift on. They are never settled. I myself bought out several of them. They came up here with the express purpose of getting a homestead and getting the certificate of title to their place, and as soon as they got that they sold it out ... and went on somewhere else or went back to the States, and that accounts for a good many of them that went away again. You see, they were people that have a wandering nature, they were never settled in any country ...' Cross charitably accorded eastern Canadian settlers the honour of being comparatively better.

CHAPTER NINE: ORGANIZED CATTLEMEN AND THE CATTLE TRADE EMBARGOES 1919–22

1 GAI, Cross Papers, B110, F88, F.R. Mohler, Chief, United States Department of Agriculture Bureau of Animal Industry to Dr F. Torrance, Veterinary Director General, Ottawa, 5 Jan. 1918

2 *Ibid.*, George E. Hilton, Acting Veterinary Director General to A.E. Cross, 11 Jan. 1918. Of the seven diseased shipments, four came from Alberta and three from Saskatchewan.

3 Canadian cattle sent to Chicago from the quarantine area were sent to a special section of the stockyards and many buyers of stocker and feeder cattle refused to bid on these cattle despite proof of inspection. The result was reduced prices that cost Canadian cattlemen thousands of dollars and an unfortunate label which threatened to cost them the US market altogether.

4 Cross Papers, B111, F894, D.A. Thompson, Secretary-Treasurer of the WSGA to A.E. Cross, 8 Sept. 1919; A.E. Cross to D.A. Thompson, 30 Sept. 1919; B112, F900, W. Huckvale, President, WSGA to A.E. Cross, 19 Nov. 1919. Appeals to leaseholders to renew their memberships did not meet with success. Most seem to have lost confidence in the ability of the WSGA to act effectively.

5 GAI, WSGA Papers, B1, F4, 'Cattlemen's Protective Association of Western Canada, Constitution and Minutes, 1919–1920,' 1; hereafter cited SGPA Papers

6 SGPA Papers, B12, F110, W.Wilson, Secretary, CPA to the Knight, Watson Ranching Company, 12 Dec. 1919

7 *Ibid.*

8 *Ibid.*, B1, F4, constitution and minutes 71. Officers elected: President, D.P. McDaniel; Vice-Presidents, P. Burns and G. McElroy; Directors, E. Kenny, D.P. McDonald, J.M. Dillon, M.J. Stapleton, W. McIntyre, and E. Wade

9 *Ibid.*, B12, F110, W. Wilson, to Dr Grisdale, Deputy Minister of Agriculture, 29 Dec. 1919; B12, F107, Dr F. Torrance, Veterinary Director General to Dr J.H. Grisdale, Deputy Minister of Agriculture, 7 Jan. 1920. The 'dipping' process consisted of forcing each animal to swim individually through a vat containing a solution of sulphur and lime. The mammoth task of collecting and dipping every head of stock in the range country was completed during the early summer of 1920 and the quarantine was consequently lifted by order-in-council passed on 6 Aug. Complaints were registered by many small stockmen and farmers who believed their cattle to be clean and did not wish to go to the expense of dipping. The regulations were, none the less, carried out to the letter under the supervision of the federal Department of Agriculture and the big cattlemen and their association.

10 For details regarding these activities see *ibid.*, B1, F4, constitution and minutes 1919–20, 3–12; B4, F21, Directors' correspondence, 'Report of Committee to Maple Creek and Shaunavon.' The delegation was pleased with the reception they received from the Maple Creek stockmen but they judged the members of the Saskatchewan Stock Growers' Association rather condescendingly as men of a different class. 'At Shaunavon the majority of the delegates were of a different class from those at Maple Creek; they consisted chiefly of farmers who were running small bunches of stock, in some cases on deeded land ....'

11 *Ibid.*, B1, F6, amalgamation of the Western Stock Growers' Association of Western Canada, W.F. Stevens to J. Mitchell, Medicine Hat, 26 Feb. 1921

12 *Ibid.*, A.E. Cross to W. Huckvale, 18 Mar. 1921. Cross had been advocating union for over a year. See Cross Papers, B112, F905, A.E. Cross to W. Huckvale, 21 Apr. 1920.

13 W. Huckvale, last president of the WSGA, was named Honourary President, A.E. Cross was elected Second Vice-President, and J. Mitchell of Medicine Hat was chosen as a Director. Others elected to the executive included: D.E. Riley (later Senator) of High River, President; G.M. McElroy (Calgary), First Vice-President; Directors: J.M. Dillon (Calgary), E. Kenny (Calgary), C. Bartsch (Gleichen), D.P. McDonald (Cochrane), M.J. Stapleton (Jenner). SGPA Papers, B1, F4, Constitution and Minutes, 73

14 See, for example, Cross Papers, B113, F906, Clay, Robinson and Co. to A.E. Cross, 21 Mar. 1921. 'I think it would be a good plan for your statesmen at Ottawa to make a big fight towards allowing your live cattle to come in free of duty. They could also use the argument there is no duty on cattle from the [states] going into Canada, also the fact that there is not enough cattle coming from Canada to affect our market, in fact, they ... do us a lot of good ... as our cattle feeders like the young Canadian cattle for fattening purposes.'

15 SGPA Papers, B9, F64, W. Dunbar of Walters and Dunbar, Chicago to J. Dillon, CPA, 28 June 1922. 'We have canvassed the situation locally and are strongly of the opinion that all of the Live Stock Exchanges at the northern markets are absolutely friendly to the suggestion of your people for placing Canadian feeding steers on the free list in the new tariff bill now pending in Washington, but as a matter of policy they are compelled to keep silent when it comes to a matter of politics, as you are well aware that the cattlemen here in the States are very much divided in their views when it comes to matters of politics and the tariff.' The above is representative of the many letters in F64.

16 See, for example *ibid.*, Kay Wood of Wood Brothers, Chicago, to J. Dillon, CPA, 13 June 1922; F. McGurk of Miller, White and Woods to J. Dillon, 26 June 1922

17 *Ibid.*, F. McGurk of Miller, White and Woods to J. Dillon, 28 June 1922. See also F. McGurk to J. Dillon, 23 June 1922; B9, F65, K. Wood of Wood Brothers to J. Dillon, 12 June 1922.

18 *Ibid.*, B10, F66, copy of Emergency Tariff Bill presented in House of Representatives, 12 Apr. 1921

19 The association was disappointed to learn later that only 41 per cent of Canadian steers arriving at the Chicago market were taken back to the country, leaving 49 per cent to go directly to slaughter. While this said a lot for the quality of the western Canadian grass-fed steer, it was not publicized. *Ibid.*, B9, F64, Miller, White and Woods to SGPA, 6 July 1922

20 *Ibid.*, B9, F64, SGPA to W.R. Motherwell, Minister of Agriculture, 23 June 1922; see also SGPA to D. Marshall, Commissioner of Agriculture, 23 June 1922; SGPA to the Hon. G. Hoadley, Alberta Minister of Agriculture, 22 June 1922. Hoadley, a stockman, volunteered to travel to the United States on the association's behalf.

21 *Ibid.*, B9, F65, SGPA to J.A. Walker, Chairman, Calgary Clearing House, 20 June 1922. The details of the computation are included in this letter. The SGPA gained the support of the Bankers' Association of Western Canada.

22 *Ibid.*, B9, F64, D. Marshall to M. Dillon, 30 June 1922

23 *Ibid.*, J. Mitchell to Secretary, SGPA, 31 July 1922. The delegation to the Minister consisted of some of the most important members of the new ranch establishment including A.E. Cross, J. Dillon, M. Stapleton, D. Hardwick, A. McHugh, W. McHugh, R. Macleay, D. McDonald, D. McDaniel, and J. Mitchell.

24 *Ibid.*, Walters and Dunbar to J. Dillon, 28 June 1922

25 *Ibid.*, SGPA to the Hon. J.L. Perron, Quebec Minister of Public Works, 27 June 1922. The letter identifies the groups supporting the ranchers' campaign. Perron was a friend of D. Riley, President of the SGPA, and he promised to take the matter up with Sir Lomer Gouin, federal Minister of Justice and former Premier of Quebec, to ensure the Canadian government acted energetically on the ranchers' behalf.

26 *Ibid.*, American National Live Stock Association to J. Dillon, 30 June 1922

27 *Ibid.*, Clay, Robinson and Co., to SGPA, 1 July 1922

28 In addition to tacit support of the Chicago commission house, the SGPA gained the friendly press of the *Chicago Daily Drovers Journal*. Noting that Canada was America's best customer for manufactured goods, the *Journal* argued that it would not 'hurt us any to be just a little generous in considering the tariff claims of our neighbour on the north.' *Ibid.*, clipping, 2 July 1922. See also letter to SGPA re editorial of 18 July 1922. The big city newspapers seem also to have been anti-protectionist. See *ibid.*, *Chicago Tribune*, 3 July 1922, clipping.

29 *Ibid.*, Theodore M. Knappen to J.F. Langan, 3 July 1922. Theodore Knappen, of the Knappen-Ulm Service, claimed a thorough understanding of Canadian-American relations, having specialized on the subject for twenty-five years and having resided for a number of years in Canada. Knappen was well-known to the Canadian Bankers' Association and through his efforts the British Columbia lumber interests had gained a number of tarriff concessions. See *ibid.*, SGPA to Secretary, Canadian Bankers' Association, 26 July 1922.

30 *Ibid.*, T. Knappen to J.F. Langan, 3 July 1922. The tariff bill passed in the House carried a duty of one cent a pound on live cattle. The Senate adopted this portion of the bill but raised the tariff to two cents.

31 *Ibid.*, T. Knappen to J. Dillon, 18 July 1922

32 *Ibid.*, SGPA to T. Knappen, 26 July 1922, statistics supplied by the Bureau of Markets in Washington. The above refers to all cattle; if only grass-fed western animals were included the percentages would be even smaller. The Canadian tactic from the beginning had been to emphasize the very modest percentage of the market that they held and wished to retain, as it was believed that this section of the bill was not particularly aimed at Canada, but was drafted to stop the importation of heavy refrigerated beef from the Argentine and other South American countries. See Cross Papers, B114, F916, A.R. MacInnes, Vice-President, CPR, to A.E. Cross, 12 Dec. 1921.

33 SGPA Papers, B9, F64, T. Knappen to J. Dillon, 10 July 1922

34 *Ibid.*, 29 July 1922

35 Great Britain, Public Record Office, Colonial Office Confidential Print, Canada, CO, 880 / 15, 170 (Papers Relative to the Importation of Canadian Cattle into Great Britain April 1894), Report of a Committee of the Privy Council of Canada, 6 February 1894, 3

36 *Ibid.* 4

37 *Ibid.*

38 *Ibid.*, Board of Agriculture to Colonial Office, 16 Apr. 1894, 14

39 *Ibid.*, confidential memorandum on the importation of Canadian cattle into Great Britain, 19 Apr. 1894, 2

40 Debates (Senate), XLVI (1896) 415

41 J.R. Fisher, 'The Economic Effects of Cattle Disease in Britain and Its Containment, 1850–1900,' *Agricultural History* 54 (Apr. 1980) 278–93. Hugh J.E. Abbot, 'The Marketing of Livestock in Canada' (MA thesis, University of Toronto 1923)

42 North-West Territories, Department of Agriculture, *Annual Report* (1901) 72. Of the 115,000 head exported from Canada to Great Britain in 1900, over 48,000 head were from the North-West Territories.

43 North-West Territories, Department of Agriculture, *Annual Report* (1901) 72. In 1907 the matter was brought to the attention of the Imperial Conference by Sir Wilfrid Laurier and was followed by another attempt by the Canadian Minister of Agriculture in 1913. See PAC, Borden Papers, MG26, H1(b), 157, Confidential Report re Cattle Embargo, 7 Feb. 1917, 83968 and 83969.

44 Borden Papers, MG26, H1(b), Vol. 157, 83867, A Plea for the Development of the Agricultural Resources of the Empire: the Present and Future Meat Supply and the Question of Free Importation of Canadian Cattle (Dec. 1915) 15, 22. The main argument was to reduce beef prices and, for those who still accepted the disease allegation, the tract pointed out that between 1912 and 1914 there had been 144 outbreaks of foot and mouth disease in Ireland and yet hundreds of

thousands of animals had still been shipped to England from that country, whereas the disease has not been found anywhere in Canada since 1870.

45 *Ibid.*, 83894-8, memorandum, Canadian Cattle Trade, Col. H.A. Mullins, MP, to Sir Robert Borden, 26 Jan. 1917; 83899, M. Burrell, Minister of Agriculture to Sir Robert Borden, 7 Feb. 1917

46 *Ibid.*, 83911, Sir Edward Watson, Chairman, FICCA, to Sir Robert Borden, 17 Mar. 1917; 83914, F.M. Batchelor to Sir Robert Borden, 6 Apr. 1917. The arrangements for the meeting on 11 April at the North British Station Hotel in Edinburgh were made through Col. H.A. Mullins, a Conservative MP from Winnipeg and former western rancher.

47 *Ibid.*, 83922, W. Henderson to Sir Robert Borden, 16 Apr. 1917 memorandum of Scottish position as requested by Borden at the meeting. See also accompanying documents 83924 and 83926 regarding information received from the FICCA before Borden opened the matter at the Imperial War Conference.

48 Great Britain, *Parliamentary Papers, Imperial War Conference, 1917*, 'Extracts from Discussions at the Imperial War Conference on the Admission of Canadian Cattle into the United Kingdom,' Cd 8673 (Sept. 1917) 2, 6. Borden's conviction was in part based on Prothero's statement: 'I can assure you that so far as the English Board of Agriculture is concerned, we are in favour of the removal of the embargo. We do not believe that there is now, or has been for a good many years past, the slightest ground to exclude Canadian cattle on the score of disease.' At another point he stated that the change should come when the war was concluded. See also Borden Papers, MG26, H1(b), Vol. 157, 83928, Sir Robert Borden to W.H. Long, Colonial Secretary, 27 Apr. 1917.

49 Borden Papers, MG26, H1(b), Vol. 157, 83931, Sir Robert Borden to Blount, 27 Apr. 1917

50 *Ibid.*, 83935, W.H. Long to Sir Robert Borden, 9 May 1917

51 *Ibid.*, 83956, R. Rogers to Sir Robert Borden, 16 June 1917. 'I note, with regret, that everything in respect to the cattle embargo has been dropped, and I am sure you will agree with me that we cannot afford to allow this to pass unnoticed and we should insist on it becoming part of the record.'

52 *Ibid.*, 83957, Sir Robert Borden to G.H. Perley, 18 June 1917

53 *Ibid.*, 83973, W.H. Long to Lord Devonshire, Governor General of Canada, 28 June 1917. The original exclusion from the minutes was justified on the grounds that the discussion was intermingled with the question of meat supplies and therefore had to remain confidential. At the same time Prothero informed the Scots that the present was not a good time to introduce the embargo question in Parliament as it would be strongly opposed by many members and in any case, there certainly would be no tonnage available for carrying the animals. See 83975, Board of Agriculture and Fisheries to Gentlemen [FICCA], 28 June 1917.

54 Great Britain, *Parliamentary Papers, Royal Commission on the Importation of Store Cattle*, Cmd 1139, Aug. 1921, 'Report of His Majesty's Commissioners Appointed to Inquire into the Admission into the United Kingdom of Livestock for Purposes Other than Immediate Slaughter at the Ports' 4. The statement was issued to the press by Lord Ernle on 26 July 1919. See also Borden Papers, MG26, H1C(c), Vol. 98, 52547–50, Dr J.W.M. Robertson, Canadian Commissioner of Agriculture, to Lord Ernle, 10 Mar. 1919, 'Cattle Embargo'; 1(b), Vol. 157, 83996, memorandum, 'British Embargo on Canadian Cattle,' prepared for Minister of Agriculture, 1919.

55 SGPA Papers, B12, F100, W.T. Ritch to W.F. Stevens, 5 Nov. 1920. See additional correspondence between Ritch and Stevens during Oct. 1920.

56 *Ibid.*, B8, F45, J. Lennox to W.F. Stevens, 30 Sept. 1920. The local Scottish press, for the most part, could also be relied upon. See, for example, B12, F95, 'Press Clippings,' *The Penrith Observer*, 12 Apr. 1921; *The Scottish Farmer*, 25 Apr. 1921.

57 *Ibid.*, E. Watson, Chairman, FICCA, to W.F. Stevens, 15 Nov. 1920

58 *Ibid.*, W.F. Stevens to J. Lennox, 10 Feb. 1921; R.B. Bennett to W.F. Stevens, 31 May 1921. Bennett speaks of his most recent discussions with Beaverbrook on the embargo question. Evidence suggests that it was Bennett who originally approached Beaverbrook on the ranchers' behalf. Bennett and Beaverbrook had been close business associates when the latter lived in Calgary.

59 *Ibid.*, B12, F95, 'Press Clippings,' *Calgary Herald*, 24 Feb. 1921

60 *Ibid.*, *Calgary Herald*, 3 Mar. 1921

61 *Ibid.*, B8, F45, J. Lennox to W.F. Stevens, 7 Mar. 1921

62 Great Britain, *Parliamentary Papers*, Royal Commission on the Importation of Store Cattle 5; SGPA Papers, B8, F45, W.F. Stevens to Lennox, 12 Mar. 1921. Lennox arranged for a representative of his group to speak at the meeting.

63 SGPA Papers, B8, F45, 'Press Clippings.' See, for example, *The Glasgow Herald*, 15 Mar. 1921; *The Meat Trades Journal*, 24 Mar. 1921.

64 SGPA Papers, B8, F45, E. Watson to W.F. Stevens, 1 Apr. 1921

65 Great Britain, *Parliamentary Papers*, Royal Commission on the Importation of Store Cattle 5–10. Among others, the National Farmers' Union of Scotland, the Scottish Chamber of Agriculture, the Free Importation of Canadian Cattle Association of Great Britain, and the Corporations of London, Edinburgh, Glasgow, Birmingham, and Manchester, Dr S. Tolmie, Canadian Minister of Agriculture, and D. Marshall, Minister of Agriculture for Alberta, spoke for removal of the embargo. The main groups presenting evidence in opposition were the National Farmers' Union of England, the Royal Agricultural Society of England, the Live Stock Defence Committee, which was comprised of a large number of Agricultural and Breeding Societies, Agricultural Societies in the West and Central Highlands, the Irish Farmers' Union, the Munster Agricultural Society, the Royal

Ulster Agricultural Society, the Irish Cattle Traders' and Stockowners' Association, and Lord Ernle.

66 *Ibid.* 14–15
67 *The Times* (London), 15 June 1922; see also 3 May 1922, regarding Sir Robert
Borden's views on the history of the pledge; 6 May 1922, a letter to the editor
from Lord Ernle justifying his position
68 Great Britain, *Parliamentary Debates*, 5th ser. (Commons), CLVII (1922) 63–178
69 *Ibid.*, 5th ser. (Lords), LI (1922) 354-404
70 SGPA Papers, B8, F50, 'Cattle Shipment, September 1921.' An experimental shipment by the SGPA to Great Britain in September 1921 accumulated total expenses
of $77.65 per head, leaving a total net return per head of $82.99, or an average
price of 5.84¢ per 100 pounds. This return was slightly less than would have been
gained in Calgary. Returns improved after the embargo was lifted. When cattle
did not have to be slaughtered on arrival, the price was bid higher by farmers
anxious to feed the animal over the winter months.
71 RG15, B2a, Vol. 175, 145330, Pt 9, W.W. Cory to B.L. York, 22 Oct. 1920; copy
of order-in-council, 4 Nov. 1920. Notice was changed to four years in Oct. 1921.
72 Cross Papers, B113, F908, A.E. Cross to A. Meighen, 11 Nov. 1920.
73 SGPA Papers, B11, F84, W.F. Stevens to J. Mitchell, 26 Feb. 1921. Lougheed's
intention is also revealed in an internal departmental memorandum from the
Deputy Minister to the head of the Timber and Grazing Branch. 'The Minister
explains that with the possibility before us of a transfer of the natural resources to
the Province, it is not desirable to tie up in closed leases for ten years any large
tracts of lands like this, and he thinks that we [should] issue from now on a clause
that will enable us to cancel on two years notice.' See RG15, B2a, Vol. 175,
145330, Pt 9, 7 Oct. 1920. A.E. Cross suggested more deep-seated reasons for
the Senator's hostility. 'I have known for a long time,' Cross informed a delegate,
'that the Minister of the Interior is not favourable to the lease holders from early
impressions of the old cattle men which I feel were quite wrong, but hard to
change.' Cross Papers, B113, F911, A.E. Cross to D. Hardwick, 27 Apr. 1921
74 SGPA Papers, B11, F84, W.F. Stevens to A.M. Firth, Secretary, Edmonton Board
of Trade, 27 June 1921
75 RG15, B2a, Vol. 175, 145330, Pt 9, resolution regarding grazing leases, UFA executive, autumn 1921
76 Cross Papers, B113, F911, A.E. Cross to C.A. Magrath, 11 Feb. 1922; C.A.
Magrath to A.E. Cross, 15 Feb. 1922. C.A. Magrath was elected the first mayor
of Lethbridge in 1891. He served in the Northwest Assembly from 1891 to 1898
and in 1908 was elected to the House of Commons as a Conservative for Medicine Hat. From 1914 to 1936 he was Canadian chairman of the International Joint
Commission.

77 SGPA Papers, B11, F84, W.F. Stevens to D. Hardwick, 25 May 1921, enclosed article for *The Grain Growers' Guide*

78 For discussion of this problem see Cross Papers, B113, F911, A.E. Cross to C.A. Magrath, 11 Feb. 1922.

79 SGPA Papers, B11, F84, Dennis Riley, Canadian Bank of Commerce, Calgary to W.F. Stevens. 'We are now informed that representations have been made by the Canadian Bankers' Association to the Minister of the Interior urging the Government to give careful consideration to the question of retaining for ranching purposes lands which are unsuitable for farming and requesting that an early announcement should be made of their decision.' Bank interest also might have had something to do with the large loans carried by some bigger ranchers. See also A.T. Lyster to W.F. Stevens, 1 Mar. 1921.

80 *Ibid.*, D. Hardwick, SGPA to Interior Stock Association of British Columbia, 1 Mar. 121

81 *Ibid.*, SGPA to the Rt Hon. Arthur Meighen, nd; SGPA to R.B. Bennett, 7 Sept. 1921

82 *Ibid.*, W.F. Stevens to D.E. Riley, 4 May 1921. Riley was asked to 'write a personal letter to the Hon. Duncan Marshall and suggest to him that he and his Government would have more to gain in a political way by keeping out of this inquiry entirely and by letting the Dominion Government deal with it.'

83 *Ibid.*, W.F. Stevens to D. Hardwick, 30 July 1921; D.E. Riley to W.F. Stevens, 4 Aug. 1921; J.A. Lougheed to C. Stewart, 25 July 1921

84 *Ibid.*, W.F. Stevens to D.E. Riley, 4 May 1921

85 RG15, B2a, Vol. 176, 145330, Pt 10, 'Synopsis of Meeting Held at Medicine Hat with Ranchmen and Grazing Lessees, Saturday March 4th, 1922'

86 SGPA Papers, B11, F84, proposed alteration, nd; B.Y. York, Controller, Timber and Grazing Branch to W.F. Stevens, 25 Apr. 1922, lists the changes that have been made.

87 *Ibid.*, D. Hardwick, Chairman, SGPA, Grazing Committee to C. Stewart, 5 May 1922; see also SGPA to C. Stewart, 13 Apr. 1922; D. Hardwick to W.W. Cory, 10 May 1922

88 RG15, B2a, Vol. 176, 145330, Pt 10 B.L. York to L. Ripon, 21 Feb. 1922, enclosing submission regarding community grazing from UFA; Hamilton, Saskatchewan Minister of Agriculture to W.W. Cory, 23 Feb. 1922

89 SGPA Papers, SGPA to C.G. Dunning, 23 May 1922

90 *Ibid.*, D. Hardwick to SGPA, 10 May 1922

EPILOGUE

1 C.W. Vrooman, *et al.*, *Cattle Ranching in Western Canada, Publication No. 778* (Ottawa: Department of Agriculture 1946) 73. After 1926 Canadian cattle exports to Great Britain began an equally rapid decline and to a lesser extent the American market also began to shrink after 1927.
2 The name of the cattlemen's association remained the Stock Growers' Protective Association until 1923, when it was changed back to the more familiar Western Stock Growers' Association.
3 GA1, WSGA, 'minutes of the thirtieth annual convention 7

Bibliographical note

This book depends essentially upon four extensive and outstanding manuscript collections. The first is the PAC records of the Department of the Interior, Timber and Grazing Branch. Here, in minute detail, is recorded the evolution and administration of federal land policy on the southern plains. In addition to policy files are individual records of most large leaseholders, numerous petitions from ranchers and farmers, as well as thousands of letters describing the character of settlement in the dry country. These files are complemented by the outstanding collection of papers from the key federal bureaucrat in the field, William Pearce. There is no aspect of settlement, land use, or resource policy between 1880 and 1920 that is not widely covered in these papers, located at the University of Alberta Archives. At the Glenbow Archives in Calgary, the A.E. Cross papers document in detail, from the mid-1890s, the operation of one of Alberta's most successful ranches as well as the activities of an outstanding western entrepreneur. The Western Stock Growers' Association Papers (records of the Cattlemen's Protective Association and the Stock Growers' Protective Association of Western Canada are included in this collection), also at the Glenbow Archives, offer the best view of the range cattle industry. Any assessment of the cattlemen as a political group must use this source.

There are other lesser but still very helpful manuscript collections at the Glenbow Archives that students of the ranching frontier should consult. The W.F. Cochrane Diary and Letterbook is one of the few sources that deals with day-to-day operations of the first of the great cattle companies. In the G.E. Goddard, Bow River Horse Ranch Papers, one can follow for thirty years the trials of the rancher who acquired Cochrane's northern leasehold near Calgary. The Inderwick Diary and Personal Letters from the North Fork Ranch shed light upon the social setting in the foothill cattle country before the turn of the century, while the minutes of the Calgary Ranchmen's Club are helpful in drawing the relationships between town, country, and national élites. Cross-boundary and international connections among the ranching fraternity can be assessed in the Sir

Horace Plunkett Ranching Correspondence with Earl Grey, Ottawa and Moreton Frewen, Wyoming. The actual operation of one of the most successful of the large trans-border cattle companies is revealed in the papers of the Matador Land and Cattle Company at the Public Archives of Saskatchewan.

Two of the most useful published sources for the period before 1900 are the *Macleod Gazette* and the *Calgary Herald*. The *Gazette* began publication just as the big cattle companies were being established and 'ranch news' was an important feature of the paper's early years. By the time the ranching industry had become well established in late 1880s, the *Herald* emerged as a key voice of the cattle interests and the Conservative party in the south-western prairie region.

This book also relies heavily upon certain published government documents. At the federal level, the *Annual Reports* of the Department of the Interior and the North-West Mounted Police are pertinent. The North-West Territories Department of Agriculture *Annual Reports* from 1897 to 1905 are useful, as are those of the Alberta Department of Agriculture after 1905.

Contemporary accounts of the ranching frontier in Canada are not numerous and only a few are of substantial assistance to the researcher. From his vantage point as an early ranch manager, John R. Craig in *Ranching with Lords and Commons, or Twenty Years on the Range* (Toronto 1903) comments upon the cattle company era and the problems of working with the British upper classes. Captain Burton Deane spent most of his career in the cattle country and enjoyed a close rapport with the ranching fraternity. His *Mounted Police Life in Canada: A Record of Thirty-One Years' Service* (London 1916) provides a sympathetic view of the cattlemen from the outside, as well as a contemporary view of life in the region from the 1885 rebellion onward. Alexander Stavely Hill headed a group of titled British investors in a western ranch and his *From Home to Home: Autumn Wanderings in the Years, 1881, 1882, 1883, 1884* (London 1885) offers some insight into the values and attitudes of this segment of the early ranching community. L.V. Kelly's *The Rangemen: The Story of the Ranchers and Indians of Alberta* (Toronto 1913) is the first published history of the Canadian cattle kingdom. It is a detailed and 'colourful' account that must be used with caution. 'A Lady's Life on a Ranch,' by Moira O'Neill, in *Blackwood's Edinburgh Magazine* (January 1898) reveals the social setting of the well-to-do in the grazing country at perhaps the height of the community's social and economic development.

Index